CLASSICAL RHETORIC A

ARTS IN EARLY MODERN EUROPE

In this book Caroline van Eck examines what roles classical rhetoric played in visual persuasion in the arts and architecture of early modern Europe. Rhetoric is the study of persuasive communication. Originally its main concern was persuasive speech, but from its first systematic treatments by Aristotle, Cicero and Quintilian it gave great importance to the use of visual means of persuasion – gesture, facial expression or vivid description. This is the first full-length study to look at the issue of visual persuasion in this period, both in architecture and the visual arts, and to investigate what roles rhetoric played in visual persuasion from the perspective of artists and of viewers.

Caroline van Eck is professor of architectural history at Leiden University, The Netherlands. In 2004 she was the first art historian to be awarded one of the prestigious VICI grants from the Dutch Foundation of Scientific Research (NWO). She has published widely on Renaissance architecture, rhetoric and artistic theory; edited *British Architectural Theory* 1540–1750*: An Anthology of Texts* and co-edited *Dealing with the Visual: Aesthetics, Art History and Visual Culture*, and *The Concept of Style in Philosophy and the Arts*, which was also published by Cambridge University Press.

CLASSICAL RHETORIC AND THE VISUAL ARTS IN EARLY MODERN EUROPE

CAROLINE VAN ECK

Leiden University

CAMBRIDGE
UNIVERSITY PRESS

CAMBRIDGE
UNIVERSITY PRESS

32 Avenue of the Americas, New York NY 10013-2473, USA

Cambridge University Press is part of the University of Cambridge.

It furthers the University's mission by disseminating knowledge in the pursuit of education, learning and research at the highest international levels of excellence.

www.cambridge.org
Information on this title: www.cambridge.org/9781107687851

First published 2007

A catalogue record for this publication is available from the British Library

Library of Congress Cataloguing in Publication data
Eck, Caroline van.
Classical rhetoric and the visual arts in early modern Europe / Caroline van Eck – 1st ed.
p. cm.
Includes bibliographical references and index.
ISBN 978-0-521-84435-2
1. Art – Language. 2. Persuasion (Rhetoric) History. 3. Visual communication – Europe – History. I. Title.
N72.L36E35 2007
701′.17–dc22 2007008730

ISBN 978-0-521-84435-2 Hardback
ISBN 978-1-107-68785-1 Paperback

This book was published with financial support from the Netherlands Organization for Scientific Research (NWO)

FOR HENDE BAUER

CONTENTS

ILLUSTRATIONS

ACKNOWLEDGEMENTS

In writing this book I have incurred many debts. It gives me great pleasure to acknowledge them. My first debt is to the Dutch Organization for Scientific Research (NWO) for providing such generous and liberal funding over the last 12 years to various research programmes on rhetoric and the arts and towards the publication of this book. In particular I would like to thank Piet van Slooten, Mies Wijnen and Annemaries Bos for their support at crucial moments. Auke van der Woud offered unconditional loyalty and what is sometimes its best expression, acute criticism, as my Ph.D. supervisor and subsequently colleague at the Vrije Universiteit in Amsterdam and Groningen University. The Dutch Institute in Florence and Rome, the Warburg Institute, Yale University, the University of York and Ghent University were very generous academic hosts. Nicholas Mann made it possible to spend three months at the Warburg and thereby opened up wide intellectual horizons. Christy Anderson, Karen Koehler and Chris Wood, together with the staff of the Yale Centre for British Art and the Beinecke Library, made the six months I spent there a highly successful intellectual mining expedition. David Peters Corbett, Anthony Geraghty and Jeanne Nüchterlein welcomed me at their department in York and enabled me to test out many of the ideas contained in this book on their BA students. At Ghent, Bart Verschaffel and Dirk Demeyer offered me the opportunity to teach architectural theory to architects and develop some ideas on architectural rhetoric in the research seminars of the Theory and History Cell of the Department of Architecture and Urbanism. Maarten Delbeke and Lionel Devlieger were great colleagues in these seminars, on one memorable excursion to Rome, and several conferences. Sophie Ploeg very generously allowed me to use materials from her (as yet) unpublished Ph.D. thesis on Wotton, Hawksmoor and Vanbrugh, and to use some of her excellent photographs. The staff of the Royal Library in The Hague, the British Library, the Soane Museum and the Warburg Institute were very helpful; the Centre for Art Historical Documentation of the Radboud University in Nijmegen offered essential help in finding images and was very generous in its support.

For their crucial role in the early stages of this project I am much indebted to Marc Fumaroli, Michael Podro and Brian Vickers. While writing the book I had many enlightening conversations, in particular with Stephen Bann, Barry Bergdoll, Lina Bolzoni, Reindert Falkenburg, Jan de Jong, Harry Malgrave, Alina Payne, Jürgen Pieters, Nicholas Savage, Robert Tavernor, Paul Taylor, Aron Kibédi Varga, Edward Winters, Chris Wood and Robert Zwijnenberg. Stijn Bussels, Pamela Edwardes, Edward Grasman and Lex Hermans read the entire manuscript and much improved it. Lex also allowed me to use the manuscript of his book on speaking statues in the Veneto. Conversations with Pamela about the theatre have done much to shape the argument about rhetorical visuality developed here. Lucy Gent read parts of an earlier version of this book, and though I fear she still does not approve of the final result, her comments made me rethink the whole project. Without that shake-up the book could not have been finished. In the background the unbroken interest of my mother, even in times of great illness, was a great and much appreciated support. All errors that remain despite the efforts of these friends and colleagues are entirely my own. At Cambridge University Press Beatrice Rehl had great and I hope justified confidence in this book. The two anonymous readers' reports were helpful in shaping and refining the argument. Earlier versions of some parts of Chapters Four and Six were originally published, in a different context and shorter form, in my introduction to David Brett's translation of Germain Boffrand's *Livre d'Architecture*, published by Ashgate in 2003, and in an article on English translations of Longinus in the *Georgian Group Journal* of 2006.

The greatest debt, however, is to Hende Bauer. Not just for always being there in spite of my compulsive habit of extended visits to libraries abroad, but also because many of the ideas that shaped this book were born during our conversations in front of art works all over Europe over the past 20 years.

INTRODUCTION:
RHETORIC AND VISUALITY

Andrea Buonaiuto di Firenze's large fresco of the militant and triumphant church in the Spanish Chapel of Santa Maria Novella in Florence, painted from 1365–67, includes a scene in which two Dominican preachers address the crowd (Fig. 1). On the left Saint Thomas confronts the heretics with argument, which he counts on the fingers of his right hand. The listeners express their reactions through gestures and the expressions of their faces: rejection, rebuttal, skepticism and derision. On the right, the word of God, held up by Saint Peter the Martyr, embodies the ultimate in persuasive power: while he silently points to the text, his audience starts to ponder these words, some among them falling to their knees with hands folded in prayer. To contemporary viewers these gestures appeared not chosen at random from the personal repertoire of the artist and his sitters for their expressive force. They recognized them as part of a generally used, codified repertoire of gesture and expressions that had been in use since classical antiquity. Many of them were described in Quintilian's *Institutio Oratoria*, an outline of the ideal education every orator ought to receive. Supporting a series of arguments by counting them on your fingers for instance was advised to visualize the structure of a speech.

Andrea Buonaiuto's fresco is probably one of the most straightforward cases of a rhetorical practice adopted by a painter, but it nonetheless raises many questions. The fresco shows rhetoric in action, but had to speak to its viewers too. In the painting the saints use argument and gesture to persuade, but what are the means of visual persuasion the painter can use? Is it really possible to transpose the advice Quintilian gave to young orators onto the canvas or a wall and retain the efficacy of speech? Is the depiction of a gesture as effective as looking at a real person using such a gesture? Classical rhetoric offered many techniques and strategies to influence the audience: from simple tricks such as the avoidance of unfamiliar words or looking the audience in the eye, to technical virtuosity in the use of metaphor, pathos or wit, and sophisticated strategies in the selection and highlighting of arguments or the projection of the right kind of image.

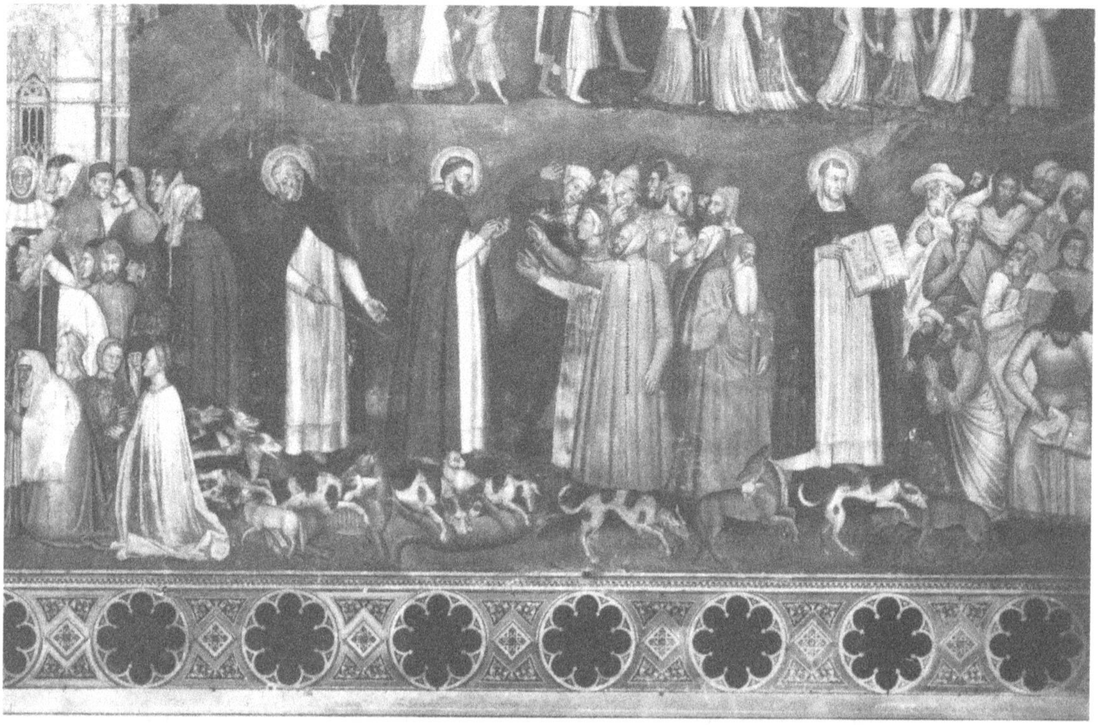

1 Andrea di Firenze, *Church Militant and Triumphant*. Florence, Santa Maria Novella, Spanish Chapel *c.* 1365–67 (photo: Centre for Art-Historical Documentation, Radboud Universiteit Nijmegen).

But can the persuasive strategies developed originally for persuasive speech be used in the arts?[1]

This book examines the role of rhetoric in the visual arts and architecture of early modern Europe. But to understand how architects, painters, patrons and viewers used rhetoric, we need to look first at visual persuasion in classical rhetoric. A good place to begin is gesture.

When Cicero was killed in 43 BC, his murderer, Marc Anthony, ordered that not only his head, but also his hands be nailed to the *rostrum* or speakers' platform in the Forum, to demonstrate that he could no longer speak, nor use the much more powerful language of gesture.[2] Cicero was not only the acknowledged master of telling gesture; he had also argued, associating gesture, acting, colour and painting in a way that would inspire many Renaissance artists, that the orator's use of gesture should not copy everyday gestures, but should highlight, clarify and intensify them:

> For nature has assigned to every emotion a particular look and tone of voice and bearing of its own; and the whole of a person's frame and

> every look on his face and utterance of his voice are like the strings of a harp, and sound according as they are struck by each successive emotion. For the tones of the voice are keyed up like the strings of an instrument [and all can be] regulated by the control of art; they are the colours available to the actor, as for the painter, to secure variety.[3]

Quintilian too has left a very detailed discussion of the use of the eyes and the glance, attitudes of the body, in particular of the head, and the meaning and effect of gesturing with the hands:

> For other portions of the body merely help the speaker, whereas the hands may almost be said to speak. Do we not use them to demand, promise, summon, dismiss, threaten, supplicate, express aversion or fear, question or deny? Do we not employ them to indicate joy, sorrow, hesitation, confession, penitence, measure, quantity, number and time? Have they not the power to excite and prohibit, to express approval, wonder or shame? Do they not take the place of adverbs and pronouns when we point at places and things? In fact, though the peoples and nations of the earth speak a multitude of tongues, they share in common the universal language of the hands.[4]

Gesture gave visual expression to what went on in the mind of the speaker and could thereby excite emotions in the audience. Orators also made use of their surroundings to visualize what went on in a speech. By pointing at significant buildings and sites, they created a stage set for their speech and activated the emotions associated with them. Gaius Gracchus, the Roman aristocrat who, together with his brother, defended the cause of the people as *tribuni plebis* in the second century BC, demonstrated his unhappy situation in one speech by asking again and again: 'Where can I turn?' After each repetition of that question he mentioned a place that might have offered refuge, such as the Capitol or his home, and then told the audience why he could not go there. Each time he acted out his plea by stretching his arm to the place he had mentioned.[5] The silent urban scene could become part of the emotional choreography. Public spaces, temples and statues of the gods could also be used to stage a speech, and as a silent, suggestive commentary to what was spoken aloud. In his first speech against the conspirator Catilina Cicero addressed the senate in the Temple of Jupiter Stator, which commemorated the salvation of Rome from an enemy, thus silently magnifying the danger from which Rome had been saved. In his speech *Pro Lege Manilia* he appealed to the gods from the *rostrum* in the Forum Romanum, 'and in particular [to] those who watch over this sacred site'. Sometimes he even changed the site, as in the third speech against Catilina, which he delivered in the Forum, but next to a conspicuous new statue of Jupiter he had put there. In the speech he asked his audience how they could stand there under the very eyes of Jupiter, the upholder of the state and of justice, and not take action.[6] The theatrical character of delivering, or rather performing, such speeches was acknowledged by Cicero, when he compared addressing the public assembly of Roman citizens with appearing on a stage where emotions could be manipulated.[7]

Settings were not the only visual elements employed to persuade. Orators could also introduce objects and even persons. Quintilian mentions 'swords encrusted with blood, bits of bone taken from wounds, and the bloodstained clothing of the victim'.[8] The introduction of Julius Caesar's bloodied garments and a wax effigy of his body covered in wounds, strengthened the effect of Marc Anthony's eloquence, causing a riot culminating in the spontaneous cremation of his body.[9] When the future emperor Galba, while governor of Spain, heard rumours that Nero was planning to murder him, he decided to have himself proclaimed emperor instead. He presided over the tribunal as usual, but instead of hearing cases he gave a speech deploring the condition of the empire under Nero. To support his words he had filled the tribunal as if it were a stage with as many portraits and statues of Nero's victims as could be found.[10]

Orators could also speak by silent means: simply by looking or pointing at significant objects. The impoverished grandson of the famous Republican orator Hortensius remained silent in front of the Senate, but glanced at the portraits of his ancestor and that of Augustus, who had once given him a million sesterces to restore his family's fortune.[11] For Quintilian, the power of the eyes was second only to that of the hands in silent persuasion.[12]

All these examples show that ancient orators were very much aware of the persuasive powers of the visual. Gesture was thought to allow all people to identify with what was put before their eyes. Nowadays the meaning of gesture is considered to be conventional and a cultural construction: an apotropaic gesture in one country can be an obscenity in another. But within the closed communities of classical Antiquity and early modern Europe gesture was considered to be a language that everybody acquired while growing up. According to Lucretius, gesture preceded spoken language as the means by which primitive humanity communicated.[13] Therefore gesture was felt to be closer to the emotions, less prone to misunderstanding than words, and hence more powerful in swaying the emotions. As Cicero observed, it is the task of the orator to 'play' his own body to appeal to the emotions of the public; persuasion is achieved not through sophisticated philosophical argument, but 'to sway [the emotions] is victory; for among all things it is the single most important in winning verdicts'.[14]

Gesture, the eyes and the expressions of the face externalize thought, emotion or memory.[15] It was an essential part of *actio* or action, the last of the five stages in which classical rhetoricians divided the process of writing and delivering a speech: invention, disposition, elocution, memory and action.[16]

After finding his material, ordering it, giving it the most fitting and eloquent formulation, and memorizing the speech, the orator had to deliver his speech, using not just words, but his entire body. Oratory, like opera or ballet, was not a static result, but a process of preparation leading to a performance drawing on various arts, taking place in public, in an organized and sometimes ritualized setting in front of an audience that was just as aware of the conventions governing public speech as the speaker himself. As Shakespeare put it in *Coriolanus*: 'Action is eloquence, and the eyes of th'ignorant/More learnèd than the ears'.[17]

Gesture was not simply a silent accompaniment, illustration or counterpoint to what the orator said. It was not merely an addition to a speech to enhance its persuasive power. Gesture and speech were also connected in a more profound way. In Book II of the *Institutio Oratoria* Quintilian urges the orator to observe decorum, but at the same time advises him to avoid traditional order when expedient. To illustrate this, he introduced a statue (Fig. 2). The curves and torsions of Myron's *Discobolus* suggest movement and life, whereas earlier statues, with their bold upright position and arms hanging by the side, cannot hold the attention of the viewer. The same interest, Quintilian argued, as that

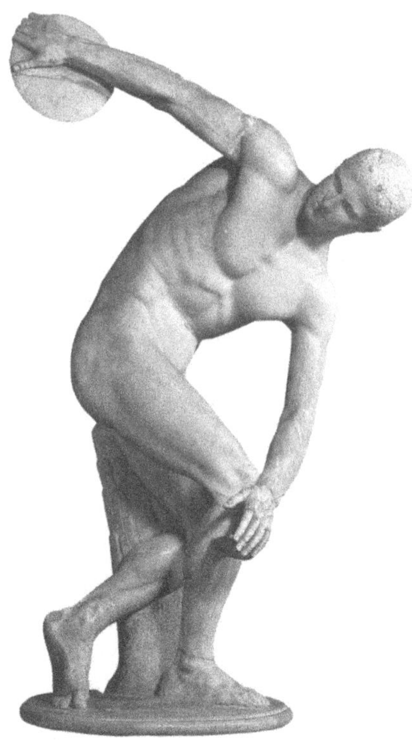

2 Myron, *Discobolus*. Rome: Museo Nazionale Romano (Museo delle Terme), *c.* 450 BC (photo: Centre for Art-Historical Documentation, Radboud Universiteit Nijmegen).

exercised by the daring, novelty and variety of the *Discobolus* is achieved by the use of figures of speech in oratory. They too 'involve a certain departure from the straight line and have the merit of variation from the ordinary usage, whether they be figures of thought or figures of speech'.[18] To define the complex and elusive topic of the figures of style, Quintilian drew on the visual arts. Playing on the original meaning of the Greek term 'tropes' – to turn away – for departures from the normal use and meaning of words Quintilian used the visual arts to illuminate the nature and role of figural speech.[19] The connection between the arts and figures of style goes further than providing examples. All rhetorical attempts to define them draw on a system of visual metaphors, all playing on the original meaning of the Latin *figura*, which etymologically is related to the verb *fingo*, to form or shape.[20] *Figura* can refer normal usage but also to deviations from it. In a general way it is used for any form or shape (*forma*) in which thought is expressed, just as *figura* can be used to refer to any shape or attitude of the body. The use of visual and spatial metaphor when trying to describe the process by which thought is expressed has become so widespread and ingrained that it has almost petrified into a dead metaphor. But it is nonetheless a metaphor, and actually forms the bridge to the second, more restricted way in which *figura* is used. It then means 'a [. . .] change in meaning or language from the ordinary and simple form, that is to say, a change analogous to that involved by sitting, lying down on something or looking back', and more specifically poetical and rhetorical changes. The changes in a body's aspect caused by motion are here used to illustrate modifications of normal use and meaning. Hence *figura* can refer to what we would now call figurative language, to expressions that have 'received a new aspect'.[21]

Figures of style are thus first connected to the gestures of the human body; but next they are defined in terms of visuality: as shapes and aspects. But Quintilian did not stop there. Figurative language is among the strongest means of persuasion an orator has at his disposal, particularly to arouse the emotions. Its force surpasses that of gesture and the expressive use of the face or eyes, because, as he put it, the 'vultus orationis', that is the face of speech seen as a whole surpasses the power of its parts. The 'face of speech' serves in particular to establish a bond with the public. Most translations normalize this metaphor, translating 'vultus' as aspect, which can be used to refer to dead matter and living beings alike. But 'vultus' was used almost exclusively of the human face, its countenance or features.[22] Cicero called it the 'image of the soul' and the 'silent language of the mind'.[23] Just as the gestures of the hands can give visible form to the emotions, the expressive movements of the face offer a visual statement of what goes on in the mind. In the same line of thought the figures of style can be called 'the face of speech': through their movement away from ordinary usage they highlight and thereby give visible shape to the emotions of the speaker.

The brilliance – another visual metaphor, caught by Cicero when he called striking arrangements of words 'quasi lumina', almost lights or even eyes – lent to speech by figurative language ultimately results in an illusion of life.[24] In the visual metaphors used by Quintilian and Cicero speech becomes alive: it has hands that gesture, eyes that see and a face that expresses emotion. Without figurative language speech is lifeless and without force; but if rightly used it endows a speech with life and the power to act on the public. One stylistic strategy that was considered particularly effective to achieve this was *enargeia* or *illustratio*, description that is so vivid and lifelike that the audience believe they are seeing what is described, not listening to somebody speaking. It can be achieved both by the use of figures of speech, in particular metaphor, and by what we would now call narrative techniques, such as detailed description constructed with telling details, the introduction of an eye witness or a sudden address to the public. If successful, speech seemed to dissolve into what it described.

Enargeia (vividness) and its Latin equivalents *evidentia* or *illustratio*, and *energeia* (actuality), were considered to be among the most important, if not the main instruments of persuasion.[25] The Greek *enargeia*, derived from *argès*, shining light, meant clearness, distinctness or vividness; and by extension putting something before the audience's eyes by highlighting it. In Aristotle's *Rhetorica* the latter stylistic strategy is defined together with the etymologically unrelated term *energeia* in his discussion of particularly persuasive stylistic techniques: a vivid representation (*enargeia*) puts what is discussed before the eyes of the audience by using words that signify motion or actuality (*energeia*).[26] A particularly effective strategy to achieve this effect is to use metaphors that animate the inanimate. Quintilian argued that 'oratory fails of its full effect [. . .] if its appeal is merely to the hearing [. . .] and not displayed in [its] living truth to the eyes of the mind'.[27] The orator should act on the eyes, not the ears, of the public, and should excite vivid images before their mind's eyes. '*Enargeia*', as Quintilian put it, 'makes us seem not so much to narrate as to exhibit the actual scene, while our emotions will be no less actively stirred than if we were present at the actual occurrence'. As we have seen, Quintilian literally called figurative language the gestures and face of oratory and 'the lights or as it were the eyes of eloquence'. Eloquence itself comes alive.[28]

All this suggests that the belief in the persuasive power of vividness and living presence was rooted in the conviction, shared by speakers and public alike, that among all visual representation, the living human form was considered most significant; but also that the ability to see is the most important sign of life. By creating a strong suggestion of life, the orator could blur the boundaries between gods and men, in the sense that the capacity to make dead matter seem alive or the absent present was a capacity generally attributed to the gods. The result was not persuasion by force of rational argument, but fascination exploiting ancient fears and ambitions.[29] Cicero and Quintilian were not unique in this.

Longinus for instance, developed the experience of the sublime in terms of a sensation of extreme vividness.[30]

Quintilian also compared gesture to the silent, but powerful, eloquence of painting:

> For we can indicate our will not merely by a gesture of the hand, but also with a nod from the head: signs take the place of language in the dumb, and the movements of the hands are frequently full of meaning, and appeal to the emotions without any aid from words. The temper of the mind can be inferred from the glance and gait [. . .]. Nor is it wonderful that gesture which depends on various forms of movement should have such power, when pictures, which are silent and motionless, penetrate into our innermost feelings with such power that at times they seem more eloquent than language itself.[31]

Quintilian here used words usually reserved for human beings ('tacens': not using articulate speech, and 'habitus': the attitudes or bearing acquired through education) to describe the power of the silent languages of painting and gesture to animate the inanimate. About 1,300 years later Leonardo da Vinci would follow the same stylistic strategy in his observations of idolatry:

> Men will speak to men who will not hear, who will have their eyes open without seeing. They will speak to them but receive no response, ask favors of those with ears who hear not. They will light candles for the blind.[32]

Considered superficially, Leonardo ridiculed those who treat inanimate images as living beings, but actually he used the language reserved for the living to designate these objects.

Rhetorical thought and practice of persuasion centres on the visual, both in the way it defines main instruments of persuasion such as gesture or figurative language, and in the way it presents some of the effects of oratory. The aims of oratory are to delight, instruct and move, but some of the most powerful means of persuasion are visual: speech literally acts on the public, establishes an affective bond through the use of the speaker's eyes and gesture, or through its creation of the effect of lifelikeness. In such experiences of vivid lifelikeness, *evidentia* or *enargeia*, representations appeared to dissolve into what they represent. Speech and, as we shall see in this book, images or buildings, are transformed into agents. Visual persuasion therefore is not a matter of speeches presented in stone or paint, putting across a message that could have been put as well, or better, in words.

In the chapters that follow we will encounter many instances of visual persuasion in the arts and architecture of early modern Europe that were shaped and influenced by classical rhetoric. This book argues that a major key to understanding them lies in the view held by rhetoricians such as Aristotle, Quintilian or Longinus that persuasion is achieved through what we might call figuration: giving an outward, visible shape to emotions, thoughts or memories that creates the illusion of human life and agency. This includes gesture or facial expression, but also the use of figurative language, in particular metaphor, or the use of *enargeia.* Considered in these terms it becomes possible to articulate visual persuasion: to show, for instance, that one of its main instruments was the creation of a common ground between works of art and their viewers, which served as the basis for a sense of shared identity. The ultimate instance of this is the viewer's experience of living presence, which transforms the boundaries between the spectator and inanimate paint into a sense of shared humanity, or even of divine presence. In architecture, which is mainly non-figurative and therefore less fit for suggesting illusions of human presence, the common ground would often be achieved by creating a sense of a shared past or cultural memory. We could call this the paradox of visual persuasion: art, in order to be of the highest quality and at its most persuasive, must cease to look like art. Through this powerful illusion of living presence, it was thought by classical rhetoricians and their early modern followers, art acts on the viewer, exciting emotions and inciting to belief or action. As I hope to show in this book, such visual persuasion was not exclusively the domain of the figurative arts in early modern Europe; architectural persuasion can also be understood in such terms.

This book looks at the roles rhetoric played in visual persuasion through works of art and buildings in early modern Europe. It takes as its starting point that classical rhetoric, though originally developed for persuasive speech, always attached great importance to visual means of persuasion. In the following pages the uses early modern artists and viewers made of rhetorical visuality and visual rhetoric will be examined. Part I looks at the use of rhetoric in artistic theory, as a provider of terms, concepts and methods to deal with visual persuasion. In Chapter One, one of the clearest and most straightforward uses of rhetoric in painting is discussed: the employment of gesture to appeal to the viewer and express emotions. In *De Pictura* Alberti explicitly advised the painter to include a figure who looks out from the painting at the viewer, and the liminal character of such pictorial strategies serves as an introduction to what is the conceptual basis of the use of rhetoric in the arts: an awareness of the representational character of art. Or, put in rhetorical terms, a distinction can be made between *res* and *verba,* between what to say and how to say it. Alberti's use of rhetorical concepts such as *compositio* or *perspicuitas* is based on that distinction. His new reading of the Narcissus myth, in which he credits him with the invention of painting, also shows Alberti to be the first early modern theorist of art who considered painting not in terms of the activity or product, but in terms of representation. In Chapter Two the attempts to provide architectural theory with a basis that is both scientific and rhetorical are studied. Daniel Barbaro, Gherardo Spini and Vincenzo Scamozzi were all strongly influenced by an Aristotelian view of architecture as a *scienza*, that is, a rational activity based on knowledge of general principles. This Aristotelian theory accorded rhetoric a double role. In presenting his designs the architect becomes an orator, the advocate who can use all the persuasive strategies rhetoric has to offer to present his work. But rhetoric is also used to articulate the design process. Like the orator, the architect has to go through the five stages of preparing and delivering a speech, and can use various manners of building just as the speaker has several ways of speaking at his disposal.

Part II examines various strategies rhetoric offered for persuasive design. Chapter Three identifies what early modern artists and viewers considered to be the *sine qua non* of visual persuasion in the arts: the creation of a common ground which allowed the viewer to identify with what a painting or statue shows. Paintings by Giovanni Bellini, Titian and Caravaggio display various compositional strategies to achieve this, including the use of linear perspective, the blurring of the boundaries between the pictorial world and that of the viewers, and the suggestion of the living, acting presence of what is represented. Chapter Four argues that architectural persuasion is not a matter of speeches in stone, of direct projections of verbal communication onto architecture, but a more subtle process in which buildings serve to create memories and identities. Throughout the seventeenth and eighteenth centuries, English architects used buildings to excite memories, trigger associations, and more generally direct the way viewers experienced their work. This chapter examines a series of strategies through which their buildings acted on the mind. In his notes for a reconstruction of Stonehenge and his masque designs, Inigo Jones attempted to create a new, classical past for the recently formed kingdom of Great Britain. His designs and reconstructions acted as the visual embodiment of a cultural memory, and by offering a classical example incited to virtuous action. Picturesque landscape design aimed to create or activate cultural memory. It sought to move the viewer by playing on a sense of shared identity; it suggested and exploited a common ground between landscapes, buildings and viewers. In Sir John Soane's houses, fragments of buildings that were to trigger emotions and associations were to direct the viewer's experience; but ultimately Soane staged the visits to his houses, expecting the visitor to approach them in the same frame of mind as a person who goes to watch a tragedy.

Part III is devoted to interpretations of the arts and architecture informed by rhetoric. It looks at the concepts and competences viewers brought to the analysis of arts but more in particular at their understanding of visual persuasion. In Antiquity rhetoric was not only considered as the theory and practice of persuasive speech. Writing and interpretation were considered as two, closely related, aspects of the same activity, the mind expressing itself through a process of understanding in word, gesture or image. It was a very widespread view, continually repeated in early modern Europe, often combined with the Aristotelian view, stated in *De Anima*, that thinking takes place through images. Rhetoric thus becomes the capacity to grasp the images before the mind's eye and transform them into coherent and persuasive speech.

Chapters Five and Six explore various manifestations of rhetoric's interpretive potential. In Chapter Five Bartolommeo Maranta's essay on an Annunciation by Titian documents the use of the distinction between *res* and *verba*, between what to say and how to say it, as a strategy of interpretation. *Ut pictura poesis* functioned not only as advice on how to write or paint but also as another interpretive strategy, because it directed viewers to what the visual arts and poetry have in common: not only several strategies of representation, but also the aim of creating an illusion of life. In Chapter Three this was discussed from the perspective of design; here we will look at how rhetoric informed reactions by viewers who were struck by the *enargeia* of paintings or statues. Francesco Bocchi's essays on Florentine art show that painting was considered to be like poetry, not so much because it resembles the latter, but because both have as their aim to imitate life. Life, however, is taken in a very specific sense: that of plot and character, of human beings engaged in events and situations with which spectators can identify. They are no longer critics; they become the audience at a play. The poems written in the early decades of the sixteenth century in response to the rediscovery of the *Laocoön* take this kind of response even further. Viewers were so struck by the pathos and suffering of the statue that they claimed it was not only alive, but had the transcendent power to render them either into speechless observers, more dead than the statue, or into fully human beings, sympathizing with the suffering before their eyes.

Chapter Six argues that rhetorically informed attitudes and responses to architecture are in important respects similar to the response to art highlighted in Chapter Five. In early modern Europe architecture was often considered as a natural sign: to explain its appeal, the viewer attributed characteristics usually restricted to the natural world, and in particular human beings, to architecture. Such an interpretive strategy ties in with the view that the natural world, including mankind, was first of all God's creation. Therefore the seventeenth-century English interpretations of architecture examined here draw not on Vitruvian iconography but on techniques of interpretation that originated in the hermeneutics of the Bible on the natural world considered typology or figural interpretation as God's creation. The concluding part of Chapter Six traces the introduction of the concepts of style and *caractère* in architectural history and theory around 1750. The wide currency gained by *caractère* in French architectural discourse after 1750 is often considered a symptom of the decay of the authority of the Vitruvian paradigm; just as the analysis of works of art on the basis of stylistic characteristics is generally regarded as a founding moment in the formation of modern architectural history. Nevertheless the art-historical use of style as an analytical tool ultimately goes back to the rhetorical distinction of *res* and *verba*, and *caractère* is yet another variety of the humanizing tendency that was so often a part of rhetorical response to art.

Beginning with the work of Rensselaer W. Lee, Ernst Gombrich, Michael Baxandall, Marc Fumaroli and David Summers, the influence of classical rhetoric on the visual arts and architecture of early modern Europe has now been the subject of scholarly attention for almost 50 years.[33] Many aspects of that influence have been studied in great detail: the formation of a Humanist critical vocabulary or the rhetorical bases of the artistic thought of Michelangelo and his entourage by Baxandall and Summers; the role of rhetorical attitudes to biography in Patricia Rubin's study of Vasari, or of rhetoric in the perception of early Florentine Quattrocento architecture by Christine Smith; the rhetorical culture that shaped viewing attitudes of Counter-Reformation art by Marc Fumaroli, to name but a few.

The particular brief of this book is to show in what ways rhetoric informed processes of artistic design, theory, perception or interpretation that all centre round visual persuasion. It also offers a view on the conceptual basis of rhetoric's roles in the arts of early modern Europe. It is not a historical survey of the roles rhetoric played in the arts of early modern Europe, and has no pretence at completeness. Nor is it yet another contribution to current debates about word and image, arguing for the inherently textual nature of all objects of interpretation, or offering a view on the irreducibly visual character of the visual arts.[34] Scrutinizing the use in the visual arts of a theory originally developed to achieve persuasive speech does raise the issue of the relation between word and image, but the perspective adopted here is different: to discern how persuasion in the visual arts and architecture was thought to work, and how classical rhetoric can help us to understand it. The book therefore focuses on visual persuasion, using a series of case studies that show the range and variety of rhetoric's adaptations and interactions, in particular in architecture, which is still a relatively neglected field in this respect. It asks in what ways works of art or buildings acted or were thought to act on their viewers and what it may have been they tried to make them think, feel, believe or do. Most of these case studies centre on Italian art and artistic discourse of the fifteenth and sixteenth centuries. In some cases, particularly where architecture is concerned, material was used from seventeenth- and eighteenth-century England and France because some aspects of visual persuasion, particularly political, were much more explicitly discussed outside Italy and after the Renaissance, in contexts of appropriation and transformation.

Notes

1 For a general discussion of the problems of connecting the verbal and the visual see Mitchell (1994), pp. 11–111. For a fundamental hermeneutic reflection on these problems see Boehm (1978), (1980), (1981) and (1988).

2 Though Marc Anthony's decision might also be understood in terms of the Roman tradition of ritual derision and defamation: see Pauly/Wissowa (1894–1997), s.v. 'damnatio memoriae' and 'defamatio'.

3 Cicero, *De Oratore* III.lvi.214–15.

4 Quintilian, *Institutio Oratoria* XI.iii.86–7. Despite its importance in eloquence, delivery or *actio* is relatively neglected in the main histories of rhetoric, but the study of gesture is a flourishing academic specialism. Thus Kennedy (1972) devotes only 20 out of almost 700 pages to delivery. For recent overviews of gesture see Roodenburg and Bremmer (1993); for gesture in ancient rhetoric, art and society see De Jorio (2000); Sittl (1890); Brilliant (1963); Maier-Eichhorn (1989); Aldrete (1999) and Corbeill (2004). On gesture in Renaissance art see, for instance, Eisenbichler and Sohm (1983) and Rehm (2002).

5 Cicero, *De Oratore* III.214; *Institutio Oratoria* XI.iii.115.

6 Cicero, *In Catilinam* I.xi.33; *Pro Lege Manilia* 24; *In Catilinam* III.vii.20; cf. Aldrete (1999), pp. 25–6.

7 Cicero, *De Amicitia* 97.

8 *Institutio Oratoria* VI.i.30.

9 Cf. Kennedy (1968).

10 Suetonius, *Galba* X.

11 Tacitus, *Annales* II.37–8.

12 *Institutio Oratoria* XI.iii.72–7.

13 Lucretius, *De Rerum Natura* V.1031.

14 Cicero, *De Oratore* III.216 and II.178; *Orator* 69; cf. Aldrete (1999), p. 6.

15 Quintilian XI.iii.72–82 is very detailed on the role of the eyes and face in giving visible expression to emotions, roles, attitudes or characters.

16 For discussions of these five stages in preparing and delivering a speech see *Rhetorica ad Herennium* I.ii.3 and III.viii.15; Cicero, *Partitiones Oratoriae* I.ii.5; Quintilian, *Institutio Oratoria* V.x.94.

17 Shakespeare, *Coriolanus*, III.2, ll. 75–7.

18 *Institutio Oratoria* II.xiii.8–11.

19 *Institutio Oratoria* IX.i.1–2.

20 Cf. Lewis and Short, *A Latin Dictionary*, s.v. 'figura'.

21 *Institutio Oratoria* IX.i.10–14.

22 Cf. Lewis and Short, *Oxford Latin Dictionary*, s.v. 'vultus'.

23 Cicero, *De Legibus* I.ix.27 and *De Oratore* III.lix.22.

24 Cicero, *Orator* XXXIX.134: 'Et reliqua, ex collocatione verborum quae sumuntur, quasi lumina [...].' In *Institutio Oratoria* VIII.v.34 Quintilian calls epigrams 'lumina orationis'.

25 On *enargeia* see Zanker (1981); Onians (1980); Scholz (1999); Calame (1991); Walker (1993); Watson (1988), pp. 69–70 and Manieri (1998). On Stoic explanations of *enargeia* see Elsner (1995), p. 26, and Watson (1988). For early modern developments, mainly from the perspective of literary history see Galand-Hallyn (1993), (1994) and (1995); Hazard (1975); Graf (1995); Cave (1976), pp. 5–19, and (1979), pp. 27ff.; for Italian Quattrocento art see Kemp (1977); for the Cinquecento see Von Rosen (2000).

26 Aristotle, *Rhetorica* 1411b24ff. Cf. Kennedy (1991).

27 Quintilian, *Institutio Oratoria* VIII.iii.62.

28 Ibid., VI.ii.32; see also Longinus, *Peri Hupsous* XV.1

29 As Gordon (1979) put it: '[These] clichés are a genuine form of cultural negotiation of boundaries, of human self-definition'.

30 Longinus, *Peri Hupsous* XV.i–xii; for a view that the experience of the sublime is actually an experience of living presence see Ankersmit (1995).

31 *Institutio Oratoria* XI.iii.66–7.

32 Leonardo da Vinci, *Notebooks*, vol. II, p. 375. For this and many similar responses by Renaissance viewers see Trexler (1980), pp. 61–71.

33 There exists no overview of the roles of rhetoric in the visual arts. On rhetoric and the arts in ancient Greece and Rome see Elsner (1995); Goldhill and Osborne (1994), and Onians (1999) for the role of rhetoric in shaping ancient thought about the arts and viewers' responses. For early modern Italy see Baxandall (1971); Payne (2000); Onians (1988); Smith (1992); Thomas Puttfarken (2000); Rubin (1995) and Fumaroli (1994). Interestingly, books on the relation between works of art and their spectators, such as Shearman (1992); reception studies, for instance, Kemp (1985), or the history of response like Freedberg (1989), have given little attention to rhetoric. More recently, Elsner (1995); Bolzoni (1995) and Barkan (2000) have each in different ways opened up the study of the role of rhetoric in the arts, by drawing attention to important sources and considerations outside the range of antique artistic theory in the case of Elsner, or by thinking in new ways about the place of visuality in rhetoric itself, in the work of Bolzoni and Barkan.

34 For a recent attempt to argue for an irreducibly visual character of the visual arts and architecture see Van Eck and Winters (2005).

PART I

THEORY

ONE:
REPRESENTATION AND PERSUASION IN ALBERTI'S 'DE PICTURA'

Gesture between presence and representation

In Masaccio's *Trinità* the Mother of God draws the beholder's attention to the crucified body of Her son with a resigned gesture that accords with her expression of stoic forbearance, but somehow is also its translation: they present the viewer with two, coherent and complementary, ways of expressing a complex emotion (Fig. 1.1). She is alone among the figures depicted to reach out, literally, and to gaze out of the picture, even though it is not entirely clear whether she looks at the viewer, or is too much exhausted by grief to focus. Her behaviour certainly seems to echo the words of *Jeremiah* 1.12: 'Behold and see, if there is any trouble like unto my trouble'. Leon Battista Alberti may very well have had Masaccio's fresco in mind when in *De Pictura*, written in 1435/6, he advised painters to include a witness: a figure who looks out of the picture at the spectators and draws them into what is happening.[1] Gesture is used in painting to show emotions, interactions between the figures, or to address the viewer. This is one of the most straightforward instances of a rhetorical practice adopted by painters and developed by theorists as an instrument of persuasion. Where orators use *apostrophe*, turning from one topic or person to another, painters make their figures turn away from the pictorial space they inhabit towards the viewer. Their action invites the spectator to participate in what the painting offers to their view.

In classical rhetoric gesture, as we have seen, was an integral part of the delivery or *actio* of a speech. It was the most straightforwardly visual part of rhetoric, but also blurred the boundaries between representation and presence. When overwhelmed by grief or anger the orator could stop speaking and let gesture take over. It thus became the enactment of emotion. But this was so highly conventionalized that it almost became a representation, recalling the gestures ordinary people make in normal life when faced, for instance, by overpowering grief.[2] Framed by the setting of the speech and rhetorical convention gesture was robbed of the spontaneity often associated with it. But it was also

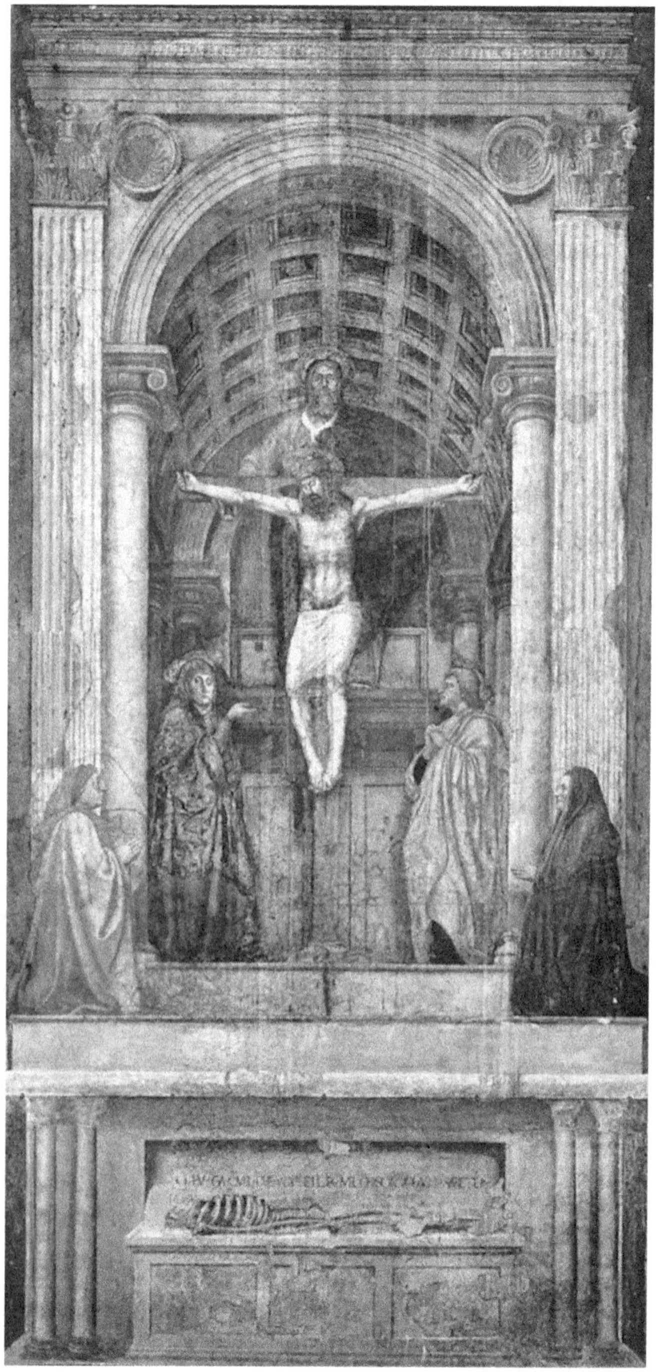

1.1 Masaccio, *The Holy Trinity.* Florence, Santa Maria Novella, *c.* 1425 to 1427 (photo: Centre for Art-Historical Documentation, Radboud Universiteit Nijmegen).

represented: described, listed, codified or decoded. Its use was discussed in the handbooks as a major strategy of persuasion because of its directness, universal character and immediate impact on the emotions. At the same time for Quattrocento artists and theorists gesture offered one of the easier ways of connecting with classical art, from the adoption of gestures taken from Roman sarcophages by Mantegna and Botticelli to Alberti's advice to painters. Leonardo da Vinci would advise painters to depict speakers using gestures that closely resemble the gestures, attitudes and behaviour described by Quintilian: counting arguments on the fingers for instance, or looking at the audience and waiting for a few moments before starting to speak.[3]

A factor complicating the history of gesture in the arts is a shift in function that seems to have taken place in the sixteenth century: whereas in ancient rhetoric and the precepts of Alberti gesture serves as a conventional expression of emotion, used in oratory to support, and sometimes act in counterpoint to the words, it increasingy became an indicator of character and personality. In Aristotelian terms gesture gradually changes from being mainly an expression of *pathos* or transient emotions to being the outward sign of *ethos*, the more permanent character or moral qualities of a person.[4]

Here, however, I will look at the ways in which gesture provides a first bridge between rhetoric and painting in Alberti's *De Pictura*, and how its double character – both mediated in representation and unmediated in its enactment – gives a first clue to understanding the play of presence and representation in visual persuasion. *De Pictura* is both the starting point of early modern theoretical discourse about painting and, in its treatment of the Narcissus myth, a thematization of this oscillation between presence and representation. Although Mary's gesture in the *Trinità* may not be a copy of an ancient gesture as described in the rhetorical treatises, in the way it reaches out from pictorial space into real space, it crosses the border between a representation of the Trinity and its actual presence. Thereby the gesture reinforces what Masaccio probably tried to achieve by the location of his fresco and the use of linear perspective because, upon entering the church, the fresco appears as a small chapel, not a painting on a wall: a blurring of the boundaries between 'real' and pictorial space. This resembles the rhetorical ideal of dissolving the representational character of a speech into what it describes, by means of all the stylistic strategies that help to achieve *enargeia*.

Leonardo's observations on the relation between poetry, rhetoric and painting throw some more light on the power of gesture to fuse representation and what is represented. In the *Paragone* he argues that the painter is capable of exciting much stronger emotions in his public than the poet:

> The elements of narrative paintings ought to move those who look at or contemplate them in the same way as him whom the narrative painting represents. That is, if the narrative painting represents terror,

> fear, flight, sorrow, weeping or lamentation; or pleasure, joy, laughter and similar conditions, the minds of those who view it ought to move their limbs so that they seem to find themselves in the same situation the figures in the narrative painting represent. If they do not do so, the skill of the painter is in vain.[5]

The depiction of emotions ought to be so lifelike that the viewers are forced to feel them too, and act, move and gesture accordingly. They are compelled to identify with the figures in the painting, and in that process the representational character of the painting, or the border between extra-pictorial 'reality' and pictorial illusion is dissolved. Leonardo then mentions a painter who 'once made a picture which made everybody who saw it yawn and yawn repeatedly as long as they kept their eyes on the picture, which represented a man who was also yawning'. For Leonardo this was a sign of the painting's quality, because it compelled the viewer to identify with what he saw and act in a certain way. In the same section he observed, turning to the poet: 'If you say with words you will stir up people to tears or to laughter, I say that it is not you, the poet, who moves them, but it is the orator (*oratore*), and oratory is another science, and is not poetry'.

Now what could be the difference between poetry and oratory that Leonardo had in mind here? It is not the medium, for both use words. The difference lies in the intensity of the emotions excited, and in the fact that in oratory as in painting they are not described but shown and highlighted, through movement of the limbs and face. A successful painting forces the viewers to move their limbs in the same way as the figures in the painting. When these yawn, *they* yawn; when they laugh or cry, *they* will laugh or cry. This is where rhetoric is fundamentally different from poetry, by which Leonardo here meant written literature: although they both use words, rhetoric also acts out emotions by employing the visual language of gesture and facial expression. Thereby it compels the viewer to identify bodily with what he or she sees.[6] Gesture is therefore one way in which a painting can touch the viewer. In the next section we will consider other uses Alberti made of rhetoric to develop a theory of painting as persuasive communication.

Rhetorical concepts in 'De Pictura'

In Book II of *De Pictura* Alberti divided the art of painting into three parts: *circumscriptio*, *compositio* and *luminum receptio*.[7] Alberti used the last term to describe the varying hues of a surface as a result of the changing intensity of light.[8] *Circumscriptio* and *compositio* are both terms that originate in classical rhetoric. Cicero used *circumscriptio* in *De Oratore* in the sense of a description.[9]

Alberti spoke of *circumscriptio* as the drawing of contours, the indication of the boundaries of an object that is to be painted. In the Italian version of *De Pictura* it is translated as '*disegno*'. This division, he wrote in Book II:

> [W]e learn from Nature herself. As painting aims to represent things seen, let us note how in fact things are seen. In the first place, when we look at a thing, we see it as an object which occupies a space. The painter will draw around this space, and he will call this process of sketching the outline, appropriately, circumscription. Then, as we look, we discern how the several surfaces of the objects seen are fitted together; the artist, when drawing these combinations of surfaces in their correct relationship, will properly call this composition. Finally, in looking we observe more clearly the colours of surfaces; the representation in painting of this aspect, since it receives all its variations from light, will aptly here be termed the reception of light. Therefore, circumscription, composition and reception of light make up painting.[10]

As Michael Baxandall has shown, in formulating the criteria for the successful depiction of a *historia*, in the most basic sense a story taken from classical mythology or the Bible, Alberti used a series of key terms used in classical rhetoric for stylistic prescription and analysis:

> The *historia* you might justly praise and admire will be of a kind to show itself so pleasant and *ornata* with allurements that it long holds the eyes of the *doctus* and *indoctus* beholder with a certain *voluptas* and *animi motus*. For the first thing to bring *voluptas* in a *historia* is precisely *copia* and *varietas* of things [. . .] in all things the mind is much delighted by *varietas* and *copia* [. . .]. I will declare that the *historia* is most *copiosa* in which there are mingled together in their places old men and men in their prime, youths, boys, mature women and maidens, young children, pet animals and puppy-dogs, small birds, horses, cattle, buildings and stretches of country; and I will praise all *copia* provided that it is appropriate (*conveniens*) to the event that is represented here. For it is usually the case that, when the beholder lingers over his examination, then the *copia* of the painter gains favour. But I should wish this *copia* to be *ornata* with a degree of *varietas*, and also *gravis* and *moderata* with *dignitas* and *verecundia* [. . .].[11]

Underlying this description of good painting are the three tasks of the orator: to instruct (implicit in the demand that paintings appeal to the educated and uneducated alike), to charm, and to move. Alberti has comparatively little to say about the first task, but quite detailed advice about the other two. *Copia* (abundance) and *varietas* (variety) are both important instruments to attract and hold the attention of the viewer. As Michael Baxandall and Brian Vickers, among others, have shown, these terms all have quite articulate and well-circumscribed meanings in rhetorical analysis of style. *Copia* refers to an abundance of subject matter and words, *varietas* to their diversity.[12] It is therefore a composition strategy, guiding for instance the use of figures of speech.[13] *Copia* is subordinated to *compositio*; if it is allowed free scope a painting will become *dissolutus*, disorderly and disconnected, displaying only a loose connection between its parts.[14] *Convenientia* is related to *decorum*, the most important stylistic quality of all: it regulates the use of all stylistic means and strategies and ensures that what is said is in keeping with the subject, the occasion and the public. *Copia* and *varietas* together bind the attention of the public by their pleasing variety. But *varietas* is presented as an absolute value. Much of Book II is devoted to analysing how variety of figures, attitudes and colours can make a painting persuasive. Alberti, however, substantially limits the use of *copia*: its use should be convenient, that is governed by considerations of decorum; it must be serious (*gravis*) and keep within the bounds of dignity and modesty, both terms loaded with rhetorical connotations; and copiousness should be enhanced (*ornata*) with *varietas*.[15] An important instrument to achieve variety is the use of *antithesis* or *contrapposto*, the figure of speech in which opposites are combined. In the passage quoted above Alberti advises the juxtaposition of the young and old, men and animals, buildings and the country. It is a powerful compositional device, but it is also a stylistic strategy with an interesting rhetorical pedigree, because Quintilian's fundamental comparison between oratory and the visual arts was made during his discussion of *antithesis* in oratory and sculpture, as we have seen in the Introduction.

Ornatus and *convenientia* (appropriateness) were all used by Cicero and Quintilian to characterize an effective style, that is one that manages to move the soul of the public, causes the movements of the soul or *animi motus* which are also the effect a properly represented *historia* achieves. To move the emotions of the spectator Alberti advises *verecundia*, truthfulness:

> A *historia* will move spectators when the men painted in the picture outwardly demonstrate their own feelings [*animi motum*] as clearly as possible. Nature provides – and there is nothing to be found more rapacious of her like than she – that we mourn with the mourners, laugh with those who laugh, and grieve with the grief-stricken. Yet these feelings are known from movements of the body.[16]

That is, truthfulness does not mean naturalism or photographic realism. *Verecundia* helps to blur the boundary between the artificial space of the painting and the 'real space' of the beholder by drawing on the human and cultural context shared by artists and their viewers. The use of linear perspective is one way of creating such a common ground, to which we will return in Chapter Three of this book; here Alberti suggests that persons and their emotions should be represented in a way all the viewers would recognize, so that the spectator can identify with the *historia* and feel the same emotions. Hence too Alberti's suggestion to include a witness:

> I like there to be someone in the *historia* who tells the spectator what is going on, and either beckons them with his hand to look, or with ferocious expression and forbidding glance challenges them not to come near, [...] or points to some danger or remarkable thing in the picture, or by his gestures invites you to laugh or weep with them.[17]

Renaissance art abounds with examples of such figures. Alberti himself cited Giotto's mosaic of the Navicella for Old St Peter's (now lost), the only modern painting he mentions.[18] By drawing attention to the power of gesture and expression to move the feelings of the public he further developed the connection between rhetorical theories of *actio* and artistic theory that had been opened by Quintilian's comparison between lively speech and the *Discobolos*. Before that Cicero had called *actio*, the union of voice and gesture, the 'dominant factor in oratory': 'In gesture the body talks, so it is all the more necessary to make it agree with the thought; and nature has given us eyes [...] to indicate the feelings of the mind [...].'[19]

'COMPOSITIO' AS A CARDINAL VIRTUE OF STYLE

All these strategies to represent a *historia* in a moving and persuasive manner are determined by *compositio*, the central concept of *De Pictura*. In rhetoric, *compositio* refers to the structure of sentences. It was a technical concept, which did not mean what we would now call literary composition; instead, it referred to the construction of a complex sentence out of words and clauses. Aristotle first systematically discussed *compositio* in the *Rhetorica*, but Quintilian also discussed it quite extensively.[20]

Traditionally three elements are distinguished in a sentence: a complex, hypotactical sentence considered as a whole was called a *periodos* (*ambitus, continatio, conclusio*); the composing elements were called *kolon* (in Latin: *membrum*, 'member'), a group of three to five words, either as main clause or as subordinate clause; and a group of two to three words belonging together was called a *komma* (*incisum*). From such *kola* and *kommata* the *periodos* should be constructed in a logical and well-balanced way.[21] Cennino Cennini had used the related term 'comporre' and 'componire', by which he probably meant the first actual drawing of a figure on a *tavola* or wall as opposed to preliminary sketching. He also associated it with poetical convention, comparing the poet's freedom to that of the painter in what is probably a misunderstanding of *ut pictura poesis*.[22] But as Michael Baxandall has shown, Alberti gave it a new sense. In his definition of *compositio* he made use of the fact that the Latin *membrum* can mean both 'member of a body' and 'part of a sentence':

> Composition is the procedure in painting whereby the parts are composed together in the picture. [. . .] Parts of the *historia* are the bodies, part of the body is the member, and part of the member is the surface. The principal parts of the work are the surfaces, because from these come the members, from the members the bodies, from the bodies the *historia*, and finally the finished work of the painter.[23]

To obtain a better understanding of what Alberti meant by *compositio* we have to take a closer look at Section 21 of *De Pictura*. Here he stressed – rather unexpectedly – the importance of *compositio*. This section appears to be added like an afterthought to his discussion of linear perspective. After starting the analysis of his method of construction in Sections 19 and 20, he writes:

> This method of dividing up the pavement pertains especially to that part of painting which, when we come to it, we shall call composition; and it is such that I fear it may be little understood by readers on account of the novelty of the subject and the brevity of our description. As we can easily judge from the works of former ages, this matter probably remained completely unknown to our ancestors because of its obscurity and difficulty. You will hardly find any *historia* of theirs properly composed either in painting or modelling or sculpture.

Linear perspective is here presented as a part of *compositio*. Its use enables the painter to compose and paint a *historia*, but it is more than a technique enabling the painter to suggest three-dimensional space on a flat surface. Perspective also becomes an instrument of visual persuasion. In rhetoric *perspicuitas* or clarity is one of the four cardinal qualities of style or *virtutes dicendi*; in the phase of *elocutio* the orator has to take care that his oration meets the demands of *latinitas* (correctness, that is pure Latin), *perspicuitas* (clarity), *ornatus* (ornateness) and *decorum* (appropriateness).[24] According to Quintilian, *latinitas* and *perspicuitas* are two qualities that every language user must strive for to be understood at all;

the other two need the special attention of the orator, who wants to persuade his audience. In *De Pictura* three of the four *virtutes dicendi* are also qualities of a good *historia*: *perspicuitas*, *ornatus* and *decorum*. In agreement with Quintilian, Alberti declared *ornatus* to be the most important guide for the composition of surfaces, the composition of members and the composition of bodies, with *decorum* as a concluding and covering quality.[25] *Ornatus* is generally translated as 'ornament', but does not have the modern sense of decorative bits and pieces to be added or left out at will. For the Romans *ornatus* suggested distinction and excellence, and having resources at hand to meet with any challenge; *ornamentum* could not only signify ornament but weapons as well, equipment or a soldier's accoutrements.[26] *Perspicuitas* is a principle of clarity, of rationalization and unity; it aims at the avoidance of obscurity (*obscuritas*) and ambiguousness (*ambiguitas*). When he described how to avoid that a *historia* appears to be *confuse et dissolute* the ultimate goals is a representation distinguished by *perspicuitas*:

> I disapprove of those painters who, in their desire to appear rich or to leave no space empty, follow no system of composition, but scatter everything about in random confusion with the result that their *historia* does not appear to be doing anything but merely to be in an turmoil. [...] In a *historia* I strongly approve of the practice I see observed by the tragic and comic poets, of telling their story with as few characters as possible.[27]

Linear perspective is obviously an important technique to obtain clarity or *perspicuitas*, because it achieves a clear visual structure. Therefore the concept of *compositio*, in rhetoric a subdivision of *ornatus*, is the centre of Alberti's conception of the pictorial represention of a *historia*, with *perspicuitas* as its basis and *decorum* as an all-embracing criterium. This is consistent with the three-part structure of *De Pictura*. Linear perspective is presented in Book I. Book II is about composition guided by *decorum*. But this sense of *decorum* is something that the painter has to learn, and that is the subject of Book III. Linear perspective is the basic technique for painting a clear and well-organized *historia*; one might almost call it not only a pictorial technique to create the illusion of three-dimensional space on a flat surface, but a narrative instrument as well, in that it helps the painter to impart visual hierarchy to the *historia* he depicts. In paintings from *c.* 1450 onwards we can observe experiments with the location and decoration of the principal vanishing point, in order to give the perspective construction a narrative meaning. For instance, painters placed figures or symbolic objects on the principal point. The best-known case is Leonardo's *Last Supper*, where the vanishing point is located in Christ's head.[28] Linear perspective is based on the selection of a point of view; it structures the depiction of a *historia* and gives visual emphasis to the vanishing point because it directs the gaze towards it. It thereby imposes a visual hierarchy, and in this respect the use of perspective can be described as the painter's equivalent to the orator's task to choose a disposition that is most conducive to persuasion.

Painting considered as pictorial representation

Alberti was the first to formulate a theory of art based on a minute and sustained analysis of works of visual art, not from the painter's perspective but developed from the point of view of the viewer. In *De Pictura* the image is discussed, independently of its maker or the material aspects of its production, as a hierarchical structure of lines, planes and bodies that together represent a *historia*. This is not to suggest that he was a formalist *avant la lettre*. But doing so enabled him to say of the image not only what it represents, or on which biblical, historical or mythological story it might be based, but also to say something about its composition, the way it is structured, and to analyse its effect on the beholder. Producing a painting is no longer the focus of interest, but its appearance as an image. Alberti's analyses of *compositio* and linear perspective are not only instructions to the painter; they provide a vocabulary for the beholder's analysis and interpretation.

In a sense this interest in paintings considered as representations is already present in classical writings on art (for instance in the ekphrastic tradition) when the power of painting to imitate nature is described, and the author shows an awareness that to achieve such imitation something else is needed than a skilled use of painting materials. The passages in Pliny where he describes the mimetic power of painting, and presents *trompe-l'-œil* as the highest aim of painting, as in his narration of the rivalry between Zeuxis and Parrhasius also display this interest in the representational aspects of painting.[29] But *De Pictura* differs from these descriptions because it rises above the level of anecdote or biography through its thematization of paintings as pictorial representations, based on *compositio*. Alberti's new treatment of the myth of Narcissus in Section 26 shows this:

> I used to tell my friends that the inventor of painting, according to the poets, was Narcissus, who turned into a flower; for, as painting is the flower of all the arts, so the tale of Narcissus fits our purpose perfectly. What is painting but the act of embracing by means of art the surface of the pool?

Alberti seems to be unique in ascribing the discovery of painting to Narcissus. Painting plays no role in other versions of the myth. The most influential version is that in Ovid's *Metamorphoses* III.339–512 (written shortly before 8 BC). Here Narcissus is the son of the nymph Liriope and the rivergod Cephisus. Teiresias had predicted that he would only have a long life if he would never know himself. Narcissus grew into a beautiful young man, who rejected the love of men and women alike. Among them was the nymph Echo, who died of despair and was transformed into an echo. One of the rejected boys prayed to the gods that one day Narcissus would also fruitlessly fall in love. Nemesis, the goddess of revenge, heard his prayers. Tired after the hunt Narcissus knelt to drip into a deserted pond. In its clear surface he saw a beautiful young man and instantly fell in love, without realizing he was gazing at his own reflection. As soon as he realized this, he became desperate: when he turned away from the water his mirror image disappeared. Realizing that his love was impossible made him ill and he withered away; his body was transformed into a flower. In his reinterpretation of the myth Alberti leaves out most of the defining elements of this myth, sterile self-love and the role of Echo, but credits Narcissus with the invention of painting. Alberti only used the motif of the change into a flower, which fits in well with his praise of painting, because it is a powerful illustration of its power to bring about metamorphoses.[30]

According to Alberti painting is nothing 'but the act of embracing by means of art the surface of the pool'. His main interest appears to be in the moment when Narcissus is looking at the surface, desires to embrace his reflection, and then suddenly realizes that he has all the time been in love with his mirror image. In Ovid's version as well this sudden insight is the crux. He actually used the term *imago* to suggest Narcissus' insight:

> Oh, I am he! I have felt it, I know now my own image, I burn with love of my own self; both kindle the flames and suffer them.[31]

In other words, Narcissus suddenly becomes aware that nature has the capacity of creating images. This insight makes him indeed the discoverer of the natural principle of painting conceived as the representation of empirical reality in reflecting surfaces. Whereas Narcissus literally tried to embrace his reflection, the painter attempts to do so in a figural sense by his art. Representation thus becomes one of nature's processes, and painting is not only an imitation of the creations of nature, but also of the way these appear to the viewer. Alberti repeatedly stressed the power of painting to create an illusion of life. And in this context it is interesting to note that Philostratus the Elder, the author of the *Imagines*, a series of descriptions of paintings, written in the third century AD, wrote a description of a painting of the Narcissus myth which begins with the lines: 'The pond paints Narcissus, and the painting represents both the pond and the story of Narcissus'.[32]

Painting is based on the mathematical and optical laws of nature, and these are used in linear perspective. Its aim is to represent visible nature. The principles and objects of painting are given by nature, but so is the discovery that there exists something like an image that is faithful to nature and lifelike. But Alberti's version of the myth of Narcissus also shows that he considered the essence of painting to be its power to transform absence into living presence. This is stressed in Section 25:

> Painting possesses truly a divine power in that not only does it make the absent present (as they say of friendship), but it also represents the dead to the living many centuries later [...] Through painting, the faces of the dead go on living for a very long time.

In a successful painting the representation is so vivid that the viewer is persuaded to elide the representation with what it represents. Not surprisingly Alberti quoted the Plinian anecdote that Alexander the Great's generals grew pale with fear when after his death they saw his portraits. These pictures became agents on Alexander's behalf, ensuring his continuing presence in the minds of their viewers, and influencing their behaviour. Alberti was not alone, nor the first, in attributing to painting the power to make the absent present. When Pliny praised the Roman polymath Varro for inventing the art of portraiture, he credited him with 'a gift that even the gods might envy, since he not only granted immortality, but even dispatched it throughout the world, so that people could be present everywhere just as the gods can'.[33]

Painting as persuasive representation

Although it is a small book, *De Pictura* announces almost all applications of rhetoric to the visual arts that were to be made during the Renaissance and after: from Filarete's treatise on architecture of the 1430s to the seventeenth-century theories of Bellori and De Piles and the last complete statement of neo-classical artistic theory, Sir Joshua Reynolds's *Discourses*. Alberti used the terms and concepts of rhetoric to formulate a humanist Latin vocabulary to discuss the arts; he drew on the way rhetorical handbooks were structured when he divided *De Pictura* into three books dealing with the elements of painting, the art itself and the training of the artist.[34] Also, he used the rhetorical distinction between *res* and *verba*, between what to say and how to say it, in his development of linear perspective, not as a technical device, but as a means of pictorial representation allowing the painter to put across literally and figurally his point of view on the *historia* he painted. Using rhetoric thus enabled him to develop a *theoria* of painting in the Aristotelian sense: a consideration of the general principles of cause and effect underlying any particular human activity.[35] In the next chapter we will see how a century later a similar effort was made to develop a theory of architecture that integrated rhetoric and Aristotelian *theoria*. But developing a theory about painting as a representational art of persuasion also set in motion a complex oscillation between representation and presence, as we shall see in Chapters Three and Five. Early modern artists would negotiate the bounds of representation to create the sense of living presence that so much visual persuasion depends on. They would explore all the compositional strategies offered by that very awareness of the representational character of painting.

Notes

1 L. B. Alberti, *De Pictura*, Section 42. On recent interpretations of today's gesture see Goffen (1998), pp. 43–68, and Walliser-Wurster (2001), pp. 122–34.

2 The passage in which Quintilian describes how Agamemnon veils his head when sacrificing his daughter Iphigenia because his emotions overwhelm him, returns in an ongoing series of discussions of vivid description and visual persuasion from Pliny through Quintilian to Valerius Maximus, Alberti and Giannozzo Manetti: see Van Eck (1998), pp. 460–2.

3 Leonardo, *The Literary Works*, ed. Richter, vol. I p. 345, nr. 594; cf. Quintilian, XI.iii.94.

4 Aristotle, *Rhetorica* 1450a18ff., 1454a16ff.; Pliny, *Naturalis Historia* XXXV.98, describing Aristides, 'who was the first to paint the soul and to give expression to the affections of man – I mean what the Greeks call *ethe* – and also the emotions'. On the gradual change in the function of gesture see Barasch (1991). Barasch argues that Francesco Bocchi was the first to consider the face, rather than the hands or entire body, as the main part of the body to represent emotions and character. He attributes this to Bocchi's innovative use of physiognomics when discussing the representation of character and emotion in Donatello's *Saint George*. But the evolution was not as straightforward as Barasch seems to suggest. Pomponius Gauricus thought of gesture as *èthos*; and he could reach back to the ancient physiognomists who also read character from gesture, gait, or manner.

5 Leonardo, *Treatise on Painting*, nr. 267, p. 110.

6 Cf. *The Literary Works of Leonardo da Vinci*, vol. 1, nr. 654, p. 369: 'Poetry describes the action of the mind, painting considers what the mind may effect by the motions [of the body]'.

7 Alberti, *De Pictura*, Section 31. Alberti may have taken this tripartition from Pliny's *Naturalis Historia* (XXX.v.16 and xi.29) and from Quintilian (XXXI.x.4–6); cf. Wright (1984), p. 63. Although the Italian version is now more widely read than the Latin, judging from the numbers of manuscript copies the Latin seems to have had a wider audience in the fifteenth century. *Della Pittura* of 1436 appears to be a rather hastily made version. Sixteenth-century Italian printed editions were new translations after the Latin versions. Cf. Grayson (1953) and (1968).

8 Vickers (1988), p. 343 quotes Thomas Wilson's *The Arte of Rhetorique* (1533; rev. edn. 1560) where *circumscriptio* is defined as 'a briefe descrybing or declaryng of a thyng'.

9 Cicero, *De Oratore*, III.liv.207.

10 Alberti, *De Pictura*, Sections 30–1.

11 *De Pictura*, Section 40. Quoted from Baxandall, (1971), p. 136, where the translation has kept the original Latin to remain as close as possible to the rhetorical connotations of the terms Alberti employed.

12 On *copia* see Quintilian X.i.15, VIII Pr. 13ff. and most of Book VIII; on *varietas* see Cicero, *De Inventione* I.xli.76 and Quintilian II.xiii.8ff., and Drijepondt (1979).

13 Cf. Quintilian X.ii.1: 'verborum sumenda copia est et varietas figurarum et componendi ratio [...]'.

14 Cf. Baxandall (1971), pp. 136–7.

15 See, for instance, *Rhetorica ad Herennium* IV.xiii.18: 'dignitas est quae reddit ornatum orationem varietate distinguens'.

16 *De Pictura*, Section 41.

17 *Ibid*, Section 42.

18 But see Grafton (2003), who argues that Alberti's comments on *historia* were inspired for a large part by Donatello's reliefs for the Baptisterio in Florence and other recent developments in sculpture.

19 Cicero *De Oratore*, III.lvi.213. Cf. Vickers (1988), pp. 347–8.

20 Aristotle, *Rhetorica* III.8–9; Quintilian, *Institutio Oratoria* IX.iv. Baxandall (1971), p. 130 drew attention to the use of *compositio* by Vitruvius (III.I.i) in connection with buildings and by Cicero (*De Officiis*,

I.xxviii.98) in connection with bodies. On the history of the term 'composition' see Scaglione (1972).

21 Cf. Baxandall (1972), pp. 135ff., and Vickers (1988), p. 343, n. 13, for other meanings of *compositio*. See also Chapter Three of this book for further discussion of *compositio* and painting.

22 Cennini, *Il Libro dell'Arte*, pp. 2, 42–3, 75. Cf. Puttfarken (2000), pp. 49–50.

23 Alberti, *De Pictura*, Section 35: 'Est autem compositio ea pingendi ratio qua partes in opus picturae componuntur. [...] Historiae partes corpora, corporis pars membrum est, membri pars est superficies. Primae igitur operis partes superficies, quod ex his membra, ex membris corpora, ex illis historia, ultimum illud quidem et absolutum pictoris opus perficitur'.

24 The most extensive treatment of these four qualities of style is by Quintilian, *Institutio Oratoria*, VIII–XI. But see also the *Rhetorica ad Herennium* IV.xi.17, where *compositio* is considered as one of the three qualities every suitable style should possess: 'To be in fullest measure suitable to the speaker's purpose such a style should have three qualities: Taste (*elegantiam*), Artistic Composition (*compositio*), and Distinction (*dignitatem*)'.

25 *De Pictura*, Section 38.

26 Cf. Quintilian VIII.iii.2, Kennedy (1969), p. 81 and Ong (1958), p. 277.

27 Alberti op. cit. Section 40: 'Improbo quidem eos pictores, qui quo videri copiosi, quove nihil vacuum relictum volunt, eo nullam sequuntur compositionem sed confuse et dissolute omnia disseminant, ex quo non rem agere sed tumultuare historia videtur. [...] Atque in historia id vehementer approbo quod a poetis tragicis atque comicis observatum video, ut quam possint paucis person is fabulam doceant'.

28 Cf. for discussion on this issue and examples of paintings Elkins (1994), pp. 146–54.

29 Pliny, *Naturalis Historia* XXXV.65ff.

30 Alberti op. cit. Section 25. Recently this passage has been analysed by Stephen Bann in Bann (1989), pp. 165–205 and in Baskins (1993). These studies do not discuss the relation between Narcissus and painting. According to Damisch (1987), p. 350, Alberti's use of the myth can only be meaningful when it is connected with linear perspective, but he gives no arguments for this suggestion. For discussions of Ovid's version from a psychoanalytical perspective see Elsner (2000).

31 Ovid, *Metamorphoses* III.463–4: 'Iste ego sum: sensi, nec me mea fallit imago; uror amore mei: flammas moveoque feroque.'

32 Philostratus, *Imagines* XXIII, p. 89; see also Vinge (1967), pp. 29–32 and Bann (1989), pp. 108 vv. Alberti may well have known Philostratus' *Imagines*, because manuscript copies of the text circulated in Western Europe in the fifteenth century. Thus the Florentine Humanist Ambrogio Traversari (1356–1439) possessed a copy around 1432. Alberti probably knew him because they both stayed in Florence in the 1430s, and Traversari was in close touch with the Papal court. See E. Kalinka's edition of the *Imagines*, pp. 64–6 and Borsi (1979), p. 259.

33 Pliny the Elder, *Naturalis Historia* XXXV.ii.11: '[...] inventor muneris etiam diis invidiosi, quando immortalitatem non solum dedit, verum etiam in omnes terras misit, ut praesentes esse ubique ceu dii possent'. On living presence in Roman portraiture see Stewart (2006).

34 See Baxandall (1971), p. 126 n. 11, who refers in very general terms to the rhetorical origins of the division elements-arts-artist, particularly in isagogic or elementary treatises; cf. Fuhrmann (1960), in particular pp. 7–28 and 122–59. For other well-known classical cases of scientific method based on division and definition not discussed by Furhrmann see Theophrastus' *Enquiry into Plants* I.1.4. See also below, Chapter Two for the use of rhetorical methods of exposition and structuring treatises in architectural theory.

35 For discussions of what distinguishes arts from crafts and a general division of all human pursuits and knowledge see Aristotle, *Rhetorica* 1354a2. Cf. also his *Metaphysics* 980a1–982a, in particular 981a. Cf. also McKeon (1973), pp. xv–xvi. Quintilian, *Institutio Oratoria* II.xvii–xviii.5 addresses the question where rhetoric belongs in the terms of the Aristotelian classification into theoretical, practical and productive sciences. It is a practical art, because it is concerned with action, like dancing. However, it draws largely on the other two kinds of arts: it has theoretical aspects because it often rests content with the examination of a subject, and it has productive aspects because in the results an orator obtains by writing speeches or histories, features can be discovered which are similar to those of the productive arts painting, architecture or poetry.

TWO: THE FOUNDATIONS OF PERSUASIVE ARCHITECTURE

Introduction

The foundations of visual persuasion are twofold: the work of art or building must be designed in such a way that it moves or persuades the viewer; but to achieve this a particular mindset is needed as well, a way of thinking that considers the arts not as made for their own sake, but to play a role in society. This attitude was rarely made explicit, but there are a few notable exceptions: the position formulated by the Council of Trent on the role of the arts in propagating the Catholic faith for instance, and the writings on architectural theory of three comparatively neglected authors of the late sixteenth century: Gherardo Spini, Daniel Barbaro and Vincenzo Scamozzi. The Counter-Reformation authors Borromeo, Paleotti or Politi have been widely studied, though they had little to say about architecture except church design and were almost silent on how visual persuasion is actually achieved. Paradoxically, Spini, Barbaro and Scamozzi all started from an attempt to show that architecture is really a science, but ended by presenting a strongly rhetorical view of architecture, that was quite eloquent about the importance of architecture for society, the relations between rhetoric and architecture, and in what ways architecture or the architect can move the viewer. They knew each other, if not personally then through their writings; all three held that there existed a fundamental relation between rhetoric, architectural theory and its design, and they were all well-schooled in Aristotelian thought. To understand this development, and to see how their ideas clarify visual persuasion by buildings is the purpose of this chapter.

The first Renaissance treatise on architecture, *De Re Aedificatoria* by Alberti, was a learned Latin treatise, addressed to fellow humanists and discerning patrons or amateurs such as its dedicatee Lorenzo de' Medici. It owed much of its intellectual and conceptual framework to Aristotle and the classical tradition of scientific methodology.[1] After the 1480s another strand of architectural theory became prominent: treatises became more practical and were written for the architect or builder who was actively involved in the activities of the building site. Sebastiano Serlio famously declared in the opening pages of Book IV of his treatise that it would help to give 'ogni mediocre', every person of average talent, the means to acquit themselves honourably by teaching how to represent a design with the help of geometry and linear perspective.[2] His visual codification of the five orders at the opening of Book III is the result of intense scrutiny of the remains of Roman architecture and Vitruvius' treatise, but no longer resonated with the humanist learning Alberti gave to his treatment of the orders. In Vignola's *Regola* of 1563 this process had reached its culmination; instead of a textual analysis the reader is presented with plates of the orders showing their visual codification that allow their use in any design simply by applying the module calculus Vignola had devised. In Vasari's *Vite* the treatment of architecture in the *Introduzione alle tre Arti del disegno* focused on the knowledge and handling of materials and techniques for covering spaces.

In the 1550s the Aristotelian strand in architectural theory was taken up again by three authors: Daniel Barbaro published extremely erudite Latin and Italian editions of Vitruvius in 1556 and 1567 with a commentary that is almost a treatise in itself; the Florentine Gherardo Spini wrote an unfinished treatise on architectural ornament in 1568, which remained unpublished until 1980; Vincenzo Scamozzi spent his entire working life on a treatise that was to be a *summa* of architectural knowledge both theoretical and practical. The *Idea dell' Architettura Universale* was published in 1615. These books are very different in what they offer and how they look, but they all distinguished between architectural design, which they considered to be a skill, similar in many respects to rhetorical composition, and architectural theory, which they took great pains to present as a science in the Aristotelian sense, that is as knowledge of the general principles that rule cause and effect in a particular domain of nature or human pursuits and artefacts. Like Alberti in *De Re Aedificatoria* they aimed to show that taken in this sense architecture is a science. They considered architecture not as a fine art, buildings were not unique, unrepeatable products of individual genius, and design for them was an activity guided by rules which can be made explicit. Spini considered architecture to be similar to poetry and painting; Barbaro and Scamozzi linked the art of building not to the representational arts that deal in fiction, but to the natural sciences.

But their Aristotelian outlook did not result exclusively in an epistemological view of architectural design as a productive art or architectural theory as a natural or mathematical science. Aristotle's division of human knowledge and pursuits into theoretical, practical and productive sciences or arts is ultimately based on the role these activities play in and for society. Architecture embodies or exemplifies knowledge of the society in which the architect lives, for which buildings provide the stone setting. As Gherardo Spini put it, architecture does not consist merely of building, but of knowing the nature of all things.[3] Similarly Spini, Barbaro and Scamozzi always thought of architecture as part of, or even an actor in society, and as an activity with social consequences. As a result they were much more inclined than the design theorists Serlio or Vignola to think about architecture in terms of other arts or pursuits. Indeed they considered it, like rhetoric, as one of the foundations of civilized society. What did they mean by this, and what was the relation between architecture and rhetoric in their thought? What, for instance, did Barbaro have in mind when he equated the *maniere del dire*, the styles of rhetoric, with the *maniere del edificare*, the ways of building, of architecture? How are we to understand Spini's identification of the figures of speech in poetry with ornament in architecture? As we will see, the answers are complex; at the same time their conception of the connections between architecture and rhetoric clarifies much that remains implicit or unclear in later statements of their closeness for instance by Sir John Soane, which will be discussed in Chapter Four.

Very little is known about Gherardo Spini, the author of a treatise on architecture in ten books, of which only the first three survive in manuscript. These were written in or before 1568, and are devoted to ornament. Spini was born in 1538, became a member of the Accademia Fiorentina, and was secretary to Cardinal Ferdinando de' Medici. He wrote poetry, some of his sonnets were published in the prestigious volume recording the funeral of Michelangelo, and in 1570 he wrote a commentary on Egnazio Danti's treatise on the astrolabe. Benvenuto Cellini mentions him as 'intendentissimo dell'arte del disegno e dell'architettura' in the dedication of his architectural treatise to Ferdinando de' Medici. After 1570, the year Spini returned to work on his book on architecture, there are no more traces of his literary or artistic activities in Florence or Rome.

In his linking of architectural and poetical ornament Spini had in fact been shown the way by the Venetian scholar, architectural patron and Patriarch-Elect of Aquileia Daniel Barbaro (1514–70), who in his editions of Vitruvius, published in 1556 and 1567, had equated the *maniere del dire* and *maniere del edificare*.[4] Spini and Barbaro are connected in other ways too: the letters included among the prefatory material to Spini's treatise on ornament include some by the mathematician Antonio Maria dei' Pazzi, who also exchanged letters with Barbaro and had sent him some instruments.[5] Other mutual friends and associates included Benedetto Varchi and Pietro Bembo. Although we do not know whether they actually met, Barbaro and Spini were both involved in the foundation of the earliest Italian academies: Barbaro in that of the Infiammati in Padua; Spini of the Accademia Fiorentina.

Barbaro (1513–70) came from a prominent family of Venetian humanists, churchmen and politicians. He designed and directed the botanical gardens in Padua, published the first Latin translation of Aristotle's *Rhetoric* by his great-uncle Ermolao, and collaborated closely with Palladio, both in the design of the Villa Barbaro in Maser and in the first Vitruvius edition Barbaro prepared in 1556, for which Palladio made the illustrations. Barbaro's revised translation of 1567 was the first to be based on a philologically sound comprehension of the original, and for that reason this remained the most authoritative edition, together with the one by Claude Perrault, until the eighteenth-century version by Galiani. Barbaro's edition includes notes that are longer than Vitruvius' own text and almost form a treatise in themselves. They are in fact a reformulation in Aristotelian terms of Vitruvius' original text, in particular of the first three chapters of Book I. Here Barbaro provided a definition of the art of building, analysed the design process, and constructed an aesthetics of architecture. In doing so he made extensive use of Aristotle's *Metaphysics*, *Nicomachaean Ethics* and *Rhetoric*.[6]

The Renaissance cycle of architectural treatises ends with the *Idea dell'Architettura Universale* of the Vicentine architect Vincenzo Scamozzi, who lived from 1552 to 1616. Architecturally he was Palladio's heir, but intellectually he was very much part of the Aristotelian tradition to which Barbaro belonged.[7] He intended the *Idea* to be a synthesis of classical architectural theory, but the book, published in 1615, just before he died, is unfinished and provides only a compendium not the systematic summary of available knowledge Scamozzi had intended.[8] Nonetheless it had a huge impact, in particular outside Italy, where editions of Book III and VI appeared as early as 1640 with the Dutch translation of Book VI by Cornelis Danckerts, followed by an English edition in 1669.[9] But the price of this success was a considerable loss of the book's intellectual scope. All these early editions only reproduced, often in severely reduced form, the practical parts of the *Idea*: Book III, which is mainly about domestic architecture and includes famous ancient and contemporary buildings, such as the Palazzo Corner in Venice or the Palazzo Strozzi in Florence; and Book VI, about the orders. The intellectually very ambitious discussion of architecture as an intellectual pursuit in Book I was largely ignored, and the *Idea* was reduced from an Aristotelian presentation of architecture as a *scienza* to a design manual, destined not for the educated and discerning amateur, but for builders and craftsmen. Architectural historians have followed this trend, and it is only recently that the intellectual stature of Scamozzi has been recognized outside Italy.

Architecture is a science

Spini's treatment of architecture takes up the humanist tradition of treatise writing begun by Alberti. Its aim is not instruction in the practical aspects of building, but to give it a place among the liberal arts. The first chapter opens with the same words 'many and various' that Alberti used to open the Prologue to *De Re Aedificatoria*, followed by a praise of architecture extolling its age, usefulness to human civilized society, in particular as the stone embodiment of society's memory, Architecture also draws on a wide range of knowledge and skills. This observation serves as the link to a definition in Aristotelian terms as the *arte*, the theory or science of building: 'simple practice without Theory is worth little or nothing'.[10] Architecture is the body uniting all arts and sciences in its practice. It is not only the science of building, but knowledge of the nature of all things.[11] The art of building has become a science; the knowledge it deals with is that of the Vitruvian encyclopaedia. The conceptual framework in which such knowledge is acquired and used is that of Aristotelian philosophy, but its presentation as a treatise and the discussion of the ornament both use rhetoric.

Taking its cue from the opening of Vitruvius' first book, 'architectura est scientia', Barbaro's commentary takes the issue of the scientific character of architecture further, aiming to show in what sense architecture can indeed be said to be a *scientia*. Accordingly, in the *Proemio* architecture is defined in terms of the Aristotelian classification of mental activities directed at contingent truths. These activities can be ranged under either *prudenza*, foresight, or *arte*. The art of building is one of the latter, although there is also a practical part to building. *Prudenza* is a regulating habit of the mind, which disposes the mind to action based on rules and reason in the material world, that is in the sphere of useful action and behaviour.[12] Experience guides the activities of craftsmen, but operates without reason; art is closer to wisdom or *sapienza* because it is based on an understanding of the causes and effects that rule its products. Barbaro considered the arts in two ways: as an intellectual, discursive activity searching the causes, reasons and purposes for the activity guided by the art; in that sense architectural theory might be called the 'art' of building. Or he saw it as 'prontezza di mano'; a readiness of hand, or the capacity to impose on matter what the mind has conceived. Defined in these terms, architecture is very close to mathematics, with which it shares a high degree of exactitude, in its grasp of the calculations necessary for architectural design, but also to rhetoric where design and its presentation are concerned.[13]

Book I of Scamozzi's *Idea* consists of an analysis of architecture in Aristotelian terms.[14] Scamozzi takes Barbaro's intellectualization even further in that not only architectural theory, but architectural design as well is presented as a *scienza*. The imitative or operative arts, painting or sculpture for instance, imitate nature, do not operate 'per via delle cause' (literally by way of the causes, that is through a knowledge of cause and effect) and therefore cannot offer any certain knowledge. Architecture, like mathematics, is perceived here as a speculative science concerned with the general principles of cause and effect ruling all natural phenomena and human artefacts.[15] Its principles are derived from mathematics, in particular geometry, and to a lesser degree the other liberal arts, astronomy or music. The subject matter of this science is architectural design conceived as applied geometry: the manipulation of geometrical shapes and bodies by means of ruler and compass, based on general knowledge of the mathematical structure God has given to the universe. This knowledge is both constituted and communicated by means of drawing. With an appeal to Vitruvius' distinction of *ratiocinatio* (reasoning) and *opus* (work), Scamozzi, like Spini and Barbaro, distinguished between *artificium*, that is the activity of building or *opus* in Vitruvian terms, and *ratiocinatio*, that is the theory and rational method underlying architectural design. *Opus* or the activity of building is specifically architectural, but *ratiocinatio* is the complex of knowledge through which the art of building is linked to all other scientific disciplines.[16] Architectural design starts with an idea in the mind of the architect; the builders who execute the design based on such ideas are the hands of the architect.[17]

But at the same time architecture is close to rhetoric because they share a universal character. The architect and the orator both need to have knowledge of everything under the sun, and both need to win their public's favour. Scamozzi also draws a parallel between rhetorical and architectural composition, to which I will return later. To the modern reader this association of architecture, mathematics and rhetoric looks somewhat academic, if not disconcerting, because mathematics, as an exact science, has little to do with the art of persuasion, which aims at the manipulation of opinion through the use of emotions. On the basis of the stress on the mathematical character of architecture one would expect an exposition of architectural theory in the form of a calculus – the way Nicolaus Goldmann would attempt in the seventeenth century – or of rules for the geometrical generation of architectural form.[18] How could such conflicting disciplines be reconciled in formulating architectural theories? Many recent studies of Barbaro and Scamozzi, in particular by Pierre Gaye and Branco Mitrovic, have concentrated on the mathematical aspect. But as we will see, the Aristotelian conception of architecture as one of the productive sciences, sharing its general nature with mathematics and rhetoric, allows for an interpretation that reconciles the mathematical with the persuasive aspects of architecture.

Architecture and rhetoric provide the foundations of society

To understand why architecture is linked so closely to both mathematics and rhetoric we need to take a look at the praise of architecture that figures so prominently in both Barbaro and Scamozzi. Barbaro devoted a substantial part of Book I to its merits.[19] His *laus architecturae* culminates in a celebration of architecture's great use to humanity, the scientific knowledge its buildings embody and its practitioners command, and its power to bend nature to human needs.[20] Scamozzi even gave Book I the formal structure of an epideictic speech in praise of architecture, as we will see.

This consideration of architecture as a social art is the basis for the similarities between architecture and rhetoric Barbaro develops. Ultimately these are based on the great social usefulness of both arts to human society. Architecture is not an entirely intellectual pursuit, existing only in the mind of the architect; like an orator's speech a design has to be presented to an audience to become effective, and therefore both have to take into consideration the reactions of the public. Not surprisingly because they share a social view of architecture's *raison d'être*, Barbaro is the first architectural theorist after Alberti to explicitly stress the importance of considering the viewer's needs: 'the quality [of a design] cannot be considered in itself, [. . .] because it is necessary that a design has a certain quality, which satisfies the eyes of the beholders and delights them [. . .]'.[21] In the annotations to the Italian translation of Aristotle's *Rhetoric* by his great-uncle Ermolao he had observed that 'we teach with arguments, move with affects, conciliate with speech, to teach is what we ought to do, to reconcile is honourable, but to move and persuade is necessary, not for reasons of the art, but for the sake of the public'.[22]

Scamozzi's Book I is also an extended epideictic speech in praise of architecture. As in Alberti's Prologue, both the definition of architecture and the assessment of its merits are deeply indebted to Book I of Aristotle's *Metaphysics*. Both Alberti and Scamozzi considered architecture to be the origin of society: it gives shelter to human beings and houses their institutions, gods and main civic rituals; by its beauty it also gives dignity to human life and elevates the mind. For Alberti architecture is the supreme expression of a civilized, well-ordered and prosperous society which is able to defend itself, give its citizens a happy life, and honour the gods. Architecture is not only the stage of civic life, but also provides stone monuments to keep the collective memory of society alive. For Scamozzi, the ultimate aim of architecture is simply to 'give order to all things'.[23] Alberti's praise of architecture as both the most useful and the most beguiling human art in fact aims to overcome the division Aristotle had set up in Book I of the *Metaphysics* between useful and recreative arts.[24] The connection with the *Metaphysics* is much more explicit in Scamozzi, who also wanted to bridge this division and simply opened with a paraphrase of Aristotle's opening sentence: 'All men by nature desire to know [. . .]'. Men want to know the causes of things, the sciences and arts provide these, and architecture is no exception to this.

THE USE OF RHETORIC IN FORMULATING TREATISES AND ARTICULATING THE DESIGN PROCESS

To understand the coupling of architecture and rhetoric in Barbaro's Vitruvius editions we have to turn to the treatment of both disciplines in his early dialogue *Della Eloquenza*, written when he was a student in Padua, and published in 1557.

As we have seen, he defined architecture as a *scienza*, unlike Serlio or Vignola who considered it as an artistic practice based on design. In doing so Barbaro forged connections between the working of the human mind and the kind of knowledge architecture conceptualized as a *scienza* embodies. In terms of the Aristotelian psychology of human faculties with which he had become familiar at Padua, architecture is the object of *prudenza* and *arte*: of rational, discursive consideration by the intellect, leading to contingent truths. Architecture is therefore considered primarily as knowledge. In his early dialogue on eloquence he performed the same classifying operation, this time for rhetoric. Again he did not follow the standard pattern, in this case that of antique rhetorical textbooks such as Quintilian's which follow the process of writing and delivering a speech in their treatment of rhetoric. Instead he located the practice of eloquence in an Aristotelian classification of mental activities, which at the same time brings out the similarities between architecture and rhetoric in such an Aristotelian mindset. Like architecture, eloquence is based on close observation of nature; like architecture, rhetoric is concerned not with absolute certainties, but with contingent truths and opinions, and acts upon the reason, will and emotions of the public. And, perhaps most interestingly, where the architect needs to give visible form to his design ideas, the orator needs to give audible or readable shape to his *sentenza*, the idea or concept he has of a speech. More than that, he needs to give body to his thoughts, so that they can penetrate, literally move and act upon the mind of the public. A speech may therefore be compared to the human body, and figures of speech are compared to parts of a body or aspects of its appearance.[25]

In this way Barbaro could draw a detailed parallel between writing and delivering a speech on the one hand, and designing a building and presenting it to the viewers on the other. The *maniere del dire* are qualities or styles of a speech appropriate to the subject and public; just so the *maniere del edificare* are the qualities, we would say style, of a building that fit its function or purpose and its public. Both the orator and the architect need intellect and the ability to develop a *concetto*. They need words to express it, or the three Vitruvian ways to represent a design: groundplan, section and façade. The orator has to present his thought with the help of figures of speech; the architect by means of order or disposition. The rhythm of speech, Barbaro argues, corresponds to proportion in buildings. Both speeches and buildings need purposive planning to achieve their aims. Decorum is essential, in regard of persons as well as things, in particular in the use of ornament.[26]

Barbaro subsequently returned to this equation of the rhetorical process of composition and delivery with the architectural process of design and its execution when he discussed temple design in his commentary to Vitruvius' Section III.i. He singled out the different effects various temples have on the beholder. They can inspire delight, veneration or awe. Oratory can excite responses from the public and move it from one position to another, when words, figures of speech, the composition of a speech, its rhythms and purpose combine to persuade. Just so the division of a plan, material texture and ornament, proportion and collocation of the parts together make up the form of a building, and render it decorous and simple, awe-inspiring or delightful. A speaker differentiates the use of words, figures of speech and verbal artifice according to the variety of speech he chooses: elegant, clear and pure, or vehement, grandiose, rough and severe. Similarly the architect uses different orders, proportions, or dispositions of the parts when he aims for grandeur, richness and veneration, or when he wants to achieve simplicity, delicacy or beauty. Some of what we would now call stylistic categories may be combined: purity and grandeur, magnificence and beauty, beauty and simplicity, simplicity and splendour. These combinations show that a speaker may be a true 'Architetto dell'oratione'. But in architecture there is no such freedom for Barbaro: proportions and ornaments taken from various types of buildings ought not to be mixed. The simple should go with the plain and unadorned, and from thence buildings may gradually be made richer and more ornate. The architect will not combine whatever pleases the crowd, but only those stylistic qualities or *maniere del edificare* that are linked by some innate or hidden similarity.[27]

Although Barbaro's analogies between architecture and rhetoric are sometimes a little forced, as in his attempts to equate rhythm in speech with numbers and proportion in architecture, he did achieve a new degree of detail in his rhetorical analysis of architectural design. A comparison with Serlio's development of a critical vocabulary in Book VII is illuminating: Serlio here tried to define 'judicious architecture', in particular in the design of ornament by listing pairs of opposing qualities, one of which is good and to be pursued, the other bad and to be avoided. Thus a design or building may be *soda* (solid, strong), *schietta* (simple, plain or unaffected), *dolce* (sweet), and *morbida* (soft). But on the other hand a building can be *debole* (weak), *gracile* (flimsy or superficial), *cruda* (delicate, affected, hard), and therefore obscure and confused. He illustrates this with three plates (Figs. 2.1–2.3).

As John Onians has shown, this was the first attempt to develop architectural criticism through five pairs of opposing terms that each refer to another aspect of design. *Soda* and *debola* refer to the presence or absence of solidity and constructive force; *schietta* and *delicata* are about the degree of incrustated ornament; *morbida* and *cruda* about the degree of unity and softness or abruptness in transitions between parts. The explanatory woodcuts each show a wall decorated with a different order. Serlio wrote, for instance, about the Corinthian plate that:

> It can be called *gracile* and *delicata* and also *cruda* and *secca* [dry]; it is *gracile* because of the thinness [*sottilità*] and slenderness [*sveltezza*] of the columns, which nevertheless are fitting in that order. It is also *delicata*

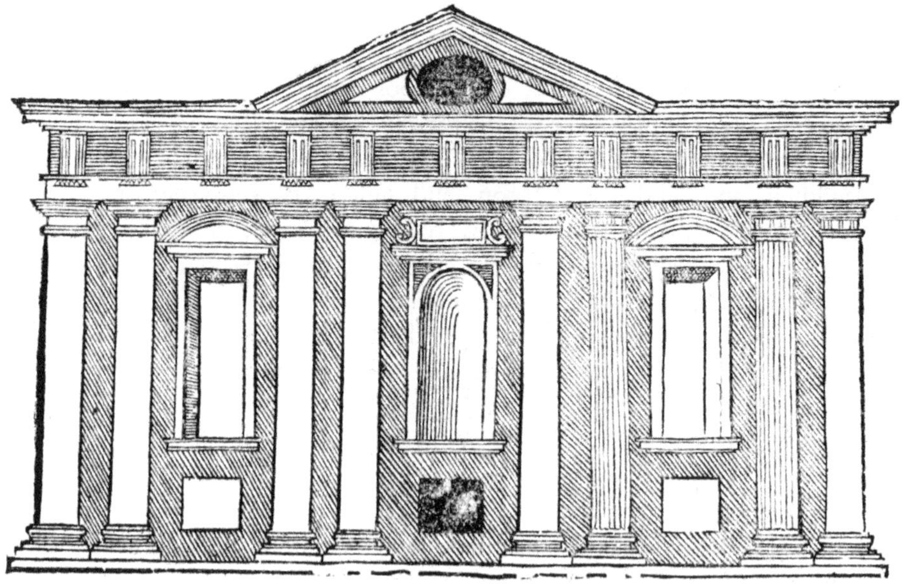

2.1 Sebastiano Serlio, Doric façade. *Il Settimo Libro d'Architettura di Sebastiano Serlio*, Frankfurt 1575, p. 123 (photo: Leiden University Library, Special Collections Research Centre, Thyssia 1463).

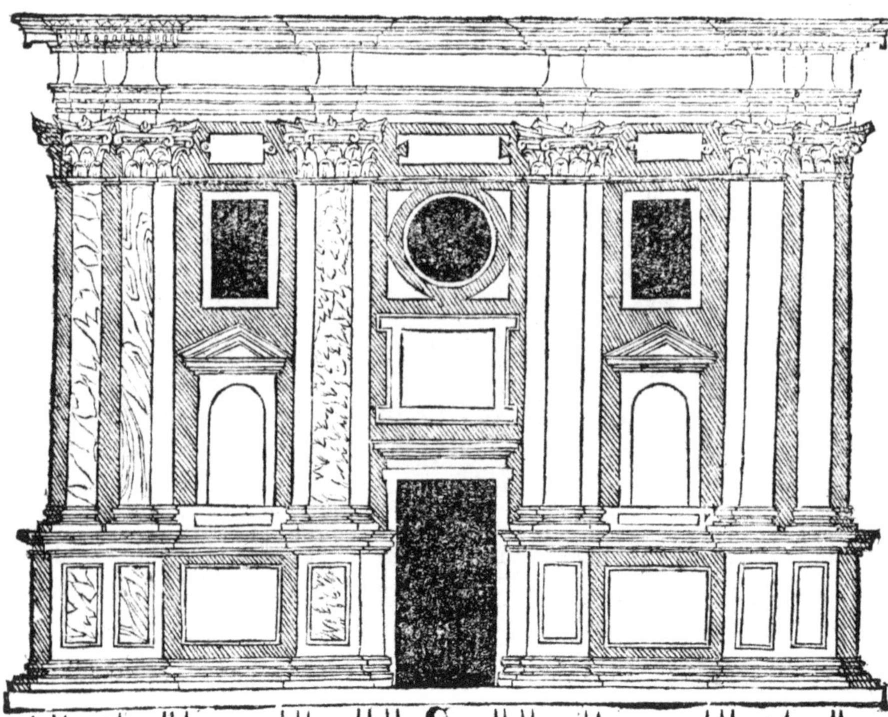

2.2 Sebastiano Serlio, Composite façade. *Il Settimo Libro d'Architettura di Sebastiano Serlio*, Frankfurt 1575, p. 125 (photo: Leiden University Library, Special Collections Research Centre, Thyssia 1463).

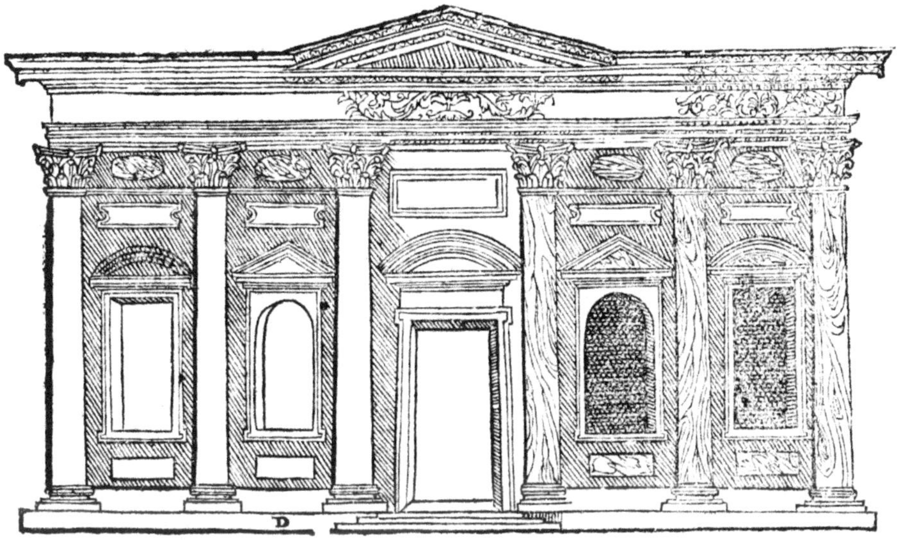

2.3 Sebastiano Serlio, Corinthian façade. *Il Settimo Libro d'Architettura di Sebastiano Serlio*, Frankfurt 1575, p. 127 (photo: Leiden University Library, Special Collections Research Centre, Thyssia 1463).

> because of the refinement of the workmanship and because of the *intagli*. It can be called *cruda* because of the darkness of the columns and because of the coloured marbles of the pedestals. It is dry [*secca*] because that is the opposite of *morbidezza*.[28]

The aim of these visual analyses is not only to develop a critical vocabulary, but also to train and educate the eye of the beholder. The pairs of terms he used, together with the underlying pattern of binary criticism, is largely derived from rhetoric, where it originated in oppositions of the *genera dicendi* or local varieties of speech such as Asian versus Attic oratory. Just as ancient orators had contrasted the simplicity and purity of Attic speech with the pomposity and bombast of Asian oratory, Serlio distinguished a use of the orders that is *schietta* and *semplice* from a handling that is *confusa* and *affettata*. The Attic style was thought to appeal to the educated and judicious public, the Asian to the illiterate masses.[29]

But whereas Serlio discussed actual cases of the handling of the orders, Barbaro developed his analogies between rhetoric and architecture in a more abstract way. Discussions of actual buildings in his commentary are rare, and occur only when Vitruvius discusses an individual building. The analogy between rhetorical and architectural composition is not made here exclusively to enable the viewer to judge a building, but above all to show that architecture shares the sophistication, importance for society and intellectual standing of rhetoric.

There is also an ulterior aim, entirely in line with the Aristotelian framework of Barbaro's book. It is to rationalize architecture, to move it on the one hand away from the sphere of manual activity based on practical experience, and on the other to remove it from the atmosphere of intangible and unique artistic creativity that cannot be taught or subjected to rational and discursive rules. Paradoxically, in Serlio's treatises an opposite movement had occurred. By showing how the visual presentation of architectural design through linear perspective could be learned by 'ogni mediocre', design itself became more mysterious and inaccessible. The subject of his treatise was no longer design itself, but its visual presentation by means of perspectival drawing. Whereas Barbaro's redefinition of architecture as a science, which considered superficially makes it less accessible, in fact opened it to the educated layman, Serlio's apparently transparent visual presentation made architecture the specialist domain of the trained artist who possessed the talent to design.[30] Not surprisingly, Barbaro was very dismissive of Serlio, because he taught 'how to paint, not how things are'.[31]

Scamozzi made these connections between architecture, mathematics and rhetoric even more explicit. Rhetoric plays various roles in the *Idea*. It helped to shape the treatise, and in particular Book I, which as have we seen is not only a definition of architecture but also an extended and wide-ranging epideictic speech extolling the virtues of architecture.[32] Rhetoric also shaped the conceptualization of architectural design in the *Idea*: it is articulated into the three stages of invention, distribution and decorum. Design consists of seven key aspects: invention, ordination, disposition, distribution, correspondence, beauty and decorum. They are all based on the architect's *idea*. This is in fact a rhetoricized simplification of Vitrivius' description of the design process and its social, practical and aesthetic norms.[33] Invention is here defined as the explanation of difficult questions (echoing the traditional rhetorical presentation of *inventio* as providing the answer to the questions who, what, where, when) and the rationale underlying new designs.[34] Invention leads to distribution consisting of a groundplan, façade and section of the building. These are born from the ideas of the architect and the faculty of invention. Knowledge of mathematics is essential here to draw outlines, planes and three-dimensional bodies. In all this a sharp distinction must be made between the intellectual understanding of causes and effects, resulting in universal knowledge, and 'la prattica semplice' based on empirical experience of individual instances or a comparison between them.[35] Scamozzi compared the architect giving a visible form to the basic, abstract geometrical structure of a design to an orator who finds the right words, expressions and figures of speech for what he wants to say, thereby also including *elocutio*. Finally, rhetoric is also used when the architect wants to present his designs persuasively in drawings, models or words, because then all the 'colours of rhetoric' can be used. Although Scamozzi never says this in so many words, this activity can be compared to the *actio*, the final stage of the rhetorical process in which the audience, or in this case the client, has to be persuaded. The basis for this use of the five stages of rhetorical composition to analyse architectural design is the universal nature which rhetoric and architecture share: they both are part of, and affect all aspects of human society. Scamozzi here drew on Aristotle's definition of rhetoric and logic in the *Rhetoric* as the two universal sciences, whose subject matter ranges over everything under the sun, but deftly substituted architecture for rhetoric.[36]

For Scamozzi design is primarily an intellectual activity, mathematical in nature; hence the first plates of Book I are of elementary geometrical shapes and the operations by which they are generated (Figs. 2.4 and 2.5). But the abstract mathematical structure of a building becomes visible and tangible through the use of forms mainly derived from the orders, and the resulting design has to be communicated in drawings, models and words. This is the second main role of rhetoric in the *Idea*. The architect conceives in his mind 'singular, unusual, and wondrously beautiful forms' with the help of mathematics, but these ideas have to be presented to the public, both in visual form by means of drawings and models, and through persuasive speech.[37] Architecture is a design discipline, and in Scamozzi's mathematical conception a speculative science, but rhetoric's province is demonstration and persuasion in all its guises, be they visual or verbal.[38] Hence the moment the architect moves from the abstract manipulation of geometrical forms and shapes to dressing that shape in concrete material form, his design activities become similar to those of the orator, who chooses the right words, phrases and ornaments to find the most persuasive form for what he has to say. Just as the orator has to speak in an orderly and convenient way, using the 'colours of rhetoric', the architect has to show in a clear way his inventions, designs, the disposition of the parts and their arrangement. Just as the orator chooses proper and persuasive figures of speech, the architect applies the right order. The orator draws on testimonies and the authority of authentic texts to prove his case; similarly the architect uses examples taken from antique buildings and well known architects, particularly to make his use of ornament and the articulation of his design acceptable and persuasive.[39]

Although in the rest of the *Idea* this detailed comparison of the composition of a speech and architectural design is not sustained, it is nonetheless one of the most explicit and consistent articulations of architectural design in rhetorical terms before the late eighteenth century. The geometrical design is, one might say, the *res* which has to be given visible form through the *elocutio* of a transparent use of a module, the appropriate use of the orders, and ornament, whose selection should be supported by antique precedent. In this view the orders are presented not as an integral part of the structure of a building, but purely as ornaments, as the architectural equivalent of the figures of speech. The architect should think and act like an orator when he produces a visible and tangible form of the design itself, as a drawing or a model, but also when he presents it to clients.[40]

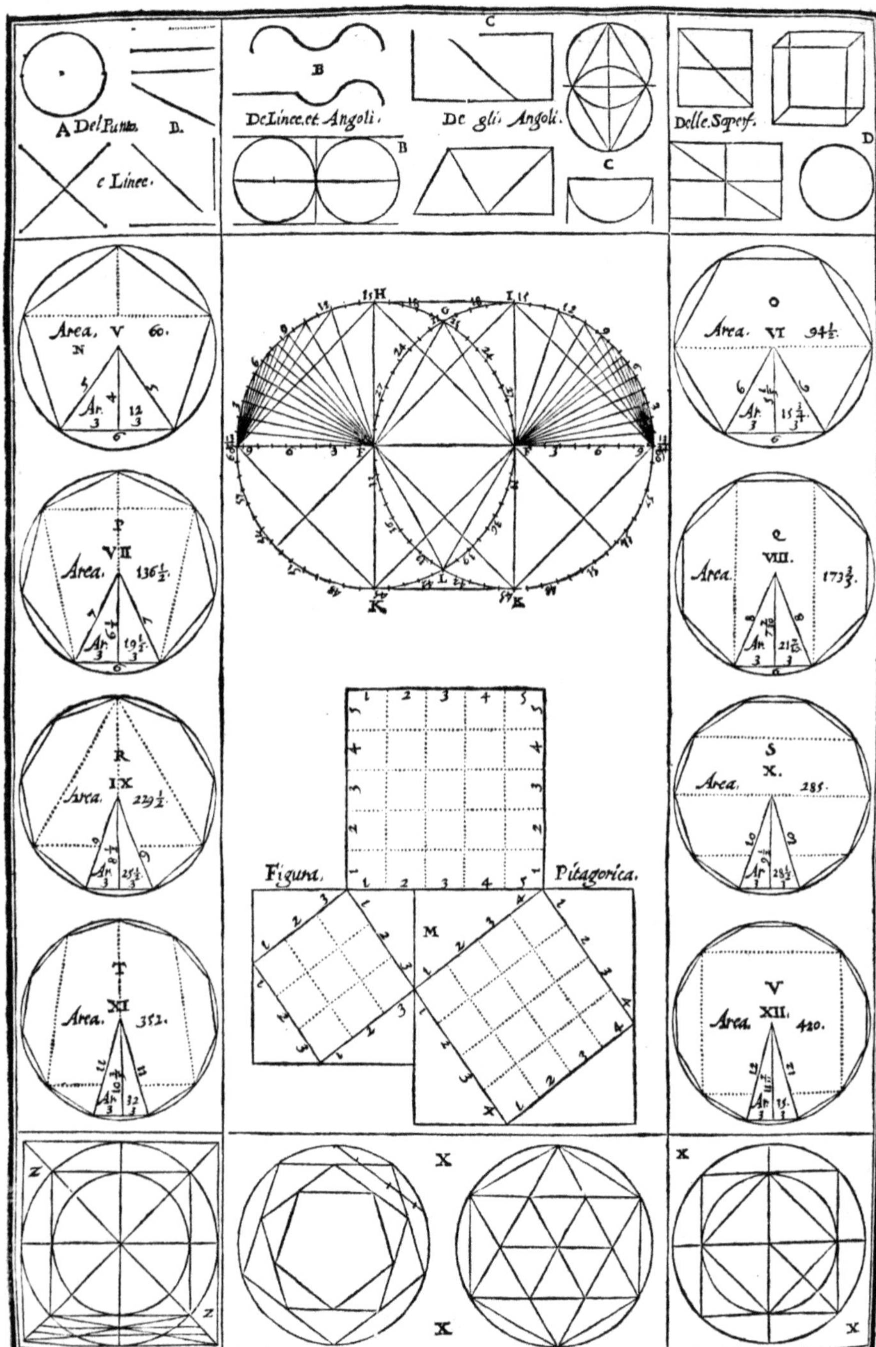

2.4 Vincenzo Scamozzi, regular surfaces. *L'Idea dell'Architettura Universale*, Venice 1615, p. 32 (photo: Leiden University Library, Special Collections Research Centre, 679 A 17).

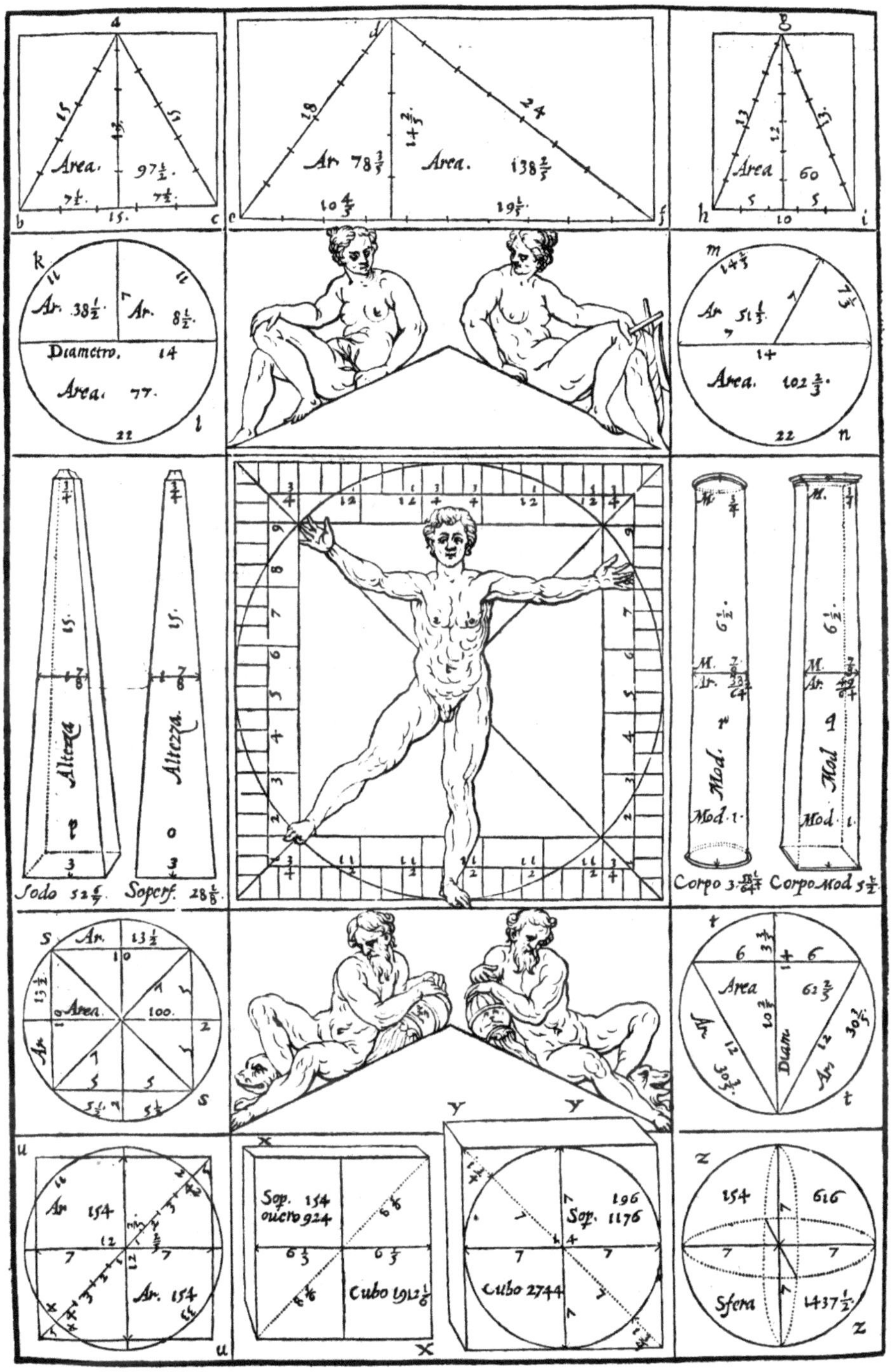

2.5 Vincenzo Scamozzi, proportions of the human body and artifical forms. *L'Idea dell'Architettura Universale*, Venice 1615, p. 40 (photo: Leiden University Library, Special Collections Research Centre, 679 A 17).

In this Aristotelian concept of architectural design and its presentation to others, designing a building has become an activity that is almost entirely intellectual, and insofar as it is intellectual, textual and *livresque*. The manual labour involved in executing a design is excluded from this view of architecture as a *scienza speculativa*. Design has become an exercise in applied geometry. Where forms are involved that cannot be construed by geometrical forms, such as the irregular shapes of many of the mouldings linking the main parts of the orders, classical examples may be followed.[41] But antique architecture and the works of contemporary distinguished architects no longer function as an example to be imitated. They have become an authority, identical to the textual authors Scamozzi quotes so frequently, to be cited to make the design persuasive. The Aristotelian framework implies not only that architectural design has become a rational activity, in the sense that it can be adequately described as a variety of applied mathematics (even though only the best and most elevated intellects can produce truly excellent designs), but also that it has become profoundly textual. The architect starts by composing geometrical forms in his mind; but the moment he wants to give shape, mass and outline to these designs and communicate them, he proceeds like an orator. And like the orator, his relation to tradition is *livresque*: the architecture of the past is the provider of suitable authorities. Beautiful and ingenious buildings are to be collected like the striking passages a student of rhetoric notes in his common-place book. Just like any author educated in the classical tradition the architect builds his case not by stressing its novelty, but by citing authoritative passages.

Is architecture an art of representation?

Are these similarities between architecture and rhetoric limited to the presentation of design and speech? Or did Barbaro, Spini and Scamozzi also assume that architecture, like rhetoric, is an art of representation, comparable to painting or poetry? The only author who addressed this issue openly was Spini. For him architecture and rhetoric are both very ancient arts that are essential to human society. Just as human beings are not content when speaking with a naked statement of truth, but have an innate desire for eloquence and ornamented speech, they are not satisfied to dwell in plain and simple buildings that merely protect them against the sun and weather. They need dignity, grace and delight as well, which ornament provides for buildings.[42] That rhetoric imitates nature, both in the sense that eloquence is innate in human beings, and in the sense that the natural and lifelike should always be pursued, is a traditional rhetorical view which is also found in Cicero and Quintilian's reviews of the history of rhetoric. But Spini includes architecture among the imitative arts, not primarily because it imitates the laws of physics, or because the orders imitate human and plant forms, but because like every other imitative art it deals with representations. On the opening page of his manuscript Spini gives a division of the subject:

> Architecture – what is it, by whom and when (...).
> Architecture is divided, or consists
> rather of building ('fabbrica') and ornament.
> Ornament – if it exists, what it is, by whom it exists, for what reason, the correspondence and similarity between poetical and architectonic ornament.[43]

Spini here applies to architecture and ornament the questions an orator asks about his subject or brief in the stage of *inventio*: what is the nature of the event or deed, where, when and how did it happen, who were involved, who caused it? He then divides architecture into *fabbrica* or building, and ornament, and proceeds to ask of ornament whether it exists, what it is, whence it comes, why and wherefore it exists. The second rhetorical element occurs when he lists as the next aspect of ornament to be treated its *convenientia*, a Ciceronian philosophical term denoting harmony, suitability, symmetry or fitness.[44] Spini treats *convenientia* in the context of the similarity between poetical and architectonic ornament, and he is the first to do so in such an explicit fashion. This does not mean that the rest of his treatise is structured along these lines. The Ciceronian heuristic functions within a larger Aristotelian conceptual framework, but rhetoric continues to be present as a formative element in Spini's treatment of architectural ornament.

All human artefacts use ornament according to their aptness to do so; therefore any art that imitates nature cannot limit itself to bare necessities or plain truths, but should also attempt to offer as much beauty as is possible through ornament. In the case of architecture ornament is mainly the correct and decorous use of order, both in the abstract sense of a regular structure based on a building's purpose, and in the particular sense of the five orders of architecture. *Fabbrica* is the process of constructing the framework, the undecorated substance of a building, one might almost say the *res* of architecture; this is embellished by the addition of decoration or the use of superior materials such as marble or terra cotta instead of wood, brick or plaster. This is the basis of beauty, which may be perfected by adding door and window decorations, columns, cornices, statues and the like. If these are used in correct proportions and according to the rules of decorum, a typically architectural variety of beauty will result. To achieve this the parts of a building must be handled the way nature does, that is with the order that results from symmetry and proportion. Just as we notice immediately when a human hand lacks a finger and thereby becomes odd, the ornaments of architecture, and particularly those of the orders, must be located in the right place. The most sublime ornaments must be placed at the top or the head of the building; other parts must be placed according to their beauty and prominence, and the rules of nature. Spini here refers to Horace's rejection of combinations of heterogeneous elements in the opening verses of Horace's *Ars Poetica*.[45]

That reference is not accidental. As in all visible objects, the aspect of ornament pleases through the nature of the material employed, the excellence of the manufacture or the artist, of which Spini cites Michelangelo's Biblioteca Laurenziana and Sacrestia Nuova in Florence as conspicuous examples, or through the discourse or explanation ('discorso o ver ragione') of the architect. This is the artifice, the ingenuity through which a building shows the spectator that each part was not designed at random, but by observing its purpose and the rule of design.[46] This rule has four parts: imitation, correspondence, invention and decorum. Here the similarity between the poet and the architect again become manifest: both delight by these same four means. The similarity is not entirely straightforward where imitation is concerned, because a poet cannot imitate his predecessors as literally as an architect can reuse the ornaments he found in a building he admires. But both represent and make copies of the works of nature and art, and both delight their public in doing so, since people delight in representation because it is instructive. Spini here follows Aristotle's observation in the *Poetics* that we delight in representation because by nature we want to learn and take no greater pleasure than in recognizing the things we see.[47] Like poetry architecture deals with fictions. As Aristotle put it in his *Rhetoric*, extending the scope of *mimesis* from the drama to the visual arts and rhetoric:

> Now since both understanding and wondering give pleasure, an example of *mimesis*, for instance, as painting and statuary and poetry do, and in general any instance of successful *mimesis*, even if its object does not itself give pleasure. For the pleasure is not just pleasure in the object; instead there is an inference that 'This is that' so that the result is our coming to understand something.[48]

That is, for Spini as for Aristotle, art is essentially representational. A similar point was made by Plutarchus in *De Audiendis Poetis*: '[. . .] poetry is an art of imitation, a capacity analogous to painting. [. . .] We praise not the action represented by the imitation but the art shown in the appropriate reproduction of the subject'.[49] Painting is like poetry because it is representational, and it is representation, not the object represented, that we analyse. The arts make us see or realize things we did not understand before. The object of representation is in particular significant human action. With this brief discussion Aristotle had determined the parameters of most classical and Renaissance writing about poetry, rhetoric and the arts. In doing so he grouped the arts, eloquence and drama together in what we may call a theatrical view of the arts: what they are about is the representation of human action in front of an audience. But as we shall see below in Part III he also forged a close connection of composition and impact, making and judging, inventing and interpreting.

Spini is probably the first to say that architecture resembles poetry because they both deal with representation. The largest part of what was completed of his treatise consists of a detailed analysis of the various parts of the orders as representations of their origins in wood or their structural role in a building. Imitation of nature combined with the use of mathematics is the basis and the norm for architectural ornamentation, both in the use of proportion and the handling of the orders. If it is ignored, Spini warns, monsters will result. Like the poet, the architect imitates not individual or special cases as they actually appear, but the general and the ideal. Just as Aristotle studied many authors, ranging from Homer and Hesiod to Sophocles and Euripides to transform the writing of poetry into an art, Vitruvius travelled widely to deduce from the most beautiful temples at Ephesus, Priene and Rome how beauty and grace would result, and how to avoid brutishness or a lack of decorum. With the help of philosophy and mathematics he discovered the laws that would reduce various building practices to the rule-bound activity or art of architecture.[50] Whereas sculptors, for instance, select the best parts of several models, the architect takes *utilitas*, fitness for purpose, as his ideal. Interestingly Spini held up Michelangelo's sculpture and architecture as the best models for the architect. Invention therefore consists in the ability to design ornament that has not yet been used by others, but flows from the talent of the designer. It will move the spectator with 'maraviglioso diletto'.[51]

It is clear what Spini meant by his note on the opening page that ornament in architecture and poetry are similar: both are representations of things seen or observed in nature or art, their use is regulated by the demands of decorum and the capacity to invent, and ultimately its use – and the delight readers and viewers take in it – is grounded in the same need for ornament and embellishment that drives humanity to transform simple and unadorned speech into eloquence, and plain houses and sheds into architecture. Together with Spini's inclusion of material and manufacture in the category of ornament this suggests that his view of ornament is ultimately more close to the rhetorical concept of *ornatus* than to that of *ornamenta* in the Albertian sense of bits and pieces that may be added or taken away without significant change or loss of quality.[52] Here the original meanings of these terms continue to resonate, particularly in Spini's innovative inclusion of the use of material and finishing, which are integral aspects of a building's design, in his definition of ornament. In this stress on fitness for purpose as a prerequisite for the appropriate use of ornament he echoes Quintilian, who ended his general discussion of *ornatus* by stating that true beauty (*vera species*) can never be separated from utility.[53]

Conclusion

The treatises by Spini, Barbaro and Scamozzi are just as interesting for what they set out to achieve as for their failures. The pleas of the latter two that the architect (and by extension the writer of an architectural treatise, like any author of a text intended for the public) should use 'all the colours' of rhetoric in the presentation of their ideas, is a precept they did not exactly follow to the letter. The dominant impression left by their books is that of a compulsion to force architectural theory and design into an Aristotelian system, so that they would look like *scienze*, resulting in prose that is dry as dust. But in writing their splendid failures they did achieve something new: a very precise demarcation of the domain of rhetoric in architecture. All three avoided easy comparisons such as saying that buildings are speeches in stone. Architectural design is fundamentally mathematical: it consists of the creation and manipulation of forms through geometrical operations. But its presentation is the province of rhetoric, in two ways. In the first place, architectural ornament, for instance the orders, may be compared to the figures of speech, or more precisely, we may think of the design of architectural ornament in the same terms as the orator thinks of finding the right ornaments of speech. It is telling that neither Barbaro nor Scamozzi added a detailed examination of the parallels between architectural and rhetorical ornament. Secondly, the architect becomes like the orator when he presents his designs to the public. But here as well, a detailed examination of this proposed similarity is lacking. Spini offers a slightly different case, because he considers architecture, like poetry, to be a representational art, representing nature. He does offer a detailed analysis of the parts of the orders to support this claim, and thus may be considered an early precursor of Bötticher's distinction between *Werkformen*, the mechanical and static forces at work in a building, and *Kunstformen*, their visual representation by means of a vocabulary of forms borrowed from natural forms.[54]

The balance of these attempts to integrate rhetoric and architecture within an Aristotelian framework is therefore mixed. They all succeed in further elucidating the province of rhetoric in architectural design, its theory and presentation, but they fail mostly in filling this out in any convincing detail. What Barbaro and Scamozzi in particular do make clear though, is the need for the architectural theorist to draw on other disciplines, and the way they argue for this is remarkably consistent: architecture, as the most public of all the arts, needs to be integrated within the whole range of human knowledge. That, one might say, is the real, but hidden rhetoric at work in their treatises.

NOTES

1 Cf. Van Eck (1998a).

2 Serlio, *On Architecture*, Book IV, p. 253.

3 G. Spini, *I Tre Primi Libri sopra l'Instituzioni de' Greci et Latini Architettori intorno agl'Ornamenti che convengono a tutte le Fabbriche che l'Architettura compone*, vol. I, p. 44. On Spini see the introduction and notes to this edition by Cristina Acidini, and most recently Payne (1999), pp. 144–70.

4 *I Dieci Libri dell'Architettura di M. Vitruvio Tradotti e Commentati da Monsignor Barbaro Eletto Patriarca d'Aquileia*, published in 1556; *I Dieci Libri dell'Architettura di M. Vitruvio Tradotti e Commentati da Mons. Daniel Barbaro Eletto Patriarca d'Aquileia da Lui Riveduti et Ampliati*, published in 1567b; *De architectura cum Commentariis*, published as well in 1567a. On Barbaro's Vitruvius commentaries see Fontana (1978), pp. 49–72 and (1985); Caye (1995).

5 Very little is known about Pazzi; he lectured at the Studio Romano from 1567 to 1576 and died in Reggio, where he was also born, in 1585. The translations of the mathematical treatises by Hero and Pappus mentioned in his letter to Spini were never published, but he had a keen interest in the application of mathematics to architecture, as his letters to Barbaro show. Cf. Spini, *I Tre Primi Libri*, p. 185 and Barbaro, *De Architectura Libri Decem*, X.iii and viii.

6 Barbaro's treatment of the distinction between *fabrica* and *ratiocinatio*, for instance, can be linked to the discussion of *noesis* versus *poesis* in Aristotle's *Metaphysics* 1032b5–20; that of *physis* and *technè* in *Physics* II.i; or the two kinds of intellect, one concerned with knowledge of particulars, the other with general knowledge, in *De Anima*; cf. Caye (1995), p. 15.

7 For recent treatments of Scamozzi's career and intellectual background see the contributions by Franco Barbieri and Werner Oechslin to the new reprint of the 1615 edition of Scamozzi's *Idea dell'Architettura Universale*; Barbieri (2003); and the chapter on Scamozzi in Payne (1999), pp. 214–37. None of these address the role of rhetoric in the *Idea*. Payne points out (p. 215) that the *Idea*, through its inclusion in Roland Fréart de Chambray's *Parallèle de l'Architecture Antique et de la Moderne* of 1650, which is actually a concordance of classical architecture, very much shaped the reception of architectural theory outside Italy after the Renaissance.

8 The *Idea* shared this encyclopaedic character with a number of contemporary didactic compendia of scientific knowledge which defined architecture, like Vitruvius and Scamozzi, in terms of the entire range of human knowledge, such as J. T. Freigius' *Paedagogus* (Basel 1582) or L. Fioravanti's *Della Specchio di Scientia Universale* (Venice 1612), who both included a chapter on architecture. The most intriguing case is J. H. Alsted's *Cursus Philosophici Encyclopaedia Libris XXVII Complectens* of 1620, which defines the architect as 'Architectus ingeniarius sit vir bonus, aedificium constituendi rationem doctus'. Cf. Oechslin (1997), pp. xxxv–xxxvi.

9 On the dissemination of Scamozzi's treatise outside Italy see Hopkins and Witte (1996).

10 Spini, *I Tre Primi Libri*, p. 45.

11 Spini, *I Tre Primi Libri*, p. 44; see p. 51 for a Vitruvian list of knowledge the architect should possess.

12 Barbaro, *I Dieci Libri dell'Architettura* (1567b), p. 4

13 Barbaro, *I Dieci Libri dell'Architettura* (1567b), p. 7.

14 On Scamozzi's relation to Barbaro, his debt to Aristotle (which is also manifest in his highlighting of every passage in Barbaro's Vitruvius edition of 1567 that is indebted to Aristotle) see Payne (1999), pp. 215–16 where she describes Scamozzi's manner of writing a treatise as printing his thought process.

15 See, for instance, Scamozzi, *Idea*, I.xxiv (p. 71), with a characteristic reference to Aristotle, *Metaphysics* Book I.

16 Scamozzi, *Idea*, 'Proemio', pp. 1–3 and 5.

17 Cf. Alberti, *De Re Aedificatoria*, 'Prologue', for a similar statement of the relation between the architect and his builders.

18 On Goldmann's mathematical theory of architecture see Goudeau (2005).

19 Barbaro, *I Dieci Libri dell'Architettura* (1567b), p. 21; cf. p. 115.

20 On the possible connections between Barbaro's architectural writings and Venetian politics see Tafuri (1995), pp. 123–8. He presents Barbaro as part of the faction that tried to continue the modernizing and Romanizing work of Doge Andrea Gritti. Caye (1995), pp. 280–1 argues that Barbaro's work was meant to continue the *translatio imperii et studiorum* started by Gritti, and connects it with the political writings of two Venetian patricians, Domenico Morosini, *De Bene Instituta Re Publica* (written in 1497) and Gasparo Contarini, *De Magistratibus et Republica Venetarum* (written *c.* 1523/4, published in 1543). It should be considered, however, that such very definite connections with the particular political situation in Venice in the 1550s and 1560s argues against Barbaro's sustained attempts in his commentaries to link architecture to the workings of the human mind and the ways in which knowledge is acquired. That is, Barbaro's purpose was to give it a universal and timeless character, rather than to identify architecture with, or enlist it for the purposes of one particular set of political beliefs. As Manuela Morosini has shown in her essay introducing the 1997 reprint of the 1567 Italian edition, Barbaro effectively

eliminated most things Venetian the better to reach an international public.

21 Barbaro, *I Dieci Libri dell'Architettura* (1567b), p. 27.

22 E. Barbaro, *Rhetoricorum Aristotelis*, I.i [= Aristotle, *Rhetorica* 1355b–1356a], 14v.: '[D]ocemus argumentis, movemus affectibus, conciliamus oratione, docere debitum est, conciliare honorarium, *permovere necessarium, non ratione artis, sed auditoris*.'

23 Scamozzi, *Idea*, p. 5.

24 Aristotle, *Metaphysics* 981b17–20.

25 Barbaro, *Della Eloquenza*, vol. II, pp. 335–453, in particular p. 381: '[Arte:]... riportando il parlare per gli aurecchi alle anime degli ascoltenti la forza dell'intendere e del volere, bisogna in questo viaggio da movimento e modo ad essa parlare. Lo artificio sia la machina et il modo conveniente di levare il peso della sentenza dalla mente umana [...] desiderando condonare alle parole i suoi colori, il sito e le parti quasi membra. Chiamaremo dunque i colori figure, le parti membra, il sito composizione, il finimento chiusa e termine della orazione'. Cf. p. 379: 'L'orazione esser dee come il corpo umano, et avere principio, mezzo e fine, e che le parti sue deono corrispondere a se stesso et al tutto con dignità e decoro. E sì come nel corpo sono tutti i sentimenti del corpo, così nel principio essere deono riposti i sentimenti della orazione.'

26 Barbaro, *I Dieci Libri dell'Architettura* (1567b), p. 36. On this passage see also Payne (2000), pp. 153–4.

27 Barbaro, *I Dieci Libri dell'Architettura* (1567b), p. 115.

28 S. Serlio, *Il Settimo Libro dell'Architettura*, p. 267, translated and quoted in Onians (1988), p. 267.

29 Cf. Cicero, *Orator* XIII.lxxiv, and Payne (2000), p. 288, n. 42.

30 For a more detailed treatment of this issue see Van Eck (2002).

31 Barbaro, *I Dieci Libri dell'Architettura* (1567b), p. 14.

32 Scamozzi, *Idea*, I.i, p. 5.

33 Scamozzi, *Idea*, 'Proemio', pp. 7–8. Cf. Vitruvius III.1.

34 See e.g. Quintilian V.x.94.

35 Scamozzi, *Idea*, I.i.xiv, pp. 46–7; I.i–ii, pp. 6–8; I.i.vii–viii, pp. 22–4; and I.i.xiii, p. 43.

36 Aristotle, *Rhetorica*, I.1 (354a1).

37 Scamozzi, *Idea*, I.xvii, p. 55.

38 Scamozzi repeatedly stressed this point; see, for instance, I.iii, p. 11.

39 Scamozzi, *Idea*, I.xiii, p. 43.

40 Ibid., I.vii, p. 23, and I.xxvi, p. 77.

41 On Scamozzi's treatment of modenature see Payne (2000), pp. 229–34.

42 Spini, *I Tre Libri*, pp. 60–1: 'Percioché sì come nell'arte del dire non si quietarono gl'huomini dell' espressione nuda della verità, ché a quella vollero aggiungere l'eloquenza e i suoi ornamenti; così in questa [sc. architecture] si vede avvenire, che non contenti delle semplici fabbriche che si fanno per difendirsi dalla molestia de' tempi et delle stagioni, ma ricercarono quello che alla degnità, leggiadria et diletto pareva che si convenisse.'

43 Spini, *I Tre Libri*, p. 31.

44 Cf. e.g. Cicero, *De Inventione* II.xv.34 and *De Officiis* I.xxviii.100 and I.iv.14.

45 Horace, *Ars Poetica*, lines 1–23.

46 Spini, *I Tre Libri*, pp. 67–8.

47 Aristotle, *Poetica*, 1448b4ff.

48 Aristotle, *Rhetorica* 1, 1371a21–1371b25, as translated in Russell and Winterbottom (1972), p. 134.

49 Plutarch, *De Audiendis Poetis* ('The Study of Poetry'), 3, in Russell and Winterbottom (1972), p. 513.

50 Spini, *I Tre Libri*, p. 65.

51 Spini, *I Tre Libri*, pp. 68–9.

52 Alberti, *De Re Aedificatoria* IX.ii, edition Rykwert, p. 156. *Quintilian* VIII.iii.4–6; cf. Vickers (1988), pp. 314–15 and Ong (1958), pp. 277.

53 *Institutio Oratoria*, VIII.iii.10.

54 See C. G. W. Bötticher, *Die Tektonik der Hellenen*, pp. 20–4.

PART II

INVENTION

THREE:
HOW TO ACHIEVE PERSUASION IN PAINTING: THE COMMON GROUND

Introduction

Giovanni Bellini's *Pietà*, now in the Brera Gallery in Milan (Fig. 3.1), carries a small tablet with the inscription 'Haec fere quum gemitus turgentia lumina promant/Bellini poterat flere Ioannis opus': 'Every time these swollen eyes produce groans/it could be the work of Giovanni Bellini weeps'. For all its brevity it is a surprisingly layered and elusive statement. Is it the painting that speaks, the painter or the viewer? Who does it address? Does it suggest, because of its conditional formulation, that the Mother of God will cry when the viewers of this painting are moved to groans, and hence to repentance? Or that the viewers will groan at the sight of the Virgin's swollen eyes? That imagining Her swollen eyes made the painter so contrite that he could produce a painting that is capable of weeping? Or that Bellini's painting actually surpasses the eyes of Mary in their power to move the viewer? Or that if this image could groan, it could be moved by its own laments? That is, does the inscription suggest a close sympathy, bordering on the magical, between the image and what it depicts, so that the painting will cry when Mary cries?[1] In its suggestion that the painting itself could weep and in that sense become one with the person it depicts, and its refusal to declare what it refers to and whom it addresses, it perfectly embodies a complex of views about the relation between art, what it represents and its viewers that is the subject of this chapter and the next: visual persuasion considered as a design issue.

In early modern Europe the main purpose of visual persuasion was to move viewers and incite them to virtuous action on the basis of emotional identification with what was depicted.[2] In a seminal formula Horace wrote in the *Ars Poetica*: 'As men's faces smile on those who smile, so they respond to those who weep. If you would have me weep, you must first feel grief yourself: then, O Telephus or Peleus, will your misfortunes hurt me [. . .].'[3] Spectators or readers react to the feelings the poet or painter has experienced; but interestingly, the examples Horace gave, Telephus and Peleus, could also refer to the tragic heroes put on the

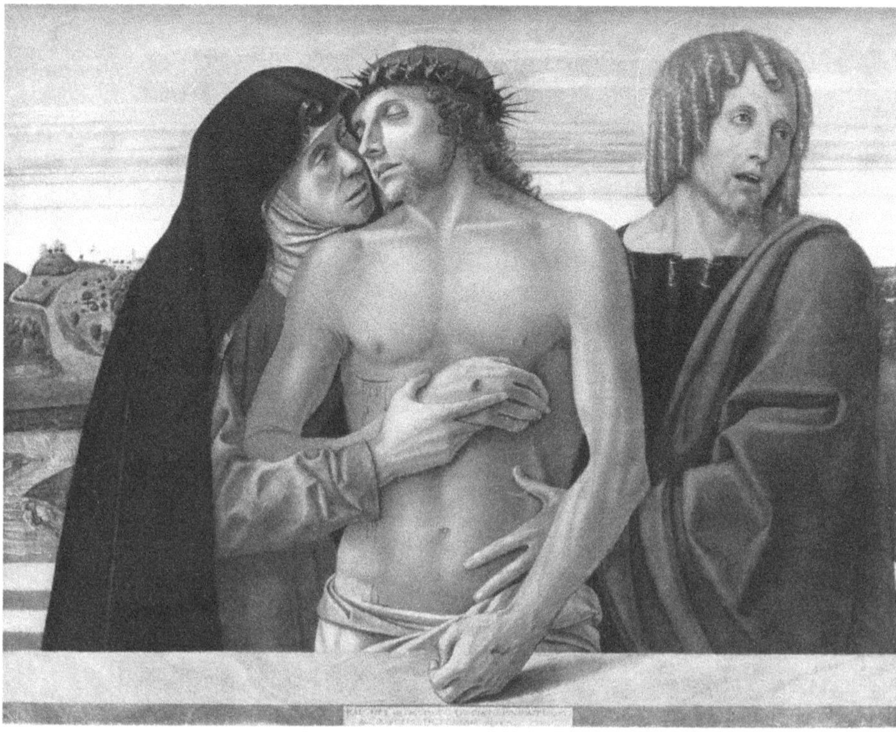

3.1 Giovanni Bellini, *Dead Christ with the Virgin Mary and Saint John the Evangelist.* Milan: Pinacoteca di Brera, 1460s (photo: Centre for Art-Historical Documentation, Radboud Universiteit Nijmegen).

stage by Euripides or Aeschylus, and hence the whole passage may refer to a theatrical mode of representing emotions and reacting to them.

This chapter is devoted to the basis, the *conditio sine qua non* of visual persuasion: the identification of the viewer with what is represented, resulting in a sense of living presence. It will consider a series of rhetorical strategies to achieve this that are all related to what we now call pictorial composition. According to Alberti such identification was the foundation of pictorial persuasion. 'An *historia*', he wrote, 'will move the soul when each man painted there clearly shows the movement of his own soul'. The explanation for this, he added, is that 'It happens in nature that nothing more than herself is found capable of things like herself; we weep with the weeping, laugh with the laughing, and grieve with the grieving'.[4] Leonardo made the same point in more detail in the notes for his *Trattato*:

> The elements of narrative paintings ought to move those who look at or contemplate them in the same way as him whom the narrative painting represents. That is, if the narrative painting represents terror,

> fear, flight, sorrow, weeping or lamentation; or pleasure, joy, laughter and similar conditions, the minds of those who view it ought to move their limbs so that they seem to find themselves in the same situation which the figures in the narrative painting represent. If they do not do so, the skill of the painter is in vain.[5]

One conspicuous example of such identification is Anton Francesco Doni's reaction to the statue of Laocoön, rediscovered in 1506 (Fig. 3.2): when a spectator sees it, he wrote, he is so overcome by compassion that he feels compelled to adopt the pose of Laocoön.[6] Viewers also reacted strongly in this manner to Christian art, where their response was often conditioned by devotional handbooks urging the reader to identify imaginatively with the Passion of Christ or the death of saints.[7]

Lodovico Dolce, the Venetian art theorist and translator of Ovid's *Metamorphoses* and Cicero's *De Oratore* articulated the importance of emotional identification for visual persuasion briefly but clearly:

> [...] it is necessary that the figures move the soul of the viewers, perturbing some of them, making others cheerful, moving some to piety and others to disdain, in accordance with the nature of the story. Otherwise it will be thought that the painter has achieved nothing: because this is the spice [*condimento*] of all his talents; as happens equally to the painter, historian and orator: that if things written or recited do not have this force, they lack also spirit and life.[8]

But the records suggest something else. Viewers indeed identified with what they saw, but this did not lead them to action or to a change in their ways. At least that is not what they deemed sufficiently important to record. What they did comment on is the basis of their identification. The paintings or statues were so vivid that they felt in the presence of living human beings. Instances of such reactions abound, both to poetry or oratory and to paintings. Aretino's letters testify to such reactions. In his contemplation of Titian's 'Cristo vivo e vero', the thorns piercing Him have become real thorns and the blood they cause to flow real blood. It is not the image that exhorts him to piety, but the pain constricting Christ's face.[9] In a less familiar instance, Francesco Bocchi described the viewers' reaction to the *Pietà* in his unpublished life of Michelangelo. After mentioning the powers of the artist to represent faces, characters and emotions he paid him the highest tribute an orator could give. No eloquence could sufficiently praise his power to infuse dead marble with living grief.[10]

Art could be so lifelike that it ceased to look like art. Visual persuasion became complete when the illusion was created that the viewer was in the

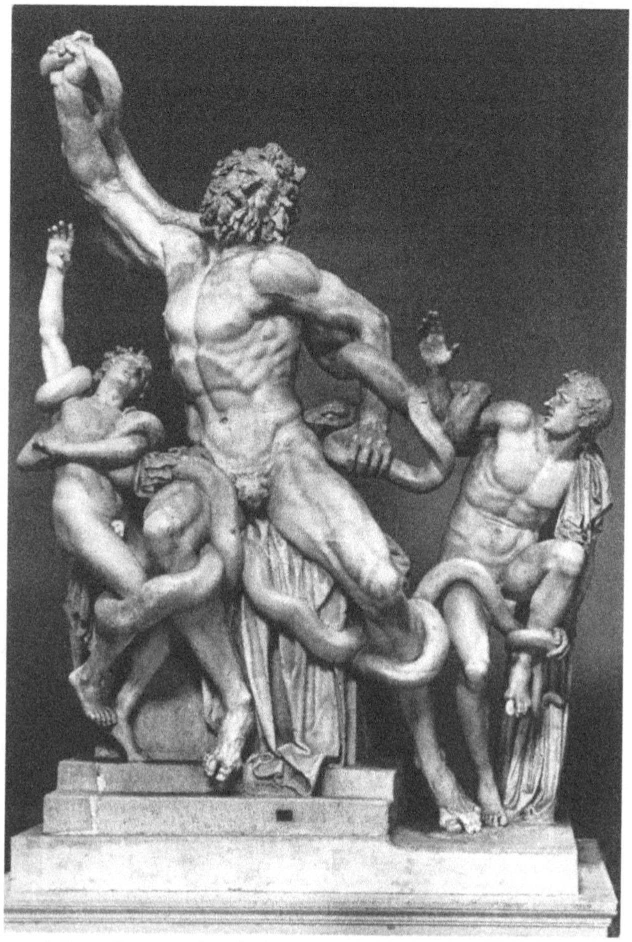

3.2 Hagesandrus, Athanodorus and Polydorus, *Laocoön*. Rome: Museo Vaticano, *c.* 200 BC (photo: Centre for Art-Historical Documentation, Radboud Universiteit Nijmegen).

presence of acting persons engaged in situations he or she could identify and engage with. Aretino reported that when he and his friend Tribolo saw Titian's *Death of Saint Peter Martyr*, Tribolo reacted to the extreme vividness of the painting with fear and pity, as if he were present at the events depicted, not looking at an image of them (Fig. 3.3). By using the words 'fear and pity' Aretino suggests that Tribolo reacted as if he were watching a tragedy because these are the emotions Aristotle famously identified in his *Poetics* as those felt by the audience: a tragedy is a representation, but also an enactment and therefore comes closer to an actual event taking place than a painting.[11] Later on in this chapter I will return to the issue of theatricality in achieving a sense of identification between the viewer and what is viewed.

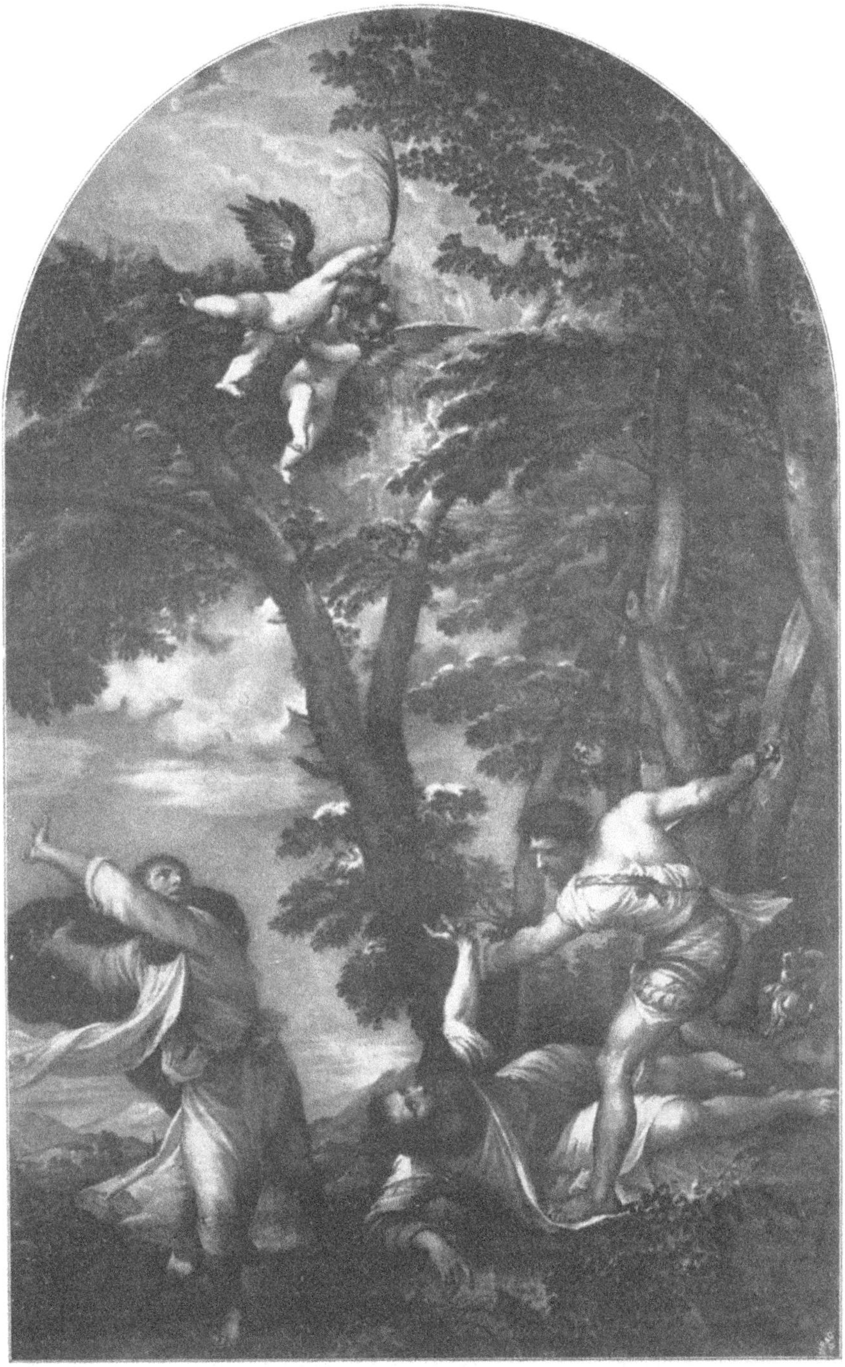

3.3 Carlo Loth after Titian, *Martyrdom of Saint Peter Martyr*, 1526 to 1530. Venice: Santi Giovanni e Paolo, *c.* 1691 (photo: Centre for Art-Historical Documentation, Radboud Universiteit Nijmegen).

As we have seen in the Introduction, to achieve this identification through speech was a key issue in ancient rhetoric. *Enargeia*, *evidentia* or *illustratio* all refer to this effect of presenting something so vividly that the public forgets it is listening to a speech, but instead thinks it witnesses the event or action described. These are all metaphorical terms with a strong visual root. *Enargeia* originally meant to single something out, for instance by putting a strong light on it, so that it became distinct and clearly visible. *Evidentia* has *videre*, to see, as its root, and was used to refer to the quality of clarity and distinctness or perspicuity in speech; *illustratio* is derived from *lux*, light, and means to illuminate and hence to elucidate, which has the same etymological root, and is in fact an accurate translation of the Greek *enargeia*.

But classical rhetoric also offered considerations of persuasion in the visual arts that addressed the specific character of images. Quintilian opened the discussion. When he wanted to illustrate the persuasive force of *elocutio*, and particularly of figures of speech, he chose, as was mentioned in the Introduction, not a fragment from a speech as an example, but the famous statue of the *Discobolos* by Myron, and compared the use of figures to the illusion of movement the sculptor had conveyed to his statue (Fig. 2). Although not explicitly identified, the basis of the persuasive force exercised by movement and figures is the illusion of life:

> The body when held bolt upright has but little grace, for the face looks straight forward, the arms hang by the side, the feet are joined and the whole figure is stiff from top to toe. But that curve, I might almost call it motion (. . .) gives an impression of action and animation. So, too, the hands will not always be represented in the same position, and the variety given to the expression will be infinite.[12]

Quintilian did not argue for a straightforward, one-to-one transposition of rhetorical figures of speech to the visual arts by assuming a direct equivalence between antithesis in speech and *contrapposto* in sculpture. Instead he suggested a much more subtle and profound relation. Curves, with their suggestion of motion, suggest life in a statue; the gestures of the hands express emotions. Similarly figures of speech serve not only to render the expression of thought more acute and hence more persuasive, but ultimately are used to establish *enargeia* or the illusion of life. In Book VIII Quintilian called the figures of speech the *lumina orationis*, the lights of speech, by which he did not mean that they provide the superfluous glitter of decoration. Rather, he used 'lumina' in the sense of the light in the eyes, which signifies life and sentient being. That same effect is reached in statuary when the use of curves, *contrapposto*, foreshortening, or other deviations from the straight line and perfect but static symmetry contribute to a heightened expression that suggests life. Statues, like speeches, should be arranged on the basis of their purpose, to persuade, for which *enargeia* is an important instrument.

This use of visual metaphor to explain the effect of figures of speech, and their adaptation to the visual arts was taken up by sixteenth-century authors. In his short treatise on rhetoric Daniel Barbaro echoed this comparison while making explicit the tacit suggestion of living presence achieved by their use. He compared them to the painters' use of colour, but also to the blood of the human body: they animate and thereby make a painting or speech more beautiful.[13] His fellow-Venetian Sperone Speroni's *Dialogho della rhetorica* is not a very original treatment of rhetoric, but it did illustrate the effect of epideictic speech by calling it the 'occhio e luce', the eye and light that illuminates the life that is praised.[14]

COMPOSITION AND THE COMMON GROUND IN ANCIENT RHETORIC

One of the most frequent pieces of advice classical orators gave their students was that they should be in touch with their audience. They should establish a common ground, creating an atmosphere of shared convictions, interests and emotions, address the feelings and agenda of their audience, and acknowledge the character of their public and the occasion of the speech. As Cicero advised: 'This oratory of ours must be adapted to the ears of the multitude, for charming or urging their minds to approve of proposals, which are weighed in no goldsmith's balance, but in what I may call common scales.'[15] Much of this is treated under the heading of decorum, but there are also more specific discussions on how to establish an emotional rapport with the public, and in particular on what to avoid. Using unfamiliar words and expressions, for instance, is fatal, because it means the audience can no longer follow the speech and becomes distracted or feels slighted.

Ignoring the public's preoccupations or the way they see themselves is also a grave error. A successful speech is not simply an act of persuasion resulting in consensus. Before that occurs an intangible process of constructing, projecting, or even performing identity has taken place, in which the identity of speaker and public alike are not fixed and stable, but can evolve and be modified during the speech. The Renaissance genre of the speech in praise of a city, the *laudatio urbis* can be used to illustrate this process. Such texts were directed primarily at the inhabitants of the city whose praises were sung. This makes one wonder why – apart from a desire to flatter – a prominent humanist such as Leonardo Bruni would spend so much trouble pointing out the virtues of his city to his fellow Florentines, just as the most famous ancient model, Aelius Aristides' *Panathenaicus* of the second century AD, was delivered before the Athenians. Such epideictic speeches are not primarily about conveying new insights, but about creating a sense of shared identity. This can be achieved by recalling significant events from the past. Aelius Aristides highlighted the role of the Athenians as defenders of democracy against the Persians 600 years earlier. In his *Laudatio Fiorentinae Urbis* of 1402 Leonardo Bruni gave Florence a Roman pedigree, and developed a powerful visualization of the Florentine *ethos* or character by suggesting a likeness between the city and her inhabitants. Delivering a speech and listening to it thus become both parts of a shared experience of identity, the performance of shared *ethos*.

Once such common ground in the sense of a feeling of shared issues and even identity had been established, persuasion, whether it is by means of words or images, needs to be direct, clear and swift to succeed. Plutarch reported an anecdote about the orator Lysias, who wrote a speech for a client. On first view the client found the speech very good, but on repeated lecture less so. Lysias explained to his client that this was the way it should be: a speech must convince the judges once and for good – there is no second chance.[16]

Another general condition underlying the belief in, and practice of, visual persuasion, was the conviction, widely shared in Antiquity as well as the sixteenth century, that sight is the most reliable of the senses, and the impact of things seen much stronger than that of things heard, read or touched. Hence the importance of gesture, and the stress on *enargeia* in speech. As Lodovico Dolce would put it:

> The eye cannot make mistakes in seeing, if it is not ill, myopic or hindered by another event. But the intellect easily makes mistakes, and very often, because it is blinded by ignorance, or by emotion.[17]

Such swiftness, clarity and perspicuity in works of art depend on individual aspects of a work of art – the use of colour and gesture for instance – but more fundamentally on a consideration of the work as a whole and the way its parts should be arranged so as to fulfil its purpose, which is to persuade: that is what we would now call its composition. As we have seen in Chapter One, *compositio* in the classical rhetorical treatises referred to the structure of sentences. It was a technical concept, which did not mean what we would now call literary composition; instead, it meant constructing a complex sentence out of words and clauses.[18]

Classical rhetoricians did discuss the arrangement and order of parts in a speech considered as a whole, but this they addressed under the heading of *dispositio*. Again Quintilian was the first to make an influential comparison between writing a speech and designing a work of art, this time comparing *dispositio* to architectural design:

> But just as it is not sufficient for those who are erecting a building merely to collect stone and timber and other building materials,

> but skilled masons are required to arrange and place them [*disponendis eis collocandisque*], so in speaking, however abundant the matter may be, it will merely form a confused heap unless arrangement be employed to reduce it to order and to give it connexion and firmness of structure. Nor is it without good reason that arrangement is treated as the second of the five departments of oratory, since without it the first is useless. For the fact that all the limbs of a statue have been cast does not make it a statue: they must be put together [. . .]. Again even a slight dislocation will deprive a limb of its previous use and vigour, and disorder in the ranks will impede the movement of an army. Nor can I regard as an error the assertion that order is essential to the existence of nature itself, for without order everything would go to wreck and ruin. Similarly if oratory lacks this virtue, it cannot fail to be confused, [and] will be guided solely by chance without fixed purpose or the least idea either of starting-point or goal.[19]

In nature, as in art, unity, and the order and arrangement that derive from it and are its outward manifestation, is essential for effectiveness. Such unity is based on the purpose for which an organism or artefact is made. Since the purpose of a speech, like that of a painting, is persuasion, its entire arrangement or *dispositio* should be determined by that goal. Accordingly Quintilian, and before him Cicero, the *Rhetorica ad Herennium* (which is the first Roman treatise on rhetoric, written first on c. 86–82 BC), and Aristotle, discussed at length how to place the arguments in a case, whether to include an *exordium* or to go straight away for the heart of the matter, how to define the issue at stake, or what evidence or witnesses to use. The overriding consideration in this was to make the best use of the available material to keep the attention of the judge or audience, stir their emotions and persuade them. Quintilian's discussion of *dispositio* is the longest, but as in Cicero's treatment devoted almost exclusively to forensic oratory. He disclaimed that there were any general principles determining arrangement, because all court cases are unique.[20]

For a systematic analysis of arrangement we have to turn to Aristotle's treatment of plot in the *Poetics*. Even though this text became widely accessible only after 1550, it prefigures – and puts into one coherent view – practically all aspects of order and arrangement in the arts of representation, both verbal and visual, that would follow in the Renaissance. According to Aristotle poetry, music and painting, although they use different media, are all arts concerned with *mimesis*, the representation of 'people doing things', that is performing significant actions, more particularly morally significant actions. A tragedy is a *mimesis* of a complete action, that is the plot, by which Aristotle meant 'the ordering of particular actions'. The plot is therefore the most important part of a tragedy, because it is its unifying principle. He called it even tragedy's principle of life, and its soul; just as in painting, 'where the most beautiful colours, if smeared at random, would give less pleasure than an uncoloured outline that was a picture of something' (1450b). Plot makes for unity and wholeness: the *Odyssey* and *Iliad* are great works of art not because of their vast subject matter, but their selectiveness and unity of action. The *Odyssey*, for instance, does not recount all the events in Odysseus' life, but only those that are directly related to the main theme, his home-coming after years of wandering. A plot is therefore the arrangement of particular actions into a unified and whole action since that is the substance, the most important element of tragedy.

This definition of a plot as a *mimesis* of a whole action has several implications. A tragedy should be a whole, with a beginning, middle and end. The plot should be of some amplitude, but no more than can be taken in at one view – the swiftness and perspicuity so many ancient and Renaissance theorists and viewers stressed. It should be a unity, in which the parts are arranged in such a way that the whole is disrupted if parts are removed or displaced. It should not be about all the actions of one man, like a biography, but about one, complete, action. A good plot should display probable connections of events; and it should contain surprises, that is events that happen unexpectedly but because of each other and not by chance, so as to excite fear and pity in the viewers. Thus theatrical representation should be highly selective in what is shown on stage. For Aristotle poetry should not be didactic, allegorical or aim for sententious meaning, but aim for a profound, shattering effect on the passions of the audience: catharsis through pity and fear. To achieve this good plots should contain at least three elements: a *peripateia* or course of events that take a turn to the opposite involving surprise; recognition, that is a change from ignorance to knowledge, and pathos, that is actions involving death or pain.[21]

The ultimate aim of tragedy is to excite fear and pity, fear for the things that might also befall the spectator, and pity for the misfortune that might befall others. Both emotions presuppose that the spectator experiences a strong sense of identification with the heroes on stage and their fate. Aristotle compared tragedy with figure painting: both the painter and the poet put the individual person before us, but though their representations are lifelike, they are also more beautiful than they are in reality, to make identification and the suspension of disbelief more easy.[22] Such lifelikeness can be achieved when the poet acts as the director and producer of tragedies acted out before his mind's eye. Only when he puts his tragedy before his eyes, and sees the events as if they are actually present, can he find the appropriate words and gestures. Similarly for Aristotle or for American method actors, 'people who actually feel passion are the most convincing'.[23]

Aristotle's criteria of unity, wholeness, order and amplitude can be applied both to tragedy and painting, because, unlike Quintilian's treatment of *dispositio* as applied to forensic oratory, they are not intrinsically and essentially temporal in character. Quintilian and Cicero had based their views about the arrangement of the parts of a speech on a keen appreciation of a speech's linear unfolding in the course of time when delivered, and what this meant in terms of keeping the audience's attention. Aristotle's account of persuasive *mimesis* of significant human action is deliberately inclusive: in the opening paragraphs of the *Poetica* he presented painting, music and poetry as closely related representational arts that only differ, but not essentially, in the media they use. Unity, amplitude, wholeness and order are not qualities inextricably linked with the narrative arts of poetry or tragedy, unfolding in the course of time; they can also be applied to painting's representation of a plot in an present moment. Ultimately the aim of all good tragedy, be it poetry or painting, is to move the audience, and from that purpose all considerations of arrangement or composition must follow.

ACHIEVING A COMMON GROUND IN RENAISSANCE PAINTING: COMPOSITION AND LINEAR PERSPECTIVE

Leon Battista Alberti was the first Renaissance theorist to address how paintings could interact with their spectators and thereby inspire a sense of identification in them, when he advised the painter in Book II of *De Pictura* to include a witness in the scene, someone who like an orator acts as a witness to what is happening and draws the viewers' attention:

> I like there to be someone in the *historia* who tells the spectators what is going on, and either beckons them with his high hand to look, or with ferocious expression and forbidding glance challenges them not to come near, as if he wished their business to be secret, or points to some danger or remarkable thing in the picture, or by his gestures invites you to laugh or weep with them.[24]

His description recalls the gesture of the grim-faced Mary in Masaccio's near-contemporary *Trinità* in Santa Maria Novella (Fig. 1.1). His advice was part of his discussion of how the painter could best represent a *historia*, which was his most elevated task, because of its subject matter – stories taken from classical mythology or the Bible – and because choosing these subjects could give the painter the same elevated status as the poet. In contemporary early Quattrocento usage the term 'istoria' was used both for painting and sculpture, in particular for relief panels representing a number of figures involved in one single, significant action in a dignified, clear and expressive manner. Alberti actually mentioned the works of Donatello, Ghiberti and Luca della Robbia, whose work came much closer to the ideals of *De Pictura* than most paintings of the 1430s. The aim of such reliefs, like that of history writing, was to exhort and persuade the viewer to act virtuously.[25] 'History', Cicero wrote in *De Oratore*, 'bears witness to the passing of the ages, is the light of truth, gives life to recollection, guidance to human life and brings tidings of ancient days; whose voice, but the orator's, can entrust her to immortality?'[26] Alberti and other Florentine artists and humanists might have answered that the arts could also be trusted with the task of keeping alive the memory of humanity, which is the subject of *historia* in its modern sense.

Alberti conceptualized this practical, pictorial problem by applying the rhetorical term 'compositio' to the visual arts. In *De Pictura* he defined a series of persuasive strategies in painting, ranging from the general to the particular: the use of linear perspective, composition, the number and arrangement of persons, and their gestures, expressions and dress. These all serve to establish an affective bond between the spectator and what is represented.

Unlike Cennino Cennini's handbook, *De Pictura* is a humanist treatise, not a primer for the practising artist, and the relation between Alberti's theory and Quattrocento artistic practice remains problematic. It is doubtful whether many artists actually read Alberti or followed his advice. But the tenuous relation between his views on painting, in particular composition and what Renaissance artists did, also points to a wider issue: the well-known fact that painters, patrons and theorists of the Quattrocento and Cinquecento hardly ever discussed composition in the modern sense of what Thomas Puttfarked has defined as

> not simpy the calculated and controlled arrangement of planimetric relationships, but the way (or the ways) in which figures and objects, settings and whole pictorial worlds refute, embody, modify, even subvert and deny the basic formal intention of the bounded image and the viewer's privilege as it is defined by it.

Nor did they consider how the parts of a painting should be related towards each other, how the handling of light and colouring should be considered in the painting as a whole, let alone the pictorial means through which such unity might be achieved. Leonardo or Vasari did not mention the spectacular innovation of their time in the way situations and events are represented: the replacement of the frontal symmetry of Byzantine painting by the highly sophisticated visual representation of narrative, action and emotion that culminated in Raphael's Vatican Stanze. That is a topic introduced in seventeenth-century French discourse about painting by Roger de Piles, continued with significant rhetorical overtones by Heinrich Fuseli in the early nineteenth century, and developed fully, but stripped of its rhetorical concern with persuasion, by Heinrich Wölfflin. This does not mean that Renaissance painters were not interested in, or unaware of the problems involved in designing a painting as a whole: Raphael's *School of Athens* and Leonardo's *Last Supper* or *Adoration of the Magi* all testify to their creators' ability to conceive of their paintings as a whole, directed at the viewer, and aiming at establishing a common ground, whether in a literal, spatial sense, or a figurative, emotional way, between the work of art and its viewer.[27] But the *topos* where such considerations could be formulated was not Alberti's *compositio*.

As Michael Baxandall has shown, Alberti's treatment of *compositio* closely followed classical rhetorical treatments of how periodic sentences should be put together. What is less prominent in his analysis, is that Alberti's main concern here is with the composition of the human figures that make up the main part of any *historia*. Alberti briefly mentioned paintings conceived as a unity, but quickly moved on to discuss how human bodies should be painted in a harmonious and well-proportioned way. Instead, linear perspective was the *locus* for considerations of paintings as a whole, unified composition. As we have seen in Chapter One, linear perspective enabled the painter to literally present his or her point of view, involve the spectator, and create a convincing illusion of lifelikeness. Because linear perspective can only be applied when the painter has thought about the image as a whole, and the relations of its parts to each other, it is in discussions of perspective that considerations of composition became explicit. We can follow this development by looking at the reception of *De Pictura* in the sixteenth century.

After Alberti's introduction of *compositio* into artistic discourse it is in Venice in the decades around 1550 that we find another series of considerations of invention and composition in rhetorical terms, possibly inspired by the new Italian translation by Lodovico Domenichi published in 1547.[28] The three Venetian treatises on painting by Paolo Pino (1548), Michelangelo Biondo (1549) and Lodovico Dolce (1557) were all influenced by *De Pictura*. But many texts by Venetian *literati* also drew on rhetoric and offered sustained comparisons between painting and rhetoric, often as part of their attempts to argue for the superiority of Titian and other Venetian artists.[29] In Venice Titian and Veronese were in close touch with learned humanist patrons such as Daniel Barbaro, who, as we have seen in Chapter Two, wrote about architecture and linear perspective, published his great-uncle Ermolao's Latin translation of Aristotle's *Rhetorica*, employed Palladio both as an illustrator for his Vitruvius edition and as an architect at the Villa Barbaro, and had a brother whose hobby was sculpture. Sperone Speroni and other writers about the arts were part of the same intellectual environment: Barbaro, for instance, wrote the dedication for Speroni's *Dialoghi*, but was also well acquainted with Lodovico Dolce. Speroni holds up Titian's portraits as a model for the orator in clarity, aptness, the choice of the right, meaningful words, and impressiveness.[30] In a reversal of Quintilian's comparison of natural and rhetorical disposition Titian is here held up to orators as a model of persuasive composition.

Alberti had defined painting as a form of composition, in which the painter designs an *istoria*. Michelangelo Biondo takes over Alberti's codification of linear perspective and like him divided painting into three parts: *circonscrizione, compositione* and *receptione dei lumini*. He also presented *compositio* as the disposition of places and bodies, their members and their parts, in accordance with the *historia* to be represented.[31] Paolo Pino remarked casually in his *Dialogo della Pittura* (thereby signalling that this was a widely accepted opinion that needed no further explanation) that 'la pittura è propria poesia, cioè inuenzione, la qual fâ apparere quello, che non è': painting is really poetry in the proper sense of the word, that is fictional invention, and makes appear that which does not exist. The art of painting is divided into *invenzione, disegno* and *colorire*, echoing the rhetorical division of the writing process into invention, disposition and elocution. *Invenzione* consists of *giudizio, circumscrizione, pratica* (which teaches the painter what to include and what to leave out of all beautiful objects in nature), and *la retta compositione*. The latter is a special category, because in it the three other competences work together. Composition ensures that a decorous painting results, consisting of an integrated image uniting the old and the young, people and animals in a well-defined manner and using fore-shortening, indicating nude forms hidden by draperies but without confusing folds, and gives depth to the image. It is, Pino concludes, the 'spirit of painting'.[32] Alberti's use of *compositio* to analyse the depiction of the human body is here extended into a much wider concept that includes arrangements of contrasting figures and an awareness of varying depth within the picture plane; that is, of the importance of *rilievo* to enhance the illusion of life in a perspectival representation of space on a flat surface.

Painting is really poetry because both arts are inventions that make appear things that do not exist. Like the writer of comedies or tragedies the painter should aim for brevity, should select, highlight and ignore, and not try to contain all the world in a frame. Just like poets use one personage to say what they want to say, the painter should compose, with the help of living nature, what he wants to depict, without stealing from others. Variety and copiousness, brevity and unity of perspective holding together the scene depicted in the vision of the painter: Pino's analysis of what the painter does may not follow rhetorical advice to the letter, but comes very close both to Aristotle's view that plots should be highly selective, and to the theatrical stage-settings of biblical and mythological life painted by Titian and Veronese.[33] The painting is a *dichiarazone*, literally a clarification, drawing something out into the light (and in that sense similar to the process of highlighting resulting in *enargeia*), but also in the more conventional sense a declaration or declamation. Therefore it is not a static product of a process either, but a performance. Pictorial composition is a dynamic process. This performative view of painting is reflected in Pino's habit to speak not of *colorito*, but of *colorire*, the process of finding the right shade of colour to put things seen under their true light before the beholder.[34] In this passage, which recalls Veronese's great set pieces, the painter is transformed into an orator or dramatic poet, whose concern is to delineate as clearly as possible the action set before the public's eyes.[35]

Pino and Dolce wrote partly out of a desire to vindicate the merits of Venetian painting, distinguished by its use of colour, against the criticism of Florentine critics, above all Vasari, who extolled the virtues of the *disegno* of Raphael, Leonardo and Michelangelo. The criticism of Venetian painting was not a very conspicuous issue in the 1550 edition. But in the preface to the 1568 edition of the *Vite*, probably written with the help of Vincenzio Borghini and other members of the Accademia Fiorentina, Vasari had defined *disegno* as '[...] having its origin in the intellect, [it] draws out from many single things a general judgement, it is like a form or idea of all the objects in nature [...]'.[36] This is an almost literal adaptation of Aristotle's definition of knowledge as derived from the senses in the Prologue of the *Metaphysics*. It is also a conceptual sleight of hand, through which Vasari manages to present drawing as an intellectual, cognitive activity. *Disegno* becomes both knowledge of the form of things, the *idea*; and the actual drawing by which the hand gives visible form to the intellectual concept or form. In this cognitive view of artistic design the generalities are more important than individual characteristics, the measurable more important than immeasurable aspects of the visual world such as colour or shading. Hence Florentine drawing was extolled at the expense of Venetian *colorire* and *chiaroscuro*. *Disegno* became the key to Vasari's theory and historiography of the arts, 'the medium of the painter's very thought as well as its concrete expression'.[37] But, as in Alberti's discussion of *historia*, it was concerned exclusively with the human figure, not with design in the modern sense of the arrangement or ordering of the parts of a work considered as a whole. Accordingly, Vasari described one single figure by Michelangelo, the *Isaiah* in the Sistine Chapel (Fig. 3.4), as the culmination and exemplification of the entire art of painting, and defined painting as 'a plane the surface of which is covered by fields of colours [...] which by virtue of *il buon disegno* of circumscribed lines define the figure'; that is, the human figure.[38]

At the same time as the *Vite* were published, in the decades around 1550, linear perspective disappeared from Italian painting as a general unifying agent. Instead it became increasingly identified with the representation of isolated elements such as buildings in the backgrounds, or was even considered as an ornament inessential to pictorial representation, as is documented by Archbishop Paleotti's instructions about religious painting. Interestingly two Florentine authors belonging to Vasari's intellectual entourage developed a way of talking about the arrangement of figures, foreground and background, and the handling of colour and light that shows an awareness of pictorial composition as a unifying agent: Vincenzio and Raffaelle Borghini. Vincenzio was closely

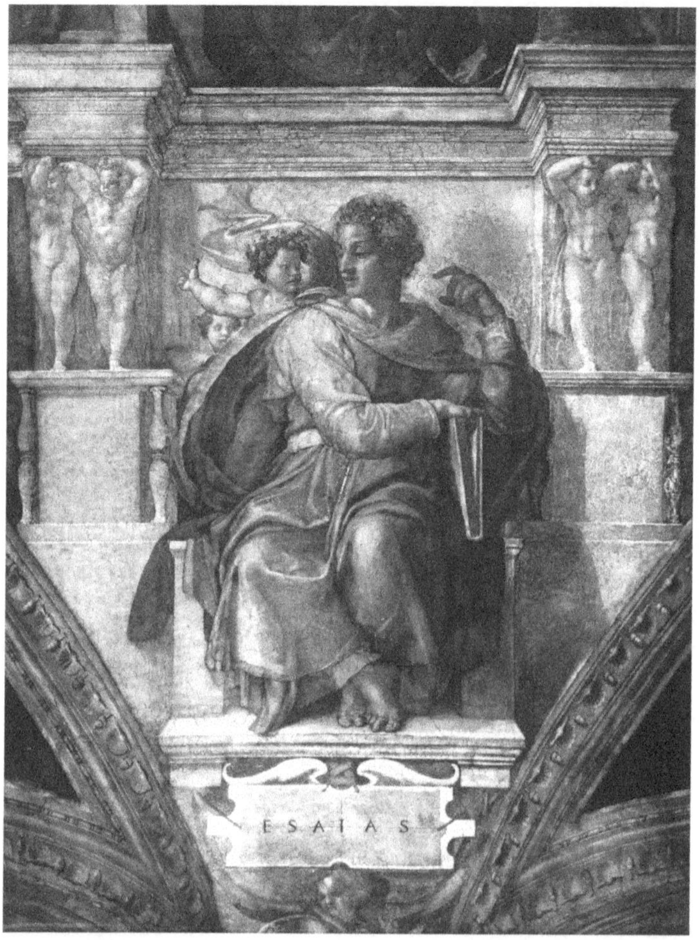

3.4 Michelangelo, *Isaiah*. Rome: Vatican Palace, Sistine Chapel, *c.* 1509 (photo: Centre for Art-Historical Documentation, Radboud Universiteit Nijmegen).

involved with editing the *Vite*, and became the first *luogotenente* or representative of the Duke to the *Accademia del Disegno* after its foundation in 1563. In his unpublished *Selva di notizie* Borghini's first concern is not with the illusion of life, or suggesting three-dimensional space, but with the overall effect of pictures:

> There is in painting a part that corresponds to [music] in a certain way and shares with it a most important and inseparable feature (I talk of the case of an *istoria*, as with poets one talks of poems, and not of a simple figure): this is a harmony, a composition [*una composizione*], a fit and appropriate disposition of the parts with each other, so that they

> do not impair each other but make the whole appear well disposed and composed, not confused and disordered. And in the same way in which high and deep voices, composed together with reason and rule, produce the sweetest harmony and consonance, so in the composition of a picture there should be a composition of large things with small ones, of distant things with things nearby, so that there results a most pleasant consonance and harmony for the eye [. . .].[39]

Borghini elucidated his conception of a painting as a unified whole resulting from the harmonious combination of opposites by comparing it with the harmony resulting in music from the reasoned, that is proportionate, combination of high and low voices. This presentation of pictorial composition as a *concordia discordantium*, a harmony of discordant elements or even a *coincidentia oppositorum*, a unity of opposites, is a very close, at times *verbatim* paraphrase of Alberti's definition of *concinnitas* in *De Re Aedificatoria*: closely knit unity, the highest beauty a building can aspire to. This book had been published in a Tuscan translation by Borghini's fellow member of the Florentine Accademia Cosimo Bartoli in 1550.[40] There Alberti had presented *concinnitas* as the beauty resulting from a unifying design of a building considered as a whole, and as the result of number, outline, and position. But he had certainly not limited its scope to numerical proportion, as is often assumed by twentieth-century commentators, nor had he restricted it to architecture. It is a general aesthetic and metaphysical principle at work in nature, society and the works of man:

> Neither in the whole body nor in its parts does *concinnitas* flourish as much as it does in Nature herself; [. . .] It has a vast range in which to exercise itself and bloom – it runs through man's entire life and government, it rules the whole of Nature. Everything Nature produces is regulated by the law of *concinnitas*, and her chief concern is that whatever she produces should be absolutely perfect. Without *concinnitas* this could hardly be achieved, for the critical sympathy of the parts would be lost.
>
> [. . .]
>
> Beauty is a form of sympathy and consonance of the parts within a body, according to definite number, outline and position, as dictated by *concinnitas*, the absolute and fundamental rule in Nature. This is the main object of the art of building, and the source of her dignity, charm, authority and worth.[41]

He then proceeded to illustrate the principle of *concinnitas* in nature and art by showing how in both realms it unites opposing parts: in nature the slender and the strong, the odd and the even; in architecture majesty and grace; in music, the high and the low.[42] *Concinnitas* does not have to be read exclusively in a Platonic sense as the unity resulting from the use of geometrical or numerical proportion that can only be grasped intellectually, through calculations and geometrical analysis, as in Rudolf Wittkower's diagrams of Alberti's façade of Santa Maria Novella that show the abstract geometrical proportion scheme underlying the dazzling variety of colour, texture and ornament in the façade. *Concinnitas* can also refer to the unity resulting from fitness for purpose, when all the parts of an artefact or organism work together to fulfill its purpose, function or end. In applying such an Aristotelian teleological view to architectural beauty Alberti was influenced by the discussions held *c.* 1440 in Rome and Florence between the Byzantine refugee scholars Plethon and Bessarion. The details of these discussions need not detain us here, but what does matter is that Alberti clearly conceived of buildings, musical compositions and paintings in terms of wholes whose unity results from the ordering of parts with a view to each other and the work as a whole.[43]

In the passage by Borghini with its Albertian echoes he called the disposition of a well-composed painting 'una atta et accomodata disposizione', an apt and coherent disposition. In *De Pictura* linear perspective is the chief instrument to achieve such unity in painting. Not surprisingly Borghini also thought this:

> This composition, this agreeable discordance [*discordanza concorde*], this harmony and proportion, [...] I would have thought should be called perspective, which contains a rule for diminishing the things on a plane according to the rule of sight [...], according to which near things appear naturally larger and distant ones smaller. And that is so not only with houses and buildings, but with all things made by nature which painters may have to imitate.[44]

A generation later Vincenzio Borghini's relative Raffaello Borghini actually presented perspective as a part of disposition, described by him as 'that beautiful order [*bella ordinanza*] which is made up of many figures, animals, landscapes and buildings, in fact of all things, so that they appear well distributed, in clothes and well placed in locations appropriate to them and well ordered'.[45] The clear arrangement of all figures within their spatial setting, that is the unity of foreground and background in an appearance of coherent space is now the basis of composition proper, resulting in a *composito unito* that can be taken in by the viewer in one glance, and in which everything is ordered with clarity, variety, propriety and overall harmony – an adaptation of the four rhetorical *virtutes dicendi* or stylistic virtues *latinitas*, *perspicuitas*, *varietas* and *decorum*.[46]

But perspective is not simply a means to achieve unity in a painting considered as an independent work of art, made for its own sake. The ultimate aim is to persuade. Alberti stressed this in the definition of *concinnitas* quoted above. The Quattrocento humanist and pioneer of art criticism Bartolomeo Fazio explicitly based his version of Simonides' dictum that painting is mute poetry on the observation that both painters and poets use *dispositio*. Without skill and discretion the poet and the painter cannot represent the outward shapes of men, or their intimate emotions and character; and precisely this ordered representation, resulting from *dispositio*, is what makes a painting 'seem to be alive and sentient and somehow move and have action'. At this point Fazio quoted Horace's injunction from the *Ars Poetica* that 'it is not enough for poetry to be beautiful, it must also be pleasing – so as to move the hearts and feelings of men in whatever direction it wishes'.[47] A century later both Borghinis also argued this. The aim of a well-composed painting is not visual harmony for its own sake, but persuasion through clarity, perspicuity and lifelikeness, which all help to involve the viewer. In this respect Andrea Pozzo, the Jesuit author of the *Prospettiva dei* Pittori of 1697, a manual on perspective that was intensively used across Europe and in her colonies, is still part of the same tradition, but more explicit. He clearly stated that the use of linear perspective is a rhetorical strategy, used to move the soul of the beholder towards the true vanishing point, that is, the glory of God: 'Therefore, Reader, my Advice is, that you chearfully begin your Work, with a Resolution to draw all the Points thereof to that true Point, the Glory of God (. . .)'.[48]

That is, Renaissance authors did not discuss composition while considering paintings as autonomous, bounded images, offering a pictorial reality *sui generis*, clearly distinguished from the 'real world' of the beholder. Instead, practically all Renaissance discussions of composition start from an assumption of continuity between reality and image. Thomas Puttfarken, for instance, has shown in his analysis of Titian's *Pesaro Madonna* and *Presentation of the Virgin* that the Renaissance concern with lifelike scale of human figures was based on the expectation that the figures depicted were at least as much part of the real world as of the represented world (Fig. 3.5).[49]

MOVING THE SPECTATOR THROUGH IMAGINATIVE INVOLVEMENT

Constructing a common ground so that the viewer could identify with what is depicted could take place in a relatively literal sense, by using linear perspective to suggest a continuum between the 'real' space of the viewer and the virtual space of the painting. Painters could also suggest a common ground by using pictorial strategies that appealed to the viewer's imagination. One of the most powerful and subtle ways of achieving this is by making viewers feel they are not looking at an image but are part of what they are looking at. Many Renaisssance paintings

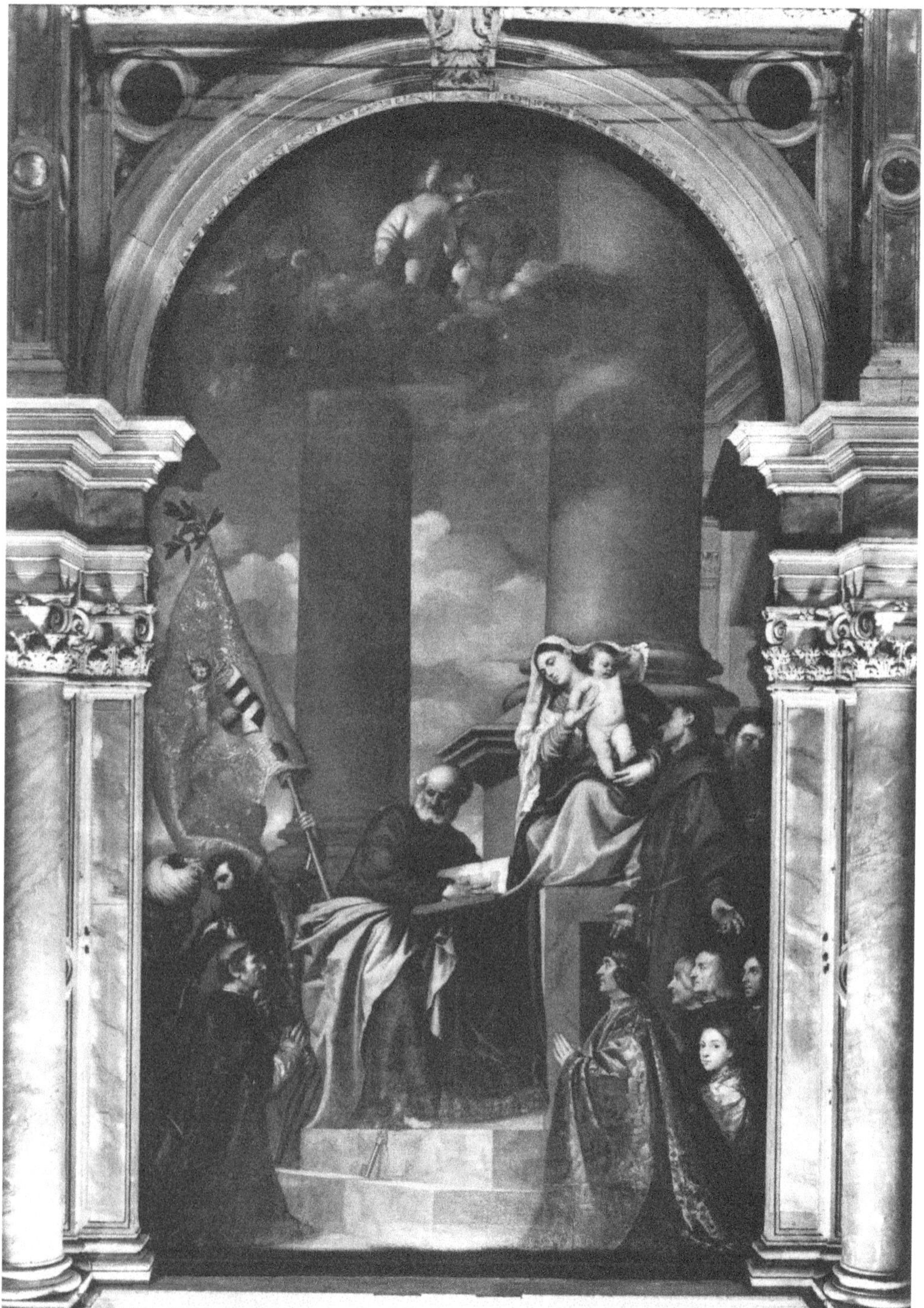

3.5 Titian, *Madonna di Ca' Pesaro*. Venice: Santa Maria Gloriosa dei Frari, 1519 to 1526 (photo: Centre for Art-Historical Documentation, Radboud Universiteit Nijmegen).

imply the presence of an external spectator: figures in the painting look out of the frame at the viewer, address him or her and gesture at the public to draw their attention. The grim stare by which Mary fixes the beholder out of Masaccio's *Trinity* in Santa Maria Novella (Fig. 1.1) exemplifies Alberti's advice to include a witness in the painting to draw the viewer's attention to what happens.

More subtle effects are achieved by suggesting continuity between pictorial space and the 'real' space of the viewer. Both Giovanni Bellini's S. Zaccaria altarpiece of the Virgin enthroned with saints of *c.* 1505 (Fig. 3.6) and Marco Basaiti's *Agony in the Garden* (1510 or possibly 1516; Fig. 3.7) for the Venetian church of S. Giobbe show a lantern painted so as to suggest that it is suspended in the chapel where the painting hangs. Giovanni Bellini's altarpiece for S. Giobbe, painted *c.* 1480, offers a dialectic of inclusion and exclusion (Fig. 3.8). The perspectival rendering of the tiled floor and the toes of St Francis that protrude over the painted tiles suggest continuity between the pictorial space and the beholder's space. In its original setting the base line is slightly below eye level, so that the feet of the saint are seen on a very much foreshortened tile floor, which adds to the effect of their feet's protrusion, strengthens the sense of their intrusion into the viewer's space, and indicates how much the perspectival composition of this altarpiece is based on the actual presence of a spectator. But at the same time the averted looks of the Madonna, the angelic musicians and the saints exclude the viewer, with the exception of St Francis who – not surprisingly in a church with important Franciscan connections – looks away in a visual *apostrophe* out of the painting and gestures at the beholder while displaying his stigmata. The Virgin and saints are visible to us, but engaged in a *sacra conversazione* that is not accessible to mortal viewers. This altarpiece was conceived by the patron and artist as part of a larger ensemble including its stone frame and altar. Relocated into this original setting these would together form a virtual chapel, consisting of a stone architectural frame and real altar combined with the fictional space of the altarpiece. It would thus correspond to the three-dimensional chapels built at the time on the opposite wall, both sides of the church nave articulating the pilgrim's progress from the entrance to the altar. This suggests that the Virgin's welcoming gesture and look, passing over the head of an actual viewer, are directed not so much at the viewer directly in front of the altarpiece addressed by St Francis, but at the pilgrims entering the church. As John Shearman has observed, this interpretation is supported by the fact that the central terracotta roundel of Christ in the Martini Chapel opposite the altarpiece is rotated anticlockwise by 45 degrees, to look also at the visitor approaching from the door of the church.[50]

Caravaggio's *Entombment* of 1602 (Fig. 3.9), now removed from its original setting above the altar in the Chiesa Nuova in Rome to the Vatican Pinacoteca, presents perhaps the most dramatic use of this compositional device. The dead weight of Christ's body is lowered over the slab of stone bordering the open tomb, and out of the pictorial space into the space where the beholder is now

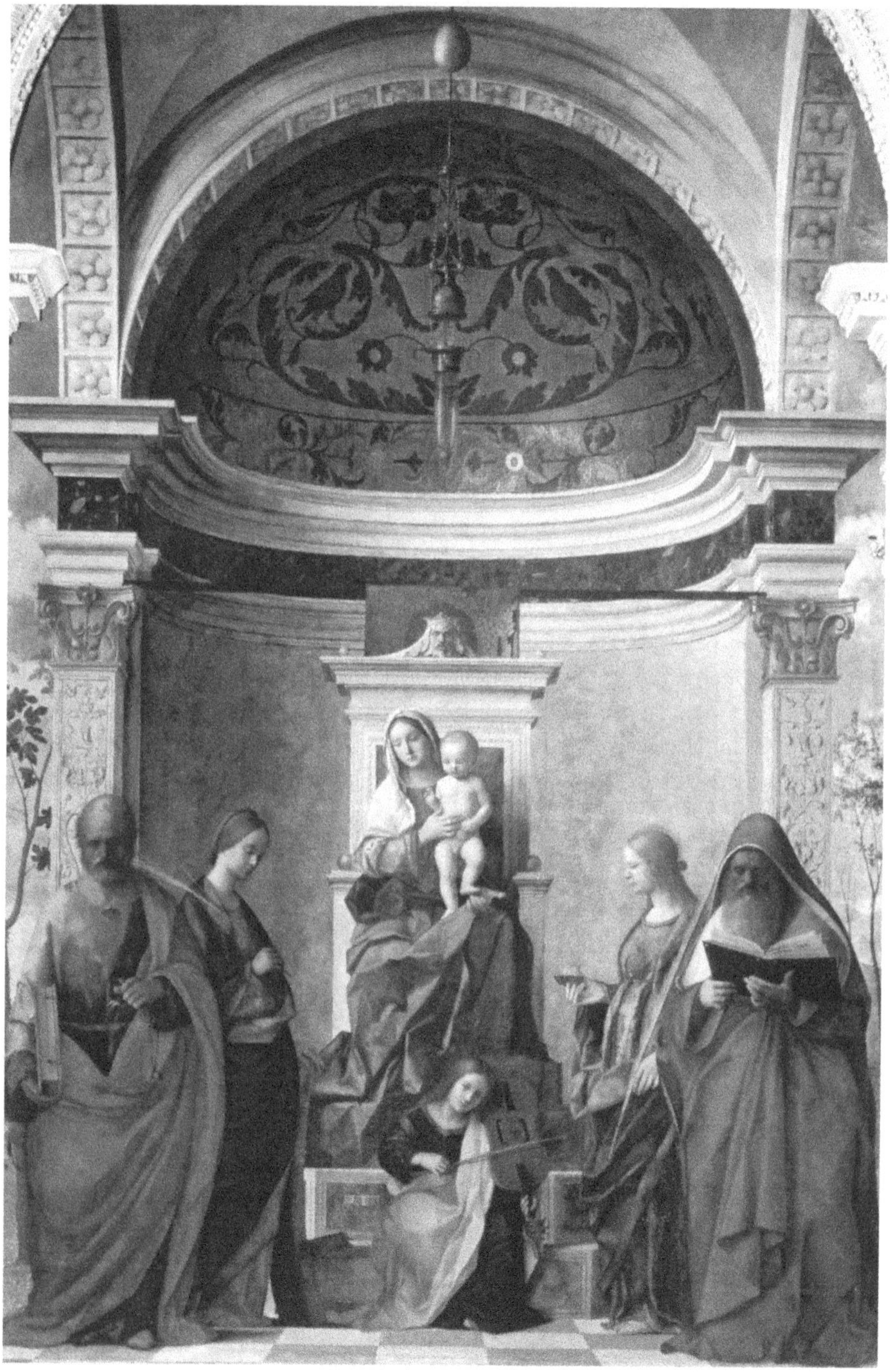

3.6 Giovanni Bellini, *Virgin and Child Enthroned with Saints*. Venice: San Zaccaria, 1505 (photo: Centre for Art-Historical Documentation, Radboud Universiteit Nijmegen).

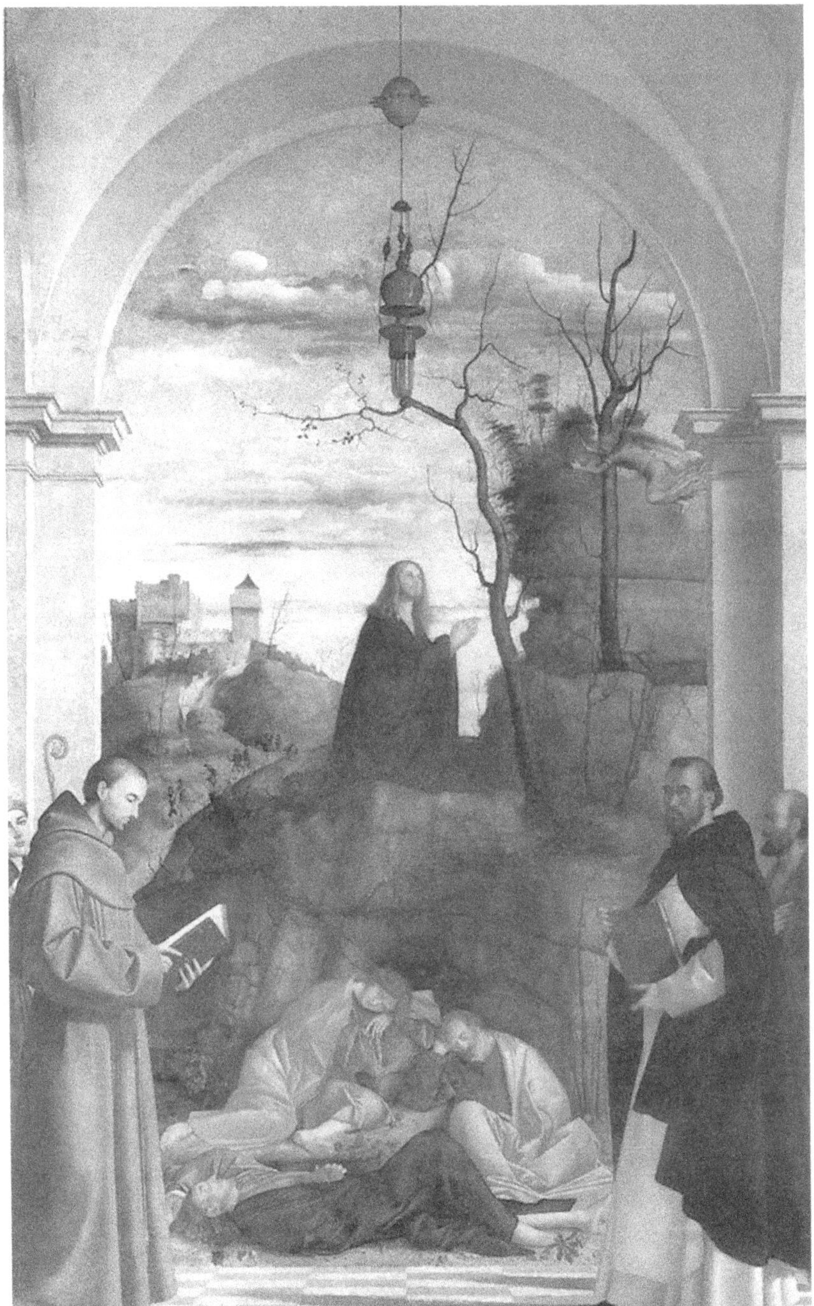

3.7 Marco Basaiti, *Agony in the Garden*. Venice: Galleria dell'Accademia, 1510 or 1516 (photo: Centre for Art-Historical Documentation, Radboud Universiteit Nijmegen).

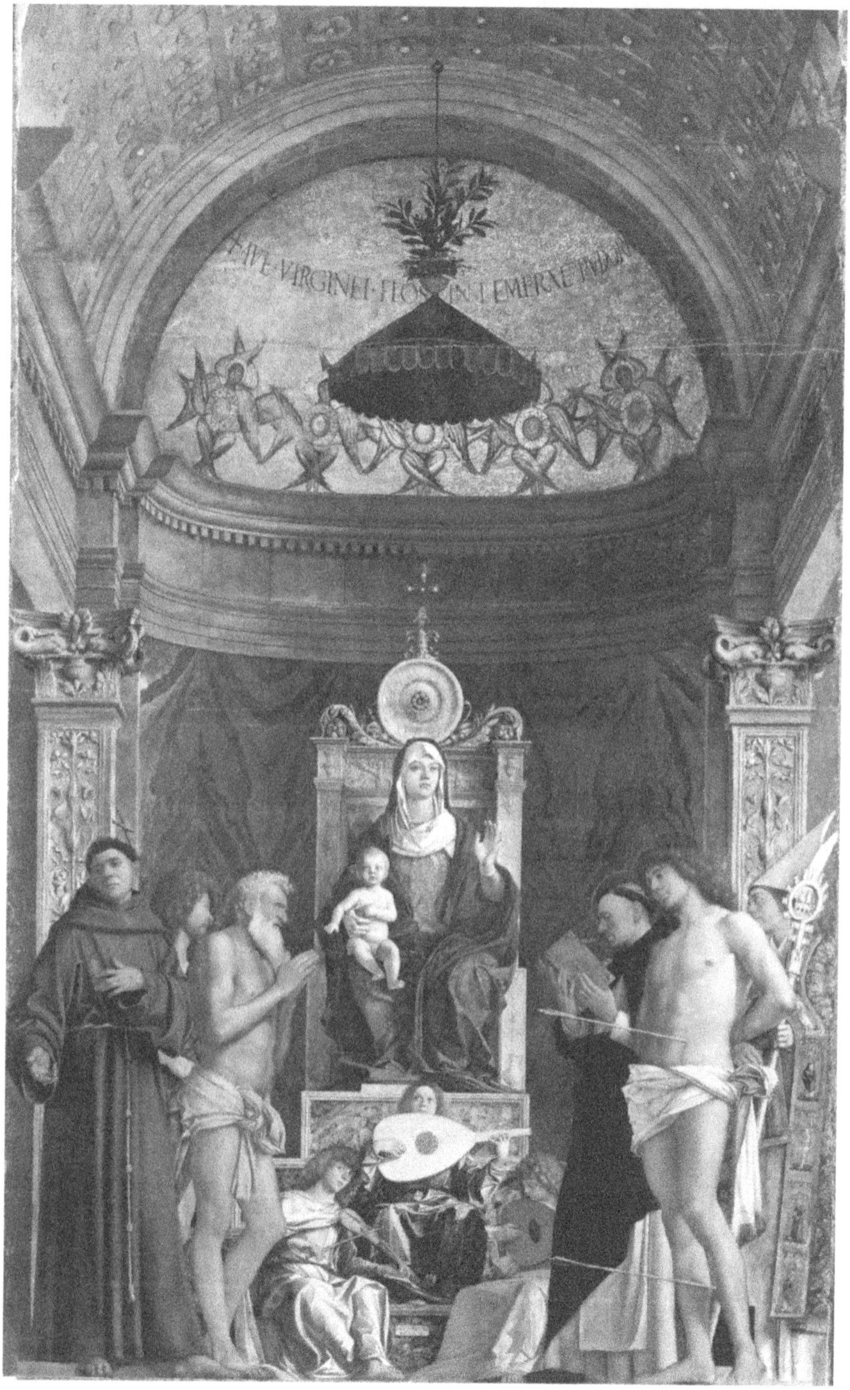

3.8 Giovanni Bellini, *Virgin and Child Enthroned with Saints* (San Giobbe Altarpiece). Venice: Galleria dell'Accademia, *c.* 1476 to 1490 (photo: Centre for Art-Historical Documentation, Radboud Universiteit Nijmegen).

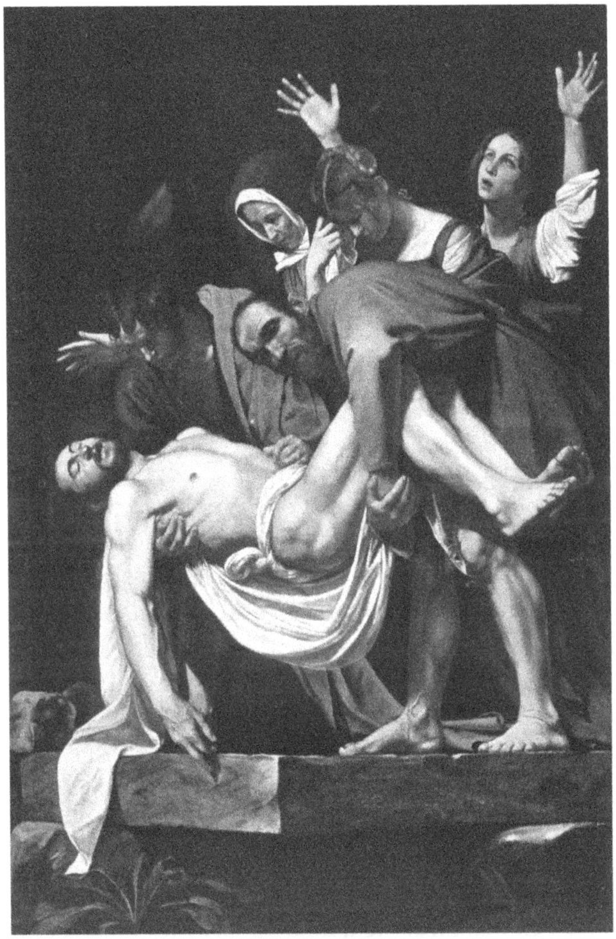

3.9 Caravaggio, *Entombment*. Rome: Pinacoteca Vaticana, *c.* 1602 to 1604 (photo: Centre for Art-Historical Documentation, Radboud Universiteit Nijmegen).

standing, suggesting that His true resting place is the heart of the believer.[51] In the Chiesa Nuova this painting was placed right behind the altar, so that the worshippers would immediately grasp that the adoration of the Host is in fact a bloodless re-enactment of Christ's original sacrifice. As the priest lifts the Host and says 'hoc est corpus meum' the eyes of the communicants were directed to the painting. But the *Entombment* does not depend entirely on its original spatial and liturgical setting to exercise its appeal on the viewer. Even in its present museum setting the viewer is still compelled by the strong downward diagonal and outward direction of the composition to consider how the action of the figures affects him or her, and to react to it. Its composition assumes the presence of a beholder who is addressed through the glance and gestures of the figures depicted; in this process the viewer is made to assume the role of a believer, an assistant at the grave or a worshipper of the Host.[52] Caravaggio here echoed Greco-Roman reliefs of heroes brought back from the battlefield such as the famous Meleager sarcophagus mentioned in *De Pictura*, and entombment scenes by Titian or Michelangelo, but he replaced idealized suffering by an image of real pain and grief, and transformed the biblical characters of Mary, St John the Baptist and Nicodemus into seventeenth-century Roman figures of the poor. This is a real scene from contemporary life unfolding before the viewer's eyes. Sacred history is enacted before the eyes of the viewer, recalling Cicero's praise of history as a *testis temporum* and *lux veritatis*.

Although Renaissance painters rarely spoke of their work in theatrical or even poetical terms, it was a quality often noted. Discerning observers like Aretino or Ridolfi thought of the work of Titian and Veronese in terms of theatrical representation. I have already quoted Aretino's description of the reaction of his friend Tribolo to *The Death of Saint Peter Martyr* in terms that clearly allude to the Aristotelian view of the impact of a tragedy on the audience. But this was not a unique instance. Titian's San Salvadore Annunciation breaks with the Renaissance tradition of representing this event as a private encounter between Mary and the Angel by giving it a dramatic staging that is close to Aretino's description in his *Vita di Santa Maria*. There Aretino wrote of the persons that they gesture as Titian would have painted them. In the *Humanità di Christo*, a life of Christ in the form of a series of tableaux-vivants he even mentions a 'theatre of clouds'.[53] When discussing *ordine*, one of the main aspects of *disegno* or pictorial composition, Dolce mentioned in the first place that painters should take care to observe chronological order in the *istoria* or narrative they depict. The classical authority quoted is Aristotle's *Poetics*.[54]

Such Aristotelian reactions were not exclusively Venetian. In *Il Figino* the art critic Gregorio Comanini argued, following Aristotle's *Poetics*, that both drama and painting should represent one single action or plot. The most highly regarded genres of painting (history and religious painting, not landscape, still-life or portraiture) resemble poetry because, like poetry, they represent plots or stories and offer visual narrative. As an example Comanini took Raphael's fresco of the Fire in the Borgo in the Vatican, and argued that, although Raphael included some details that suggested a resemblance to the fire of Troy, it did represent a unified narrative.[55]

In the early seventeenth century Carlo Ridolfi singled out the tears Veronese's religious scenes could excite like Bellini's *Pietà*, calling them 'precious pearls which, liquefied in the heart's alambic by fire of ardent emotion possess the power to wash away the stains of inveterate error'. He described the setting of the *Feast in the House of Levi* as a 'maestoso Teatro' (Fig. 3.10), and described the action of Titian's *Crowning with Thorns* (Fig. 3.11) as taking place in a theatre.[56] As David Rosand has shown, the composition of Veronese's paintings depicting feasts, weddings or the Last Supper, use architectonic settings that are very close

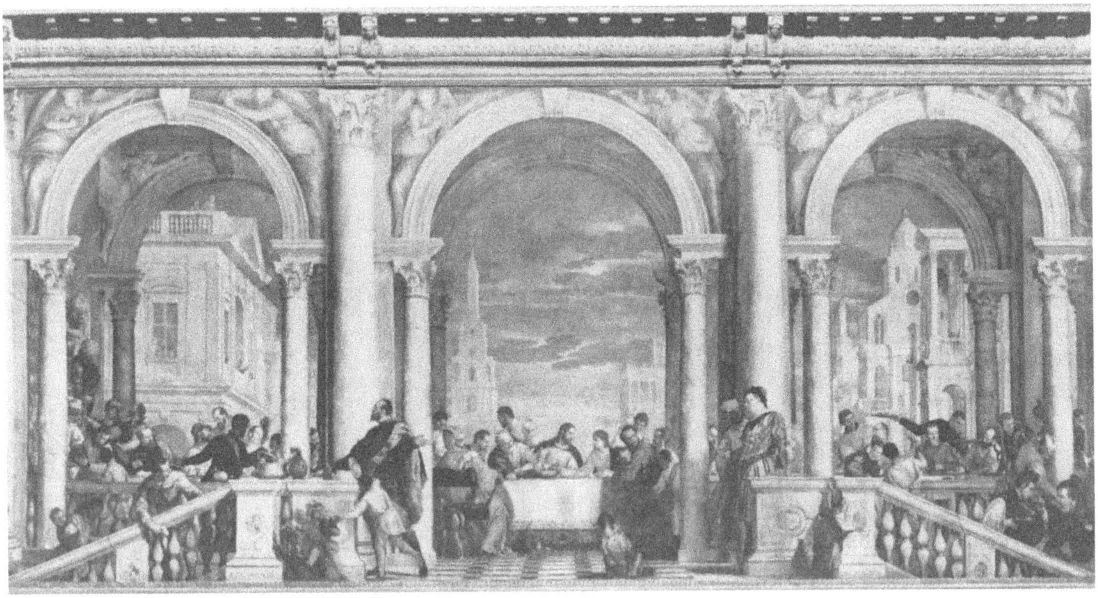

3.10 Veronese, *Feast in the House of Levi*. Venice: Galleria dell'Accademia, 1573 (photo: Centre for Art-Historical Documentation, Radboud Universiteit Nijmegen).

to Serlio and Palladio's reconstructions of Roman theatrical backdrops as described by Vitruvius.[57] These architectonic frames are not a representation of real, three-dimensional stone architecture, because they cannot be reconstructed as such, but a theatrical stage-setting, and thereby signal that the viewer is looking at the enactment of some drama or comedy.[58] At the same time they are not simply dramatic scenes represented as if on stage: Veronese handled the sacred and the secular, the elevated and the mundane in a subtle way that could not have been achieved on a real stage. In the *Feast in the House of Levi*, for instance, there is no central, unified linear perspective; instead each zone of the painting obeys a different visual order, probably because a unified perspectival system imposed on such a vast scene would look very unnatural. The receding orthogonals are broken, which forces the eye to linger on the surface before moving to the next zone; only after all parts of the painting have been taken in can the spectator form an idea of the composition as a whole. Thus the spatial, two-dimensional pictorial representation of an event is transformed into a temporal succession in the act of looking at it, not unlike the way we watch a play and only grasp the whole when we have seen all of it. At the same time the spectator keeps looking because he or she is engaged by the amazing variety and copiousness of invention Veronese displays.[59]

Variety was not the only stylistic strategy painters used to catch and hold the viewer's gaze. In Veronese's as in Titian's painting, the attention of the beholder

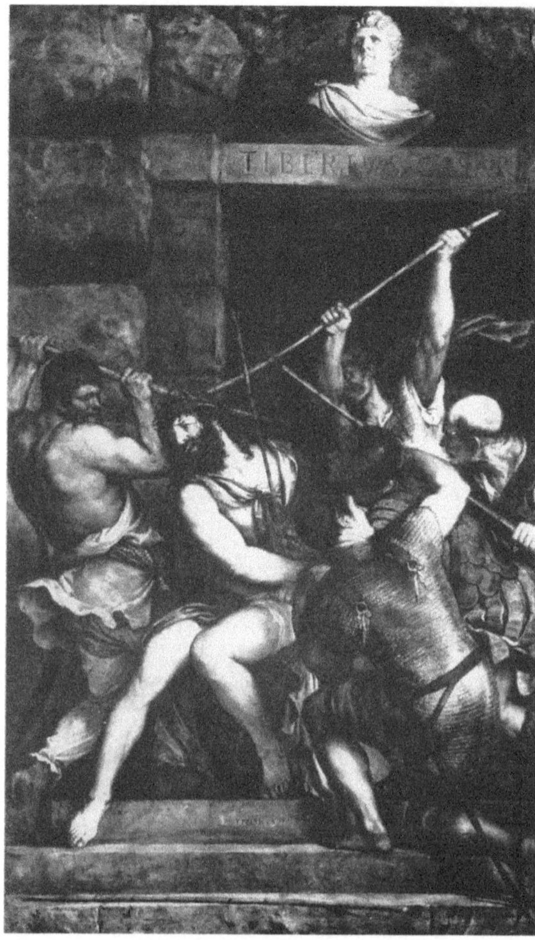

3.11 Titian, *Crowning with Thorns*. Paris: Louvre, *c.* 1540 to 1542 (photo: Centre for Art-Historical Documentation, Radboud Universiteit Nijmegen).

is also kept by another theatrical feature: the selection of what is to be depicted. Venetian painting of the second half of the sixteenth century shows how Aristotelian considerations of a good plot may be combined with an Albertian use of perspective as means both for creating a common ground and conveying the painter's point of view. Both painters chose not to represent the entire story, but only the most important moment: when the crisis, or the *periegesis* or turning-point in the plot occurs. These make the viewer aware of the larger drama and hence of looking at a pictorial representation conceived as a whole.

In *The Death of Actaeon*, for instance, Titian did not depict various scenes from the myth, but telescoped two successive moments into one scene (Fig. 3.12). On the left we see Diana shooting an arrow at Actaeon; her hand

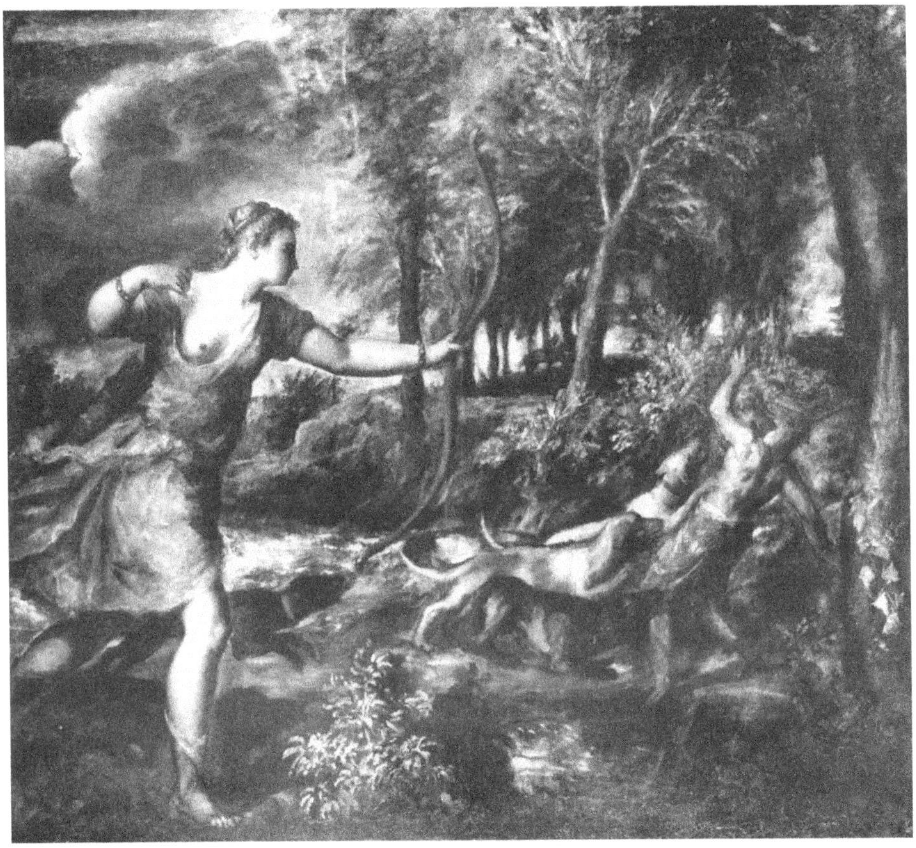

3.12 Titian, *The Death of Actaeon*. London: National Gallery, 1559 to 1576 (photo: Centre for Art-Historical Documentation, Radboud Universiteit Nijmegen).

is still on the string of her bow. In the centre, however, we see Actaeon already being transformed: his head is changed into that of a stag, and Diana's hounds are tearing at his legs, which are turning into those of a stag. This conflation of a well-known myth into the turning-point of its plot engages the spectator's attention because it breaks with accustomed linear progress. Titian, following Aristotle, turns this distillation of the myth into one scene into a powerful means of visual persuasion. At the same time, it helps the spectator to identify with what happens because the conflation of Diana's shot and Actaeon's transformation forces the viewer to re-enact in his or her mind the process which is so selectively represented. Watching Actaeon's transformation into an animal and his death, Aristotle or Aretino would have argued, fills us with fear and pity; just as looking at Actaeon watching Diana and her nymphs at her bath would force us to identify with his feelings, and fear for his imminent end. Through Titian's scenic enactment of the drama we would become involved emotionally in its plot. The viewer cannot simply enjoy the beautiful imitation of individual beautiful objects and persons, but has to engage with the drama as a whole.[60] Although Pino or Dolce did not mention them, we might add to the emotions of fear for imminent death and pity for the protagonists that of the fear for the dissolution of the human into the animal, which is such a recurrent theme in the classical Greek tragedies and Ovid's *Metamorphoses*, and so powerfully conveyed by Titian's paintings. Actaeon is transformed before our eyes into an animal; Europa is dragged away from civilization by a bull; Diana and her nymphs bathe in an environment in which it is difficult to distinguish the man-made from animal remains; and perhaps most poignantly in Titian's last painting, the *Deposition* in the Accademia in Venice, a Corinthian capital, that symbol of the triumph of life over death in classical civilization and of Christian splendour, is no longer decked out with acanthus leaves, but shows a grimacing lion's head. The vivid representation of metamorphosis is taken so far that in each case the boundaries between the human and the animal threaten to dissolve. The viewer is not a passive follower of what is set out in full detail, but is forced to become an active participant in the re-enactment of myths that probe the boundaries of human identity, poised between the divine and the human, the civilized and the bestial, life and death.

This chapter opened with a burial scene, and ends with scenes of death, entombment and dissolution of the human into the bestial. Through its *subscriptio* Bellini's *Pietà* thematized the ambiguities and transgressions of the borders between art and life involved in visual persuasion when it depends on lifelikeness. The short distich added to Bellini's painting drew attention to its power to act on the viewer, and perhaps even to the power of this image or what it depicts, to act on itself: as we have seen, one possible interpretation would suggest that the swollen eyes of the Mother of God make the work of Bellini weep. The other works of art discussed in this chapter are not so explicit; they achieve with pictorial means what the Bellini *subscriptio* puts into words: drawing spectators into the world of the painting, and exercising their agency by making them live what is before their eyes. In the words of the Venetian critic Pino, 'painting is that poetry that makes you not only believe, but *see* [...]'.[61] Such seeing is not a passive scrutiny of the painted surface, but an imaginative act on the part of the beholder which is part of being alive and human.

NOTES

1 The Latin is difficult to translate; here I have chosen to translate 'fere' as 'every time' instead of 'almost' or 'just' (which it can also mean), and to read the second line as an accusativus-cum-infinitivo construction; but many other translations have been offered, usually taking 'opus' as the subject of 'poterat'; for grammatical reasons this seems less likely. On Bellini's *Pietà* see Arasse (1993), Goffen (1989), pp. 67–89; Charles Brink was the first to argue that the inscription is based on Propertius, *Elegies* Book I.xxi, line 3: 'quid nostro gemitu turgentia lumina torques?' (not 21.1.3 as Goffen writes on p. 300 n. 56); see Robertson (1968), p. 55 n. 1. Propertius' elegies were available in Venice in manuscript before the

first edition of 1472, as Goffen notes. Hans Belting has argued in Belting (1985), pp. 28–36, that this is a visualization of Horace's (and Alberti's) demand that poems and paintings express emotions felt by their author to make the audience feel the same emotions. Arasse argued that here mimesis becomes so effective – the painting appears to weep – that it almost performs the miracle of sacred images to be able to weep. But in stopping short of this and thereby making the viewer aware of the limits of mimesis, the painting achieves a transference of the feelings of devotion the viewer feels from the image to those represented, and it highlights the autonomy of the image. All modern authors go along with the identification of Propertius as a source for the inscription, but ignore the context in which the phrase occurs. In Propertius' poem a dead Roman soldier asks a passing fugitive why he turns away his staring eyes. In the rest of the poem the dead soldier asks the passer-by to inform his sister that he survived the battle at Perusia in 41 BC to be killed by unknown hands, and see to a proper burial. This raises more questions than it answers: why quote from a pagan poet in a devotional Christian context, and why quote from a poem in which a dead soldier asks for a reburial executed with the proper, in this case pagan, rites? Cf. Propertius, *Elegies Book I*, ed. Camps, pp. 98–9.

2 To cite just a few examples of this attitude, which was not restricted to Counter-Reformation authors, though they offered the most explicit statements: S. Speroni, 'Della Rhetorica', p. 124 verso; L. Dolce, *Dialogo della pittura di M. Lodovico Dolce, intitolato L'Aretino*, fol. 19v–20r; A. Gioioso, *Degli errori de' pittori circa l'historie... et in che modo vogliono esser dipinte le Sacre Imagini*, p. 27 and also p. 77: 'anco le pitture edificano e scandellezzano'; G. Paleotti, *Discorso intorno alle imagini sacre e profane*, p. 215: the painter of Christian images had as his purpose to 'move men to proper obedience and subjection to God, or to penitence, or to voluntary suffering, or to charity, or to disdain of the world, or other similar virtues which are all instruments to unite men with God. This is the true and principal goal to be undertaken in these images'; G. B. Armenini, *De' veri precetti della pittura di M. Gio[vanni] Battista Armenini da Faenza libri tre*, pp. 151–2; J. Molanus, *De Historia ss.[sanctarum] imagimum et picturarum pro vero earum usu contra abusus libri IV*, pp. 183–4. Cf. Hall (1999), p. 268 on the Counter-Reformation's use of classical rhetoric and Renaissance humanist teaching to further its programme of religious reform; Freedberg (1971).

3 Horace, *Ars Poetica*, ll. 101–4.

4 Alberti, *De Pictura*, Section 41.

5 Leonardo, *Treatise on Painting*, no. 267, p. 110.

6 A. F. Doni, *Il Disegno*, pp. 118–20.

7 On medieval devotional treatises and their Renaissance readership see Ragusa and Green (1961), pp. 317–20, and the quotation from *Zarlino de Oration* in Baxandall (1972), p. 46. Cf. also Roman D'Elia (2005), p. 48. For an explanation of this phenomenon in terms of sympathetic magic see Barasch (1997), p. 317. For criticism of the magical explanation see Gell (1998), pp. 99–101.

8 Dolce, *Aretino*, fol. 41r.: '[...] bisogna, che le figure movano gli animi de' riguardanti, alcune turbandogli, altre rallegrandogli, altre sospingendogli a pietà, & altre a sdegno, secondo la qualità della historia. Altrimenti reputi il Pittore di non haver fatto nulla: perché questo è il condimento di tutte le sue virtù: come aviene parimente al Poeta, all'Historico, & all'Oratore: che se le cose scritte o recitate mancano di questa forza, mancano elle ancora di spirito e di vita.' Cf. the edition by Roskill, p. 301. Incidentally, Speroni was involved in the public controversy over the nature of tragedy sparked off by his tragedy *Canace* (published in 1546), but which was really about conflicting Horatian and Aristotelian views about tragic poetry: should it restrain itself to decorous expression of emotion, or not shy away from showing on the stage acts of cruelty and inhumanity? As Puttfarken (2003) has argued, this may have influenced Titian's paintings of exceeding cruelty, such as *The Flaying of Marsyas* or the *Death of St Peter Martyr*.

9 P. Aretino, Letter to Titian of January 1548, describing a copy of Titian's *Ecce homo*, in Aretino, *Sur la poétique, l'art et les artistes*, p. 60 (= *Lettere* ed. Procaccioli vol. IV, pp. 199–200): 'Di spine è la corona che lo trafigge, ed è sangue il sangue che lor punte gli fanno versare; [...]. Il dolore in cui se restringe la di Giesù figura, conmuove a pentirsi qualunche Cristianamente gli mira [...]'.

10 Fr. Bocchi, *Oratio Francisci Bocchij de laudibus Michaelisangeli Florentini Pictoris, Sculptoris, atque Architecti Nobilissimi*, fol. 8: '[A]ut quae vox, quae latera sufficerent, quae matrem eiusdem laudarent, quae dolorem vivum spirat in mortuo marmore. Vis autem maxima divinitatis apparet in mortuo Christo qua nostros animos non religiose solum, verum etiam terrore afficit; redigitque nobis in memoriam, cum sanctissima nobilissimaque membra contemplamur, quantopere illius mors acerba fuerit'.

11 Aretino, *Lettere sull'Arte*, vol. I, p. 73. Cf. Lomazzo, *Idea*, vol. II p. 99, where he states that 'The Passion is a tragedy; paintings of it should move the viewers to tears'.

12 Quintilian, *Institutio Oratoria* XII.xiii.9–11.

13 D. Barbaro, *Della Eloquenza* (1557 edition), pp. 73–91; cf. also A. Minturno, *L'Arte Poetica*, p. 435. Quintilian's analogy was also echoed in Daniello's use of sculpture to explain the importance of *dispositio*: Bernardino Daniello, *Della Poetica*, p. 272. See also G. Camillo, *L'Idee, ovvero forme della oratione da Hermogene considerate, & ridotte in questa lingua*, fol. 86v.

14 Speroni, *Della Rhetorica*, p. 13.

15 Cicero, *De Oratore* II.xxxviii.159. For Renaissance statements of this view see, for instance, D. Barbaro, *Della Eloquenza*; Dolce, *Aretino*, fol. 14r, and Stefano Guazzo, *La Civil Conversazione*, vol. 1, pp. 86–7.

16 Cf. Plutarch, *Moralia* 504 e. On clarity and lack of ambiguity as essential to persuasion see Aristotle, *Poetica* 1451a, and the *Rhetorica ad Herennium* 4.12.17, 4.53.67; for velocity see Barbaro, *Eloquenza*, 38–9. *Claritas* is a variety of *perspicuitas*, one of the four cardinal virtues that distinguish a good speech or *virtutes dicendi*.

17 Dolce, *Aretino*, p. 14 verso. Cf. G. Bonifaccio, *L'Arte de' Cenni*, p. 551. See also Cicero, *De Oratore* II.lxxxvii.357 and III.xli.163 on the primacy of sight as the reliable source of knowledge.

18 Aristotle gave its first systematic discussion in the *Rhetorica*, but Dionysius of Halicarnassus and Quintilian also discussed it quite extensively: Aristotle, *Rhetorica* III.8–9; Dionysius of Halicarnassus, *De Compositione Verborum*, Quintilian, *Institutio Oratoria* IX.iv. Baxandall (1971), p. 130 drew attention to the use of *compositio* by Vitruvius (III.I.i) in connection with buildings and by Cicero (*De Officiis*, I.xxviii.98) in connection with bodies. On the history of the term 'composition' see Scaglione (1972), p. 24. Traditionally three elements are distinguished in a sentence: a complex sentence considered as a whole was called a *periodos* (in Latin: *ambitus, continatio, conclusio*); the composing elements were called *kolon* (in Latin: *membrum*, 'member'), a group of three to five words, either as main clause or as subordinate clause; and a group of two to three words belonging together was called a *komma* (*incisum*). From such *kola* and *kommata* the *periodos* should be constructed in a logical and well-balanced way. Cf. Baxandall (1972), pp. 135f., and Vickers (1988), p. 343, n. 13, for other meanings of *compositio*.

19 Quintilian, *Institutio Oratoria* VII. Prooemium i–ii.

20 *Rhetorica ad Herennium* I.ii.3 and III.iv.7; Aristotle, *Rhetorica* III.13; Cicero, *De Oratore* II.lxxvi.307 and 317; Cicero, *De Partitione Oratoria* Section 9; Quintilian, Book VII.

21 Aristotle, *Poetica*, 1447a–1453a. I have relied heavily on the excellent translation and notes in Russell and Winterbottom (1972), pp. 85–112.

22 Aristotle, *Poetica*, 1454b.

23 Aristotle, *Poetica*, 1455a.

24 Alberti, *De Pictura* Section 42, edition Grayson p. 83.

25 Cf. Grafton (2003) and (2001), pp. 111–51.

26 *De Oratore* II.ix.36, quoted with some changes from the translation by E. W. Sutton for the Loeb edition, p. 225.

27 Puttfarken (2000) p. 30 Cf. Hall (1999), p. 9, who puts the use by Renaissance artists and viewers of rhetorical theories about composition and persuasion in a wider perspective by observing that 'a change occurred in what artists wanted from antiquity [...] around 1500. They no longer studied antique remains as if they were another copybook; they studied the whole culture to assimilate it, so that they could recreate it. In addition to looking, measuring and copying, they read and discussed the instructions of Cicero and Quintilian on rhetoric in order to deduce certain principles of creativity: *varietas, decorum*; and differences between reporting bare facts and appealing to the audience and winning its assent'.

28 Cf. Puttfarken (2005), pp. 42–8.

29 See Puttfarken (1991), pp. 75–101 on Vasari's presentation of Florentine art based on *disegno* as superior to Venetian painting as the incitement for these treatises to be written.

30 S. Speroni, *Della Rhetorica*, p. 140 verso: 'Adunque egli è l'ufficio dell'Oratore dir parole non solamente ben risonanti, ma intelligibili, & a concetti significati correspondenti che si come nei ritratti di Titiano, oltra il dissegno, la simiglianza consideriamo; & sendo tali (si come son veramente) che i loro essempij pienamente ci rappresentino, opera perfecta, & di lui degna gli essistimiamo: cosi anchora nell'oratione con la testura delle parole, con i loro numeri, & con la loro concinnità l'intentioni significate paragoniamo [...]'. See also p. 123 recto for a comparison between words and colours (which are produced naturally, without effort) and style in speech and composition and movement or variety in painting, which results from the efforts of the speaker/painter to be persuasive.

31 M. Biondo, *Della Nobilissima Pittura*, pp. 3 recto, 11 recto and 13 recto.

32 P. Pino, *Dialogo di Pittura* (ed. 2000), p. 107. Circumscription here does not only refer to the outlines of figures, but also to giving all objects light and shade; *practica* includes not only good draughtsmanship but also the arrangement of objects or models in a good light; a knowledge of what will be beautiful in a painting, and a grasp of one's inventions, investigated in sketches and drawings, where chiaroscuro is the best method because it allows one to make a unified composition ('perchè si puo ben unire il tutto'). Composition is geared, not as in Alberti, towards the representation of an *istoria*, but towards the unity of the whole painting: the *integrità dell'opera* or *il tutto*. Invention, the second main part of painting, is what makes painting similar to poetry: it is not the imitation of what is visible, but the representation of a theme as a whole (*un solo tutto*), the composition of a subject as a unity.

33 Pino, *Dialogo di Pittura*, pp. 108–9: 'E per che la pittura è propria poesia, cioè inuenzione, la qual fà apparere quello, che non è, però util sarebbe osservare alcuni ordine eletti da gli altri poeti che scriuono, iquale nello loro comedie, et altre compositioni ui introducono la brevità, il che debbe

osseruare il pittore nelle sue inuentioni, & non uoler restrignere tutte le fatture del mondo in un quadro [...]. Usano ancho di *far pronuntiare à un solo tutto quello*, che s'hà da dimostrate, cosi die fare il pittore, comporre (con l'aiuto del uiuo) lui solo, & da se senza altro latrocinia la sua historia [...]'.

34 Pino, *Dialogo di Pittura*, p. 110.

35 Ibid.

36 Cf. Puttfarken (1991), p. 175.

37 Rosand (1995), p. 11.

38 Vasari, *Le Vite de' più eccellenti pittori scultori e architettori* (1967 reprint of the 1568 edition), vol. I, pp. 115ff.; cf. Puttfarken (1991) pp. 175–6.

39 V. Borghini, 'Selva di Notizie', printed in P. Barocchi (ed.), *Scritti d'Arte del Cinquecento*, vol. I, pp. 611–13; I quote the translation by the author in Puttfarken (2000), p. 181. Nick Scorza prepares a new, complete edition.

40 L. B. Alberti, *De Re Aedificatoria* IX.5, ed. Orlandi and Portoghesi, p. 815; ed. Rykwert, pp. 301–5.

41 Alberti, *De Re Aedificatoria* IX.5, ed. Rykwert, pp. 302–3; ed. Orlandi and Portoghesi, p. 815.

42 Alberti, *De Re Aedificatoria* VI.3 (ed. Orlandi and Portoghesi, p. 453; ed. Rykwert, p. 158) is even more explicit about the unity of opposites achieved in architectural design: 'Paria quidem [im]paribus, recta flexis, prompta subobscurioribus permiscendo, intuebatur, an quasi ex maris foeminaque connubio tertium quippiam oboriretur'. Unlike Orlandi and Portoghesi, who were followed in this by Rykwert *et al.*, I have preferred here the version of the manuscript V (*Vat. Urb. Lat.* 264, which dates from 1483, cf. Alberti edition Orlandi and Portoghesi, p. 1005, which has 'Paria *im*paribus', whereas Orlandi and Portoghesi follow the text of mss. EFL, which have 'paria quidem paribus'. Given the structure of the sentence as a whole, which is antithetical, it seems more consistent to follow the reading of ms. V. The antithetical tenor of the passage is strengthened by the sequel, in which Alberti speaks of '[...] aequavit similia dissimilibus'. Orlandi and Portoghesi obscure the possibility of a non-mathematical reading by their over-interpretative translation 'Mescolando elementi di pari proporzioni'.

43 For a more detailed discussion and further explorations of the rhetorical origins of the term *concinnitas* see Van Eck (1994), pp. 48–56, and Van Eck (2000a). The points of view of Plethon and Bessarion were published as G. G. Plethon, *Platonicae et Aristotelicae Philosophiae Differentiae* (1439), and J. Bessarion, *De Natura et Arte adversus Georgium Trapezuntium Cretensem Liber Sextus*, pp. 105ff. For a wider exploration of these discussions on teleology in art and nature and the impact of Byzantine refugee scholars in the fifteenth century see Rüther-Weiss (1991), and Smith (1992), pp. 80–96.

44 V. Borghini, *Selva di Notizie*, vol. I, pp. 648–50.

45 R. Borghini, *Il Riposo*, Book I, p. 52 (= *Scritti d'arte* vol. I, p. 936); translated here by T. Puttfarken in Puttfarken (2000), p. 183.

46 V. Borghini, *Selva di Notizie* as reprinted in *Scritti d'Arte* vol. I, p. 342 and pp. 938–44.

47 Bartolomeo Fazio, *De Viris Illustribus*, fol. 38r, quoted from Baxandall (1964), pp. 98–99. The Latin original has: 'Est enim ars magni ingenii et solertiae. Nec temere alia inter operosas maiorem prudentiam desiderat. ut pote quae non solum ut os ut faciem ac totius corporis liniamenta. sed multo etiam magis interiores sensus ac motus exprimantur postulat. ita ut uiuere ac sentire pictura illa et quodam moueri ac gestire uideatur.' The Horace quotation is from *Ars Poetica*, lines 99–103.

48 A. Pozzo, *Rules and Examples of Perspective for Painters and Architects* [...]. 'To the Lovers of Perspective'. The original has: 'al vero punto dell'occhio che è la Gloria Divina'. Cf. L. Pascoli's 'Vita di Andrea Pozzo', p. 192: 'Più prodigiosa però di tutti mi pare la prospettiva, la quale ingannando a suo piacere la vista ci tira a vedere qual che non è, e fa cadere su' nostri sensi cioche poscia veduto, o da piu vicino, o da piu diverso punto non trova'. And cf. Pascoli's remark on rhetoric: 'All'energia dell'eloquenza che si gloria di trarre il cuore dell'uome ovunque vole, e di movere lo al suo arbitrio all'ira, al diletto, allo sdegno, e all'amore.' A similar connection between linear perspective's vanishing point directing the viewer ultimately to God is also suggested in Daniel Barbaro's dedication of *La Prattica della prospettiva*.

49 Cf. Puttfarken (2000), pp. 30, 121, 123–47 and 169.

50 Shearman (1992), pp. 94–100.

51 Cf. Langdon (1998), pp. 241–7, who draws attention to the interest of the patrons, the Oratorians of the Chiesa Nuova in Rome, as expressed by Cardinal Baronio in 1564, in works of art that were direct and simple, suited as Baronio put it 'to make those weep who contemplate it attentively'.

52 For a reconstruction of the original setting and its liturgical meaning see Wright (1978), pp. 35–42.

53 Aretino, *Vita di S. Maria*, pp. 152ff., and *Humanità di Christo*, pp. 63–75; cf. Roman d'Elia (2005), p. 107.

54 L. Dolce, *Aretino*, ed. Roskill, pp. 120–1.

55 G. Comanini, *Il Figino, ovvero del Fine della Pittura*, in Barocchi vol. III, pp. 345 and 347: 'Della favola, dice il vostro Aristotele che ella dee essere una e rappresentante una sola azzione d'un solo [...]. Corrisponde a questa unità di favola poetica l'unità dell'invenzione del buon pittore, il quale non dipinge dentro una tavola diversi azzioni, ma una sola. [...] E quantunque l'Incendio di Borgo, [...] abbia alcuni accidenti da me accennativi, co'quali par quasi che risomigli quello di Troia, [...] Quale adunque sia l'unità dell'invenzione del pittore, corrispondente a l'unità della favola del poeta'. Cf. Von Rosen (2000), pp. 195–7. Badt (1959) has argued

that Raphael was doubly dependent on classical sources: on Vitruvius and Aristotle's *Poetics*, and that the composition of the fresco closely follows Aristotle's precepts for successful dramatic plotting. See also *Il Figino* p. 345 for a comparison between painting and dramatic poetry: '[...] il pittore non cede punto al poeta nell'arte dell'imitare, anzi, che col medesimo artificio, col quale il poeta imita, imita anch'egli e finge le cose. E perchè io non vi sembri parlare a caso, poichè la pittura più rassomiglia la poesia rappresentativa che la narrativa, e tra le poesie rappresentative principale sappiamo essere la tragedia; io voglio che consederiamo tutte le parti di questo poema, non le quanto, che sono il prologo, l'episodio, l'essodo e'l coro, ma le quali, che sono la favola, i costumi, il verso, la sentenza, l'apparato e la melodia [...]'.

56 C. Ridolfi, *Le Maraviglie dell'Arte*, edition 1919–24, vol. I. p. 315: 'Pregiatissimi pianti, pretiose perle, che liquefatte nel lambico del cuore al fuoco d'un ardente affetto haveste virtù di lavar le macchie d'un inveterato errore. La mensa è situato nel seno di maestoso Teatro, nel cui circuito girano molte colonne [...]'. Cf. C. Ridolfi, *The Life of Titian*, p. 91.

57 Rosand (1982), pp. 150–82.

58 Cf. Rosand (1982), p. 160.

59 Cf. Puttfarken (1991), in particular 94ff., (2003) and (2005), where he argues for a reading of Titian's late *Poesie* in terms of Aristotle's *Poetics*. In his interpretation of the *Danae*, *The Rape of Europe*, and *Actaeon and Diana* (in the National Gallery, Edinburgh) he shows how Titian's way of representing these *istorie* selected precisely these moments from the story that are the turning-points of the plot: scenes of recognition and *periegesis* that may be read to correspond to Aristotle's analysis in the *Poetics* of Greek viewers' awareness that they were looking at selected scenes from the myths on which these tragedies were based. Puttfarken contrasts this attitude of the viewers strongly with that positioned by Horace and Alberti, who aim for empathy rather than narrative or dramatic involvement with the ultimate aim of edification or moral improvement, but it would seem that when he argues that the viewers of Titian's *Poesie* become emotionally involved because they see what Actaeon or Venus see, the result is in fact empathy, albeit realized through different pictorial means.

60 Cf. Puttfarken (1991), pp. 90–3.

61 P. Pino, *Dialogo di Pittura* pp. 10 recto and verso and p. 16 recto.

FOUR: MUTE ELOQUENCE. VISUAL PERSUASION IN ENGLISH ARCHITECTURE OF THE SEVENTEENTH AND EIGHTEENTH CENTURIES

Introduction

Buildings, like paintings, were not designed in early modern Europe for the sake of art alone. They had practical purposes, housing public institutions in the appropriate manner, or offered a stage for civil life; they also acted on their viewers. As we have seen in the previous chapter, an important instrument, if not the foundation for visual persuasion through painting, was to achieve a strong sense of identification by the viewer with what was depicted. The condition for this was the figurative character of early modern painting: identification was achieved by establishing a common ground, the basis for a sense of *enargeia* or living presence of the figures depicted. But for architecture the situation is different, because it is not a figurative art. One of the best-known examples of a church building thrusting religious conviction on the person in the street is Saint Peter's in Rome with its colonnade and piazza. As Bernini, its architect, said of his design (1656–67): 'it embraces Catholics to reinforce their belief, heretics to re-unite them with the Church, and agnostics to enlighten them with the true faith'.[1] Bernini's description of the persuasive action of the piazza recalls the three types of rhetoric as they were traditionally distinguished: epideictic associated with pomp and circumstance in praise of God and the Church for the Catholic believer; forensic, dealing with proof for the heretic; and deliberative, or exhortative oratory addressed to the agnostics, helping them to reach a conclusion about the truth of the faith. But Saint Peter's is such a powerful statement of the nature of the Catholic Church, not because of Bernini's subtle and sophisticated adaptation of the three kinds of rhetoric to three varieties of persuasion, but because the form of the piazza and its colonnade resembles two arms extended in an embrace. The colonnade speaks to the eye because it recalls a universally recognized human gesture. In this case, iconicity, the representation of a human gesture by its conventional sign, is the basis of architectural persuasion. But what happens if there is no iconic basis for visual persuasion?

This issue was not widely discussed in Italy during the fifteenth and sixteenth centuries. Alberti is one of the very few Renaissance authors to address explicitly the persuasive power of architecture, when he observed how beautiful church interiors take the viewers outside themselves with delight and thereby move them to greater piety, or that a building's beauty may act as a defence against the vandalism of the crowd.[2] But how this persuasive effect is achieved, or what parts of a building or aspects of architectural design play a role in it, is left very implicit.

Authors and architects living outside Italy, and after the sixteenth century, were more explicit about these issues. Controversies surrounding architecture *all'antica* that were largely absent in Italy generated much debate, particularly in Britain and produced a wide range of written sources that document the appropriation of Renaissance architecture in British contexts and its manifold transformations.[3] English critics and architects of the seventeenth century offer a very rich range of discussions of architectural persuasion, for two reasons: both Anglican church design and the introduction of Renaissance architecture in England were highly controversial and heavily politicized issues. The need for new churches, made urgent by the Great Fire of London in 1666, produced a debate on religious architecture that had no equal on the Continent because architects and churchmen, historians and laymen interested in art contributed to it, and because it gave unparalleled scope to discussions of aspects of church design that received little attention in the Italian treatises on architecture of the preceding centuries. Among these the attention to a building's impact on its beholders stands out. The introduction of Renaissance architecture by Inigo Jones and Sir Henry Wotton during the reign of James I and Charles I was equally contested.[4] It was not a triumphant entry of Italianate good taste, in the course of which Renaissance architecture was introduced or appreciated entirely for its aesthetic qualities, and immediately dispelled all remains of the Gothic. Patrons and courtiers had to be educated in this new approach to architectural design and taste, and from the outset monarchs, churchmen and their entourage had a very clear grasp of the political potential of Renaissance architecture, in particular its usefulness in dynastic and religious propaganda. The aim of this chapter is therefore to show, in a roughly chronological course, how classical architecture was put to persuasive use in seventeenth- and eighteenth-century Great Britain.

'Art became a piece of statecraft'

The first uses of classical forms in England occurred not in buildings, but in portraits and tombs: the widely disseminated engraving by Crispijn De Passe the Elder of Elizabeth I of 1596 flanked by composite columns, the portrait of her courtier Sir Robert Dudley (Fig. 4.1), or preceding these instances, the design by Torrigiano for the tomb of Henry VII and Elizabeth of York in Westminster Abbey (commissioned in 1512). The orders were first used in a coherent way in the triumphal arches erected for the London entry of James I in 1604. All these instances show a use of classical forms that is heraldic or dynastic, not architectural. This is part of the English sixteenth-century tendency to consider the orders of architecture, not from the point of view of structure or tectonics, or their correct Vitruvian handling, but as heraldic devices or emblems. In Edmund Bolton's *Elements of Armouries* (1610), coats of arms are called the natural hieroglyphs of nobility.[5] The combination of the orders with coats of arms or

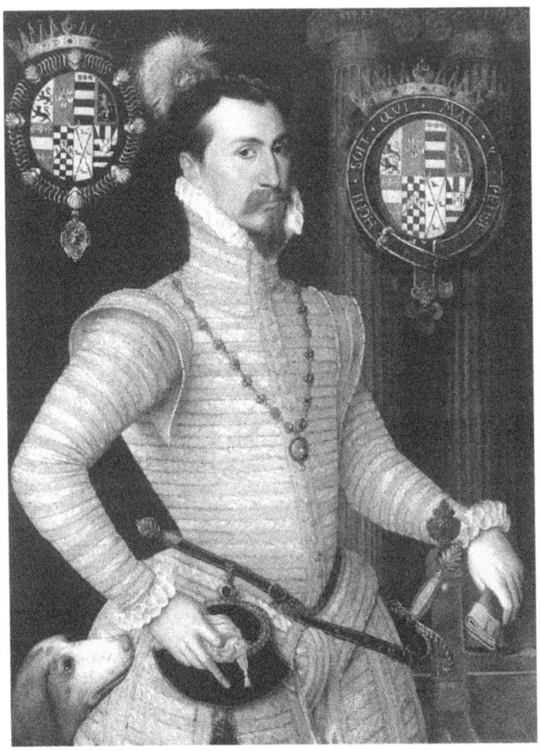

4.1 Anglo-Netherlands School, *Robert Dudley, Earl of Leicester.* Waddesdon Manor, The Rothschild Collection, *c.* 1564 (photo: Centre for Art-Historical Documentation, Radboud Universiteit Nijmegen).

other heraldic devices often occurs in frontispieces of books: John Guillim's *A Display of Heraldrie* of 1610, for instance, shows a Corinthian broken pediment, with columns flanking coats of arms on both sides. In the opening poem the author explains that the 'Display of Heraldrie' or 'Edifice' is put before the eyes of the reader in this frontispiece, in which:

> First, *England*, being thy Scene thou doest present,
> In a Triumphall *Arch* her *Regiment* [. . .]
> And Head of every Priviledge, the KING
> is set above: From whom those *Six* beside,
> Betweene the *Pillars* by their *Coats* descri'd.[6]

In *The Elements of Architecture* of 1624, the first complete English treatise on classical architecture, Sir Henry Wotton used terms taken from heraldry to analyse the orders and their meaning. The Doric order is considered not from the perspective of its structural role, proportion or its Vitruvian iconography, but as a heraldic emblem:

> [. . .] there are fiue Orders of Pillers, according to their dignity and perfection, thus marshalled:
> The Dorique.
> The Ionique.
> The Corinthian. [. . .]
>
> The *Dorique Order* is the grauest that hath beene receiued into ciuill vse, preserving, in comparison of those that follow, a more *Masculine Aspect* [. . .]. To discerne him, will bee a peece rather of good *Heraldry*, then of *Architecture:* For he is best knowne by his place, when he is in company, and by the peculiar ornament of his *Frize* [. . .] when he is alone.[7]

That is, the orders are not presented as in the Italian treatises by Serlio, Palladio or Vignola, in a series of increasing size and ratio between length and diameter, but heraldically (hence the term 'marshalled'), on the basis of their rank. The poet Ben Jonson explained the use of heraldry and of the orders in the triumphant arches erected for James I's London entry in 1604 in the same, emblematic terms:

> The nature and propertie of these Devices being, to present alwaies some one entire bodie, or figure, consisting of distinct members, and each of those expressing it selfe, in the own active spheare, yet all, with that generall harmonie so connexed, and disposed, as no one

> little part can be missing to the illustration of the whole: where also is to be noted, that the *Symboles* used, are not, neither ought to be, simply *Hieroglyphickes*, *Emblemes* or *Impreses*, but a mixed character, partaking somewhat of all, and peculiarly apted to these more magnificent inventions.[8]

Jonson drew here both on the original meaning of *concinnitas* in carpentry to describe a well-knit, closely connected unity of parts, and on Alberti's definition of *concinnitas* in *De re aedificatoria* as the foundation of persuasive beauty in architecture to which nothing may be added or taken away without damaging the overall effect. The unity achieved here, however, is not structural, but the persuasive expressive unity of the decorative apparatus. To these belong coats of arms and *imprese*, but the orders as well.

Sir Henry Wotton (1568–1639) was a diplomat, collector and writer. He spent much of his life as English ambassador in Venice, where he was involved in the acquisition of works of art for the Stuart court. That he had a keen appreciation of Italian art and was at home in the vocabulary of Italian art criticism is shown by his praise of the art collection of King Charles I:

> [...] what more learned then to behold the tongueless eloquence of lights and shadows, and the silent poesie of lines and (as it were) living Marble? Here would the spectator swear the limbs and muscles design'd by *Tintoret* to move; there the birds of *Bassano* to chirp, the oxen bellow, and the sheep to bleat: Here the faces of *Rafael* to breath, and those of Titian even to speak: there a man would commend in *Correggio* delicatenesse, in *Parmesano* concinnity [...].[9]

The *Elements* were written after his return to England in 1623, to support his application for the provostship of Eton College. This was successful, and among the things he brought to Eton is one of the rare illuminated manuscript copies of Leon Battista Alberti's *De re aedificatoria*, which is still kept in the Eton library. Although Wotton assumed a pose of modesty and wrote in great haste, his book was the fruit of extensive, first-hand study of classical and Renaissance sources, both built and written, and of his acquaintance during the periods of his life spent in Italy with important artists, theorists and patrons. The first copies of the *Elements* were presented to King James I and Prince Charles.[10] It was read widely, in a Latin edition which appeared in 1649 as part of Johannes de Laet's edition of Vitruvius, published in Amsterdam, in a Spanish version published in 1698, and in various English editions.[11]

One would expect from such an author steeped in Italian Renaissance discourse on the arts that he would follow Vasari and state that the visual arts and architecture share a common basis in *disegno*, the idea in the mind of the artist that subsequently receives material form as a design drawing. But Wotton takes a very different approach: his definition is political, not artistic or aesthetic:

> [...] true it is indeed that the Marble *Monuments & Memories* of well deseruing Men, wherewith the very high wayes were *strewed* on each side was not a bare and transitory entertainement of the *Eye*, or onely a gentle deception of *Time*, to the *Travailer*: But had also a secret and strong *Influence*, euen to the aduancement of the *Monarchie*, by continuall representation of vertuous examples; so as in that point *ART* became a piece of *State*.[12]

Wotton refers here to the Roman Via Appia, which was lined on both sides by the graves of Roman families, and hence became one long extended monument to Roman history. These were built not for aesthetic enjoyment or variety, but to instil in the mind of the viewer a persuasive image of Roman virtue, and thereby to incite to virtuous action. Art in this view is politics by another means, and in calling art a 'piece of state' Wotton follows the classical rhetorical view of art not as an object of aesthetic appreciation for its own sake, but as a means of persuasion.[13] One way in which such visual persuasion works is by its appeal to one's innate tendency to imitate. At the end of the *Elements* he announced another book (which he never completed), this time on education or 'how to build a man'. He plays here on the similarity in sound not etymology between edification and education, but the basis for this pun is his conviction that building is not merely construction but also the projection of a certain view of the builder as a learned gentleman, conversant with the latest developments in Italian art and with a keen awareness of the political dimenson of every gesture;[14] conversely education is not simply putting learning into a child and thereby leading it out of infancy, literally the inability to speak, but the construction of a civil person. In what may therefore be called the moral sequel to his treatise on architecture, he observed:

> That Parents should mark whether their Children be naturally apt to imitate: wherewith certainly all fine fancies are caught, and little less then ravished: and we have a tradition of *Quintilian* himself, that when he saw any well-expressed Image of grief, either in *Picture*, or *Sculpture*, he would usualy weep: For being a Teacher of Oratory in School, he was perhaps affected with a passionate Piece of *Art*, as with a kind of *mute Eloquence*: True it is indeed, which a great Master hath long before taught us [in margin: *Aristotle in Rhetoricis*], That Man is of all Creatures the most Mimicall, as a kind of near Adjunct to Reason: Arguing necessarily in those that can do it well, whether it be in

Gestures, in *Stiles*, in *Speech*, in *Fashion*, in *Accents*, or howsoever, no shallow Impression of Similitudes and Differences [. . .].[15]

That is, man learns through imitation, as Aristotle had argued in the *Poetics* to account for the apparently perverse pleasure viewers take in watching tragedy, and by implication for its fundamental role in society. The monuments of the ancients, classical rhetoric or contemporary art all persuade because they appeal to humanity's innate pleasure in imitation. They present the viewer with an image or visual object that is familar in the sense that it belongs to a shared culture, but at the same time alludes to a desired tradition, that of the Roman empire.

Wotton was not alone in this political consideration of art and architecture. That statues incited to virtuous action was a widely held view among the Romans. The historian Sallust recorded in *Bellum Iugurthinum* (*c*.41–40 BC) that Roman patricians felt 'that their spirit was incensed to virtue' when they looked at the wax masks of their ancestors. This did not happen because these wax figures had conspicuous aesthetic qualities, but because they were believed to excite memories of their actions.[16] Cicero too was a firm believer in the persuasive power of statues. In one of the *Philippicae* (44–43 BC) he argued that for this reason the memory of virtuous men should be kept alive by erecting statues for them.[17] Continuing this line of thought after the Restoration Sir Christopher Wren began his notes for an architectural treatise (*c*. 1670) by observing that:

> Architecture has its political Use; publick Buildings being the Ornament of a Country; it establishes a Nation, draws People and Commerce; makes the People love their native Country, which Passion is the Original of all great Actions in a Common-wealth. The Emulation of the Cities of *Greece* was the true Cause of their Greatness. The obstinate Valour of the *Jews*, occasioned by the Love of their Temple, was a Cement that held together that People, for many Ages, through infinite Changes. [. . .] Modern *Rome* subsists still, by the Ruins and Imitation of the *old*; as does *Jerusalem*, by the Temple of the Sepulchre, and other Remains of *Helena's* Zeal. Architecture aims at Eternity [. . .].[18]

In this explicit interest in the political uses of classical architecture, English architects and theorists of the seventeenth century, as in many other things, were quite unique. What makes these passages even more original is that they say something about how they felt the political use of classical architecture actually worked. Both Wotton and Wren play here on the Latin root of 'monument': 'monere', which means both to warn and to recall, and is also the basis for the

Latin *moneta*, money.[19] Monuments, whether they were buildings, tombs, altars like the Ara Pacis in Rome, or coins, are not direct, iconic imitations of what they refer to. Latin usage, unlike Greek, differentiated between imitation (*imitare*, the copy of an object's appearance) and representation (*repraesentare*, recalling its presence). Imitation affects the senses in a direct way by offering a more or less iconic substitute for what is imitated. Representation is directed at the mind, although it of course addresses the senses too, and aims at a reconstruction, at making again present before the mind's eye what is no longer before the eyes by conjuring up images already stored in memory and the emotions that come with them. Hence Quintilian distinguished between showing and saying, between imitation and representation, when he stressed the difference between the orator imitating emotions *ad oculos* or representing them.[20] Whereas imitation is restricted to the visual and the iconic, representation is more varied and abstract, and can use words, images, stones or any other material or medium. Accordingly, architecture cannot imitate the glorious Roman past, but it can represent it, particularly through its power to appeal to memory. In his *Agricola* (52 AD), one of the most intensely read Latin texts in seventeenth-century England because it contained a description of Roman Britain, Tacitus noted the relation between speech, memory, and by implication other ways of keeping memory alive when speech is impossible: 'Along with speech, we should have lost memory itself, had it been in our power to forget as much as to keep silent'.[21] Speech and memory are intimately linked, but do not exist only in outward, public manifestations. Even when speech is forbidden, memory is a silent storehouse of images of the past, and can be kept alive both in language and by non-verbal records. Buildings thus become visual rhetoric, because they are the construction in stone of a nation's memory, built to incite to virtue. According to Wren patriotic sentiments need visible objects: monuments serve as the visual and tangible expression of feelings of national identity.

The political use of architecture is based in part on the rhetorical view of all human expression as persuasive communication. But on the opening page of the *Elements of Architecture* Wotton states that 'In Architecture as in all other Operative Arts, the end must direct the Operation. The end is to build well'. In calling architecture an 'operative', that is a productive art, Wotton follows the Aristotelian definition of all human activities, and this offers another clue on Wotton's views about architecture as visual persuasion. From Antiquity until the end of the eighteenth century, two main classifications of all human activities and pursuits were current. One was the division into the mechanical and liberal arts, codified by Martianus Capella in the fifth century AD in *De Nuptiis Philologiae et Mercurii*. To the first belonged all activities we would now call crafts, concerned with the practical aspects of human survival: for instance, shoemaking, housebuilding, or medicine. The seven liberal arts were concerned with scientific knowledge and contemplation, reasoning and language, geometry, music, astronomy and physics (which made up the quadrivium), and grammar, logic and rhetoric (together forming the trivium). The other classification was developed by Aristotle, and was based on a distinction between doing, making and knowing. Architecture was a productive art, as were music and poetry. Rhetoric was considered by Quintilian to be both a practical art because its aim is to do something, namely, to speak persuasively, but also a productive art, because the orator writes speeches or history, that is, produces lasting texts.

In Wotton's view architecture is not singled out from the other arts, as would be done in modern classifications of the arts, because of its utility or practical aspects. Instead it is considered on the same footing as rhetoric, poetry, or erecting monuments: as a productive art, concerned with making durable objects that have both a practical and a more ideological function: to uphold the state. The question then is, how can buildings perform that role?

One clue is provided by Wotton's discussion of a building's situation, in which he did not limit himself to practical considerations:

> Some againe may bee said to bee Optical? Such as I meane as concerne the Properties of a well chosen Prospect: which I will call the Royaltie of Sight. For as there is a Lordship (as it were) of the Feete, wherein the Master doth much joy when he walketh about the Line of his owne Possessions: So there is a Lordship likewise of the Eye which being a raunging, and Imperious, and (I might say) an usurping Sence; can indure no narrow circomscription; but must be fedde, both with extent and varietie. [...] Lastly, I remember a private caution, which I know not well how to sort, unlesse I should call it Political. By no meanes, to build too neere a great Neighbour; which were in truth to bee as unfortunately seated on the earth, as Mercurie is in the Heavens, for the most part, ever in combustion, or obscuritie, under brighter beames then his owne.[22]

Wotton advises here that buildings should be placed on the top of a hill, or at least that their situation be unencumbered, so that they can be seen from all sides, but more importantly, that their owners or inhabitants can enjoy a free and varied prospect.[23] This is no disinterested aesthetic enjoyment, but the visual expression of the gazer's dominion over what he can survey; just as there is a 'dominion of the feet', in which the owner sets out his own territory by walking along its boundaries. The architect should try to achieve a panoramic view by situating the building in such a way that it forms the centre, the viewpoint from which its surroundings can best be seen. Persuasion, that is, works not just through the triggering of remembrance, as in the Roman monuments cited above, but also in a more abstract way, through the construction of the visual domain.

STATECRAFT AND STAGECRAFT: CONSTRUCTING A CLASSICAL PAST

Whereas only a few major building projects were actually completed in seventeenth-century Britain before the Restoration, much ephemeral architecture was produced in the masques designed by Inigo Jones. The masques were very costly, highly conspicuous and prestigious events at the early Stuart court, and consisted for a large part – and in the masques performed after the rupture between the poet Ben Jonson and the designer Inigo Jones in 1631 – principally of paper architecture, constructed to last for only one night; the architectural stage-sets and backdrops were made of painted paper attached to wooden props, and were burnt immediately after the performance.

Until Jones' appointment as Surveyor of the King's Works in 1614 masque design was his main artistic activity; in them he experimented with classical design on a scale and with a variety that was impossible to explore in real architecture. As has often been noted, the Stuart masques were not plays: they were allegories or emblems of kingship. Jones and others often spoke of the principal 'invention' or 'devise' that was the basis of a masque, using terms that were also used in emblematics. The masques also functioned as a laboratory for the introduction of classical architecture and design in Britain. Practically all elements of Jones' designs, from the costumes, attitudes and gestures to the architectural setting, are derived from Italian and French models, found both in architectural treatises and in publications of Italian *apparati* and festivals. This was not because of a lack of creativity. Imitating respected examples was an integral part of Renaissance artistry and of the rhetorical curriculum, in which *imitatio* was succeeded by *aemulatio*, and an artist could show his talent by choosing and combining the best models.[24] But there is also another aspect to Jones' imitation of continental models: by integrating them into his English masques he made them part of the English artistic repertoire. In their design the masques integrated Renaissance art and architecture on English soil; in their performance these forms were seen by the court, which was thus educated into Renaissance taste. And because the masques are all celebrations of ideal Stuart monarchy, the classical tradition and its Renaissance renewal were thus integrated into a visual and verbal enactment or staging of idealized kingship. In their conscious revival of classical drama, buildings, costume and gesture the masques offered antiquity spectacularized.

Jones observed after the break with Ben Jonson that his masques were 'but pictures with light and motion'. This brief remark points to the importance of pictorial techniques, in particular linear perspective, in creating these spectacles of antiquity and kingship. In the performance of masques a complex dialectic between reality and theatrical illusion was acted out, in which perspective and architecture were constitutive factors. The proscenium is a typical liminal marker, providing the demarcation between the world of theatrical enactment and that of the spectators. Its form was ultimately derived from Roman triumphal arches, which were also powerful boundaries, representing the moment when a Roman general was transformed from the leader of an army into an unarmed citizen.[25] Behind it was the stage on which the masquers performed, but often there was also a narrow stage in front of it, with steps leading to the audience. In his description of the last Stuart masque, *Salmacida Spolia*, Jones called it 'the border that encloses the scene and made a frontispiece to all the work'.[26] His use of the porticoes of classical temples follows Palladio and Scamozzi's adaptation of temple fronts to the façades of Christian churches, and their use of portico-based title pages in their architectural treatises (Figs. 4.2 and 4.3). All the authority and majesty of

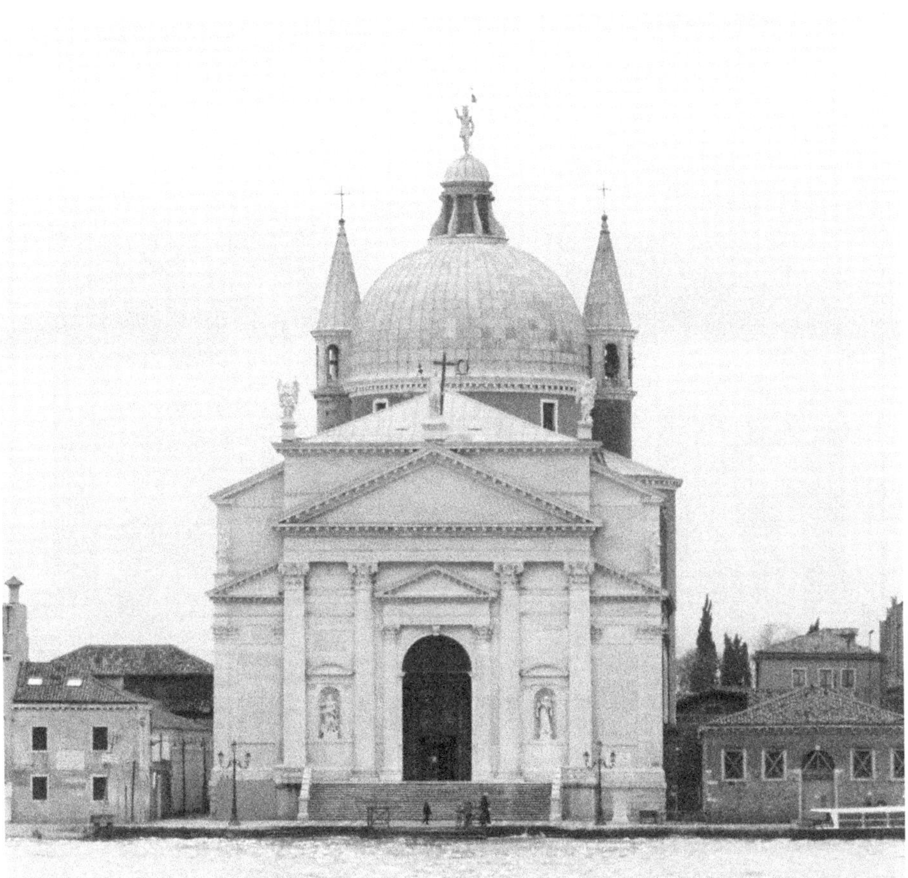

4.2 Andrea Palladio, façade of the Redentore. Venice, 1577 (photo: Lex Hermans).

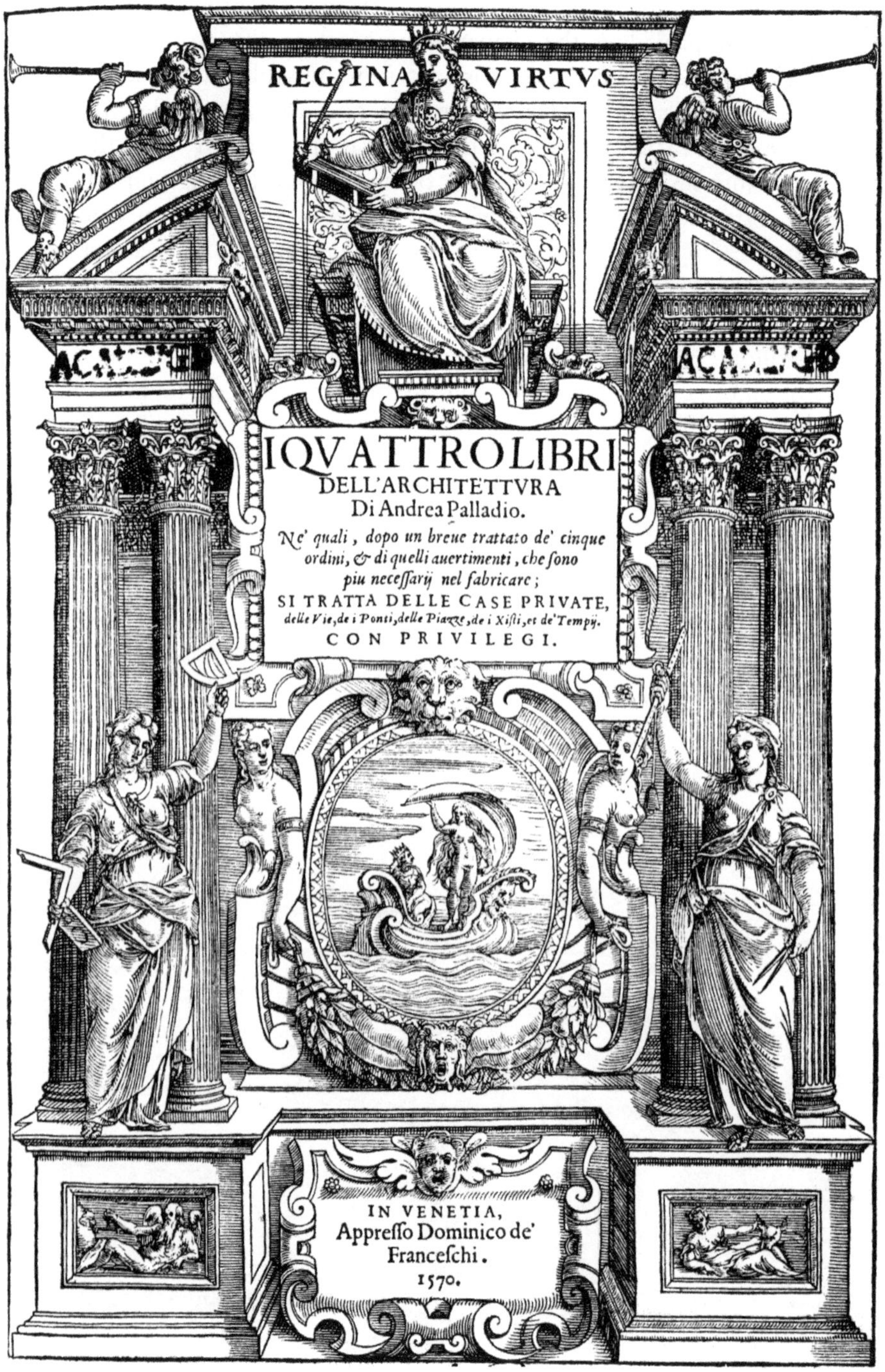

4.3 Andrea Palladio, Frontispiece of *I Quattro Libri dell'Architettura*, Venice, 1570 (photo: Leiden University Library, Special Collections Research Centre, 679 A 16).

classical temples was thus added to the paper design of treatises and the theatre. But Jones' remark also suggests a temporal dimension to the liminal function of the proscenium, suggesting that this framing device directs the gaze of the viewer from the borders of the stage to what is going to happen at the centre of the scene, in the depths suggested by linear perspective.[27]

Linear perspective also served to direct and change the viewing habits of the audience. As John Peacock has argued, Jones deliberately used perspective to change the viewing attitude of his public. As the puzzled reactions to his early masques document, Jacobean spectators did not always know what to make of his perspectival illusionism. At the time the viewing competences they brought to the masques, as to all visual art, were very much that of readers of texts. Elizabethan portraits and miniatures explored the flatness of their medium; they do not suggest much depth, let alone that of three-dimensional space. When linear perspective was introduced, its use was initially reserved to royal portraits and the stage sets of the masques. Viewers had to adapt to Jones' perspectival illusions of buildings set in three-dimensional space. One could perhaps say that this process of adaptation was thematized by Jones, for instance in the grand classic tableau that forms the backdrop to the first scene of *Albion's Triumph* of 1632 (Fig. 4.4), which uses a fragment of a cornice in the collection of the Earl of Arundel.[28] By using one fragment of a classical temple and integrating it in a new design showing a seventeenth century reconstruction of a Roman ritual and its architectural setting, Jones' backdrop thus shows something of the archaeological and artistic process that led to Renaissance reconstructions of antique architecture.

The seating arrangements also show that linear perspective was not only seen as a very powerful instrument of pictorial composition, determining the exact position and relations between the parts of a painting. It also very much determined viewing positions. During the masque, the main point of interest was not the masque itself, but the king watching it. James I was well aware of the theatrical character of kingship. As he observed in *Basilikon Doron* of 1599, the treatise on monarchy he wrote for his son Prince Henry: 'A King is as one set on a stage, whose smallest actions and gestures, all the people gazingly do behold'.[29] Accordingly the king was placed exactly on the point from which he, and he alone, could fully enjoy the spatial illusion, that is the viewpoint corresponding to the vanishing point of the perspectival construction used in the stage sets. Courtiers were seated around him in an order which reflected their closeness to the king.[30] The use of linear perspective therefore was not simply a neutral pictorial strategy to create the illusion of three-dimensionality on a flat surface; it could be used as a powerful rhetorical instrument, because through its ordering of sight lines and viewing positions, as in Wotton's advice on the location of country houses, it established hierarchy by visual means. Stagecraft thus becomes a means of statecraft.

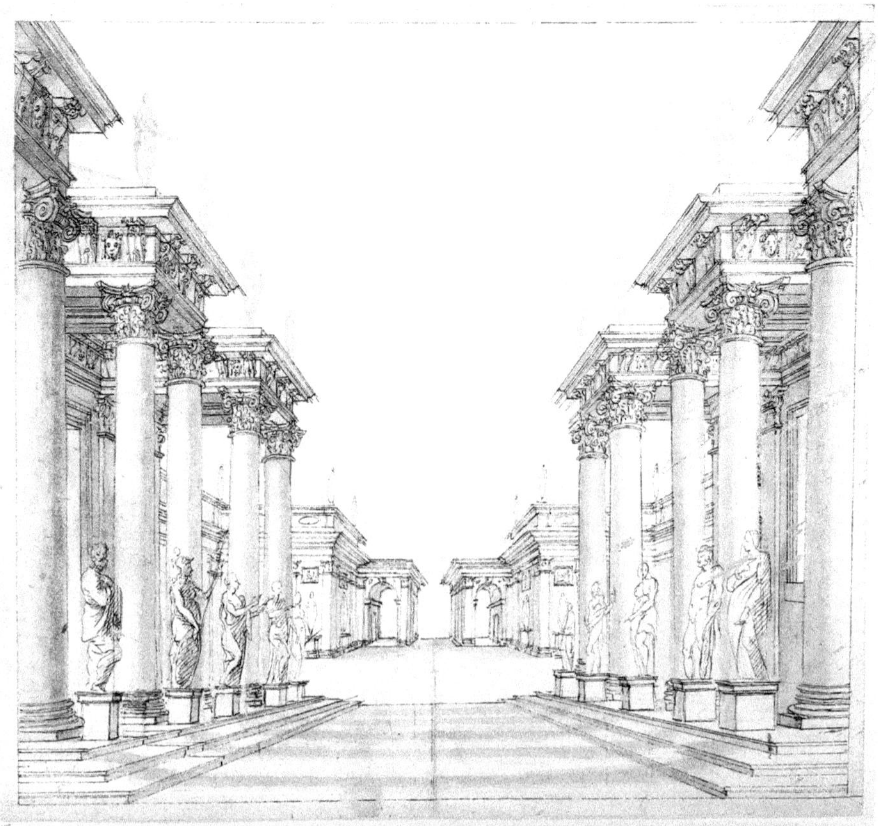

4.4 Inigo Jones, design for scene 1, 'a Roman Atrium' of *Albion's Triumph*. Chatsworth, 1631 (photo: Department of Art History, Leiden University, Netherlands).

Inigo Jones reconstructs Stonehenge

Linear perspective also had other powerful associations for Jones, with the representation of Roman monuments in the architectural treatises of Palladio and Scamozzi. He exploited these in another context, that of Stonehenge. In its representational techniques, use of classical architecture and persuasive purpose, his notes on stonehenge are related to his masque designs and Wotton's *Elements of Architecture*.

As Sir Christopher Wren observed on the first page of his notes for an architectural treatise quoted in section two of this chapter, 'Architecture aims at Eternity'; but he added: 'and therefore the only Thing uncapable of Modes and Fashions [are] its Principals, the *Orders*'. Thereby he made explicit one of the deepest, but mainly implicit, convictions held by anybody involved with classical architecture as a designer or patron: that the formal vocabulary of classical architecture, based on the five orders and the temple, somehow represent the eternal, fundamentally unchangeable essence of Western architecture. One reason for this conviction is tectonic: the system of columns and trabeation as exemplified in the Greek temple front embodies the essence of architecture; the interaction of load bearing and thrust from which spaces are created. The other is cultural: classical architecture is the building style of the Greeks and Romans, and thereby stands for everything their classical culture implies, ranging from democracy to the idea of the Empire, and the post-classical complex of ideas associated with *translatio imperii*, the notion that after the end of the Roman Empire its ideals could be resumed in Northern Europe, by Charlemagne, the Habsburg emperors, or even, as we shall see, by King James I of Great Britain.

It is against this background of the appropriation of classical architecture for dynastic purposes that Jones' treatment of the enigmatic prehistoric remains at Stonehenge, usually rather neglected in Jones studies, becomes interesting.[31] In 1620, when King James I stayed at Wilton, he sent Inigo Jones to Stonehenge to prove that it had been built by the Romans (it is of course much older, dated now to *c.* 2000–1600 BC). Jones made extensive measurements and drawings of the stones, a groundplan and a reconstruction; these were published posthumously in 1655 under the title *The Most Notable Antiquity of Stone-Heng*, by his pupil John Webb on the basis of the notes Jones had left (Figs. 4.5–4.9). According to Jones, Stonehenge was originally a Roman temple. The argument is in three parts. First alternative theories are refuted, chief among them the prevalent view that Stonehenge was built by Druids. Next he offered a reconstruction in word and image based on the measurements he made on the spot. Finally the plates show in one glance what it took Jones about 60 pages to argue: that these are the remains of a circular Roman temple dedicated to Coelus or the Sky, the sun, and the moon because of its roofless structure, open to the skies. The argument presented by the text for the Roman origins of Stonehenge is based on a careful listing of statements by Roman authorities such as Vitruvius and Tacitus about temple architecture and the Roman presence in Britain. The plates argue for the same thesis with different means. They show the groundplan, façade, section, orthogonal and perspectival projection, all carefully drawn to scale, to be compared by the reader with a view of the temple in its present, crumbling and weather-beaten state, and its irregular groundplan.

Jones thus followed the procedure recommended by Leon Battista Alberti in *De Re Aedificatoria*. Architects should follow the humanist method of collecting as much classical source material as possible, read the best authorities, and on the basis of such philological comparisons make their text editions. Similarly the architect should inspect Roman monuments with his own eyes, measure and draw them, compare them with the remains of other similar buildings, and base his reconstruction or design on the notes taken on the spot. The result should be published as a set of drawings: groundplan, section and façade, or a model,

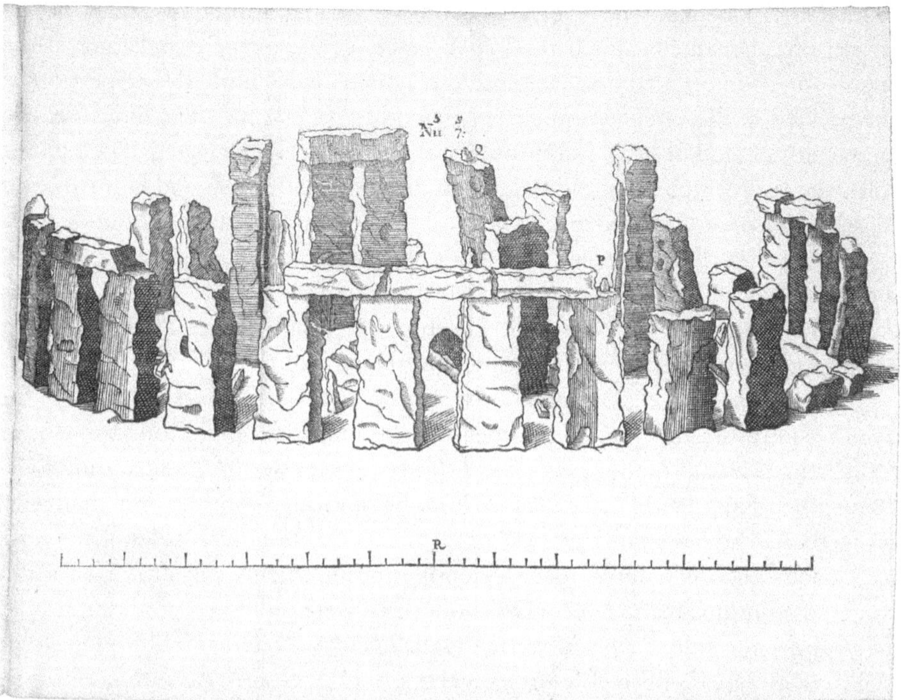

4.5 Inigo Jones, view of Stonehenge in original state. From: *The Most Notable Antiquity of Great Britain, vulgarly called Stone-Heng, on Salisbury Plain. Restored by Inigo Jones*, 1655, plate 7 (photo: Koninklijke Bibliotheek, The Hague, Netherlands, 3318 B 30).

as shown for instance in the paper reconstruction Palladio made of the Pantheon (Figs. 4.10 and 4.11).[32] The decision itself to give Stonehenge the treatment usually reserved to Roman antiquities was highly unusual, and cannot be explained from a stylistic, aesthetic or engineering interest, as is shown by the reconstruction Jones made and what he deemed worthy of mentioning. No other English prehistoric remains were singled out for the same kind of analysis or reconstruction, and until the Gothic Revival gained momentum at the end of the eighteenth century, such treatment was restricted to Roman and Greek antiquities.[33] But when we look at Jones' groundplan and reconstructions, it becomes clear that he was not interested in archaeology or antiquarianism for its own sake. Instead, what he set out to do was to assimilate Stonehenge, the oldest British building known at the time, into the Vitruvian tradition, by giving the same representational treatment to Stonehenge as the Roman antiquities received in the treatises of Serlio or Palladio.

In his opening statement, Jones straightaway declared that the Druids could not have built Stonehenge because there is no trace of academies of art among them, and no trace of any pursuit of the liberal arts or sciences needed to educate

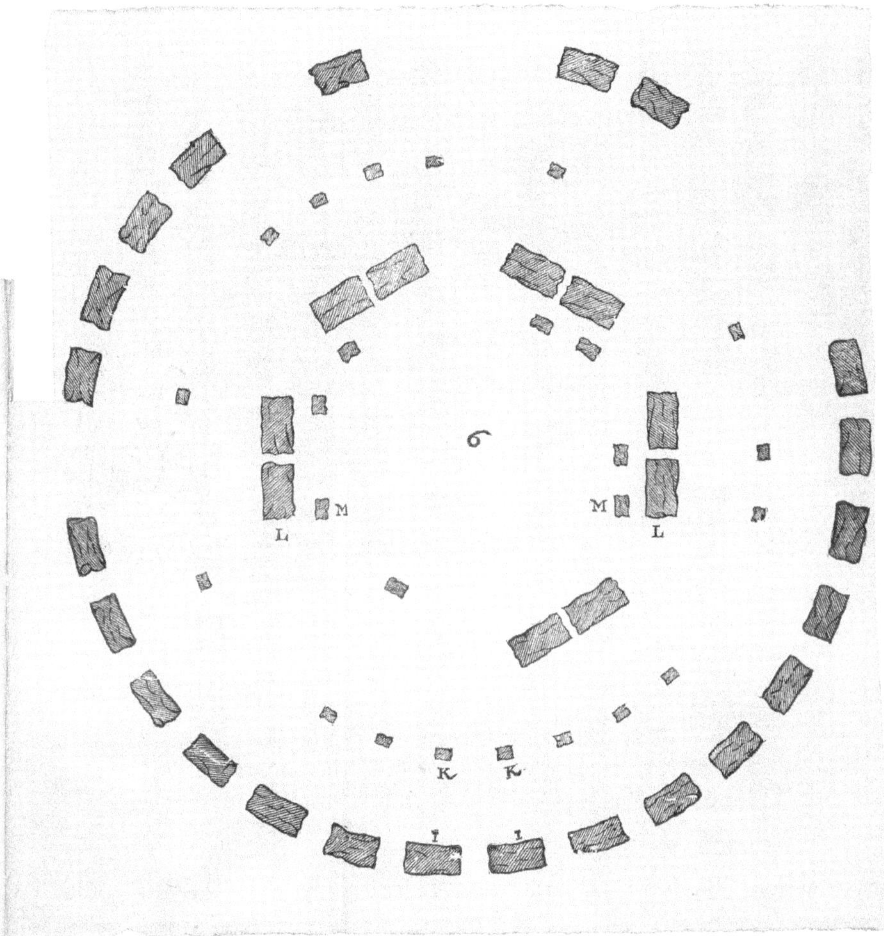

4.6 Inigo Jones, groundplan of Stonehenge in original state. From: *The Most Notable Antiquity of Great Britain, vulgarly called Stone-Heng, on Salisbury Plain. Restored by Inigo Jones*, 1655, plate 6 (photo: Koninklijke Bibliotheek, The Hague, Netherlands, 3318 B 30).

an architect in the Vitruvian sense.[34] Even the explanation of its name Jones offers is part of the assimilating strategy: 'This *Antiquity* [. . .] because the *Architraves* are set upon the heads of the upright stones, and hang (as it were) in the air, is generally known by the name of *Stoneheng*'.[35] From the very beginning Jones' inquiry is not an attempt to grasp the unique character of prehistoric Britain on its own terms; instead it is judged according to the standards of classical culture. After the reconstruction, he asks who may have been the builders of this pile, and answers it in a typically classicizing fashion: it is so magnificent that only the Romans could have built it.[36] It uses the Tuscan order according to Jones, the one order the Romans invented, and which occurs only outside Italy in

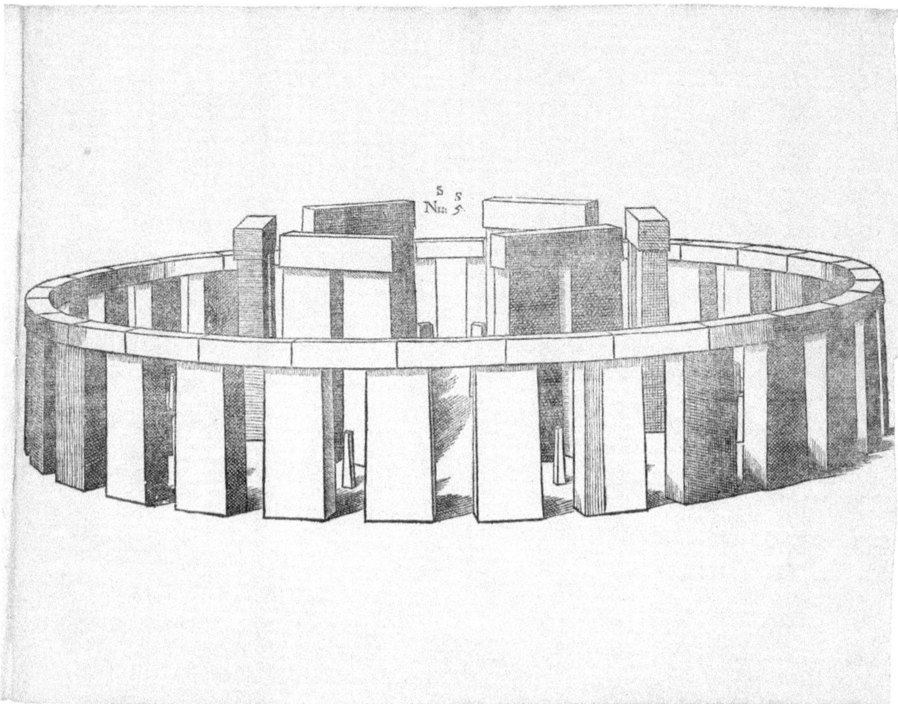

4.7 Inigo Jones, view of Stonehenge as restored. From: *The Most Notable Antiquity of Great Britain, vulgarly called Stone-Heng, on Salisbury Plain. Restored by Inigo Jones*, 1655, plate 5 (photo: Koninklijke Bibliotheek, The Hague, Netherlands, 3318 B 30).

places where the Romans had been. Hence only the Romans could have designed Stonehenge. Jones here attributed two typically Roman qualities to Stonehenge: magnificence or *magnificentia*, a characteristic of Roman public buildings; and the use of the simple, sturdy Tuscan order. The remains of Stonehenge no longer sport capitals, he argued, because of the weather and the mistreatment of the building by vandals after the Romans had left.[37] The argument ends with a dig at those antiquarians who believed it was the work of indigenuous Britains. According to Jones, they err and are deaf to rational argument supported by the authority of classical culture. In an instance of the ultimate rhetorical strategy of classicism, classical culture is presented not as one option among many, but as completely natural and self-evident. For the properly educated designing classical buildings is doing what comes naturally:

> As I have delivered my own judgement freely, all reason they should enjoy theirs. But such as sail in the vast Ocean of time, amongst the craggy rocks of *Antiquity*, steering their course, betwixt anciently approved customs, and convincing arguments, guided by good

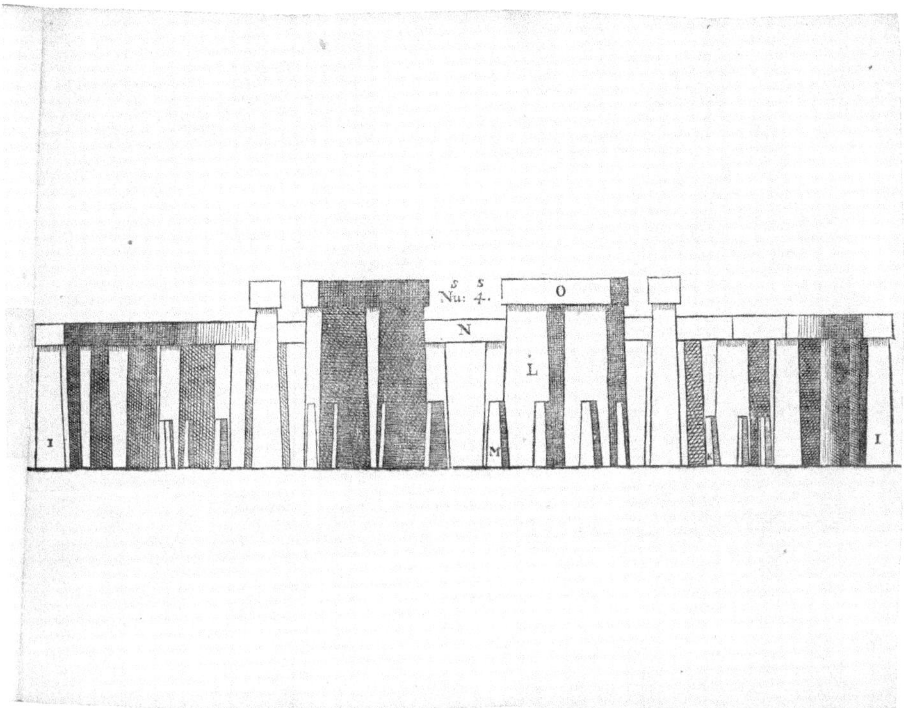

4.8 Inigo Jones, sectional elevation of Stonehenge as restored. From: *The Most Notable Antiquity of Great Britain, vulgarly called Stone-Heng, on Salisbury Plain. Restored by Inigo Jones*, 1655, plate 4 (photo: Koninklijke Bibliotheek, The Hague, Netherlands, 3318 B 30).

> Authority, and sound judgement, arrive much safer, and with better repute, in the secure Haven of undoubted *Truth*. For mine own part, I had rather erre happily with venerable *Antiquity*, then so much as trouble my thoughts with modern conceits.[38]

Jones rests his case with a well-known and often reproduced statement of this attitude by Sebastiano Serlio, who published the first complete codification of the classical orders of architecture in 1538: 'Roma quanta fuit ipsa ruina docet'. The ruins themselves, that is without our aid, teach us Rome's greatness; or: even the ruins teach us Rome's greatness (Fig. 4.12).

The Antiquity of Stone-Heng is therefore not simply an essay in architectural history or antiquarianism, even though it is presented as such, but in cultural appropriation. And ultimately the purpose of this exercise was dynastical: by arguing that Stonehenge was built by Roman, or Roman-educated architects; that the large stones were really a rough, British variety of the Tuscan order weathered down to naked blocks of stone in the course of centuries; and that the complex had really been a temple dedicated to Coelus, Jones could give

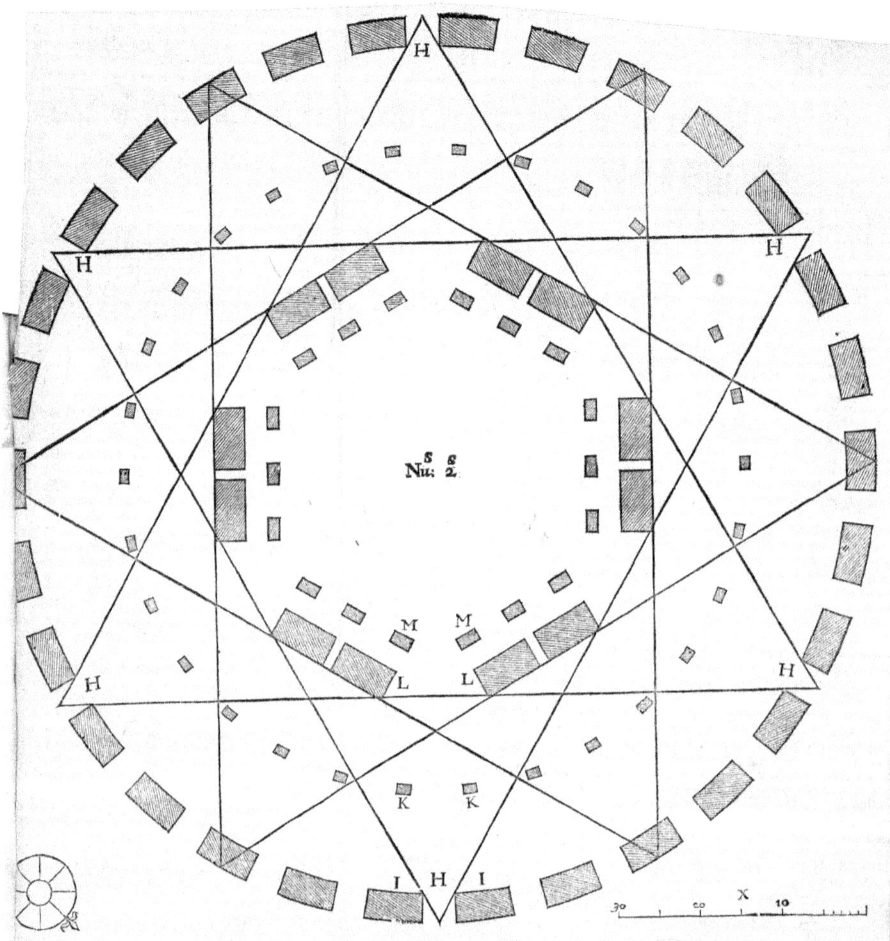

4.9 Inigo Jones, groundplan of Stonehenge as restored. From: *The Most Notable Antiquity of Great Britain, vulgarly called Stone-Heng, on Salisbury Plain. Restored by Inigo Jones*, 1655, plate 2 (photo: Koninklijke Bibliotheek, The Hague, Netherlands, 3318 B 30).

credibility to claims that Britain had a strong Roman past, whose remains were still visible. James I used such 'evidence' of a Roman past to bolster his unification of England and Scotland under one crown, to claim that the creation of the new kingdom of Great Britain was really a resumption, after the Dark Ages, of Roman rule. A *translatio imperii* that is, taking the rule of the Roman empire and transferring it to Britain.[39]

In this case the use of classical architecture is not, as it was in Italy, the effort to bring back to life a building style of the past whose material remains were present across the country. It was its opposite, the recreation in word and image of an ancient monument in the classical style, to create not a new present, but a

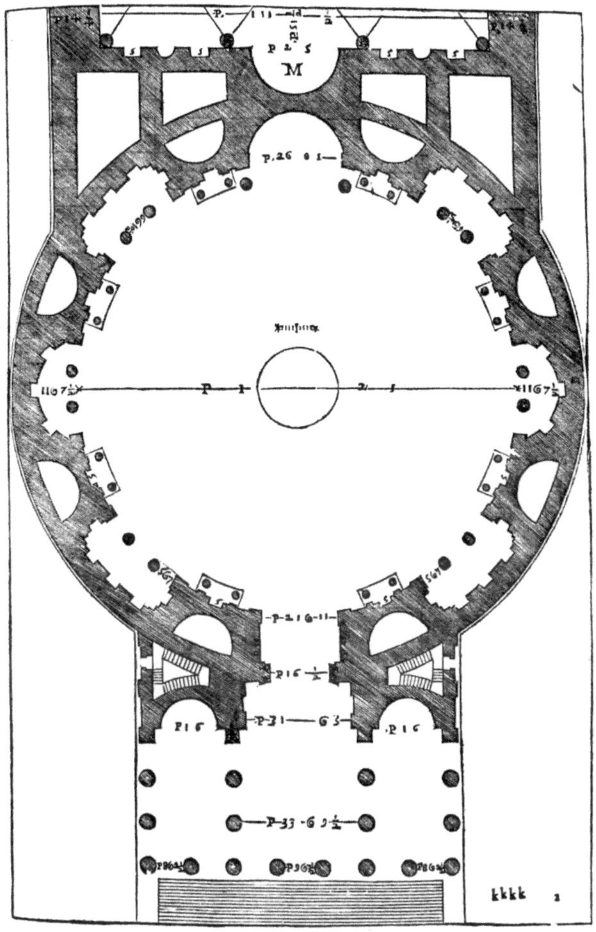

4.10 Andrea Palladio, groundplan of the Pantheon in Rome. From: *I Quattro Libri dell'Architettura*, Venice, 1570, Book IV, p. 75 (photo: Leiden University Library, Special Collections Research Centre, 679 A 16).

new past for the dynasty and the nation. In this respect Jones' reconstruction is close to his masque designs. Both were aimed at creating visible allegories of kingship based on a reformulation of Britain's mythical past. In the masques that mythical past is presented either as a lost golden age, to be restored by the Stuarts, as in *Albion's Triumph*. In *Oberon the Fairy Prince* of 1611 the victorious British prince is associated with King James' recent union of the English and Scottish crowns, and a symbolic map of the new kingdom of Great Britain was depicted on the curtain before the masque began.[40] The mythical past is also transformed, as happened to Stonehenge, into the enduring remains of a classical origin, as in *Coelum Britannicum*. That masque begins with a representation of the three kingdoms of Great Britain, which almost acts as an *orator tacens*, recalling the use of

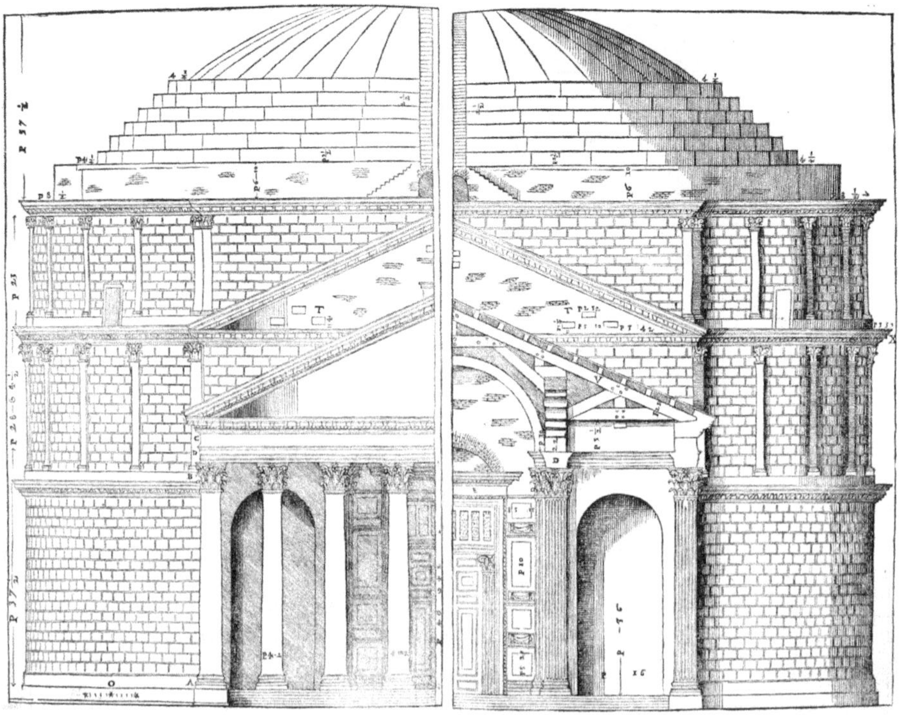

4.11 Andrea Palladio, sectional elevation of the Pantheon in Rome. From: *I Quattro Libri dell'Architettura*, Venice, 1570, Book IV, pp. 76–7 (photo: Leiden University Library, Special Collections Research Centre, 679 A 16).

silent statues by Roman orators, or one might say an acting image. In the masques as in *The Antiquity of Stone-Heng* the essentially classical nature of the British monarchy is celebrated. The last masque to be staged in Britain, *Salmacida Spolia* of 1640, ends not with the usual dance of the masquers with members of the audience, but with a large tableau of 'magnificent buildings' and eight masquers who represent the planetary spheres. It suggested an identification of classical architecture, Stuart rule and cosmic harmony.[41]

Sublime architecture

The construction of a classical past by architectural means is not the only persuasive strategy. For a closer understanding of the details of persuasive architectural design we have to turn to another source: the reception in seventeenth-century England of the first-century Greek treatise on the sublime traditionally attributed to Longinus. According to a still very widespread prejudice, the English did not produce any architectural theory to speak of before the advent

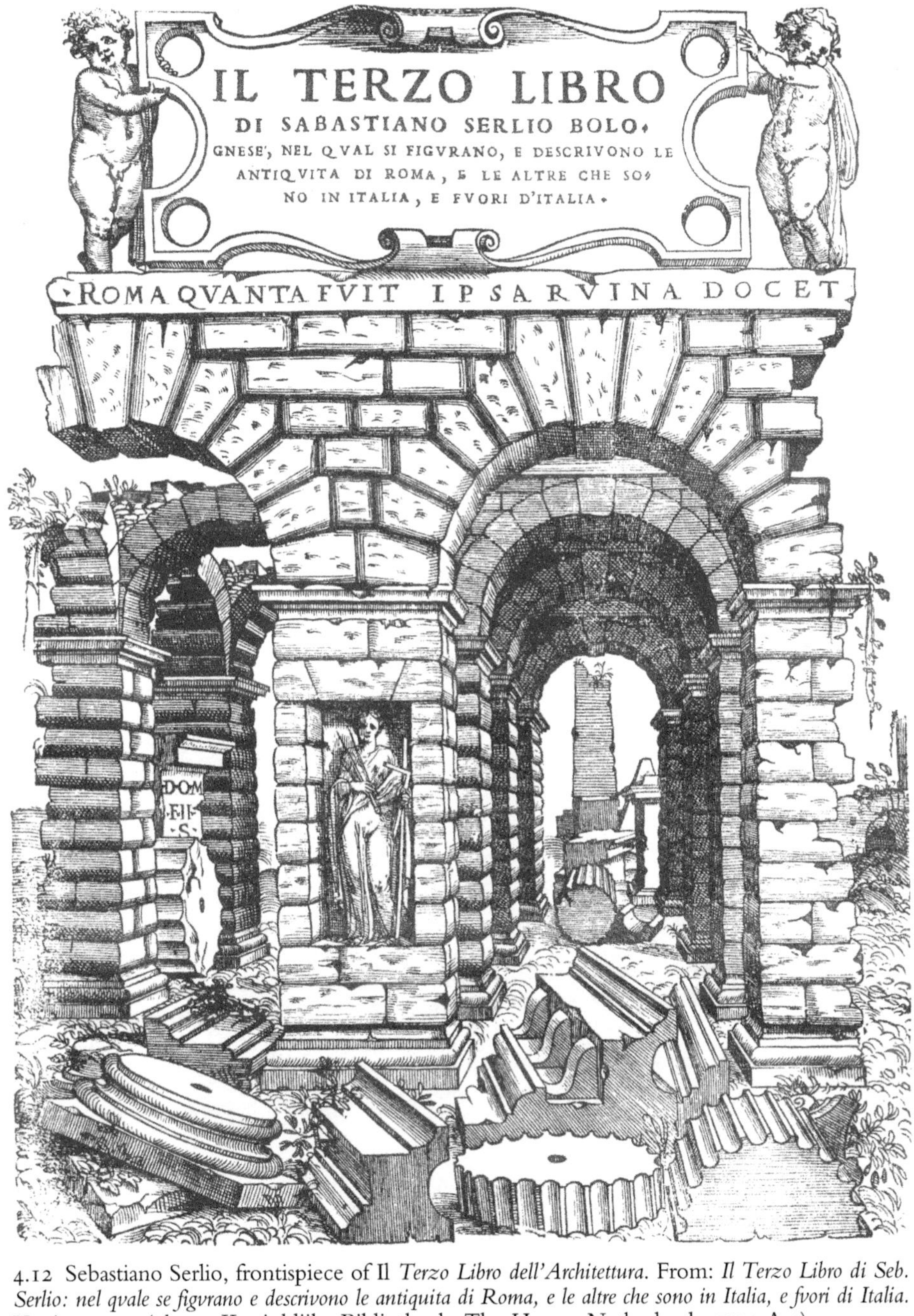

4.12 Sebastiano Serlio, frontispiece of Il *Terzo Libro dell'Architettura*. From: *Il Terzo Libro di Seb. Serlio: nel qvale se figvrano e descrivono le antiquita di Roma, e le altre che sono in Italia, e fvori di Italia.* Venice, 1540 (photo: Koninklijke Bibliotheek, The Hague, Netherlands, 1303 A 5).

of neo-Palladianism after 1715, which resulted from the efforts of Lord Burlington and his circle. His villa at Chiswick, based on Palladio's villas in the Veneto, marks the birth of the so-called Rule of Taste in English architecture. Before that, there was the eccentricity and idiosyncracy of what is called the English Baroque of Nicholas Hawksmoor, Sir John Vanbrugh and James Gibbs. It is distinguished by a great predilection for what Hawksmoor called the 'Emminencys', the very conspicuous towers and other ornaments that shape the roof-line. The churches Hawksmoor and Wren built for the City of London are immediately recognized by their highly individual spires (Fig. 4.13). Hawksmoor's work is also distinguished by his very personal handling of key features of the classical style. He covered, for instance, the entire façade

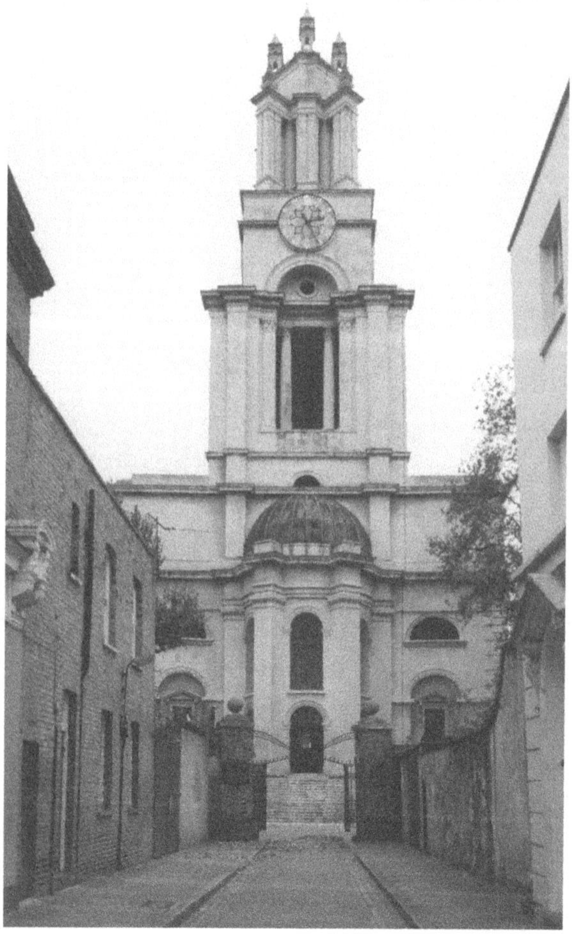

4.13 Nicholas Hawksmoor, St Anne Limehouse, spire. London, 1714 to 1719 (photo: Sophie Ploeg).

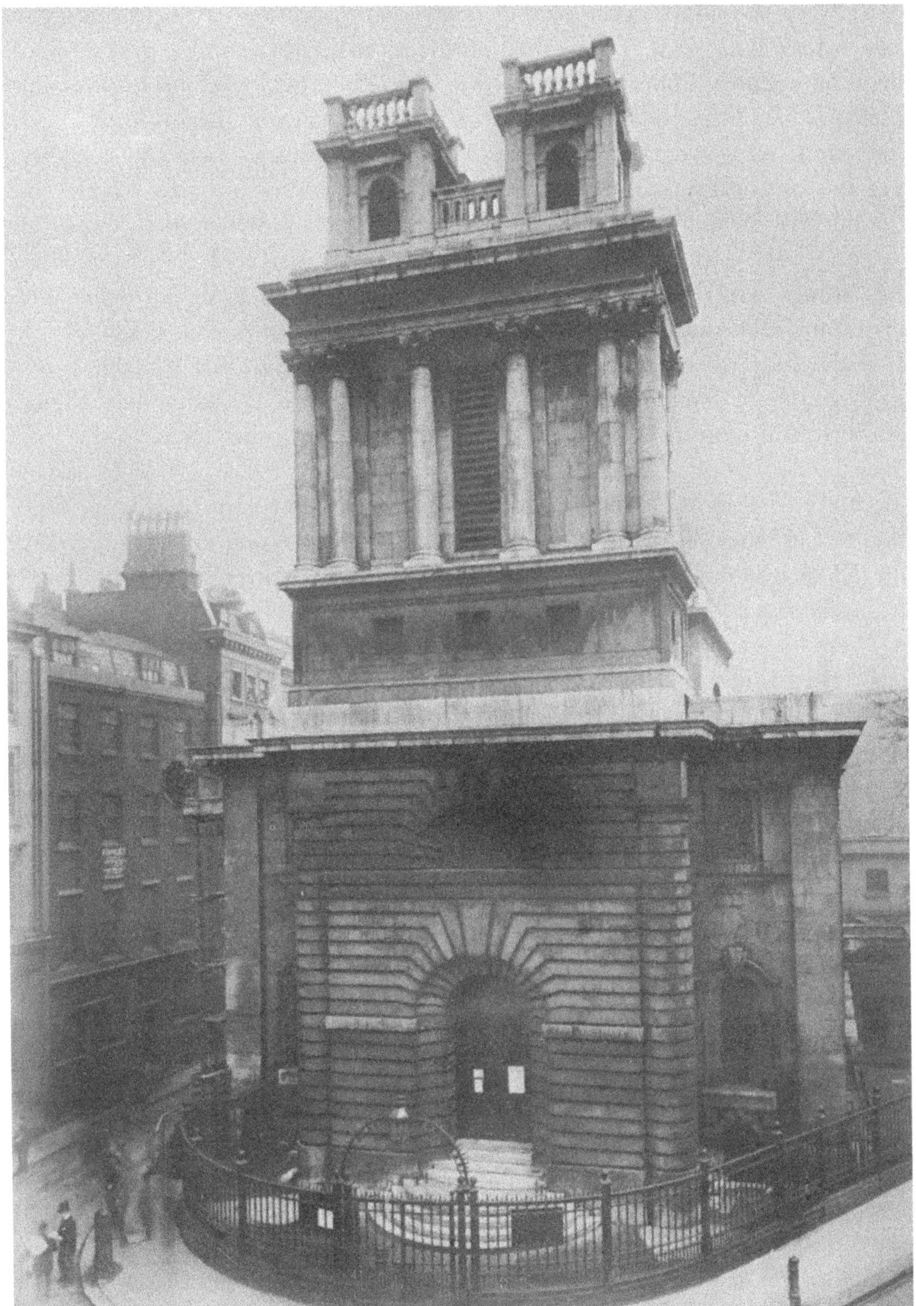

4.14 Nicholas Hawksmoor, St Mary Woolnoth, City of London, 1717 to 1727 (photo: Centre Art-Historical Documentation, Radboud Universiteit Nijmegen).

of St Mary Woolnoth in the City of London in rustication or blocks of roughly hewn stone (Fig. 4.14). The normal practice is to limit this to the ground floor, because originally rustication was used to strengthen the lower floor and express the sturdy, military, or uncouth – in a pun that can only be made in Dutch: 'onbehouwen' – character of the users and inhabitants of such floors; soldiers, peasants and craftsmen. Hawksmoor also tends to blow up very normal and unobtrusive elements of the classical style into such proportions that they are no longer recognizable as building elements, but instead evolve into something that comes very close to abstract sculpture. Such elements are no longer integrated and subordinated into a larger whole as the laws of classical design dictate, as exemplified for instance in Bramante's Tempietto, or the restrained neo-Palladianism of Inigo Jones. In St George in the East the keystones, though outsized, still perform a structural function by keeping the stones of the vault over the door in place (Fig. 4.15). But the giant keystones on the ground floor of the north front of St George Bloomsbury in London have no constructive function because they do not keep a vault in place. Through their size they transform the doorframe into abstract sculpture reminiscent of Michelangelo's Mannerist extravaganzas in the Biblioteca Laurenziana in Florence (Fig. 4.16).

Architectural historians have always found it difficult to deal with this phase of British architecture.[42] There is indeed very little seventeenth-century evidence of what architects thought: there are no treatises, no systematic treatment of architectural composition, and only a few scattered remarks by Hawksmoor, Vanbrugh and Wren. What we would need to give an account in contemporary terms of the appearance of Hawksmoor's buildings, to account for the overall effect they make, would be seventeenth-century theories of composition. Unfortunately neither Vitruvius nor his Renaissance successors Alberti, Serlio, Palladio or Vignola, offer much advice on architectural composition. What they offer instead is instruction in the correct handling of the classical orders, the ornaments derived from them and their dimensions and proportions; and they offer more general rules on how to give proportion to a building. Both kinds of advice start from the parts of a building, for instance the basic module that will relate the dimensional parts of all the order in a building to each other, and rarely discuss the composition of a building as a whole. These instructions are helpful when analysing Palladio's or Bramante's buildings, which very much obey the rules of classical architecture. But they are not much use when dealing with Hawksmoor's highly individual and idiosyncratic buildings, where it is not the individual elements in themselves that makes them highly individual, but their handling and combination with other elements.

There is one rhetorical treatise on composition, however, which was widely translated and read in Britain during the entire seventeenth and eighteenth centuries, long before Boileau and Edmund Burke put the sublime on the artistic and aesthetic map: *On the sublime* attributed to Longinus. Even before the widely read

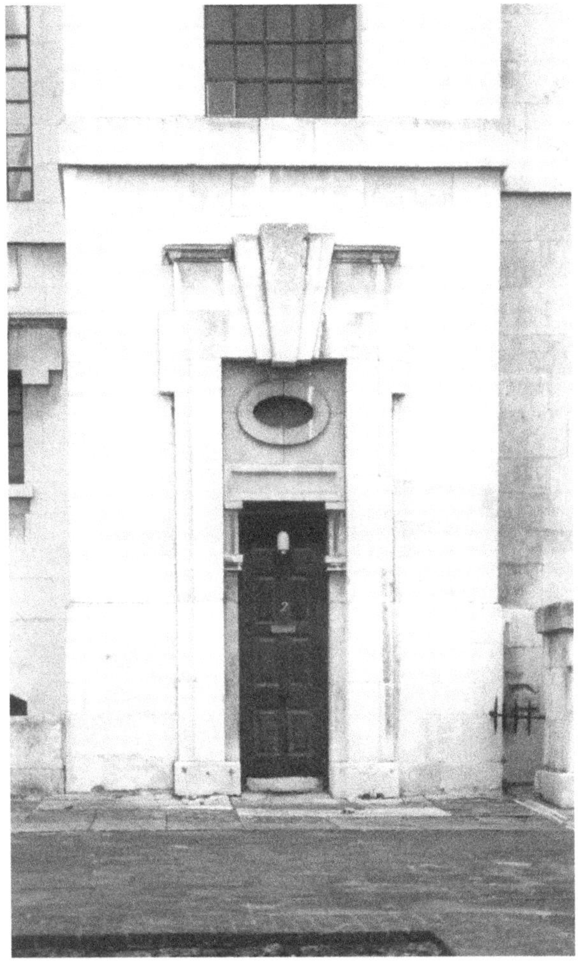

4.15 Nicholas Hawksmoor, St George-in-the-East, door to gallery staircase. London, 1714 to 1725 (photo: Sophie Ploeg).

French adaptation by Boileau was published in 1674, Longinus had been quoted by George Chapman, the translator of Homer, in *On Translating and Defending Homer* of 1611. Milton had included him in the ideal curriculum devised for the Christian poet in 1641–4.

Before 1674 a number of English editions had appeared. The first translation is that by John Hall of 1652, but this was preceded by some Latin and Greek editions. John Hall, who lived from 1626 to 1656, was educated at Cambridge and worked as a pamphlet writer for Cromwell. He died while working on a translation of Procopius of his attempts to cure obesity by eating pebbles. His translation of Longinus is by far the best, stylistically speaking, of these early English editions, and has an interesting preface in which he calls eloquence

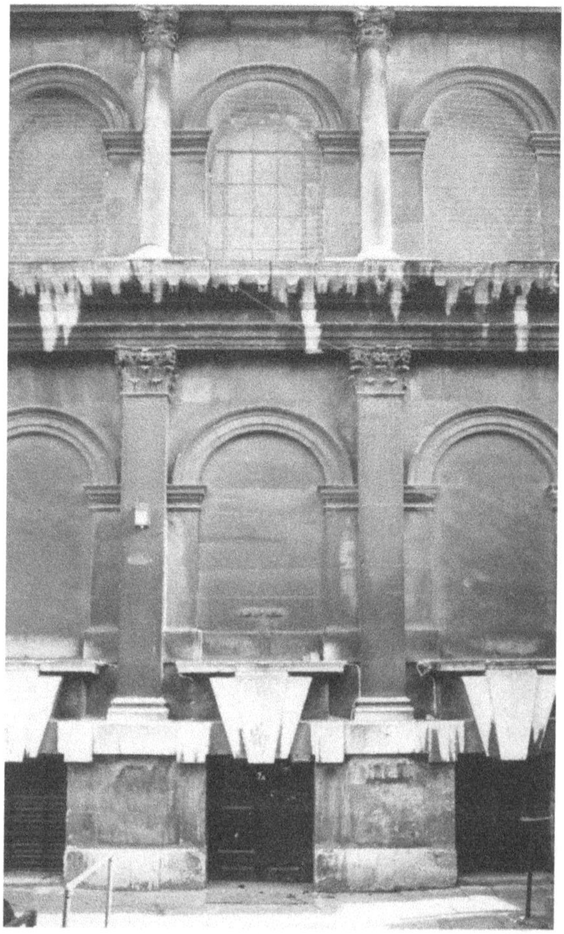

4.16 Nicholas Hawksmoor, St George Bloomsbury, north front. London, 1716 to 1724 (photo: Sophie Ploeg).

'[...] a distilling our notions into a Quintessence or forming all our thoughts in a Cone, and smiting with the Point [...]. 'tis Empire wholly commanding, yet never to be commanded'.[43] The other seventeenth-century translations all followed after Boileau's French edition of 1674, and vary in quality and completeness. These are: [Anonymous] *An Essay on the Sublime. Translated from the Greek of Dionysius Longinus Cassius, the Rhetorician. Compar'd with the French of the sieur Despreaux-Boileau* (1698); John Pulteney's version, also published in 1698; Leonard Wellsted, *Dionysius Longinus' Treatise on the Sublime* (1712); and William Smith, *Dionysius Longinus On the Sublime* (1739). Among the versions published after Boileau the one by John Pulteney is of particular interest because of his close links to some of the most important building patrons of the time.

Sophie Ploeg has recently demonstrated that many persons involved in what was the major building programme of the English Baroque were familiar with Longinus' ideas and with his aesthetics of the sublime.[44] Thus at least one group of major architectural patrons, the Commission that oversaw the building of 50 new churches in London, created in 1711, counted among its members a number of persons who possessed versions of Longinus or were closely acquainted with one or more of his translators. Even more important, Sir John Vanbrugh, who was on the committee and a close associate of Hawksmoor, wrote a memorandum on church design that shows a close affinity with the aesthetics of the sublime. He recommended, for instance, that 'the Reverend look of a Temple itself [...] shou'd ever have the most Solemn and Awfull Appearance both without and within, that is possible'.[45]

Longinus' treatise on rhetorical composition is also relevant here because of its intensely visual character; it often draws on architectural and pictorial metaphor to illustrate his points. This visuality, the visual metaphors Longinus used in defining the sublime, is often highlighted in the English translations that Vanbrugh, Hawksmoor and their circle knew. That in itself makes it a congenial document for architects and those thinking about architectural design. But more importantly, it offers an approach to composition that is very different from the standard Vitruvian account found in the architectural treatises of the Italian Renaissance. Thus Longinus helps to understand something of the strangeness, and compelling visual quality of the designs of Hawksmoor.

Longinus defined the supreme quality of style we now generally call the sublime in intensely visual terms. Subsequently these have been somewhat obscured by the general acceptance of Boileau's translation of the original Greek term 'hupsos' as 'le sublime'. It is what the earlier English editions, faithful to the original, called 'the Height of Eloquence', in itself a visual metaphor. As John Hall put it: 'Height whenever it seasonably breaks forth, bears down all before it like a whirlwind, and presently evidences the *strength* and ability of the speaker'[46] – where 'to evidence' in itself is also a profoundly visual term, related etymologically to the Latin *videre*, to see. In the previous sentence he had compared the structure of a speech to the fabric of architecture: 'And when the *vivacity* of Invention, the *harmony* and *order* of Disposition cannot be discerned out of one or two clauses, but difficultly [sic] make themselves appear a generall *Survey* of the whole fabrick'.[47] Longinus also evoked the overwhelming effect of sublime eloquence by comparing it with the light of the sun:

> For see how like a small gleam approach't by the sun in its full lustre presently disappears, so the sophistry of rhetoric is wholly overshadowed, being so circumfused and covered by Height. Not unlike this is an observation we find in pictures; for after that Lines are drawn upon a *plain* and colours *laid on* and *shadowed* and enlivened,

> thrust in the light [that] projects a pleasant brightnesse, which is so much the more visible by how much you nearer approach it: even so Heights and Passions of speech neighbouring to our souls, as knit thereunto by a straight allyance, outshine the figures, and *only* stand in sight, overshadowing their art and clouding it in obscurity.[48]

This stress on the visual also extends to Longinus' views on life in general. Life is a theatre, in which man is both a spectator and a performer. In the words of the anonymous translation of 1698:

> Nature has not design'd Man to be a Creature of a low Rank, of an ignoble Standard, but has given him Life, and brought him into the world, as unto a great Theatre, like a curious Observer of all that passes in it; and not only so, but on this mighty stage, to be an high-spirited actor, breathing after nothing but glory and renown.[49]

At the same time, this visual approach to eloquence and life in general often takes on a distinctly architectural character, for instance when Longinus discusses composition:

> What then may we not say of composition? Which is the Harmony of Speech, the use whereof is natural to man? Which does not only strike the ear, but penetrates the mind, which masters up such different words, thoughts, things, and Elegancies suitable to the affections of the soul, which by a Mixture and Variety of pleasing sounds, crept into the mind, does create in him who hears them, the same passions that the Author himself has; and which [rests] upon *this stately pile* of words which the noble Structure of loftinesse [...].[50]

Hall's version also thematizes the similarities between literary composition and architectural design, but in a different manner:

> [composition] by mixing and moulding their sounds disposes the passion of the speaker, and infects all near him, and by all this adding magnificence to the structure of words, and raizing them up to glory and majesty.[51]

A comparison with the standard modern translation by D. A. Russell shows to what degree these early English translations foreground Longinus' visual metaphors and take them further:

> The combination and variety of its sounds convey the speaker's emotions to the minds of those around him and and make the hearers

share them. It fits great thoughts into a coherent structure by the way in which it builds up patterns of words.[52]

As we have seen in the previous chapter, rhetoric offered a definition of composition, concepts with which to achieve and analyse it, and often used architectural comparisons to illustrate it. Longinus and his translators made the similarity between prose composition and architectural design even stronger:

> But these men [...] choosing the most illustrious things that have been said, and knitting them according to their severall worths into one piece, produc'd nothing that was swelling, unbecoming or Pedantick. For such things infect the whole like washes, but great Buildings are raised up by the correspondence of parts one towards another.[53]

There is one passage in Longinus on sublime composition that directly brings to mind Hawksmoor's architectural composition. Longinus defined composition as the union of conflicting or contradictory elements. Here is his analysis of a description of Odysseus' shipwreck in the *Iliad*:

> Moreover, by forcing into an abnormal union prepositions not usually compounded [Homer] has tortured his language into conformity with the impending disaster, magnificently figured the disaster by the compression of his language, and almost stamped on the diction the precise form of the danger. [...] What [Homer, Sappho and Demostenes] have done is to clean up, as it were, the very best of the main points, and to fit them together, allowing nothing affected or undignified or pedantic to intervene. These things ruin the whole, by introducing, as it were, gaps and crevices into masses which are built together, walled in by their mutual relationships.[54]

This immediately recalls the abrupt transitions and 'conflicting unions' of Hawksmoor's St Alphege, the abrupt articulation of the spire of Christ Church, the disproportional enlargement of the key stones in the North façade of St George in the East, or, as Sophie Ploeg has shown, the careful combination of conflicting façades in St Anne Limehouse (Fig. 4.17).[55] It also ties in with one of Hawksmoor's rare statements about architectural composition, a letter of 1734 in which he argues that the South and North front of his design for Castle Howard should not be taken in completely at one glance, 'nor at any time upon the Diagonall (or angular view)'.[56]

What this juxtaposition of Longinus' analysis of literary composition and Hawksmoor's architectural composition shows, is not so much that we can

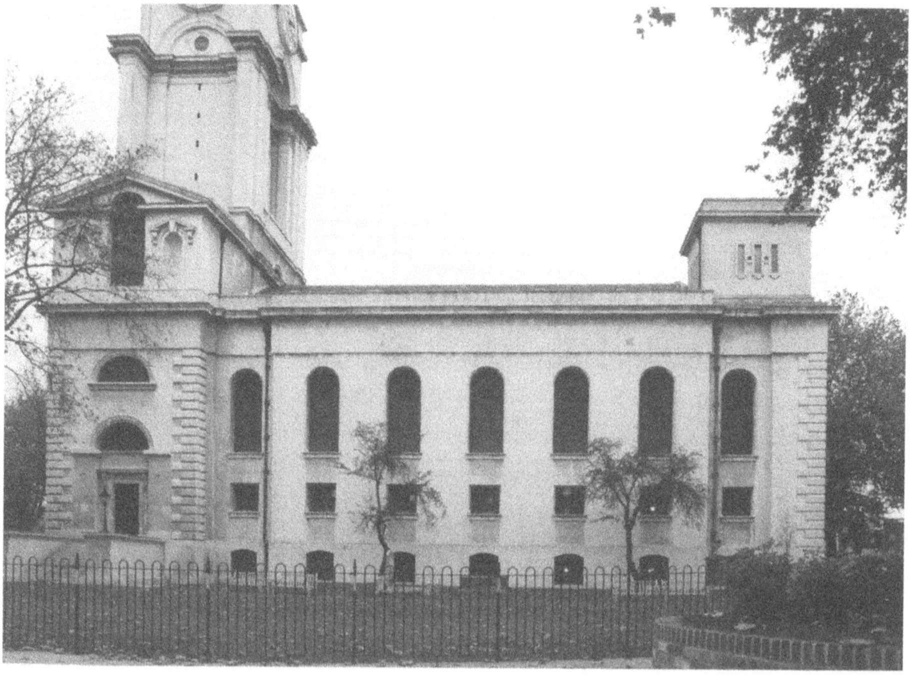

4.17 Nicholas Hawksmoor, St Anne Limehouse, London, façade and side. London, 1714 to 1719 (photo: Sophie Ploeg).

point out immediate traces or evidence that Hawksmoor or Vanbrugh had read Longinus and taken it to heart. Instead, the repeated introduction of Longinus in English both during and after the Civil War, and the publication of several Greek and Latin editions in Britain in the seventeenth century, opened up a new way of thinking about the arts and in particular composition. Up to that time relations between poetry and the visual arts or architecture had been conceived mainly in terms of *ut pictura poesis*. Now that Longinus had become accessible again, readers could become acquainted with another fusion between the arts and poetry, this time by presenting composition in visual and verbal terms, and at the same time by defining the sublime itself in intensely visual terms.

Longinus' book thereby offered architects and patrons a new way of thinking about architectural design and its perception. This differs fundamentally from modern approaches to architectural history. These tend to concentrate on stylistic analysis – asking whether a building is Baroque, Gothic or Renaissance; Continental or English Baroque – attribution, dating and authorship; they trace formal and stylistic genealogies, for instance by showing the similarities between Hawksmoor's Christ Church and the Basilica of Constantine and Maxentius in Rome, or the handling of the architectural orders and proportion.

Looking at architecture in a manner that is inspired by Longinus focuses on other aspects of a building, in particular on its composition considered as a union of conflicting opposites.

But the new editions of Longinus also made available what the whole book was about, the key concept of his aesthetic: the sublime. Before the English translations by Hall and others, the sublime aesthetic, as far as I have been able to trace, was not part of the English vocabulary used to discuss or appreciate architecture.[57] Vanbrugh's plea for a solemn and awful appearance in church design may be connected with the existing tradition of appreciating the Gothic for its sombre, imposing grandeur, but had not been used in the context of classical church design before Longinus was reintroduced. His treatise on the sublime points to an architectural aesthetic that is very different from the classical aesthetic set out in the treatises by Alberti or Palladio. These theorists all stressed harmony, simplicity, clarity and perspicuity. Longinus, and in his wake Vanbrugh, Hawksmoor and Wren, appreciated the intricate, the difficult, the dark and the awful.

In this interest in the impact of buildings on their beholders British writing on architecture of the seventeenth century is quite unique.[58] Continental writing, and in particular the main architectural treatises produced during the Renaissance in Italy, concentrated much more on the architectural object itself. Here we touch on a third point of agreement between Longinus and those involved in church building around 1700. Both Vanbrugh and Hawksmoor are concerned with the impression a building makes on the spectator. This is shown, for instance, by the memorandum Vanbrugh wrote for the Fifty Churches Commission that oversaw the large church building campaign that started in 1712 and resulted in Hawksmoor's City churches. There he stressed the importance of a solemn and awful *appearance*, not the intrinsic aesthetic qualities of the buildings themselves. Now the effect of a text on the spectator is precisely the issue that Longinus addresses in his treatise. Like so many rhetorical handbooks and treatises, it offers strategies and precepts of invention – how to compose a speech, how to move and persuade the audience, which figures of speech to use, etc. At the same time, these function also as strategies of interpretation for the reader, the public or the beholder. Longinus tells how to achieve the sublime in writings, in particular by his advice on composition, uniting the discordant for instance, or making deliberate use of the abrupt, but does so as well by showing us the effects of sublime speech and poetry on the reader. It is a typical case of the closeness in rhetoric of strategies of invention and interpretation. In this consideration of the effects of composition on the public, Longinus came very close to what we know of Hawksmoor's design practice. Hawksmoor was very interested in the appearance of a building, its effect on the spectator. In his mature professional work he often added coloured flaps to his drawings that would allow the viewer to form an idea

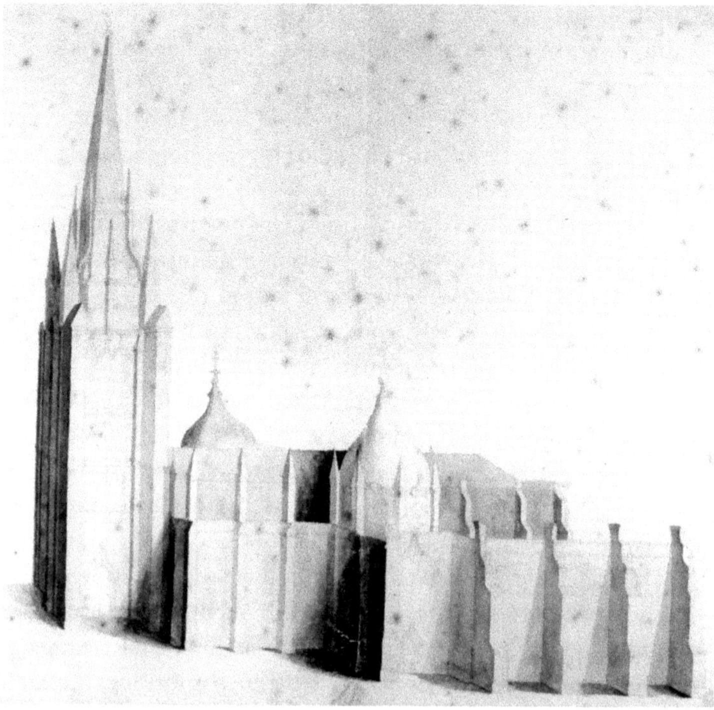

4.18 Nicholas Hawksmoor, design for St Mary, Warwick. Oxford, All Souls' College, *c.* 1694 to 1698 (photo: All Souls' College, Oxford).

of the different appearances a building could take on under varying conditions of daylight.

One of his earliest drawings shows this very clearly (Fig. 4.18).[59] In this small design for St Mary's Warwick he significantly departs from seventeenth-century practice to show architectural designs by means of drawings of the ground plan and façade in an orthogonal representation. Orthogonal projection was preferred to linear perspective because it allows the exact calculation of all dimensions. It shows you a building as you approach it frontally, whereas linear perspective shows it under one particular angle, from one, necessarily personal and individual perspective. But Hawksmoor chose a different manner: not the traditional, strongly mathematical and analytical techniques of orthogonal projection and linear perspective, but a view of the whole as it is touched by the rays of the sun which create light and shadow, and singles out projections and recesses, or clear and obscure parts. Just as a spectator would view the façade as a whole on a particular day; and just as Longinus tells us in a passage that caused his English translators to indulge in flights of visual metaphor: the blazing light of the sublime obscures the minor eloquence of isolated figures of speech.

'Architecture speaks a language of its own'

Coming at the end of the classical tradition in England, Sir John Soane (1753–1837) is probably the architect who left the most articulate statements on the ways in which buildings affect the spectator. The relation between buildings and their viewers is a major theme in the lectures he held for the Royal Academy, and he annotated the major classical rhetorical authors extensively. Architecture shares with rhetoric, he observed in his margin notes to Quintilian, the five stages of invention, disposition, elocution, memory and action. The question of course is, what he may have had in mind when saying this: what, for instance, can he have meant by architectural action or memory? Many issues that remain more or less implicit in seventeenth-century authors and architects were the object of extended scrutiny in his lectures and notes, particularly the power of architecture to speak to the beholder because it can excite memories and associations in the spectator's mind. In some respects this is part of the Picturesque aesthetic with which Soane was very familar.

The manipulation of the emotional response of the public to landscape gardens and architecture was one of the central issues in Picturesque theories as they were developed in Great Britain from the 1740s onwards. 'To move, to melt and elevate the mind' was the aim of landscape gardening according to Richard Payne Knight's poem *The Landscape* of 1795.[60] But given the importance of the impact of art on the memory and emotions of the beholder, Picturesque theories are surprisingly silent on how such direction can actually be achieved. Most eighteenth-century authors refer briefly to associationist philosophies of perception, memory and aesthetic response, some to the importance of a connoisseur's eye and a memory well-stocked with remembrances of works of art from the past. Yet the associationist view of the workings of the human mind is in an important sense rather meagre, since it only offers an explanation in formal terms of contiguity, likeness, causal or accidental connection. It does not offer a satisfactory explanation why particular works of art excite particular trains of associations and memories in one spectator, but excite entirely different reactions in another.

To find a discussion of the way these effects were actually achieved, we have to turn to a relatively late source on associationism, Archibald Alison's *Essay on Taste* of 1811, which offers the most detailed explanation of the way association works, and in particular to Francis Jeffrey's review in the Edinburgh Review of 1811. Like so many theorists on the Picturesque, Alison and Jeffrey distinguish between inquiries concerning the mental faculty that experiences the sensation of the Picturesque, and inquiries into the nature of beautiful, sublime or Picturesque objects, only to argue that the Picturesque is not a property of an object, but a sensation, 'produced [...] by the recollection or conception of *other* objects which are associated in our imaginations with those before us'.[61]

These objects affect us 'on the common and familiar principle of being the natural objects of love, or of pity, or of fear or veneration, or some other common and lively sensation of the mind. [...] All objects are beautiful or sublime which signify or suggest to us some simple emotion of love, pity, terror, or any other social or selfish affection of our nature'.[62]

The connection between these objects and the emotions they arouse is that objects may be natural signs or 'perpetual concomitants' of happiness, grief, anger or suffering; that they are accidental or arbitrary concomitants of these feelings; or that they show some analogy or fortuitous resemblance to circumstances or situations in which these emotions occurred.[63] Thus an English landscape considered as a combination of lines, forms and colours does not affect us; but we find it beautiful insofar as it presents us with a picture of human happiness that starts a train of associations and emotions in our minds:

> The mere forms and colours that compose its visible appearance, are no more capable of exciting any emotion in the mind, than the forms and colours of a Turkey carpet. It is sympathy with the present or the past, or the imaginary *inhabitants* of such a region, that alone gives it either interest or beauty.[64]

In these passages on the mechanism of association, Alison and Jeffrey formulated a theory that closely resembled David Hume's analysis of the laws of association in his *Enquiry Concerning the Principles of Human Understanding* of 1777, where all possible varieties of association are reduced to three principles: resemblance, contiguity in time or place, and cause and effect.[65]

In spite of the close resemblance between the position of the philosophers Hume and Alison on the way association works and the views of theorists of the Picturesque, the associationist position does not offer a satisfactory explanation. This is mainly because, both in the case of Hume and of Alison, the relation between objects and the emotions their perceptions arouse in the viewer is described in formal terms, varying from spatial and temporal contiguity to accidental resemblance or connection in the beholder's mind. The associationist view does not offer a satisfactory account of the reasons why a particular object sets in motion a particular train of emotions and memories, but only a general principle explaining the way associations are combined in very abstract terms. It is merely descriptive, and its view of the working of association can hardly function as a guide for design, because it does not really make clear how particular objects affect individual viewers. But there is more to the Picturesque manipulation of associations.

Picturesque theories of art do not take as their starting point the innocent, uneducated eye of the beholder. On the contrary, all authors stress the importance of education, both visual, literary, and historical, for art to make its effect.

The artistic education young gentlemen received by looking at Italian art during their Grand Tour was one of the elements that contributed to the development of the Picturesque; but as Alison, Knight and many others argued, we enjoy looking at nature or art because our education enables us to attach meanings and emotions to what we see. Archibald Alison, for instance, wrote that the beauty of the classical orders does not reside in their proportion, but in the associations of Roman grandeur, Greek culture and the classical past they evoke. This also recalls Wotton's view of Roman monuments as incitements to virtuous behaviour:

> [...] for they are the GRECIAN orders; they derive their origin from those times, and were the ornament of those countries which are most hallowed in our imaginations; and it is difficult to see them, even in their modern copies, without feeling them operate upon our minds as relics of those polished nations where they first arose, and of that greater people by whom they were afterwards borrowed.[66]

Picturesque landscapes or buildings excite memories of the past in the viewer, but only when the viewer has a well-stocked mind. Richard Payne Knight argued in *An Analytical Inquiry into the Principles of Taste* of 1805 that it is not tenable to think that the Picturesque is an inherent property of things. Instead, it consists in the effect, that is, the associations caused by it in the mind of the observer. The Picturesque – or rather, the sensation or experience of the Picturesque – consists of these effects, not of some objective and independent fitness of parks and buildings to serve as the subject of a painting. The starting-point of his *Analytical Inquiry* is the statement that there exists no fixed and definable combination of colours, lines and forms, which in itself gives pleasure to the senses or the mind.[67] The pleasure that architecture, music or paintings give us is located not in these works of art themselves, but in their association with the sensations they cause in us.[68] The connoisseur will enjoy a landscape in a higher degree than somebody with an untrained eye, because he or she is familiar with the work of Giorgione, Poussin or Claude Lorrain. Once a particular train of associations has been made, it will haunt us, whether we like it or not: 'so that we feel ourselves in a situation not unlike that of a moth fluttering around a candle'. Every work of art or nature will excite memories of those we already know, recall these works to the mind in their former vividness and throw new light on them, so that 'recollection enhances enjoyment, and enjoyment brightens recollection'. The philosopher or the natural historian will find in the insect that is thoughtlessly crushed by a peasant occasion for unlimited speculation and reflection; and the blue vault of the sky will be transformed by means of a train of associations leading from the 'lowest dregs of animated matter' to the 'incomprehensible throne of Omnipotence itself'.[69]

That is, landscapes (or gardens or buildings) can only exercise their Picturesque effect on the mind of the viewer by drawing on what we would now call cultural memory; precisely the mental faculty that Wotton and Jones also used when arguing for the persuasive powers of architecture or the theatre. That remembrances of the past were an important factor in Picturesque sensations is shown, for instance, by Thomas Whately's *Observations on Modern Gardening* (published in 1770), the first English treatise on the aims, methods and achievements of landscape gardening. He stressed the importance of considerations of character in designing a landscape garden, by which the imagination and sensibility of the visitor are affected. Ruins are particularly effective in this respect:

> [. . .] they are a class by themselves, beautiful as objects, expressive as characters [. . .] imperfection and obscurity are their properties; and to carry the imagination to something greater than is seen, their effect. [. . .] besides the characters expressed by their style and position, they suggest ideas which would not arise from the buildings, if entire. The purposes of many have ceased [. . .] and certain sensations of regret, of veneration, or compassion, attend the recollection.[70]

For Soane too, buildings speak to us because they are monuments. In the Academy Lectures the power of ruins to excite trains of associations and a wide range of emotions in the mind of the beholder is demonstrated in terms that recall those Wotton and Wren used:

> The monument of the Horatii and Curatii fills us with respect for the patriotic and the heroic deeds to which it refers, whilst the remains of many towering structures, broken arches, and massive walls, bring back to our recollections interesting, important and instructive incidents of history which call forth all the nobler feelings of the sympathetic mind [. . .]. [. . .] when such sensations are raised, if the ruins of buildings bring the recollection of such deeds fresh to the mind, as if then acting, we are only anxious for time to spare such monuments, that the same effect may produced to the latest ages. Here there is no delusion, no imaginary colouring: the effect on the mind is complete.[71]

The phrase 'recollection of deeds [. . .] then acting' suggests that the viewer of such powerfully evocative monuments is present at the actual performance of heroic actions. Soane is more detailed than most of his contemporaries on the actual working of the mechanisms of association. He noted in his preparations for the Academy Lectures, adapting Quintilian, that 'the art of architecture consists of the effect which the perfection of a work has upon the eye'. These effects depend on the union of building, painting, sculpture and landscape gardening in architectural design. In his notes for the Lectures he quotes with approval Roger de Piles' *Life of the Painters*:

> the whole, arising from the combination of several objects, must not be like a number made up of several unities, independent and equal among themselves, but like one poetical whole: all the objects, lines, colors, lights and shades of a picture, are great or small, strong or weak, only by comparison; but let their natures, qualities, or conditions be what they will, they have such a relation to one another in their combination as no one in particular can supersede. For the effect of the whole consists in a general subordination where the darks heighten the lights, and the lights set off the darks, and where the merit of each part is formed on a mutual dependence.[72]

Architects, like painters and orators, must compose their works. There is no persuasion without disposition. They must order the parts of a building, give some prominence by making them stand out, and make others subordinate by hiding them in the shade, or make important parts of a building catch the eye through their prominent decoration, whereas the background is handled more discreetly through a uniform and inconspicuous handling of materials. This recalls Longinus' advice on the use of contrasting elements in sublime composition. One of the most sophisticated cases of this approach to design is Soane's Dulwich Gallery, where the orders are treated in such an abstract manner, being simply indicated by brick relief, that they have become mere remembrances of their marble forebears. The walls, made of uniform brick, are handled as discreet, inconspicuous foils to major elements such as the entrance or roof, which stand out because their finish makes them catch the light. In other words, architects, like orators, must not only invent; they must also order their material in such a manner that it is clear what the building or speech is about and catches the eye or the ear of the public.

Soane had little to say about the architectural counterpart of elocution; but his treatment of the architectural counterparts of *memoria* and *actio* is highly original. Soane described the way in which a building can affect the mind in terms taken not from painting but from rhetoric and poetics. Antique architecture possessed an unequalled power to touch the viewer. Seeing and walking through a building may be compared with watching a play unfold on the stage:

> The front of a building is like the prologue of a play, it prepares us for what we are to expect. If the outside promises more than we find in the inside, we are disappointed. The plot opens itself in the first act and is carried on through the remainder, through all the mazes of

> character, convenience of arrangement, elegance and propriety of ornaments, and lastly produces a complete whole in distribution, decoration and construction.[73]

Looking at a building and watching a play are similar experiences, not because buildings use theatrical ornaments or are designed like theatre sets (although that happens, as in Hawksmoor and Vanbrugh's designs of Castle Howard, whose groundplan looks very much like a Baroque stage set with its receding wings meeting each other at the centre of the building; Figs. 4.19 and 4.20), but because both are *temporal* arts. Both the experience of watching a play from the prologue to the last act, and that of walking through a building unfold in the course of time. In both arts composition is built on the assumption that the viewer is able to follow the plot, or grasp the connections on which dramatic or architectural composition is based. Designing or looking at a building both draw on a cultural memory shared by the architect and the viewer, but also on the viewer's capacity to appreciate the building as a whole, an experience that unfolds in time. In Soane's buildings such experience is achieved through the activation of cultural memory and the representation of character, as his own remarks on Pitzhanger show, the London house he largely rebuilt for himself in 1800–1803 (Fig. 4.21). The mind is activated by using the visual arts, landscape gardening and even drama in architectural design. Such elements taken from other arts serve as clues for spectators to grasp what is offered to their eyes, but also as a design strategy for the artist. Thus he admonished his students that:

> In every poem we seek for a distinguishing and chief object; in every picture, a principal figure or group, a principal colour, a principal light, to which every other must be subservient; from these as so many radii, the other parts diverge.[74]

His description of Pitzhanger catalogues the use of elements taken from other arts both in creating and in perceiving allusions:

> Describe the front. No man will suppose that the architect or owner had attained civic crowns for saving the lives of his fellow citizens [...]. To judge of this species of building we should endeavour to discover the object to be attained: for example, in the building before you, if we suppose the person about to build possessed of a number of detached pieces of ornament, such as eagles and wreaths, demiboys and foliage, columns and statues, pedestals and acroters &c, and that from a desire to preserve them from ruin, or to form a building to give

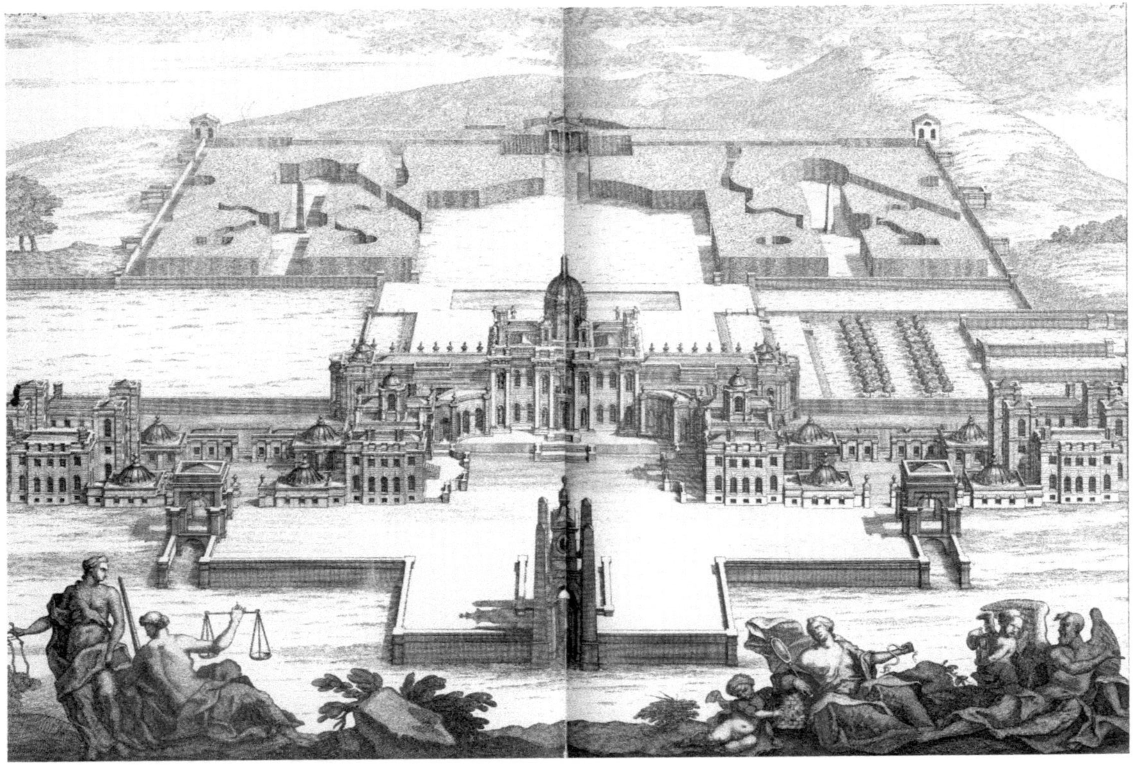

4.19 Sir John Vanbrugh and Nicholas Hawksmoor, view of Castle Howard, Yorkshire. From: Colen Campbell, *Vitruvius Britannicus*, London, volume III, 1725, plate 6 (photo: Department of Art History, Leiden University, Netherlands).

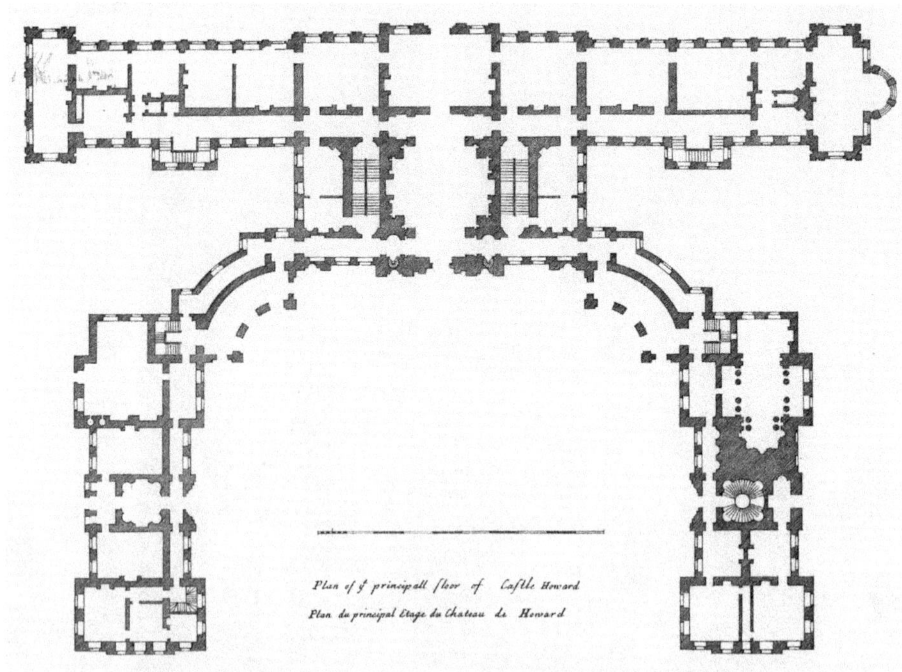

4.20 Sir John Vanbrugh and Nicholas Hawksmoor, plan of Castle Howard, Yorkshire. From: Colen Campbell, *Vitruvius Britannicus*, London, volume I, 1715, plate 62 (photo: Department of Art History, Leiden University, Netherlands).

> a faint idea of an Italian villa . . . this building may thus be considered as a picture, a sort of portrait.

That is, cultural memory, activated through the use of iconic, figurative elements borrowed from painting and poetry, is used as the material to represent character in a building.

With the representation of character we reach the last of the parallels Soane suggested between architecture and rhetoric. In oratory *actio* or delivery is the final stage. Successful delivery depends on the use of the right gesture, dress and expression, which all must serve to establish the credentials of the orator and his case. Persuasive delivery is based, at least partly, on the character, the *ethos* the speaker tries to establish. This is probably the basis for Soane's vehement identification of rhetorical action with architectural character:

> [. . .]every building whether great or small,– simple or elegant, must like the picture speak intelligibly to the beholder, – each must have a positive character, peculiar to itself; sufficient to point out the purpose and uses for which it was erected: – this cannot be attained if the

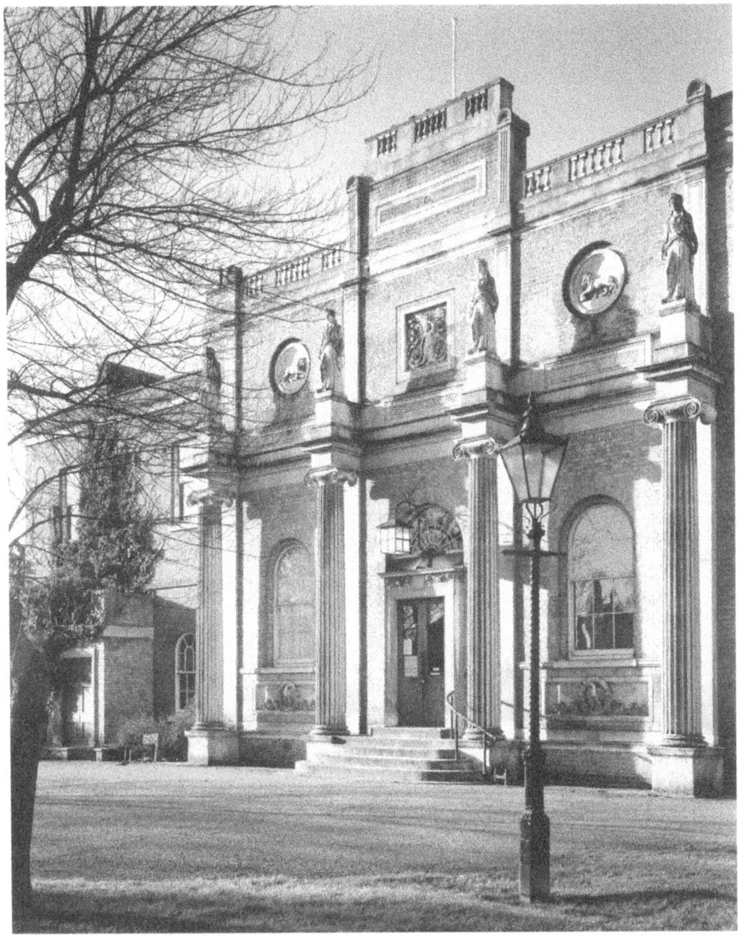

4.21 Sir John Soane, Pitzhanger Manor, Ealing, 1800 to 1803 (photo: Martin Charles).

work is deficient in character – The Athenian Orator being asked what were the great requisitions in his art, replied, action – action – action; so if it were asked what constituted the distinctive beauties in architectural composition, the answer would be, character – character – character.[75]

This is double-edged advice: the designer must show the purpose and function of a building in a way the viewer can understand, otherwise it cannot speak the language of the viewer and remains dumb. But this passage is not simply about the adequate and understandable representation of function. A building must have character like the orator, that is relate in some way to the beliefs, convictions and memories of the viewer. Somehow buildings must

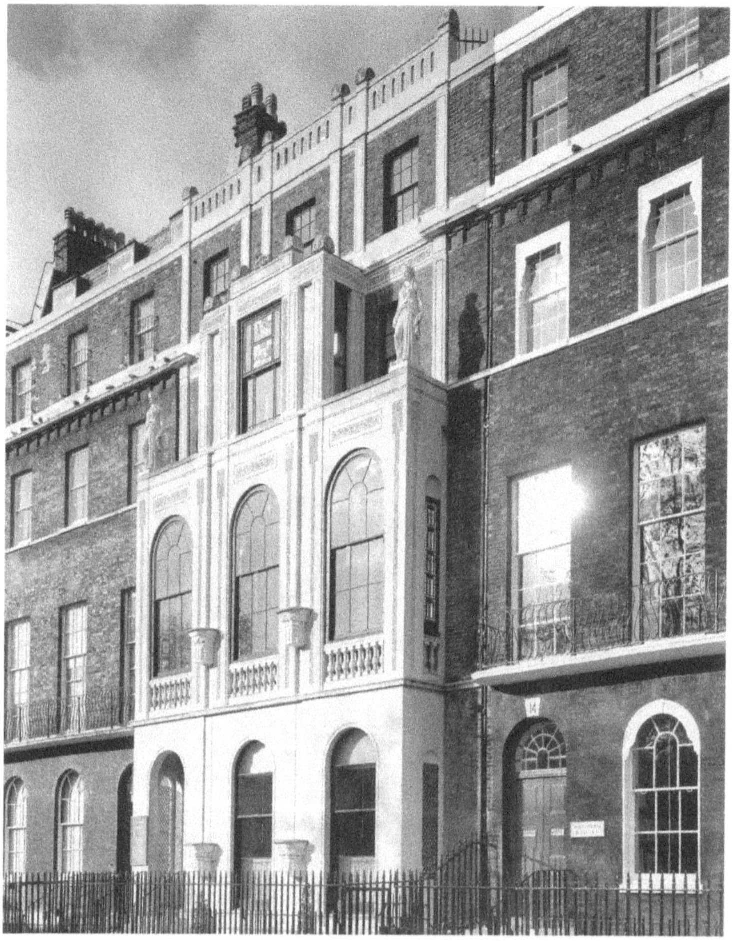

4.22 Sir John Soane, Lincoln's Inn Fields, No. 12. London, 1792 to 1794 (photo: Martin Charles).

become human or at least suggest a common ground between the built and man. This is achieved through theatricality, which conditions both architectural design and the viewers' reponse to buildings, drawing on their memories to engage with a building in the way they engage with a play acted before their eyes.

At the same time, considering buildings as portraits of characters enabled Soane to use devices of plot that are found both in historical painting and in drama. The best-known instance of their use is his own house in Lincoln's Inn Fields (Fig. 4.22), where the succeeding rooms, passages and their decoration offer a portrait of the many aspects of Soane's personality, his pursuits, his education, and the cultural milieu of which he made himself a part, gradually unfolding as the visitor walks through the house. Similarly, the façade of Pitzhanger Manor with its sarcophagi, isolated elements of the orders, and fragments of classical statuary offers a view of the architect almost as a deconstructor of the classical style: here are a number of its essential elements, together with the funerary and sacrificial associations that are so essential to its original functions and meaning, but presented almost as building blocks which the architect may assemble as he likes. But the drama in Soane's buildings is not only a drama of character; it is an architectural drama, and therefore one of the handling of light and space, of the direction of movement, and of a progression of points of view. Soane's buildings can never be grasped completely by looking at the façade and groundplan: one has to walk through them. The secret of their beauty lies not, or not only, in their handling of proportion and classical ornament, but in the way they make the spectator see and feel what it is to create and handle space by the manipulation of light, shade and mass.

In his review of Alison's *Essay on Taste* Jeffrey observed that the arousal of the emotions by art or scenery is achieved through a creative act of the mind:

> When we are injured, we feel indignation, – when we are wounded, we feel pain [...] without any effort of the imagination, or the intervention of any picture or vision in the mind. But when we feel indignation, or admiration, in consequence of seeing some piece of inanimate matter that merely suggests or recalls to us the ordinary causes or proper objects of these emotions, it is evident that our fancy is set to work, and that the effect is produced by means of a certain poetical creation, or a train of images and conceptions that are conjured up in the mind. [...] We are employed, therefore, partly in composing and delineating this inward and ideal picture of the objects of our emotions, and partly only in receiving the emotions which it excites.[76]

The experience of beauty consists of an act of creative visualization by the human mind. When we call some building or piece of scenery beautiful, we really mean to say that we are moved by it in some way; this affection sets in motion a train of associations in the mind. But this is not a passive, mechanical reaction that reactivates already formed links between objects and feelings. It is a creative act of the imagination that visualizes and composes before the mind's eye the objects that originally caused us to feel pity, anger, love or hatred. All associationists link objects or situations with the arousal of emotion, and mainly describe these links in terms of contiguity, contrast and likeness; but Alison is important because he draws attention to the active role of the mind in forging these connections. His contemporary, Soane, showed how the design activity of the architect closely resembles both the orator's and that of the viewer. *Memoria* is the basis for this resemblance: not in the sense of learning a speech by heart, but in the sense of cultural memory, which the designer needs as a formal vocabulary, the orator to find a common ground with his audience, and the viewer in order to grasp what he or she is looking at. The process of looking, considered in Picturesque terms, is an active one, in which the viewer follows the thread of the composition in the same terms of invention, composition and elocution the architect uses to articulate the design process. Both the very essence of the Picturesque, which is to move the spectator through the allusive image set before the eyes; the doctrine of the sister arts through which that richness of meaning is constructed; and the stress on active visualization as part of the aesthetic experience are core issues in classical rhetoric.[77] Active visualization is the means through which the public is moved by paintings, landscape gardens or buildings. As Richard Payne Knight observed, to the uneducated observer the night sky is meaningless, and so are the masterworks of painting and architecture. But we might also turn this around: works of art that do not in some way refer to the life and history of the community for which they are made, do not possess any meaning.

Notes

1 See Wittkower (1980), p. 195. A century earlier, Vittoria Colonna observed about Michelangelo's *Last Judgment*: '[painting] incites the melancholy to gladness and to the contented and troubled alike brings knowledge of the misery of man; the contumacious it brings to contrition, the wordly to repentance, the impious and non-contemplative to contemplation and fear and shame'. Fr. de Holanda, *Diálogos em Roma*, p. 81. According to Holanda this conversation took place in 1538.

2 Alberti, *De re aedificatoria* VII.3, ed. Rykwert, pp. 194–5.

3 For a selection of these sources see Van Eck (ed.), *British Architectural Theory* 1540–1750, pp. 143–237.

4 See Gent (1995) for a many-angled discussion of the introduction of classicism in Britain and the conflicts associated with it.

5 E. Bolton, *Elements of Armouries*, f. A1v.

6 J. Guillim, *A Display of Heraldrie*, p. a. Cf. Hart (1993), who lists many instances of seventeenth-century English connections between architecture, heraldry and emblematics; Chirelstein (1990); and Henderson (1995), p. 133 on the use of entire buildings as emblems, such as Sir Thomas Tresham's garden lodge at Lyveden New Bield, which was built in the plan of a cross and covered with symbols of heraldry and the passion of Christ.

7 Sir Henry Wotton, *Elements of Architecture*, pp. 29 and 33.

8 Ben Jonson, *Works*, vol. 7, pp. 90–1. Cf. Hart (1993), pp. 64–5.

9 Sir Henry Wotton, 'A Panegyrick to King Charles [...]', p. 159.

10 Cf. F. Hard, Introduction to the 1968 reprint of the *Elements*, pp. xlv–xlvi.

11 On Wotton see Pearsall Smith (1906); the entry on him in Harris and Savage (1992); and Ploeg (2006). Wotton's manuscript writings were published in 1651 by Izaak Walton in *Reliquiae Wottonianae.*

12 Wotton, *Elements of Architecture*, p. 102.

13 As a provost of Eton Wotton urged the pupils not to neglect rhetoric, for '*Almighty God has left Mankind affections to be wrought upon*': 'The Life of Sir Henry Wotton', p. d3. In [Izaak Walton, ed.]. Sir Henry Wotton. *Reliquiae Wottonianae*, 1672 edition.

14 On Elizabethan awareness of the importance of non-verbal communication, its political aspects and wide use see Hazard (2000), in particular pp.138–63 on the use of buildings such as Sir Thomas Gresham's Triangular Lodge as silent statements of religious belief or political convictions. Her description on p. 163 of the elaborate and highly public dinner rituals at the court of Elizabeth I is suggestive. These were 'epideictic ceremonies for which the physical [and architectural] setting was the stage. Physical elevation signified elevated social status, the ascent beginning with the climb to the upstairs location of the dining chamber [...] the ascent was kinetically enacted by a series of processions'.

15 'A Philosophical Surveigh of Education, or Moral Architecture [...] proclaiming another Worke [...] a Philosophicall Survey of Education, which is

indeed a second *Building*, or repairing of Nature, and as I may term it, a kind of *Morall Architecture*? *Reliquiae Wottonianae*, pp. 330–1. Wotton never completed this book, but announced it at the end of the *Elements of Architecture*.

16 Sallust, *Bellum Iugurthinum* IV.5.

17 Cicero, *Philippicae* IX.i.3. In *De Oratore* III.xlvi.180 he observed that in temples, as in 'oratory and most things nature contrived', usefulness is always allied with dignity, and sometimes with beauty as well. *Dignitas* for the Romans was not only a matter of private behaviour, but had important political connotations. See for similar views Florus, *Epitome* IV.2 and Martial, *Epigrams* 7 and 9.

18 Sir Christopher Wren, 'Tract I', reprinted in Soo (1998a), pp. 153–7.

19 Cf. Onians (1999), pp. 181–92.

20 Onians (1999) p. 206. Quintilian VI. ii.26–32. Other relevant places for this distinction include Horace, *Epistulae* I.xix.14 and Cicero *Pro Sestio* XI.26.

21 Tacitus, *Agricola* II.2: 'Memoriam quoque ipsam cum voce perdidissemus, si tam in nostra potestate esset oblivisci quam tacere'. See also Moore (1998).

22 Wotton, *Elements of Architecture*, p. I.

23 Wotton's use of the expression 'royaltie of sight' recalls Sir Philip Sidney's *New Arcadia*, line 91, where Basilius' lodge 'gives the eye lordship over a good large circuit'.

24 Cf. Peacock (1995), Chapter One.

25 On this ceremonial role of triumphal arches see Brilliant (1967).

26 Orgel and Strong (1973), vol. II, p. 730, ll. 22–3; cf. Peacock (1995), p. 259.

27 Cf. Peacock (1995), p. 218. He relates Jones' proscenia to the pioneering use of this feature by the Florentine Riccio's design for *L'Ortensia* of 1560. The earliest author to associate the beginning of a play or speech with a portico is probably the sixteenth-century Venetian writer about art Francisco Sansovino. In his treatise on rhetoric (*Dell'Arte Oratoria Libri Tre*, fol. 5r he wrote: 'Il Proemio nell'Oratione è somigliante a una bella e ricca entrata di un magnifico e ben inteso Palazzo di dentro debbe essere ben ornato, con perfetta Architettura composto, & insieme tutto corrispondente alle parti, cosi questa entrata dell'Oratione, è l'imagine et il dimostramento di quel si dee dire e trattare'. At about the same time the poet Torquato Tasso made a similar observation in his *Discorsi*, p. 21: the first stanza of a poem 'should be full of grandeur, magnificence and splendour, like the façade of palaces'.

28 Cf. Peacock (1995), p. 35.

29 Quoted in Orgel and Strong (1973), vol. I, p. 50.

30 Orgel and Strong (1973), vol. I, p. 7, where Orgel observes that the use of linear perspective flourished only at the court.

31 A notable exception is Orgel (1971), pp. 109–25, which sees Jones' text as the expression of Jones' tendency to classicize and christianize Britain's prehistoric and pagan past, particularly in his dedication to Coelus, but does not discuss the issue of architectural representation.

32 L. B. Alberti, *De re aedificatoria*, VI.i.

33 For an overview of seventeenth- and eighteenth-century studies of Stonehenge see Haycock (2002).

34 J. Webb (ed.), *The Most Notable Antiquity of Great Britain, Vulgarly Called Stoneheng* (1655 edition), p. 3.

35 Webb, *The Most Notable Antiquity*, p. 55.

36 Webb, *The Most Notable Antiquity*, p. 65.

37 Webb, *The Most Notable Antiquity*, p. 65.

38 Webb, *The Most Notable Antiquity*, p. 105.

39 Cf. Kishlansky (1996), pp. 68–82.

40 Cf. Peacock (1995), p. 74.

41 Cf. Orgel and Strong (1973), vol. II, p. 732. See also Hart and Tucker (2001), for an interpretation of the use of classical architecture in Banqueting House as a representation of ideals of kingship drawing on Jones' annotations to Aristotle's *Ethica Nicomacheia*.

42 Sir John Summerson (1978), pp. 84–90 for instance, developed an analysis of Hawksmoor's churches in terms of a conflict between Gothic, dynamic axiality based on East-West liturgical orientation and a classical square and static plan. Another approach, developed by Pierre de la Ruffinière du Prey, has related Hawksmoor's church designs, especially their spatial lay-out and spires, to theological concerns, in particular the Anglican interest in basing the London City churches on those of the early Christians; this has led to the discovery of much hitherto unconsidered sources and many new insights, but comparatively little insight in Hawksmoor's actual handling of the classical style. See Du Prey (1989) and (2000). Vaughan Hart has shown in Hart (2002), pp. 70–2 how elements of Hawksmoor's designs can be traced back to examples in treatises or pattern books.

43 John Hall, *Peri hupsous, Or, Dionysius Longinus on the Height of Eloquence. Rendered out of the Originall*, Preface.

44 Ploeg (2005).

45 Sir John Vanbrugh, 'Mr Van-Brugg's Proposals about Building ye New Churches' [1712], pp. 136–8.

46 John Hall, *Peri hupsous, Or, Dionysius Longinus on the Height of Eloquence*, p. iii (= I.4).

47 John Hall, *Peri hupsous, Or, Dionysius Longinus on the Height of Eloquence*, p. iii (= XVII.2).

48 John Hall, *Peri hupsous, Or, Dionysius Longinus on the Height of Eloquence*, ibid.

49 Anonymous, *An Essay on the Sublime. Translated from the Greek of Dionysius Longinus Cassius, the Rhetorician* (1698), p. 74 (= XXXV.2).

50 James Pulteney, *A Treatise of the Loftiness or Elegancy of Speech. Written originally in Greek . . . and now translated*

out of French by Mr J. P. (1698 [1680]), p. 174 (=XXXIX.3).

51 J. Hall, *Peri hupsous, Or, Dionysius Longinus on the Height of Eloquence*, p. lxxi (=XXXIX.3).

52 Longinus, *On the Sublime* XXXIX.3 in Russell and M. Winterbottom (1972), p. 497.

53 John Hall, *Peri hupsous, Or, Dionysius Longinus on the Height of Eloquence*, p. xxiv (= XXXIX.3).

54 Longinus, *On the Sublime* (1995), Section X, pp. 203–5.

55 Ploeg (2005).

56 Nicholas Hawksmoor, Letter to Lord Carlisle, 13 July 1734, reprinted in Downes (1979), p. 254.

57 Milton's *Paradise Lost* is the most familiar case of seventeenth-century sublime aesthetic in England. This is not the place to go into the complex issue of the relations between Milton's poem and Hawksmoor's designs, but in addressing it we should distinguish at least four aspects: the sublime subject matter of the epic (when Dryden and Addison called Milton 'sublime', they had this in mind); sublime style (for instance, the use of abrupt and daring juxtapositions, something shared by both artists, and very prominent in Satan's speeches); the effect of the sublime on the reader or viewer (achieved by Milton's vivid descriptions and larger-than-life subject, again something for which we can find parallels in Hawksmoor's inflation of classical elements); and the role of architecture in *Paradise Lost.*

58 For more sources on this tendency, and a more extended discussion, see Van Eck (ed.), *British Architectural Theory* 1540–1750, pp. 8–9, 25–6, 123–7 and 221.

59 Downes (1996), p. 29.

60 R. P. Knight, *The Landscape, a Didactic Poem in Three Books*, vol. II, l. 162.

61 Anon [Francis Jeffrey], review of *Essays on the Nature and Principles of Taste*, by Archibald Alison, *The Edinburgh Review*, May 1811, vol. 18, nr. xxxv, p. 3.

62 [Francis Jeffrey], review of *Essays on the Nature and Principles of Taste*, by Archibald Alison, p. 3.

63 [Francis Jeffrey], review of *Essays on the Nature and Principles of Taste*, by Archibald Alison, p. 11.

64 [Francis Jeffrey], review of *Essays on the Nature and Principles of Taste*, by Archibald Alison, p. 13.

65 David Hume, *An Enquiry Concerning Human Understanding*, pp. 23–5.

66 Archibald Alison, *Essay on Taste*, vol. II, pp. 156–7, quoted in [Francis Jeffrey], review of *Essays on the Nature and Principles of Taste*, by Archibald Alison, pp. 32–3.

67 Richard Payne Knight, *An Analytical Inquiry into the Principles of Taste*, p. 4.

68 Knight, *An Analytical Inquiry into the Principles of Taste*, p. 143ff.

69 Knight, *An Analytical Inquiry into the Principles of Taste*, p. 136.

70 Th. Whately, *Observations on Modern Gardening* (1770), quoted from Hunt (1975), pp. 301–8. For similar sentiments see William Shenstone, *Unconnected Thoughts on Gardening* (1764), also reprinted in Hunt (1975), pp. 289–98.

71 Sir John Soane, *Academy Lectures*, p. 626.

72 Cf. Soane, Soane Museum case 161/4, convolute 'P': 'Disposition should be also considered because it gives a value to everything that invention has supplied it with, [. . .] every thing that is most proper to make an impression upon the eye and the mind of the spectator'.

73 Soane, *Academy Lectures*, pp. 187–8.

74 Soane, *Academy Lectures*, ibid.

75 Soane, ms. Lecture V 1819, fols 73ff., in Soane Museum Library AL Soane Case 156.

76 [Francis Jeffrey], review of *Essays on the Nature and Principles of Taste*, by Archibald Alison, pp. 26–7.

77 Cf. Soane's strong belief in the unity of the visual arts, for instance in ms. Lecture V 1819, fols 73ff.: 'I must here recall to the minds of the students the importance of that intellectual relation, that secret charm, which in connecting one liberal art with another combines them all together: Painting, Sculpture and Architecture, when united from one grand whole, calculated to improve the intellectual feeling, and to increase the happiness and convenience of individuals'.

PART III

INTERPRETATION

FIVE:
RHETORICAL INTERPRETATION OF THE VISUAL ARTS

Invention and interpretation in rhetoric

At the end of the *Institutio Oratoria*, after the delineation of the personality of the ideal orator, Quintilian introduced a rhetorical concept that was to be most influential in art history: the concept of style.[1] The ideal orator is the gentleman expert at speaking, Cato's *vir bonus dicendi peritus*. But just as there is not one personality type everybody agrees is the best orator, there is not one single style of speaking which is most appropriate for every subject, occasion and audience. To illustrate this point he compares oratory to painting and sculpture, distinguishing various genera and species in an attempt to draw up a classification of speaking styles that is not normative. Here for the first time in European art styles of invention and elocution are used to classify art on the basis of individual and group characteristics. Painting and sculpture differ in genus (there is an Etruscan and an Athenian school for instance) and in species, because individual statues and paintings differ from each other as well. In the visual arts and oratory the artists and speakers differ, but the audience and situation in which they occur as well, and therefore there is no perfect orator or artist for all times and critics.

Quintilian then gives a brief history of painting, sculpture and oratory which was to be mined by Renaissance authors looking for a critical vocabulary. His history of painting styles singles out aspects of composition and creative ability: the handling of colour, line, light and shade, roundness and solidity in the representation of the human body; the capacity to take trouble over a painting or to depict imaginary scenes; talent and grace. Similar qualities of the artist are mentioned in the history of sculpture. Quintilian also sketches a development from the hardness of early beginnings through a less rigid style to the softness and beauty (*decor*) of Myron. This is echoed in his evaluation of Roman and Greek orators: relatively uncouth speakers such as Laelius, Cato or the Gracchi are compared to Polygnotus, Callon and other sculptors of the early, hard style. After an intermediate stage represented by Lucius Crassus and Quintus Hortensius Roman oratory began to flourish in the age of Julius Caesar.

Quintilian then described the style of the orators of this period, lasting from the first century BC to his own age, in terms that were originally used to describe characters or personalities: vigour, talent, subtlety, diligence, dignity, austerity, gravity, sharpness of wit, bitterness, mellowness, charm and elegance. That is, human or rather personal characteristics are attributed to oratory and to works of art; but to analyse the development of the art, Quintilian used concepts such as style or composition originally developed to analyse the writing process.[2]

Classical rhetoric developed manifold strategies of persuasion, but it was also concerned with interpretation. It gave persuasive expression to thought, but this was not considered merely as a matter of finding the right formulation for some thought that had already been fully expressed in the speaker's mind.[3] It was an interpretive activity that did not simply offer alternative wordings but shaped thought. The concept of style is perhaps the clearest case of rhetoric's double-edged potential. Although Quintilian did not use the term 'stilus', instead employing the biological concepts of genus and species when analysing style, his discussion is the origin of that essential instrument of art-historical interpretation, the concept of style. All rhetorical instruction and practice is based on the principle that speakers have a choice in how to say what they want to say, in the formulation of their subject matter. Similarly, modern art-historical discourse about style is based on this principle insofar as it uses style in the sense of a distinctive way in which a work of art is made: 'There can be no question of style unless the speaker or writer has the possibility of choosing between alternative forms of expression'.[4] Quintilian was not the first to do so; Cicero, for instance, presented his version of the doctrine of *genera dicendi*, and stressed the importance of a fit style of address, but Quintilian's discussion is particularly relevant for us because he is the first to talk about the visual arts in terms of style.[5]

The guidance for interpretation that rhetoric offered could be extended to the visual arts and architecture.[6] The conceptual basis for this use is the distinction between *res* and *verba*, between what to say and how to say it, or between subject matter and its representation. This distinction is reflected in the five *officia oratoris* by the division between invention, finding the subject matter, on the one hand, and elocution, its apt and persuasive formulation, on the other. It presents the orator with an analytical instrument to find the best relation between subject matter and its formulation. This relation was a frequent theme among rhetoricians.[7] Quintilian put it most succinctly: 'Every speech however consists at once of that which is expressed and that which expresses, that is to say of matter and words'.[8] Early humanists shared this awareness. In the speech Guarino Veronese held at the opening of the Studio in Ferrara in 1442 he praised rhetoric for its power to clothe and ornament the material offered by other disciplines. Without rhetoric, the other arts would be naked and bereft of speech, and would hardly dare to go out into the daylight.[9]

The rhetorical conviction that ideas may be formulated in various ways according to the aims of the speaker also served as a guide in analysing and interpreting discourse. In Cicero's *Brutus* the relation between *res* and *verba* is one of the criteria by which to judge a speech.[10] The decisions made by a speaker while writing his speech are at the same time clues for the public to understand its significance. Some awareness of the possibilities rhetoric offers as an interpretative instrument can already be found in Quintilian: he pointed out that students can decide with the help of rhetorical writing instructions whether a story is credible or not.[11] His observations in Book VIII on other orators and their speeches show how his instructions for eloquence may also serve to analyse and judge existing speeches. The instructions for determining the nature of a question and adapting a speech to it may also be used as a strategy of interpretation. Every orator must ask three questions of a new case: 'Is it the case?', 'What is it?' and 'Of what is it?'. These could well be used as the basis for the interpretation of a text.[12] The instructions of forensic oratory, for instance about determining the nature and status of the evidence or about what to do in case of conflicting law texts,[13] can in fact be considered as interpretative strategies which enable the orator to form a judgement about facts and represented opinions.

Rhetoric, that is, provided not only strategies of invention, but also of interpretation, or hermeneutics. Their closeness is also illustrated by the traditional etymological association of the Greek root of that term with the god Hermes, who brought messages of the gods to humankind (*hermeneia*). This suggests that *hermeneia* originally signified the statement or announcement of meaning rather than interpretation or exegesis. In Plato's *Gorgias* the protagonist is made to say that rhetoric 'makes one capable to speak as well as to understand what is being said'.[14] For Aristotle *hermeneia* was semiology, the discipline of signs which serves to communicate feelings and thoughts to the world. The treatise on style by Demetrius (*c.* 270 BC) was called *Peri hermeneias*, by which he meant not the selection of the right words, but the apt and persuasive formulation of thought.[15] Accordingly *hermeneia* came to mean the expression, the statement of an interpretation, and not the explanation of difficult or obscure passages in ancient poets and religious texts, which is the meaning the theological and philosophical discipline of hermeneutics subsequently acquired.[16] According to Clement of Alexandria, for instance, St Paul said that Christ was God's *hermeneus*. This does not turn Him into a scholar of biblical scripture, but into God's messenger to humankind.[17] Philo of Alexandria, a Hellenistic Jew who lived in the first century BC, developed a very detailed allegorical interpretation of the Septuagint, the Greek translation of the Hebrew Old Testament. He distinguished three mental faculties: the soul or mind which is the faculty of thought; perception, concerned with images; and speech (*logos*), concerned with *hermeneia*. That is, the mind uses speech as the messenger to express its thoughts.[18] Rhetoric is therefore the discipline that teaches the mind how to express itself; it teaches how to find the fitting formulation (*hermeneia*) for every thought or mental image.[19] Writing and interpretation in this view are two closely related aspects of the same activity, the mind's expression of itself through a process of understanding in word, gesture or image.[20] It was a very widespread view, continually repeated in early modern Europe, often combined with the Aristotelian view, stated in *De anima*, that thinking takes place through images. Rhetoric then becomes the capacity to grasp the images before the mind's eye and transform them into coherent and persuasive speech. As the English rhetorician John Hoskyns put it in his widely used *Directions for Speech and Style* of *c.* 1599:

> The conceits of the mind are pictures of things and the tongue is interpreter of those pictures. The order of God's creatures in themselves is not only admirable and glorious but eloquent. Thus he that could apprehend the consequence of things in their truth, and utter his apprehension as truly were a right orator.[21]

Style, however, would only become prominent as a classificatory tool at the end of the eighteenth century, in the new academic discipline of art history as it was developed by Winckelmann. In the preceding centuries much writing on the arts informed by rhetoric took as its starting point the doctrine of *ut pictura poesis*. Throughout the Renaissance Horace's comparison of painting and poetry was used to legitimize the application of rhetoric to the visual arts.[22] But this passage, unlike the rest of *The Art of Poetry*, which treats the writing of poetry, is also about how to understand art: how to read or listen to poetry, how to look at painting:

> A poem is like a picture: one strikes your fancy more, the nearer you stand; another, the farther away. This courts the shade, that will wish to be seen in the light, and dreads not the critical insight of the judge. This pleased but once, that, though ten times called for, will always please.[23]

Horace was not the first to compare poetry and painting. The Greek sophist Simonides (who died in 567 BC) as reported by Plutarch, is the earliest author known to have done so:

> Simonides, however, calls painting inarticulate poetry [*poièsin sioposan*] and poetry articulate painting [*zographian lalousan*]: for the actions which painters portray as taking place at the moment, literature narrates and records after they have taken place. Even though artists with colour and design, and writers with words and phrases, represent

> the same subjects, they differ in the material and the manner of their imitation[. . .][24]

In another version reported by Plutarch Simonides even called poetry a resounding painting. But in both the common ground between painting and poetry is what the ancients considered to be the defining characteristic of humanity: the ability to speak, to articulate one's thought in a way that is comprehensible to others and can sway their thoughts and actions.[25] That is where painting and poetry, by which Simonides here means history writing, ultimately meet:

> [. . .] and yet the underlying end and aim of both is one and the same; the most effective historian is he who, by a vivid representation of emotions and characters, makes his narration like a painting. Assuredly Thucydides is always striving for this vividness in his writing, since it is his desire to make the reader a spectator, as it were, and to produce vividly in the minds of those who peruse his narrative the emotions of amazement and consternation which were experienced by those who beheld them.[26]

Painting was so often called mute or visible speech, for some authors gaining in vividness what it lost in articulateness, that this particular variety of *ut pictura poesis* became a commonplace in early modern Europe. Paintings or statues were considered to speak not because of some inherently verbal or discursive characteristic, but because they were so lifelike and vivid that they seemed to possess the distinctive feature of being alive, the ability to speak. And conversely, persuasive writing was able to conjure up moving and speaking images in the mind of the beholder who was transformed into the spectator of a play set on a mental stage. How this effect could be achieved by the artist was the subject of Chapter Three; here we will look at the way spectators with a rhetorical awareness looked at art: how did they look, what kind of competences did they bring to it, what did they single out for mention, and how did they think the effect of vivid, lifelike presence was achieved?[27]

According to a widely held view of the *ut pictura poesis* tradition if painting is like poetry, readers are like spectators, and spectators like readers. This view concentrates on one public of poetry: its readers. But in comparing painting to poetry Horace was concerned with dramatic poetry. His *Art of Poetry* assumes that its addressees, the Piso brothers, are about to sit down and write plays.[28] At times therefore the *Art of Poetry* is not about how to write drama or comedy, but addresses the effect of such texts on the public, that is the audience at a theatre. In the *ut pictura poesis* tradition the public can be the silent reader of a book, but it very often is a member of the public watching the performance of a play.

Thinking about the visual arts in rhetorical terms singles out vividness and lifelikeness; pictorial composition is compared to conceiving the plot of a play and putting it on stage, as we have seen in Chapter Three and *ut pictura poesis* fosters the tendency to see paintings as representing plots and stories, speaking silently to the beholder. But there are also aspects to the comparison between painting and poetry that do not single out those aspects of painting that lend themselves well to poetical analysis (plot, composition, figures of speech), but instead accommodate the visual, the non-discursive characteristics of painting. To illustrate this I will discuss three cases: Bartolommeo Maranta's interpretation of an Annunciation by Titian; Francesco Bocchi's writings on Michelangelo, Donatello and Andrea del Sarto; and some early reactions to the discovery of the Laocoön in Rome in 1506.

Art as theatre: Bartolommeo Maranta on an Annunciation by Titian

A record of a visit to a Titian Annunciation in Naples provides a first illustration of the interpretive attitude fostered by rhetoric's close linking of invention and interpretation. Somewhere between 1559 and 1571 the Neapolitan physician and botanist Bartolommeo Maranta went with his friend Scipione Ammirato to see Titian's *Annunciation* at the Church of San Domenico Maggiore in Naples (Fig. 5.1). The text recording their conversation is an extended interpretation of one painting and in fact the first substantial text devoted to a single work of art, predating Francesco Bocchi's discourse on Donatello's statue of Saint George. Ammirato did not much like this painting: he thought the face of the angel too full, it was not a good painterly decision to show it only in profile, and Titian had not understood the proportions of the figure of the angel very well. Maranta's reply starts as a defence of Titian but develops into an extended statement of the principles of art criticism.[29] He reminds Ammirato that one should first try to grasp what Titian was trying to do here before criticizing him. Critics often miss the point, as in the case of the reactions to Michelangelo's *Last Judgment* in the Sistine Chapel, because a work may not fit in with preconceived notions. Paradoxically, there is more to painting than meets the eye; one can understand more than can be put into words: 'più vi si intende che non vi si dimostra'.[30] As all lovers of painting and beautiful women are aware, viewers are very capable of imagining all the things that are hidden from their eyes, and this binds them more closely to the object of their desire.[31]

The opening gambit of Maranta's defence is yet another comparison between painters and poets, in which he briefly alludes to Horace's *poetis atque pictoribus aeque potestas*, the licence that both groups of artists equally enjoy. But he gives this cliché an unexpected twist when he develops the comparison by stating

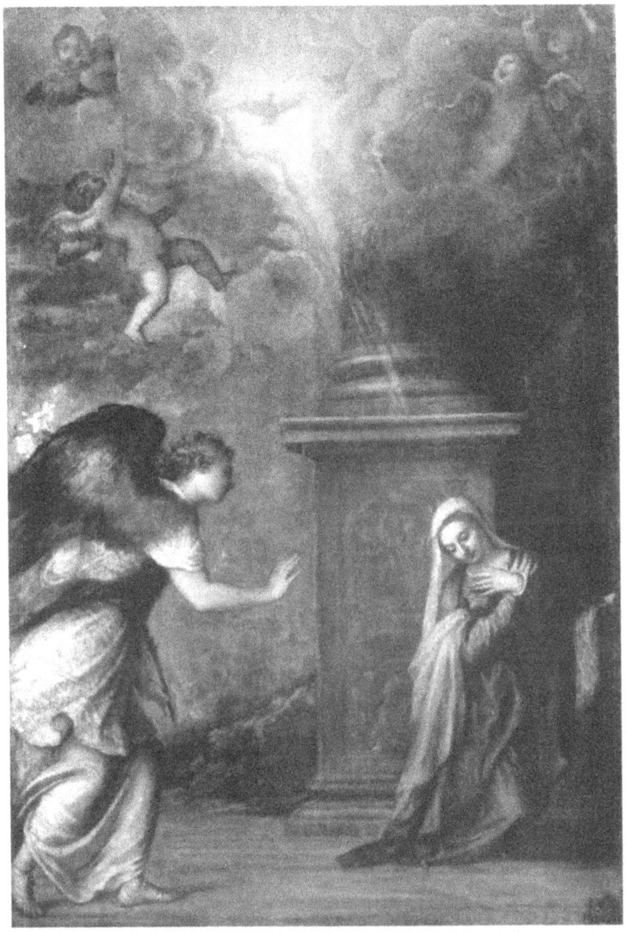

5.1 Titian, *Annunciation*. Naples, San Domenico Maggiore, *c.* 1557 (photo: Centre for Art-Historical Documentation, Radboud Universiteit Nijmegen).

that painters are at liberty to vary not the plot, or what situation they must represent, but the proportions, colours and attitudes of the figures involved, just as poets can vary the treatment of plot in their plays. In the course of his defence, he analyses this Titian in great detail. Maranta drew a parallel between various literary representations of one theme such as the story of Oedipus, and pictorial versions of an event or situation:

> And as a poet cannot alter or vary the story which has already been accepted by everybody, for instance that Laius will be killed by his son Oedipus, but can vary the actual scenes, that is the way in which this death happened, similarly the painter cannot represent the angel in any other way than that which has been accepted by everybody.

> But the manner in which he depicts the angel can vary, which corresponds to the scenes in a drama. For that reason he is at liberty to let the angel be still suspended in the air while he makes his announcement to Mary, he can make him touch the floor of the room with his feet, he can vary his figure so that it is full or thin or average and other similar things, which by their variety make the difference between one painter and another, just as the episodes distinguish one poet from another.[32]

Maranta's interpretation is based on the insight that subject matter and its representation should be distinguished: the subject, that is the sacred or mythological *historia*, is fixed, but the way in which it is represented pictorially can be varied. This reflects the fundamental rhetorical principle that *res* and *verba*, theme, or plot on the one hand and its representation on the other, although in the end result inseparable, should be distinguished in analysing the painter's work, and that this distinction can be used as an instrument of interpretation. In other words, why did Titian choose to give this particular pictorial form to the theme of the Annunciation, and in what manner does it contribute to the overall persuasive effect of this painting?

To grasp the intentions of the painter Maranta appeals to the similarity between painting and poetry. For him painting offers silent metaphors, similes, figures of speech and allegories with the help of paint. One could think of Giovanni Bellini's *Death of St Peter Martyr* in the National Gallery in London. There the cuts in the trunks and branches of the trees surrounding the scene of the Saint's murder appear as visual similes for the blows dealt to his head and body. Poetry offers speaking metaphors using language and action. Therefore what can be said of one art may be applied to the other. The alleged fatness of the angel is not a defect of taste or design, but a silent allegory of heavenly abundance, a visual sign of the 'divine food, that is love, grace and splendor' the angels enjoy in heaven.[33] But if this interpretation in terms of speaking poetry and silent painting does not convince Maranta suggests we turn to an understanding of Titian's mind: art is an imitation of what one sees, and if a painter has to paint something that cannot be seen – such as an angel or the exchange between the angel and Mary – he has to devise a composition of the most beautiful parts, and these parts have an allegorical or symbolical meaning. The angel's wings, for instance, signify its eagerness to serve divine command and its nature, which is unburdened by anything corporeal or earthly, and engaged in the road towards celestial life.

This comparison between painting and poetry shows where the licence of the painter lies: not in making free use of the generally accepted essence of a situation or event, but in varying the way in which it is put across. The *res* may not be changed, but *dispositio* and *elocutio* remain the domain where artistic freedom can be exercised. But what corresponds in painting to the *verba* of the poet or orator? According to Maranta, what corresponds to the actual scenes in a play. In the tragedy of Oedipus the poet can vary the way that killing is put on stage, that is, the words, gestures and expressions used. Similarly the painter cannot deviate from the course of events as narrated in the New Testament, but within those limits he is at liberty to introduce variations in those aspects which all painters of Annunciations vary: he can paint the angel suspended in the air, or with one foot touching the ground, with a thin or full face; he can introduce, as Titian did, a sumptuous loggia, far richer than Mary's lowly status would lead one to expect.

Keeping in mind the distinction between *res* and *verba*, between plot and scenes in poetry and painting helps to understand what Titian tried to achieve. In the course of answering some other points of critique – the angel is shown in profile, and its proportions are not properly understood by Titian – Maranta develops four criteria to judge painting which sets out to imitate human beauty: correct proportion (*debita proportione*); convenient or fitting liveliness of colour (*debita quantità, convenevole vivacità di colore*); a certain grace in these three aspects which we also call loveliness or elegance (*una certa grazia in tutte tre queste cose, che per altro nome usi dir leggiadria*). To these the painter has to add disposition (*disposizione*), which is found in living bodies and which is needed in the composition of beauty. Drawing on the two meanings of *disposizione* – design or layout and character or mood – Maranta used this word to refer to a painter's ability to select and compose his figures in such a manner that they seem to be living characters, engaged in a situation that makes sense to the viewer, and depicted with grace or *leggiadria*.

Disposition and liveliness are rhetorical terms; but Maranta's use of *debita quantità* also has a rhetorical implication because he draws attention to its effect on the spectator. By due quantity he means such dimensions that at first sight the painted object is not too large to discern its beginning and end, and not so small that its parts cannot be distinguished, and 'no convenient discourse can be held about it'.[34] Its dimensions should be such that it is capable of eliciting some response on the part of the viewer.[35]

Lively colour is a matter of handling light and shade. They convey wonderful liveliness because the angel's skin, clothes and fabrics look so lifelike that one does not seem to look at colours or died painted canvas, but at 'true and living human bodies, and very true and lifelike fabrics'.[36] The hair of the angel is of such a beautiful colour, and painted with such expert shading that it gives so much depth to its depiction as to make it part of the space of the viewer, and it seems as if one could actually touch these locks.

Similarly, *leggiadria* is sent by God and gives life to painting. It gives tremendous persuasive power to painting. The painter copies it either from some living being, or it is composed by the painter after some mental image.

The latter is more worthy of praise because it involves much more deliberation about clothes and character, depending on the mystery, story or *istoria*, its time and place, and about the persuasion or dissuasion, acceptance or denial and their attendant emotions, such as fury, piety, peacefulness or rigidity, cheerfulness or sadness. These emotions and traits of character must be shown not only in the face of the figure, but also in their attitudes, movements and clothes.

Finally the fourth critical term, disposition, is used in an analysis of the painting in terms of what is going on, of the emotional and narrative interaction between the depicted figures. This way of looking at painting ultimately goes back to the ekphrastic tradition. In Philostratus the Younger's *Imagines* the task of the painter – and the merit of painting – is to represent the characters and emotions of his figures, and to interpret the dramatic situation they find themselves in. By extension, the public becomes the spectator of these pictorial dramas:

> For he who is to be a true Master of the art must have a good knowledge of human nature, he must be able to discern the signs of men's characters even when they are silent, and what is revealed in the state of the cheeks and the expression of the eyes and the character of the eyebrows and, to put the matter briefly, what ever has to do with the mind. If proficient in these matters he will grasp every trait and his hand will successfully interpret the individual story (*drama*) of each person [. . .].[37]

In other words, pictorial composition or disposition is here used by Maranta as a way of analysing how the scene that is described in the Gospel of Luke, verses I.28–38 is represented. But this analysis could just as well have been the description of a scene in the theatre: Maranta describes the movement, gestures, clothes and expressions of the figures, and what they are supposed to say to each other, not the pictorial means by which these are represented. This is not an Albertian analysis of *compositio* in terms of the way colour, light and outlines work together on the pictorial plane, but a narrative analysis of the interaction between the figures, a way of establishing in what manner, in what kind of scenes, this particular plot or *istoria* has been narrated.

For Maranta an important aspect of disposition and its appraisal is the use of gesture. One of the reasons why Titian is such a consummate master is because he is able to convey, through the use of gesture, attitude and expression, not only that Mary is listening attentively to the angel and considering its words, but also what she is going to reply. The hands, Maranta observes, entirely in line with the rhetorical tradition, truly speak. They are the major part of a sermon, because the meanings of words vary throughout various languages, whereas the gestures of the hands are a universal language.[38] This recalls the praise by Cicero and Quintilian of the persuasive power of gesture, and its power to speak to everybody. Cicero had argued, in a seminal connection of gesture, acting, colour and painting, that the orator's use of gesture should not copy everyday gestures, but highlight, clarify and intensify them:

> For nature has assigned to every emotion a particular look and tone of voice and bearing of its own; and the whole of a person's frame and every look on his face and utterance of his voice are like the strings of a harp, and sound according as they are struck by each successive emotion. For the tones of the voice are keyed up like the strings of an instrument [and all can be] regulated by the control of art; they are the colours available to the actor, as for the painter, to secure variety.[39]

Quintilian was even more clear on the way in which gesture shares the powers of silent manifestation of thought and feeling with painting:

> For we can indicate our will not merely by a gesture of the hand, but also with a nod from the head: signs take the place of language in the dumb, and the movements of the dance are frequently full of meaning, and appeal to the emotions without any aid from words. The temper of the mind can be inferred from the glance and gait [. . .]. Nor is it wonderful that gesture which depends on various forms of movement should have such power, when pictures, which are silent and motionless, penetrate into our innermost feelings with such power that at times they seem more eloquent than language itself.[40]

Like its language, the delivery of a speech must be correct, clear, ornate and apt. Quintilian has left us a very detailed discussion of the use of the eyes and the glance, bodily attitudes (in particular of the head) and the meaning and effect of gesturing with the hands:

> For other portions of the body merely help the speaker, whereas the hands may almost be said to speak. Do we not use them to demand, promise, summon, dismiss, threaten, supplicate, express aversion or fear, question or deny? Do we not employ them to indicate joy, sorrow, hesitation, confession, penitence, measure, quantity, number and time? Have they not the power to excite and prohibit, to express approval, wonder or shame? Do they not take the place of adverbs and pronouns when we point at places and things? In fact, though the peoples and nations of the earth speak a multitude of tongues, they share in common the universal language of the hands.[41]

Maranta develops the art of gesture as the visible expression of emotion and thought through an analysis of the anatomy of the hand underlying gestures. This culminates in more praise of Titian. He is capable of ordering the muscles of the hands in such a way that we are able to see with the mind's eye what the painting hides, in this case that in the gesture of the angel the positions of the thumb and index fit together, whereas we hardly see a trace of the thumb. He makes us see things that are not depicted by suggesting them through the parts of the body he does include, not by hiding these from sight.[42]

Maranta's account ends in an ekphrastic mode of viewing, in which the beholder looks at a painting as if it were a theatrical scene, and focuses on the interaction between the figures. He looked at gesture for clues about what is going on and the emotional interaction between the figures in the painting, and considered gesture, just as Quintilian did, as a universal language, whose eloquence is at times more effective than that of speech. All these interpretative approaches will become key features of subsequent interpretations of art: in the *conférences* of the Académie Royale de Peinture for instance the distinction between invention, disposition, and elocution would often be the guiding feature of description and analysis.[43] But in a final reckoning it is the painting's *leggiadria*, its power to suggest the grace that only living beings possess, that truly affects the viewer. To gain a closer understanding of how viewers thought this illusion could be achieved we have to turn to Francesco Bocchi's writings on art.

'VIVACITÀ', LIVING PRESENCE AND HUMANITY

What, in other words, did spectators mean by that illusion of life so many of them noted, which was the common aim of painting and poetry, drama and eloquence? The Florentine art critic Francesco Bocchi's essays on Andrea del Sarto, Donatello's statue of Saint George, and Pietro Cavallini's *Annunciation*, formerly at SS. Annunziata in Florence but now lost, and his funeral oration on Michelangelo, are among the most telling records of viewing attitudes informed by rhetoric and *ut pictura poesis* produced in late sixteenth-century Italy.[44] Painting, like poetry and public government, aims to excite virtuous feelings in the audience. But perhaps more important in our context, painting is compared not to all genres of poetry, but to the drama. In Bocchi's speeches and treatises in praise of Florentine paintings works of art are not considered primarily in terms of the means of pictorial representation, but as images that are so vivid that they literally seem to turn under Bocchi's fixed gaze into tableaux-vivants, enactments of affecting dramatic situations or events. His writings testify to a particular variety of viewers' response that is not very much differentiated in response to individual works of art. All lifelike paintings or statues cause the same feeling that the representation dissolves into what is represented. It is an intensely anthropomorphic way of looking at paintings, bordering at times on magical thinking, in which viewers become fascinated, cannot turn their eyes away, and are persuaded to believe in the real and living presence of what is represented. In their fascination, viewers help the painter to complete the illusion of life: they fill in with their own imagination what the brush or the chisel can only suggest.[45]

The essay on Andrea del Sarto, written in 1567, gives the most detailed statement of Bocchi's views on art, and sets out to praise this painter by showing that his work fulfils to the highest degree the five qualities painting must display in order to achieve excellency. These are *disegno*, *vivezza* or *costume*, *rilievo*, *colorito* and a certain sweetness and facility that results from the other qualities. Of these *disegno* is the most important, because without it no successful illusion of life is possible; next to it comes *costume*. *Disegno* in painting is what the plot or story is in poetry, because actions in poetry are dependent on the plot, just as in painting *disegno* organizes the representation of actions. *Costume* fulfils the same task in painting and poetry: to reveal character, which is revealed primarily in the expression of the face, but also in gesture and movement. It is the most important means the painter has to achieve *vivezza*, liveliness or *enargeia*. Its importance is shown by the comments of poets on paintings and statues: the highest praise they can bestow is that the image seems to speak; that they believe they are able to see what in itself lacks visible shape, namely the voice. Painting shows what is invisible.[46] According to Bocchi, character can only be shown on the stage or in a painting, if actions are represented, together with the mental process of reflection and decision that precedes them. Inanimate objects do not possess *costume*, nor do beings without free will and intentions, such as most animals. Most of the examples Bocchi gives in his essay on Andrea del Sarto's work are expressions of the face: the sweetness and humility of Mary, the nobility, valour and majesty of the saints.

Yet in spite of Bocchi's stated aim to describe and define the greatness of Andrea del Sarto's work, he spent much more time elaborating the analogy between painting and poetry, and defining *costume*, than on actual, detailed descriptions of individual paintings. These are limited in most cases to quite standard descriptions of facial expression and gesture, which often turn swiftly into a reading of the personality of the person depicted. Nothing is said about what is probably for present-day viewers the most distinguishing feature of Andrea's style, a particular range of tertiary hues and colours, which distinguishes his work from that of Bronzino or Pontormo with their acid colours and harsh oppositions.

But there is one passage where Bocchi tells us a little more. While discussing *rilievo* he pauses to describe its effect and that of good *disegno* (Fig. 5.2):

> [...] while looking at [the *Disputà*] the eyes remain, together with thought, suspended, and seem unable to judge, thanks to this grand

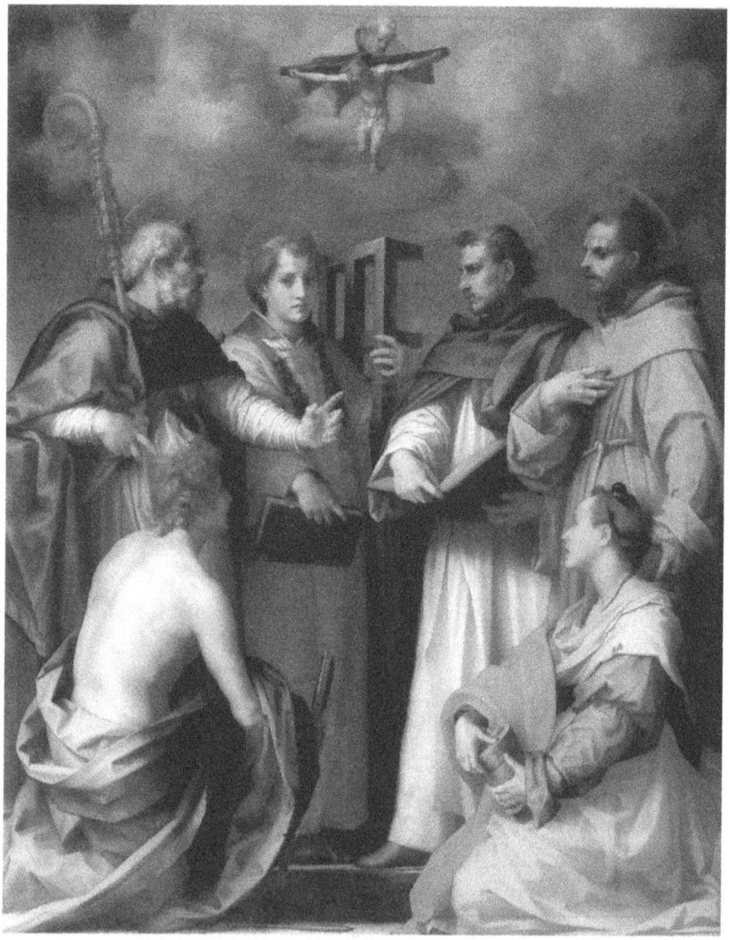

5.2 Andrea del Sarto, *Disputation on the Trinity*. Florence: Palazzo Pitti, *c.* 1517 (photo: Centre for Art-Historical Documentation, Radboud Universiteit Nijmegen).

> union of both *disegno* and *rilievo* which one sees here, doubting whether the figures are sculpted in relief or painted.[47]

Vividness again exerts its synaesthetic fascination, causing the viewer to suspend rational thought and to abandon the usual clear boundaries between painting and sculpture. As a compositional device, *rilievo* is compared to sentences in speech or poetry, probably because they have a similarly important organizing function; *colorito* is compared to *dittione* or *elocutio*, the third of the five *officia oratoris*. Bocchi does not pursue the analogy between the stages of preparing a speech and those of designing and executing a painting to any great lengths. Instead, what returns with almost obsessive frequency is his view that painting, like poetry, is a representative art. The main object in both arts is the lifelike or vivid representation of character or personality, guided by the demands of the plot or the *disegno*. But although rhetoric and poetry are the models for this analysis of painting, the visual arts surpass poetry in the effectiveness of the illusion of life they create. Spectators forget that painting is a silent, visual art and attribute speech to the silent figures they are looking at, and they even suspend rational, analytical judgement while gazing at a painting. What painting represents though is the same subject matter as poetry: plots, characters and their actions. In Bocchi's view there is no illusion of life in painting without the suggestion of living beings endowed with intentions and free will, expressed in action.

A somewhat similar statement of Bocchi's view on art can be found in his longest text about a single work of art, the *Ragionamento sopra l'Eccellenza del San Giorgio di Donatello*, dedicated to Cosimo I and published in 1571 and 1584 (Fig. 5.3). Here Bocchi argues that the excellence of a work of art depends on only three factors, *costume*, *vivacità* and *bellezza*. All three derive their effect from their power to convey the illusion of life. Bocchi's descriptions move very quickly from a description of a statue to that of the human being represented; it almost seems as if technical aspects do not interest him. What counts is the illusion of life, as if a work of art can only speak to the beholder if it seems to be a fellow human being. His next move is not to discuss the technical means by which this is achieved, but a rehearsal of the Aristotelian classification of human actions and pursuits which serves as a justification of the persuasive power of the arts. All human arts pursue the good that is proper to their nature. The virtuous part of our lives consists of action and liveliness; when we abandon these, we become lazy, forget praiseworthy actions, and become like the dead.[48] *Saint George* has this liveliness without any need for explication: the moment we see this statue, our souls are led from stone to action, and from inactivity to movement. It has a nobly uplifting effect on the eyes and mind of the beholder. In it, Bocchi wrote, the representation of the saint's noble character is so perfectly transparent that the viewer in gazing forgets all considerations of art and only considers the character, not its stone image. This response recalls Michelangelo's appreciation of Donatello's statue of St Mark for Or San Michele, as reported by Bocchi in his guide to Florence's art (Fig. 5.4). Michelangelo had never seen anybody who looked more like a gentleman [huomo da bene]: 'His face was all devotion and holiness: his entire person showed a certain horrendous gravity which transforms the holy soul entirely into faith'.[49]

Bocchi's *Opera sopra l'imagine miracolosa della Santissima Nunziata di Firenza*, published in 1592, contains a long description of Pietro Cavallini's *Annunciation*, which Vasari also described in his *Lives of the Artists* (where he located it in the convent of San Marco), and which is now lost.[50] After a discussion of the power of images to excite feelings of devotion in the viewer, and a description of the church, he sets out on yet another

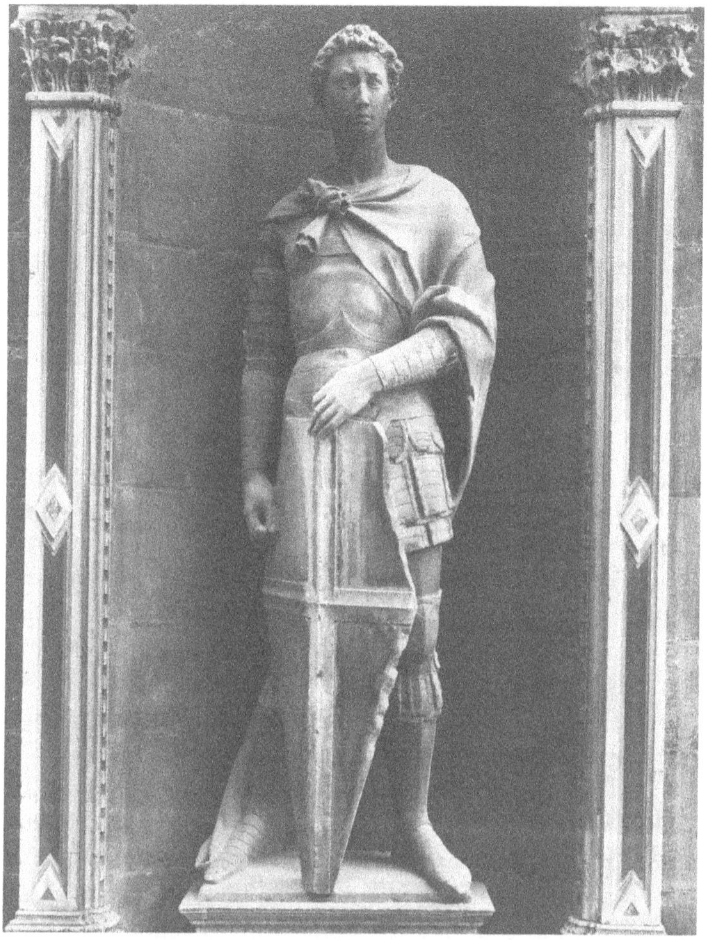

5.3 Donatello, *St George*. Florence: Museo Nazionale del Bargello, *c.* 1417 (photo: Centre for Art-Historical Documentation, Radboud Universiteit Nijmegen).

analysis of *costume* as the outward manifestation of character and emotion. His account provides a clearer view of the comparison of painting with poetry. Echoing the Greek verb *charasso* – to make an impression into wax, to stamp, engrave or seal – which is the origin of our word 'character', he defines *costume* as:

> [...] when the soul impresses itself on the face [...] it is called 'costume'; it is, as the soul is dressed ['costumato'] a manifestation of the soul. The Greeks called it ethos, the Romans *mos*, and we call it 'costume'. It is used not only in painting and sculpture, but more properly in rhetorical speech and rhetorical imitation.[51]

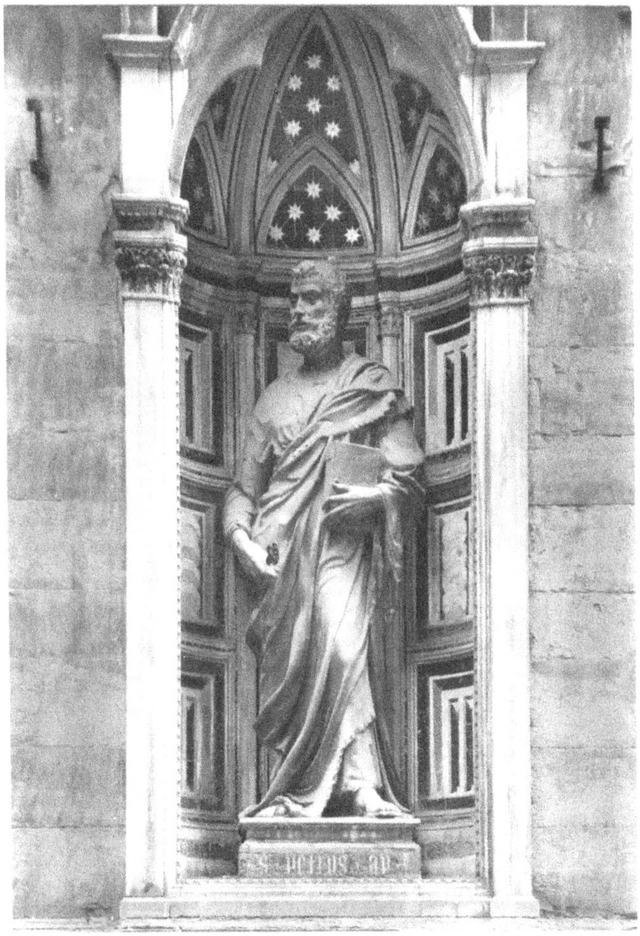

5.4 Donatello, *St Mark*. Florence, Or San Michele (photo: Centre for Art-Historical Documentation, Radboud Universiteit Nijmegen).

In a successful painting of Christ *costume* is expressed so vividly that the spectator becomes overwhelmed by feelings of piety and devotion. He or she realizes what a fragile and sad thing humanity is:

> When this most Holy face appears man realizes how low his human condition is, how fragile, how broken, how the eye cannot suffer to look at it without changing: and feeling how he is most vile and earthly of all, he sighs over his lowness, and bathed in hot tears he begs silently for help and comfort.[52]

While paintings excite feelings of devotion, tragedies cause pity and fear in the audience and thereby a feeling of release. In this lies the similarity, or one of the similarities, between painting and poetry. The painter of religious images should work very hard to make the representation of *costume* in the face of his figures so virtuous, praiseworthy and affecting, that all base feelings and thoughts in the beholder are driven away.[53]

Painting therefore is like poetry, not so much because it resembles the latter but because both have as their aim to imitate life. Life, however, is taken in a very specific sense: that of plot and character, of human beings engaged in events and situations the spectator can identify with. In giving in to the illusion of life Bocchi and other sixteenth-century viewers abandon the discursive, analytical interpretative potential suggested by the analogy between poetry and painting, exemplified by Alberti's comparison of the structure of the sentence with pictorial composition, in favour of close identification with what they see. They are no longer critics; they become the audience at a play. Spectators consider painting as a kind of theatre, behave as if they are watching actors on a stage performing a play, feel themselves to be a public, and think about the effect of the spectacle on them in terms of theatrical effects, of the impact of a drama in the Aristotelian terms of *mimesis* and *mathesis*. In this context it is interesting to note that, according to Pliny, the rivalry between Zeuxis and Parrhasius was acted out in a theatre. This response to the representational arts – painting, but also the mixed media of triumphant entries or public funerals – as a kind of theatre also appears in Aurelio Biondi's account of the Florentine *essequie* organized in honour of the deceased King Philip II of Spain in 1598:

> We have no reason to believe that the Holy Church, to whose solicitude is entrusted the care for our salvation, would have admitted the use of funereal pomp in the burials of great Princes to any other effect than our instruction; [...] she has permitted that we represent as if in an open theatre death triumphing over human nature in a lugubrious display [...].[54]

English rhetorical treatises of the sixteenth and seventeenth centuries are even more explicit than their Italian counterparts about the theatrical aspects of lifelikeness. As Leonard Barkan has put it recently: 'The theatre is England's lively pictorial culture, the answer, the compensation, the supplement in the face of all the painting and theory in European civilizations that Elizabethans dreamt about'.[55] In this view elocution is a staging of speech, just as action, the delivery of the speech, is a staging of the body. For Sir Philip Sidney, the picture that really speaks is the drama. Theatrical scenes are literally speaking pictures. In *Coriolanus*, 'Action is eloquence'; Thomas Wilson wrote that 'the gesture of man, is the speeche of his bodie'; in Thomas Nashe's preface to Sidney's *Astrophel and Stella* (1591) language is transformed into theatre, as the pages of the book are compared to the stage, and the reader to a visitor to the theatre: 'to turn aside into their Theater of pleasure, for here you shall find a paper stage streud with pearls [. . .]'.[56] Sir Henry Wotton advised his readers that they should consider, when judging a painting, that '*Affection* is the *Liuely Representment*, of any *passion* whatsoeuer, as if the *Figures* stood not vpon a *Cloth* or *Boorde*, but as if they were *acting* vpon a *Stage*'.[57]

'Laocoön I am'

The power of art to express the emotions was often explained by invoking an art that excited a much more direct emotional response from the public than painting: the theatre. Because of its oscillation between acting and enacting, representation and presence it became a powerful model for painters and theorists. The pictorial plane became a stage on which key moments in a story could be represented as if frozen in time.[58] As all the viewers' accounts discussed here show, the viewers' experience of living presence, the theatrical character of painting, and the pictorial character of drama are all related. Vivid representation suspended the awareness of looking at a representation, and created the illusion that the public was looking not at a painting but at the events, situation or actions that were depicted. The highest degree of *enargeia* or lifelikeness was achieved when representation dissolved into what was represented, and art ceased to be art. This resembles the attitude of fascination that will occur while watching a play: a suspension of disbelief, or a dissolution of representation into what is represented.[59] The effect on the public is also similar: fear and pity, resulting in catharsis.[60] The interpretive attitude fostered by *ut pictura poesis* is not that the spectator becomes the reader of a text, but that he or she becomes the audience at a play, for plays like Renaissance paintings represent significant human action by means of gesture, movement and apt composition of a scene. Painting compensates its lack of speech by visual effects, just as drama compensates its lack of visual means of representation by speech. The public of the theatre and the visual arts alike felt themselves watching the representation of significant human action. Moved by its vivid representation and instructed by what they see unfolding before their eyes, they experience how their human identity is affirmed.

There is one group of viewers' response that illustrates this kind of response very well: the poems inspired by the recovery of the Hellenistic statue of Laocoön (Fig. 5.5). When the statue of the Troian priest and his sons was dug up on 1 January 1506 near the Colosseum it caused an enormous stir. The moment it became clear that the greatest and most famous of antique sculptures had been unearthed Pope Julius II was alerted. He immediately sent one of his officers to the architect Giuliano da Sangallo to order him to the site to see

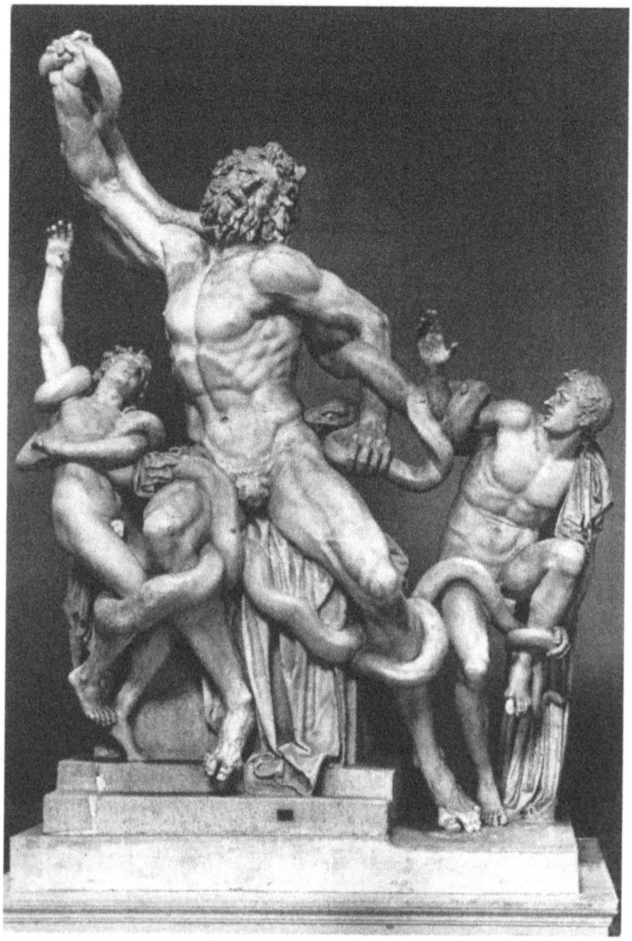

5.5 Hagesandrus, Athanodorus and Polydorus, *Laocoön*. Rome: Museo Vaticano, *c.* 200 BC (photo: Centre for Art-Historical Documentation, Radboud Universiteit Nijmegen).

what was happening. Since Michelangelo was staying at Sangallo's house, he went with him. Sangallo climbed down to the pit and said immediately: 'That is the Laocoön, which Pliny mentions'. Giuliano's son, who is the source for this eyewitness account, continued by mentioning that 'as soon [the statue] was visible everyone started to draw, all the while discoursing on ancient things, chatting as well about the ones in Florence'.[61]

It is a wonderful snapshot of the Renaissance in action: one of the most famous classical statues is recovered, two famous artists are immediately present and start drawing it, and in the background Pope Julius II immediately grasps the opportunity this event offers to augment his collection of classical art and thereby add extra substance to his lifetime project of returning Rome to its former, imperial glory, if not to surpass it. For he did not choose his papal name at random.

Sangallo's account also singles out the archaeological and artistic aspects of the event: architects are the first to witness and record the recovery of the *Laocoön*, and while doing so they talk about classical matters. But when we look at other reactions, and in particular at the immense amount of poetry written in reaction to this event, another theme becomes prominent: the statue, though made of marble, lives. In the Latin poem by Jacopo Sadoleto, for instance, the sculptors are praised because they were able to render rigid stone animate with living figures and endow the marble with living senses.[62] As a result, the beholder sees movement, anger and grief, and almost hears the groans of Laocoön and his sons. This may be described as a typical, not very original example of the cliché of the work of art that seems to breathe. But many poems offer much more original reactions. The poem by Elio Lampridio Cervo opens by exclaiming that 'the stone image lies true colours', in an interesting ungrammatical transitive use of the verb 'to lie', which here takes an object, namely, the true colours of the statue.[63]

Evangelista Maddaleni de'Capodiferro's Latin poem offers an even more original, and very subtle take on this topos: it is not the poet, but Laocoön himself who speaks: 'Laocoön I am'. Then in the course of the poem the speaker is transformed from the Trojan priest into the statue: 'you will say, when you look at me, that the pains are real for the stone, and that death and fear are not fictive for my sons'. But in a clever twist at the end the poem plays on the phenomenon of the statue's silent cries that would receive so much attention in Lessing's essay on the *Laocoön*: 'If the sculptors who were able to give death and fear and living grief to stone could also endow it with a voice and soul, they would have refused, because it is more wondrous to struggle, suffer, beg, lament, fear and die without voice and without soul'.[64]

A short poem by Antonio Tebaldi offers yet another take on the effect of the statue on the beholder. The statue is again the speaker: 'I am Laocoön, so expressive and alive/that, if you are not made of the material/out of which I am made and my sons, you will make of your eyes a sorrowful river'.[65] That is, this statue is so lifelike that looking at it the viewer, if he is a human being, is overcome by pity: I, Laocoön, though a stone statue that is nonetheless able to speak, will not cry, but you, living human being, will. Pushing the oscillation between marble and flesh, life and death even further the poet Cerva plays on the theme of life and death in an almost Baroque manner: death, or rather mortality, is presented as the supreme sign of life: 'you could believe that the stones are bitten, that they strike, or die'. That is, the vulnerability and mortality of the marble is the ultimate sign of life.[66] And in the most pre-metaphysical twist of all, Giovanni Paolo Lancelotti addresses Laocoön, again identifying the person with the statue: 'Cease, Laocoon, to lament in a sad voice/that the serpents kill you with their lethal tongues./For Death [. . .] forbids you ever to die'.[67]

As in Bocchi's essays on Florentine art, these poems describe not the statue, but what is represented. They do not single out for praise the work of art considered in itself as an aesthetic object, the way the marble is handled, or the composition of its figure. Instead in many of these it is difficult to determine with absolute certainty whether the poet is addressing the statue, the unfortunate priest, or the priest through the statue. Moreover, this blurring of the boundaries between the statue and what (or whom) it represents, is intentional, and often the *concetto* at the basis of the poem.

To some extent concentrating on the action represented rather than the representation is characteristic of the ekphrastic tradition. But in these poems a more subtle process of personification is going on: these Renaissance viewers did not only describe classical works of art that were rediscovered – and often presented enigmas to them because they could not readily be identified – in their own words; they also gave them a voice, and thereby a personality and identity of their own. This process of personification may be described with the help of two rhetorical figures of speech: first *apostrophe*, that is to turn suddenly in a speech from one subject to another, often to an inanimate object; and second *prosopopoeia*, that is to present an absent object or person as speaking. In other words, in the first an object is addressed, and in the second it answers back. *Prosopopoeia* is derived from the classical Greek *prosopon*, a mask and hence a face, and *poiein*, to make. Through its use an object is given a voice, and in the Laocoön poems the statue also receives a body, eyes and mouth, a face and thereby an identity as a person.[68] From our twenty-first-century enlightened and rational frame of mind we may scoff at such a fanciful interpretation of what surely is no more than a cliché in poems describing art works.

But that the distinction between inanimate statues and living human beings was not always crystal clear is also suggested by the perseverance, during the Renaissance, of the view that Rome had two populations: one consisting of living people, the other of statues. The sixteenth-century architect and antiquarian Pirro Ligorio, for instance, wrote that Rome had:

> two populations, the one of living men and the other of marble statues, these last being all placed in their homes, palaces, theatres and amphitheatres, arches, piazzas, and baths; so that, just like living Romans, as well as foreigners, these were transported from all the various parts of the world, not sparing even that the gods and heroes be moved from their native places to install them among all the cities of the world. [. . .] But what would Pliny have said, seeing such a large population of statues in the time of the emperor Vespasian if he had been able to observe the many emperors who succeeded,

> who brought an infinite number of statues to Rome commemorating innumerable gods [...]? I am sure he would have said that in Rome there was one population of living men and ten of marble statues.[69]

This complex dialectic between life and death, marble and humanity is neatly summarized in the poem by Tebaldi quoted above, in which the marble statue speaks, and tells the viewer that if he is not made of marble, he will weep at what he sees: that is, the marble object is able to speak and feel, two eminently human traits, and tells the viewer to become human, too.

Quintilian compared the persuasive force of the figures of speech to the movements of Myron's *Discobolus* (Fig. 5.6). Both suggest motion and thereby convey the illusion of life. The response to *Laocoön* is no exception to this: viewers were amazed by the extreme movement, bordering on contortion, of the figures. But there is more to Quintilian's comparison of the figures of speech with movement. In Book IX he called the figures of speech first *schemata* in the original Greek sense of the word, that is, attitudes or movements of the body, such as reclining, sitting or turning around, thus announcing the sculptural

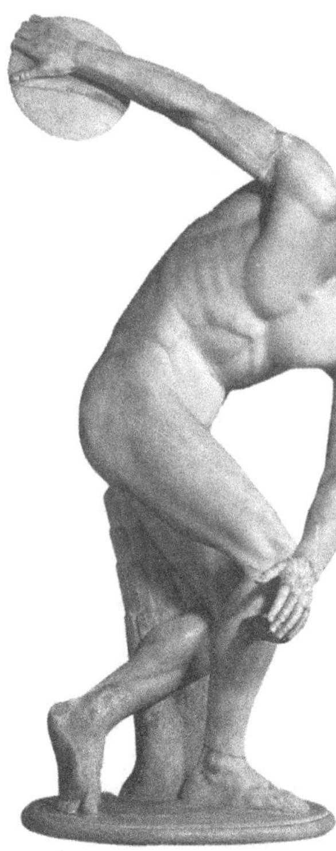

5.6 Myron, *Discobolus*. Rome: Museo Nazionale Romano (Museo delle Terme), *c.* 450 BC (photo: Centre for Art-Historical Documentation, Radboud Universiteit Nijmegen).

comparison of Book XII. These figures or *schemata* introduce movement into the text: they are, Quintilian pursues, its 'attitudes and gestures', those features whereby a text deviates from the normal and straightforward, just as the movements of the *Discobolus* or *Laocoön* present a break from the static and the obvious. They are crucial for persuasion. Just as the expression of the eyes and gestures of the hands excite the emotions, the figures of style make speech more acceptable and moving. They animate speech, and one could say, make it human. Thereby they become the gesture and attitude, and ultimately the face of a speech, the 'orationis ipsius vultus'.[70]

But there is yet another aspect to Quintilian's account of the role of the figures of speech in persuasion.[71] As Lina Bolzoni has recently shown, the laws through which the imagination in medieval and early modern Europe was thought to operate – similarity, contiguity and opposition – are also the relations that generate metaphor and metonymy. These are also the three laws of association identified by Aristotle to operate when we try to recover a memory by starting with something we do remember. Both invention and recollection are imaginative activities, in the sense that they involve the mind's *vis imaginativa*, the power to form and connect mental images. The rhetorical connection of invention and interpretation, of formulating a speech and understanding thought, suggests that interpretation, like response, is an imaginative act. Indeed, Quintilian's use of anthropomorphy enabled him to think about such an abstract and elusive phenomenon as the nature of figurative language. Drawing on the fact that the Latin 'figura' can mean both the human form, and metaphor or metonymy, he suggested that ultimately eloquence – in speech as in the arts – can only be understood in terms of human behaviour, whether of the body or the mind.[72]

Notes

1 On the history of art-historical concepts of style and their rhetorical origins see, for instance, Hendrickson (1905); on the history of the art-historical concept of style see Gombrich (1972) and (1974); Bialostocki (1961), pp. 128–52; Gumbrecht and Pfeiffer (1986); Sohm (2001), and Van Eck *et al.* (1995).

2 Institutio Oratoria XII.x.1–12.

3 Cf. *Institutio Oratoria* IX.i.19: 'Ut vero natura prius est concipere animo res quam enuntiare [. . .]': 'As, however, in the natural course of things we conceive ideas before we express them [. . .].'

4 Ullmann (1957), p. 6.

5 See for instance Cicero's *Brutus* 100 and *Orator* 71. The Latin use of 'stilus' in the sense of style does not occur before Quintilian; besides 'genus' terms as 'sermo', 'oratio', 'dictio', 'dicendi modus', 'ars' or 'forma' are used. Examples where 'stilus' does occur in the sense are, for instance, Suetonius, *Life of Augustus* 85: 'affectatione obscurabat stilum'.

6 Both Eden (1997) and a number of articles in Kopperschmidt (1990) discuss the hermeneutic potential of rhetoric in the interpretation of texts, but there has been no in-depth study devoted to the use of rhetoric in the interpretation of the visual arts.

7 See, for instance, Cicero's brief formulation of the relations between *res* and *verba*, and between *inventio* and *elocutio* in *De partitione oratoria* I.3.

8 *Institutio oratoria* III.v.1. See also I.v.2 (on the meaning of *verbum*); I.v.3 ('when we praise words, we do so because they suit the matter') and II.iv.37; II.xi on the importance of the distinction between

figure and thought; III.iii.1 and III.iii.7–11 (a discussion of the passage quoted here from *De partitione oratoria*); and VII.Pr.32–3 which is a summary of his ideas about the relations between *res* and *verba*. In IX.1.16 he put it most succinctly: 'For the same things are often put in different ways and the sense remains unaltered though the words are changed [...].'

9 Guarino Veronese, *Oratio Guarini Veronensis quam recitavit in principio studii Ferrariae coram marchione Leonello et aliis famosiis viris*, p. 489: 'Huic [sc. dialectica and topica] dulcis ac facunda comes adiungitur dicendi ratio et disciplina, idest rhetorica, cuius ea praestantia, commoditas et, ut ita dicam, beneficentia est, quod cum artes reliquae suum munus, suum finem suamque materiam profiteantur, haec una omnibus vestes, ornamenta linguamque largitur adeo, ut sine rhetorica praeceptis et exercitatione nudae ceterae, inornatae ac prorsus elinguae vix in lucem prodire audeant et ad eruditas saltem aures sese verecundius offerant.'

10 Cicero, *Brutus* xvi.65.

11 *Institutio oratoria* II.iv.18–19.

12 See, for instance, Cicero, *De Partitione Oratoria* XVIII.62 and Quintilian, *Institutio Oratoria* VIII. Proemium 8.

13 See, for instance, Book II of the *Rhetorica ad Herennium*.

14 Plato, *Gorgias* 449E. Cf. Isocrates, *Antidosis* Section 277. See also *De Oratore* III.xvi.61, where Cicero argues that to deny this principle amounts to introducing a division between heart and tongue ['linguae atque cordis'], or a dichotomy between our speech and our mind. The context of this remark is that of the Platonic polemic between philosophy, the realm of *sapientia*, and rhetoric, the domain of *eloquentia*, but Cicero's close association of speech and mind not only has implications for the relation between what is said and how it is said, or between thought and speech, but also, less often noted implications for the closeness of speaking, listening and interpretation, because these are also based on that same closeness of the mind and speech.

15 This has been traditionally attributed to the student of Aristotle Demetrius of Phaleron, but scholarly consensus now tends to date it *c.* 270 BC.

16 Cf. Augustine, *On the City of God* VII.14, which is probably based on an etymology offered by Varro but now lost. In Cicero's *De Natura Deorum* II.iv.12 angels are called 'deorum interpretes': the messengers of the gods, who announce and explain on their behalf.

17 Clement of Alexandria, *Oratio contra Gentes* 19.11, Pépin (1988), p. 106.

18 See, for instance, Philo Judaeus, *De Migratione Abrahae* II.12, XIV.78 and XV.84; see also Hahn (1965).

19 Cf. Pépin (1988), in particular pp. 97–99 and 106.

20 On the relation of hermeneutics and rhetoric in general see Gadamer (1976), p. 24; Hyde (2001), and Jost and Hyde (1997).

21 J. Hoskyns, *Directions for Speech and Style*, reprinted in Vickers, *English Renaissance Literary Criticism*, p. 399. The first sentence is a paraphrase of Aristotle's account of language in *De interpretatione* I. 16a2–8 and of Horace's *Ars Poetica* 111; see also Bath (1994), p. 157. The double use of rhetoric was also recognized by readers of Alberti's *De Pictura*, for instance his contemporary Pietro Barozzi, who wrote that 'Battista's talents, Reader, lead you to facility/In painting and in Latin volubility./He satisfies our ears and eyes:/For every hand and tongue a guide supplies.'. P. Barozzi, 'In Leonis Baptistae libellum de pictura elegantissimum' Ms.O.58 sup. fol. 64 verso: 'Pingere seu discas, seu dicere multa latine,/Baptistae ingenio, lector, utrumque potes./Auribus atque oculis fecit satis, et studiosis/Omnibus, hinc lingua profuit, inde manu.' Quoted in Baxandall (1971), p. 121.

22 See the studies by LeCoat (1975); Lee (1967); and Gent (1981).

23 Horace, *Ars Poetica*, lines 361–5:
Ut pictura poësis: erit quae si propius stes
te capiat magis, et quaedam si longius abstes.
Haec amat obscurum, volet haec sub luce videri,
iudicis argutum quae non formidat acumen;
haec placuit semel, haec deciens repetita placebit.
(Translation H. R. Fairclough, 1926 edn, pp. 479–81.

24 Plutarch, *Moralia*, 'On the Fame of the Athenians', 346F–347D.

25 Diodorus Siculus, a historian of the first century AD, for instance, wrote in *Historia* I.ii.6 that '[...] it is speech which makes the Greeks superior to the Barbarians, the educated to the uneducated; and more, it is by means of speech alone that one man is able to prevail over many'.

26 Plutarch, ibid. cf. *Moralia* 18A, where Simonides is quoted as saying 'poetry is articulate painting ('phtheggomenèn tèn poièsin'), and painting is inarticulate poetry ('poièsin sigosan'). 'Siopao' means to be silent; 'sigao' to be silent or to be quiet; 'laleo' to resound (in the case of inarticulate sounds), to babble, prattle, as opposed to 'legein', which meant to speak seriously. In the first centuries AD it increasingly lost its negative connotations, and simply meant to speak. *Phtheggomai* means to shout, raise the voice, open the mouth; to proclaim, or to speak loudly. In other words, to translate Simonides' comparison as 'poetry is articulate painting and painting is inarticulate poetry' is a bit weak, and ignores the suggestion that poetry actually can be a resounding painting. See also Longinus, *On the Sublime* XXV: 'Again, if you introduce events

in past time as happening at the present moment, the passage will be transformed from a narrative into a vivid actuality'.

27 See for instance Land (1994), pp. 5 and 10.

28 Cf. Horace's *Ars Poetica*, lines 80–90 and 99–101, and, for instance, Russell (1981), pp. 2–3 and 5.

29 B. Maranta, *Discorso all'ill.mo Sig. Ferrante Carrafa Marchese di Santo Lucido in Materia di Pittura nel quale si difende il quadro della Cappella del Sig. Cosmo Pinelli, fatto per Tiziano, da alcune opposizioni fattegli da alcune persone*. Very little has been written about this text: see Barocchi, *Scritti d'Arte*, vol. I, p. 1110 for an overview of literature published before her edition, and Freedman (1985), which places Maranta in the ekphrastic tradition, offers an analysis of his discourse in terms of the rhetorical division of forensic speech into an *exordium, narratio, confirmatio, confutatio* and *peroratio*, and suggests some connections between Maranta's views and those of Dolce.

30 Maranta, *Discorso*, p. 865.

31 Maranta, *Discorso*, pp. 872–3.

32 Maranta, *Discorso*, p. 870: 'E come un poeta non può alterare né variare la favola già così accettata da tutti, come per caso che Laio sia stato ammazzato da Edipo suo figliuolo, ma ben può variare gli episodi, cioè il modo come questa morte sia accaduta, così il pittore non può dipingere l'angelo in altro modo che in quello che è stato accettato da tutti. Ma il modo può variare, ché ha proporzione con l'episodii della poesia. Imperoché può a sua posta far che l'angelo mentre annunzia stia ancor sospeso in aria, può farlo toccare il suolo della camera co' piedi, può variar la sua figura di farla piena o scarna o mediocre et altre cose simili, le quali per la varietà loro fanno differenza da pittor a pittore, come gli episodii da poeta a poeta. E quando in queste cose si pecca, sono errori accidentali e non guastano la sostanza della invenzione.'

33 Maranta, *Discorso*, p. 866.

34 In her notes Barocchi here draws attention to the close similarity of this passage to Aristotle's *Poetics* 1450b–1451a.

35 Maranta, *Discorso*, pp. 876–9.

36 Maranta, *Discorso*, p. 879: 'Veggonsi i lumi e l'ombre di quell'angelo così attamente poste che dànno meravigliosa vivacità all'opera per la rassembranza che hanno le parti ignude con la carnatura umana, e parimente le vestite con li panni naturali. Talmente che, non già colori o pur tela colorita par vedere, ma vere e vivi membri umani, verissimi e naturalissimi panni'.

37 Philostratus the Younger, *Imagines*, Proemium. On ekphrasis see Alpers (1960); Carrier (1987); Goldhill (1994); Elsner (1995); Rosand (1990); James and Webb (1991); Land (1990) and (1994); Graf (1995); *Yale French Studies* (1981).

38 Maranta, *Discorso*: '[...] non è però membro che a tutte le varietà del dire (che sono infinite) possa i suoi atti accomodare, se non le mani, che in un certo modo si possono dire che veramente parlino. Il che si vede nei mutoli, i quali tutti i loro concetti con esse chiaramente esprimeno. [...] la mano fa un certo parlare commune a tutte le lingue, col quale ogni barbara nazione può farsi intendere dalle greche e latine, e queste da tutte quelle. È dunque così difficile far la scelta del gesto che alla mano conviene, che gli oratori famosi e gli istrioni, che in questo studio attendono più che ad ogni altro, sogliono bene spesso fallirlo.'

39 *De Oratore* III.lvi.214–15.

40 *Institutio Oratoria* XI.iii.66–7.

41 *Instutitio Oratoria* XI.iii.86–7.

42 Maranta, *Discorso*, p. 891.

43 See, for instance, Merot (1996), pp. 45–59 (Félibien) and 123 (Bourdon).

44 Fr. Bocchi, *Eccellenza del San Giorgio di Donatello* (published 1584 but written in 1571); *Discorso sopra l'Eccellenza dell'Opere d'Andrea del Sarto, pittore fiorentino* (1567); *Oratio [...] de laudibus Michaelis Angeli florentini, pictoris, sculptoris, atque architecti nobilissimi* (1564).

45 Giovanni Pico della Mirandola compared the imagination, the ability of the human soul to create images, with the painter's capacity to do so: see his *Commentary on a Canzona by Benviani*, pp. 157 and 136. Torquato Tasso described the act of viewing as one of 'reading', in which the viewer helps the painter to complete the illusion of life by supplying with their own imagination what can only be suggested in the painting: *Lezione del Signor Torquato Tasso sopra il sonnetto LIX di Monsignor G. della Casa*, p. 303; cf. Land (1994), p. 20.

46 Bocchi, *Discorso sopra l'Eccellenza del San Giorgio di Donatello*, p. 135.

47 Bocchi, *Discorso sopra l'Eccellenza dell'Opere d'Andrea del Sarto*, pp. 126–8.

48 Bocchi, *Ragionamento sopra l'Eccellenza del San Giorgio di Donatello*, pp. 152–9.

49 Bocchi, *Le Bellezze della Città di Fiorenza*, p. 30: 'Egli si dice, fermatosi un giorno Michelagnolo Buonarroti à contemplar questa statua, che un suo amico à punto sopraggiunse, & il doma[n]dò, come gli pareva bella: à cui rispose il Buonarroto: se tale fu il vivo, come stimare si de[v]e, che fosse fermamente, gli si può credere tutto quello, che egli scrisse: peroche io non vidi mai alcuno, che più di questo havesse aria di huomo da bene. Spira il volto divozione, è santità: si conosce in tutta la persona una certa horrevole gravità, che dell'animo santo fa fede interamente'.

50 G. Vasari, 'Life of Pietro Cavallini', in *Lives of the Painters, Sculptors and Architects*, vol. I, pp. 160–1.

51 Bocchi, *Opera sopra l'imagine miracolosa della Santissima Nunziata di Firenza*, pp. 1005–10.

52 Ibid. p. 1006.

53 Ibid. p. 1008: 'È la pittura alla poesia simile molto, como dicono gli uomini letterati [...]. La poesia,

come avviene nella Tragedia, per lo mezzo della misericordia, & ancora del timore, fa la purgazione; cio è netta dell'anima quelli affetti, che dal tutto alla misericordia, & al timore sono contrarij. [...] il pittore di sacre immagini altresi dee sopra tutto mirare è questo che il costume sia lodevole, che sia virtuosa, & per dir quello, che tutte le virtù abraccia [...]; onde in colui, che contempla, i vizij, & gli errori mirabilmente se purghino, & si dipartono. Perche nel modo, che nella poesia entra la compassione in altrui, & il timore quando sono espressi felicemmente questi due affetti del poeta, parimente dal costume, & dal volto, che spiramo pensier divini, e purità, entra nell'animo un disio tutto colmo di lode, per cui bracciati i vizij diviene albergo l'animo di santità, & di virtù'.

54 A. Biondi, *Essequie della Sacra Cattolica Real Maesta del Re di Spagna Don Filippo II d'Austria*, p. 6: 'Ned è menoma ragione di credere, che la S. Chiesa, nella cui sollecitudine è posta la cura della nostra saluazione, habbia ammesso l'vso della pompa funerale nell' Essequie de Principi grandi ad altro effetto, che è nostra ammaestramento; [...] permette eziandio, che quasi in aperto teatro con lugubre apparato rappresentiamo la morte trionfante dell' humana natura corrotta, [...]. Queste cose in mille soggiete rappresentate con pittura loquace, e con muta istoria [...] in comune ammaestramento contemplar si possono nell'essequie sontuose'.

55 Cf. Barkan (1995), pp. 341–2.

56 On the commonplace that all the world is a stage cf. Cicero, *De Oratore* III.lix.222, and *Oratore* XVII.55; Curtius (1948), pp. 148–54. For Sir Philip Sidney see Heninger (1989) and Kapp (1990); Barkan (1995), p. 337; cf. Attolini (1988). Even clearer is what Sussenbrotus wrote in *Pragmatographia*: 'rei descriptio [...] omnibus fucatum coloribus ob oculos ponimus, ut auditorem sive lectorem iam extra se positum, velut in theatro evocet' (1562 edition, p. 87; cf. Henry Peacham, *Garden of Eloquence* p. 139 and Quintilian VIII.iii.67–9). Conversely, the drama was often called an image of life: Franciscus Junius, for instance, quotes from the scholia by Donatus on Horace, p. 8 ll.6–7: 'Quid est enim comoedia aliud quam imago vitae humanae?' and 'Comoediam esse Cicero ait imitationem vitae, speculum consuetudinis, imaginem veritatis' (*The Painting of the Ancients. De Pictura Veterum according to the English Translation (*1638*)*, p. 51. See also Plett (1993), and Salerno (1951). On the opposite view, that a play should be like a painting, see Belkin (2000).

57 Sir Henry Wotton, *The Elements of Architecture*, pp. 82 and 85.

58 Cf. Barkan (1995), pp. 341–2.

59 On the dissolution or transparency of the sign in antique and early modern ekphrasis see Galand-Hallyn (1993).

60 Cf. Aristotle, *Poetica* 1449 b8 on catharsis, and on fascination see *Ethica Eudemia* III.ii.30 (1230b31), translation J. Solomon, in J. Barnes (ed.), *The Complete Works of Aristotle*, vol. II, p. 1949: '[I]f one sees a beautiful statue, or horse, or human being, or hears singing, without any accompanying wish for eating, drinking, or sexual indulgence, but only with the wish to see the beautiful and hear the singers, he would not be thought profligate any more than those who were charmed by the Sirens'.

61 Cf. Barkan (1999), pp. 1–4.

62 J. Sadoleto, *De Laocoontis statua Jacobi Sadoleti Carmen*: 'vos rigidum lapidem vivis animare figuris/eximii et vivos spiranti in marmori sensus/inserere'. On Sadoleto's, poem and the conditions of describing visual art see most recently Baxandall (2003).

63 Ibid., p. 122: 'Saxea quam veros mentitur imago colores/et simulat verum Laocoon lapis!'

64 Evangelista Maddaleni de'Capodiferro, *Laocoon in Titi imperatoris domo Julio II Pontifici Maximo repertus*: 'Laocoon ego sum [...]. Dices, me aspicias, veros lapidi esse dolores,/et natis haud fictum exitium atque metum./[...]/Si mortem atque metum saxo vivumque dolorem/qui dederunt, possent vocem animamque dare,/abnuerent: mirum magis est sine voce animaque/niti, ferre, queri, flere, timere, mori.'

65 Antonio Tebaldi, from his *Rime* (quoted in Settis [1999], p. 132): 'Laocoonte son, sì expresso e vivo/ che, se de la materia tu non sei/onde son io formato e figli mei,/farai de gli occhi un doloroso rivo.'

66 Elio Lampridio Cerva, *Opera latina* (quoted in Settis [1999], p. 124): 'Sibila mentiri, saniem manare cruentam/morderi credas saxa, ferire, mori'.

67 Giovanni Paolo Lancellotti, *Io. Pauli Lancellotti Perusini i[uris] c[onsulti] de Lacoonte* (quoted in Settis [1999], p. 146): 'Quod te laetiferis morti dant oribus angues/Laocoon, tristi desine voce queri./Mors etenim – invideant licet (aspera numina) Parcae –/te vetat haec ullo tempore posse mori'.

68 Barkan (1999), p. 55: 'Sculptures are representations of human beings. Underlying all the possible reactions in front of art objects [...] is a sense that, in the act of looking at ancient statues, modern individuals are encountering their own mirror images from the classical past, not in marble or bronze but in the flesh'.

69 Pirro Ligorio, Naples M. 13.B.7, quoted in Barkan (1999), p. 63 from Mandowsky and Mitchell (1963), pp. 49–50 n. Ligorio attributed this view to Pliny. Although Barkan writes he cannot find Ligorio's source in Pliny (p. 63 n. 172), Pliny wrote in the *Historia Naturalis* XXXIV.35 about bronze statues in Rome: 'Sed haec ad infinitum effloruit, multorum voluminuum opere, in quis plura persequi velit; omnia enim quis posuit'. In XXXIV.36. he mentions the 3,000 statues in M. Scaurus' temporary theatre, and the host of statues erected by Mummius and

Lucullus, all in Rome. Barkan does trace Ligorio's statement back to a passage in Cassiodorus' *Variae*; he also mentions a reference to it in Alberti, *De re aedificatoria*, VII.xvi.

70 *Institutio Oratoria* IX.i.10–21: 'Sed si habitus quidam et quasi gestus sic appellandi sunt [. . .]. Ergo figura sit arte aliqua novata forma dicendi. [. . .] Nam si frons, oculi, manus multum ad motum animorum valent, quanto plus orationis ipsius vultus ad id, quod efficere intendimus, compositus?'

71 Bolzoni (1995), pp. 135–40.

72 As Barkan (2000), pp. 106–7 put it recently: '[W]hy [should] rhetoric and visuality not be one and the same? When Quintilian finds himself at a loss to define the genres of rhetoric because his own categories of genus and species have failed him, he draws a rhetorical analogy to the history of art because it offers a nonhierarchical scheme of differences [. . .]. After all is said and done, both the represented human form and the operations of metaphor go by the same name: *figura*'. The reference is to Quintilian XII.x.3–9.

SIX:

ONLY THE HUMAN CAN SPEAK TO MAN: RHETORICAL INTERPRETATIONS OF ARCHITECTURE

Introduction

In the preceding chapter we have looked at some varieties of rhetorical interpretation and the hermeneutic concepts and competences on which they were based. Maranta's analysis of Titian's San Domenico *Annunciation* in terms of *dispositio* and *elocutio*, or the various ways in which poets can put their version of a plot on the stage, was based on the rhetorical closeness of invention and interpretation, recalling the ancient view of *hermeneia* as the eloquent formulation of thought. We have also seen how *ut pictura poesis* was not so much an expression of the representational equivalence of word and image, but rather the expression of a fundamental kinship between painting and poetry. They do not share some superficial equivalence between stylistic or compositional strategies. Instead what they have in common is their theatricality: both poetry and painting put human beings, their actions and emotions before the eyes of the viewer, be it on the stage or before the interior theatre of the imagination. The height of persuasion is attained in vivid or even living presence.

Until now we have only considered response to the figurative arts; but how did viewers react to architecture, and do their reactions tell us something about the manner in which buildings were felt to be persuasive? Does the use of figures, their effect of humanizing speech and thereby conveying the illusion of life or *enargeia*, play a role as well in responses to architecture?

Viewers' response, or in a wider sense the interpretation of architecture, is not a topic in the mainstream of early modern architectural theory. As we have seen in Chapter Three, Barbaro, Spini and Scamozzi thought about the persuasiveness of architecture, but only from the perspective of design and how to analyse this in a theory of classical architecture. There is one passage in Alberti's *De Re Aedificatoria* in which he describes the pleasure of gazing at a beautiful building, but that is quite unique, and is an illustration of the delight the scrutiny of *concinnitas* can offer.[1] It is only in the seventeenth century, and outside Italy, that responses to buildings of some length and articulateness begin to appear. Interestingly, they were produced in countries where classical architecture was not uncontested, either because it had to compete with strong native or vernacular traditions, or because it was associated – or tainted, depending on the perspective of the viewer – with the pagan culture of ancient Rome or the papacy. In England both the controversial religious aspects of classical architecture and the effort to appropriate an unfamiliar style led to quite explicit responses; two of them will be examined here in greater detail, because they offer articulate testimonies of the persuasive impact of buildings, but also show how this was perceived to work by its authors. At the same time, these records show that the persuasion exercised by these buildings was experienced in the same terms of gesture, figure and projection of human qualities onto inanimate matter we have encountered in the previous chapter. Ultimately it could even lead to a response of living presence.

Contrary to a widespread opinion, it was only in the late eighteenth century, when the classical tradition was coming to an end, that reactions to buildings informed by rhetoric did lead to the view that they are speeches in stone, or that classical architecture is a language.[2] Discussions of the meaning of architecture in the seventeenth century often turned around the question whether it is a natural sign or a conventional language. When architecture is considered to be a natural sign, the issues of closeness to nature, lifelikeness and vividness as the main instruments of persuasion return that were so prominent in the previous chapter. Perhaps the most widespread variety of this view is the tendency to humanize buildings: to attribute human characteristics, personality traits or even behaviour to them. Such humanizing readings transform architectural qualities such as proportion, relief or the play of light or shadow on a façade into the expression of character and emotion or gesture. This view, of which Sir Christopher Wren was an eloquent advocate, as we shall see below, allows for buildings to signify non-verbally in the sense that meaning is conveyed by the design of space and light, the contrast between robustness and lightness, the handling of the less iconic parts of the orders such as the corona, and other typically architectural means.

This chapter opens with two English responses to classical architecture from the seventeenth century that draw on theories of meaning that were supplanted a century later by linguistic analogies: Walter Montague's defence of the Italianate, classicizing splendour at the Court of Charles I, which uses typology or figural interpretation; and Sir Christopher Wren's response to the Temple of Peace, which is in part informed by heraldry and emblematics. They both draw on a complex of interpretive attitudes developed in Bible exegesis from the early days of Christianity onwards. Its chief characteristic is the conviction that God has used His creation as natural signs, and that Scripture and the

Book of Nature – words and things – are their main repository. This conviction led to a particular cast of mind in which every created object under the sun can be interpreted as an allegorical sign. It was the driving factor behind typology, allegorical interpretation, and the creation of *imprese*, emblems and heraldry. Rhetoric played a role in such responses in more than one way: on the most practical level, producing emblemata was part of the training school boys received at grammar school. In fact Quintilian defined emblemata as passages ready at hand to be inserted when needed by the orator; they are therefore very close to common places, *loci communes* or *topoi*.[3] Secondly, there is a strong persuasive dimension to allegory and emblems: like meditation exercises they serve to direct the mind away from sin and towards God. And in the third place the multi-media genre of the emblem like rhetoric draws on *enargeia*: on the use of images taken from the Book of Nature to add to the persuasive power of words. The final two sections of this chapter are devoted to the use of the rhetorical concept of style as an instrument to interpret architecture, and to French theories of *caractère*, another instance of the tendency to humanize a work of art in order to understand its impact on the viewer. The wide currency gained by *caractère* in French architectural discourse after 1750 is often considered as a symptom of the decay of the authority of the Vitruvian paradigm because it signalled a shift away from proportion and other qualities of the building itself towards the experience of the viewer. The analysis of works of art on the basis of stylistic characteristics is generally regarded as a founding moment in the formation of modern architectural history. Nevertheless, the art-historical use of style as an analytical tool ultimately goes back to the rhetorical distinction of *res* and *verba*, and *caractère* is yet another variety of the humanizing tendency that is so often a part of rhetorical response to art.

'THE SHADDOWES THAT SIGNIFIE'

In 1648 Walter Montague, an English courtier, published a collection of religious essays, called *Miscellanea Spriritualia*. One of them is a defence of the court of Charles I:

> [A]ll the exteriour state and Ceremony and Reverence (being truly conceived) is significative as referr'd to the images of God, and thus all the distinguished ranks of honour, which compose the formall order of Courts, are figures of those different degrees of Ministers, which attend their Originall, the King of Kings: and in this order, the Glory and Majesty which exteriorly in all sorts, resideth about the persons of Princes, may be fitly understood to represent (in such shaddowes as these materialities can make) the celestiall magnificence of the King

of Heaven: so that one who will interpret religiously the Ceremonies of Princes Courts, may say, *all things befall them in figures.*[4]

Montague (1603?–1677) was the second son of Sir Henry Montague, the first Earl of Manchester. After Cambridge he went abroad. In 1635 he abjured the Anglican faith in a ceremony presided over by the Pope after having witnessed the exorcism of the Ursuline nuns at Loudun. In spite of this highly publicized conversion he was allowed to return to England, and on his return he was well received at the court of Charles I, in particular by the Duke of Buckingham. He became a friend of Queen Henrietta Maria, to whom he dedicated the *Miscellanea Spiritualia.* The essay starts as a statement of the familar and widespread doctrine that the king is the representative on earth of God, and that his court and its organization reflect the kingdom of heaven. Its splendour and beauty are but a representation of the beauty, order and perfection of heaven.

By that time, politicians such as Thomas Strafford, churchmen like Archbishop Laud, architects like Inigo Jones and the Stuart kings themselves believed that the harmony of the body politic was based on the divine harmony with which God had endowed His creation, and that this harmony should be represented and proclaimed in architecture as well. The king was often compared to the keystone of the political edifice; but the architect was compared to God, because he too was a creator, who presented tangible and visible models of harmony and proportion. Architecture thus became more than a useful art; it aimed to be the persuasive embodiment of current ideas about what the state should be, and how its citizens should behave. In Chapter Four we have seen how Inigo Jones used his masques to present the public with a vision of Britain as a harmonious monarchy in classical dress that reflected divine order. Classical architecture and the pomp of court ceremonial were both agents in the service of that vision.

Grasping this message of classical architecture is not a straightforward matter of aesthetic appreciation of its formal qualities. It requires classical learning and specialist training in analysing proportion and the handling of the orders,. both of which had not yet become very widespread in early seventeenth-century Britain. Classical architecture was also, particularly in the decades leading up to the Civil War, very much tainted with Catholic associations, as the hostile reactions to Jones' Corinthian portico to Old St. Paul's and his wary handling of that order in the chapel he built for Queen Henrietta Maria show.[5] Surviving evidence of reactions to classical architecture displays a very wide range of references, but stylistic issues did not feature very prominently. The poet Samuel Daniel gave a memorable expression of both these mixed feelings about classical architecture and the wider cultural context of its reception: 'All our understandings are not to be built by the square of Greece and Italy. [. . .] Let us go no further but look upon the wonderful architecture of this state of England and see whether they were deformed times that could give it such a form'.[6]

Walter Montague's defence of the splendour of the Stuart court is revealing because it defends the use of classical architecture and religious ceremony at the court, and because it is unusually explicit about the terms in which that architecture and ritual were perceived, and how they made their persuasive impact. He did not use proportion, the handling of the orders or other critical categories of the aesthetics of classical architecture, but traditional religious typology, with its long roots in early Christian apologetics and rhetoric.

Typology

In the seventeenth century typological or figural interpretation was a widely used interpretation technique that was rooted in rhetoric and profoundly Christian in character; at the same time it was capable of accommodating art and architecture's visuality.[7] Invention and interpretation are closely related in rhetorical theory: stylistic strategies for achieving persuasion also functioned as strategies of interpretation, and interpretation itself aims to persuade. A similar connection between invention and interpretation characterizes typology. Not only was it one of the most influential ways of attributing meaning to nature and art alike; it was also developed in the intensely persuasive setting of early Christian writing as part of the effort to convince the heathen of Christianity's truth. Its late descendants are still with us, for instance in Freudian psychoanalysis. Through typological or figural interpretation, two real, historical objects, events or persons within the same continuing, unified history are shown to be connected. This is an important difference with allegory: whereas in allegory images are linked to abstract concepts, typology links real things with real things. As the seventeenth-century German divine Johann Gerhard put the difference:

> A type exists when something in the Old Testament is shown to have prefigured or foreshadowed something done or to be done in the New Testament. Allegory is when something from either the Old or the New Testament is explained in some new way and is accommodated to some spiritual doctrine of the holy life ... Typology consists in the comparison of facts. Allegory is concerned with words themselves, from which it brings forth some useful, though recondite doctrine.[8]

Typology resulted from the combination of rhetorical analysis of style with Christian philosophy of history, but its origins and uses are not exclusively classical or Christian. The Christian view of human history as a unified series of events, unfolding in a temporal continuum that starts with Original Sin and ends in the Last Judgement, is a continuation of the Jewish view of human history which also started with the Fall of Man, but offered a promise of the coming of the Messiah. Typology or figural interpretation combined this view of history with Greek, more particularly Hellenistic allegorical interpretation, originally developed to explain passages in Homer that were unclear, unseemly or below the usual standards of quality.[9]

As we have seen, the Latin *figura* originally meant the living shape of things. Etymologically it is related to *fingere*, *effigere* and *fictor* (to form, to feign, to make, and somebody who engages in these activities). The Greek *túpos* shares this sense of shape: it can mean both a stamp, mould or matrix or the outline, shape or impression produced by such a matrix, for instance a seal that is impressed on wax. Quintilian defined 'figura' as any 'form of expression to which a new aspect is given': they are what he calls gestures or attitudes of language, occurring when rhetorical or poetical changes to 'the simple and obvious method of expression' have been made. All these visual metaphors play on *figura*'s original meaning of form or shape, that is, physical appearance. As we have seen in Chapter Three Quintilian described the effect of figures as one of humanizing speech: through their use a speech becomes like an animate person, changing its facial expression and using gesture.[10] In the context of figural interpretation two related figures are of particular interest: *allegoria* ('saying one thing, while intending something else to be understood'), and *emphasis*, meaning something different from, or contrary to what you say. Quintilian gives as an example of *allegoria* a quotation from Virgil's *Aeneid*, where Dido asks:

> Might I not have lived,
> From wedlock free, a life without a stain,
> happy as beasts are happy?[11]

In spite of her complaints about marriage Dido implies that an unmarried life is a life not fit for man, but only for the beasts of the field. In Quintilian's time *allegoria* had become so widely used that his colleagues often restricted the use of the term *figura* to this turn of speech. It occurs when the speaker indicates or excites suspicion that his meaning is other than his words seem to imply; but the underlying meaning is not contrary to what is said, as in the case of *emphasis*; it is a hidden meaning which the hearer must discover.[12] This figure can be suitably employed when it is unsafe to speak out openly; when the hidden meaning is indecorous; or when it adds novelty and variety to the speech to leave things to be discovered by the public rather than express them directly. What is interesting about this figure of speech here is not so much its actual character but the interpretative attitude it fosters: the public is encouraged to look under the surface, to go beyond the appearances for meanings that are similar to what is expressed, but for some reason cannot be put directly into words. But the public is also asked to look for similarities.

The use of this *figura* is discussed by Quintilian as part of his advice on *elocutio*, on stylistic strategies of persuasion in writing a speech. But the interpretative attitude it engenders is tied in with existing traditions of allegorical interpretation. One of the first Greek authors we know about, Pherecydes of Syros (*fl. c.* 550 BC), had begun to realize that some of Homer's words could not be understood literally.[13]

From the third century BC allegorical interpretation became something of a stoic specialism. Chrysippus of Soli (280–207 BC) was one of the first of its exponents to apply allegorical interpretation to a painting. According to Origenes

> in one place Chrysippus [...] expounds the meaning of a picture at Samos, in which Hera is portrayed as performing unmentionable obscenities with Zeus. This honourable philosopher says in his treatises that matter receives the generative principles of God, and contains them in itself for the ordering of the Universe. For in the picture at Samos matter is Hera and God is Zeus.[14]

Quite early in its development allegorical interpretation was therefore applied to the visual arts.

Figural or typological interpretation is based on a view of history as a unified continuum in which earlier events announce or foreshadow subsequent happenings. Within the Jewish and Christian religions this was part of their view of history as sacred history, created and shaped by God. But the tendency to read history in such terms is almost universal, and may be the result of the human need to give significance to historical events.[15] The medieval and Renaissance notion of the *translatio imperii*, of Northern nations continuing the Roman Empire, which motivated Inigo Jones' classical appropriation of Stonehenge, is a case in point.[16]

Somewhat similar views of history may also be found in Roman authors, most conspicuously in Book VI of Virgil's *Aeneid*, where Rome is presented as the new Troy against the background of a cyclical view of history, visualized – not to say figured – by a wheel. In fact one could argue that the *Aeneid*, with its narrative of the destruction of Troy and foundation of Rome, separated by Aeneas' descent into the Underworld to learn both about the past and the future, is probably the best-known classical formulation of the philosophy of history on which typology is based.[17] But the most famous passage in pagan Roman literature, and one eagerly seized by Christian apologists from Augustine to Dante, is that in Virgil's fourth *Eclogue*, where the birth of a child is celebrated, and a new golden age is announced when nature will again be paradise and 'the serpent shall die'.[18]

It is against this background that the development of typological interpretation must be understood: the rhetorical use of *figura* to suggest a hidden, but similar meaning, primarily as a stylistic strategy, but with important implications for the interpretive attitude of the public; the stoic allegorical reading of important texts such as the *Iliad* or *Odyssey* to recover their sense obscured by difficulties of language or corrupt manuscripts; and the Palestinian Rabbinic tradition of reading the words of the Septuagint in such a way that they show God's deeds and intentions based on a view of history as a unified continuum of fall from grace and ultimate Messianic redemption.[19] In a few places in the Old Testament, and a substantial number of passages in the Evangelical and Apostolic writings, events that have happened before the birth of Christ are presented as shadows, patterns or models of events to come after His birth.

This way of interpreting biblical history is generally said to begin with St. Paul's Epistle to the Hebrews 5.14, in which Adam is described as a type of Christ.[20] The words used are *túpos* in the Greek version, *forma* in the Vulgate, and *figura* in the King James Version. In the first Epistle by St. Peter the baptism of Christ is presented as the antitype (again translated as 'figure' in the King James Version) of Noah's salvation of humankind from the flood (3.21).[21] What these passages show is an interpretation of biblical history as a unified continuum, in which events or persons in the Old Testament are said to announce, prophesy or foreshadow subsequent events in the New Testament, by which they are fulfilled and overwhelmed. The tree of Jesse is the type of the Cross, its antitype; the journey through the Red Sea a type of Christian baptism; the paschal lamb a type of Christ's death on the cross.

There may be said to be two rationales behind this exegetical procedure. One is hermeneutic and rhetorical, the other theological. An object or person A may be said to be the type of object or person B because of a resemblance in shape, form, or character that is so strong that it convinces. But another defining characteristic of figural or typological interpretation is that it stays with the appearances. Unlike allegorical exegesis it does not delve behind them to reveal a hidden meaning; instead, it takes the outward appearance, the shape of object A as the starting point. Both the Greek *túpos* and the Latin *figura* (like the English figure) share this reference to the appearance, in the case of *figura* even the living shape, the aspect or form of an object or person. The theological rationale is the Christian philosophy of history building on the Palestinian Rabbinic exegesis discussed above. It was formulated in the second century by Melito of Sardis in a *Homily on the Passion*, in a choice of words that would have a long resonance through the ages and across a wide range of human pursuits. He likened the types in the Old Testament to the scale-models a sculptor uses as patterns when he is carving a full-scale sculpture. The model is only of service while the statue is being made. By looking at it, the sculptor forms a mental picture of the finished work and knows how to shape the material. But when the statue is finished, the model can be discarded. In the same way:

> The people was held in honour before the Church arose, and the Law was wondrous before the Light of the Gospel was shed abroad.

> But since the Church arose and the Gospel was shed abroad upon men on earth, the type is made void, giving over the image to the natural truth.[22]

Melito used types in the same sense as St. Paul. He believed Old Testament types were powerful mysteries because of the truth they foreshadowed:

> The sacrifice of the sheep was found to be the salvation of Israel, and the death of the sheep became the life of the people, and the blood abashed the angel. Tell me, angel, what stayed thy hand, the sacrifice of the sheep or the life of the Lord? The death of the sheep, or the type of the Lord?[23]

From its earliest occurrences artistic metaphor was used to explain the working of types and antitypes. Types are compared to sculptor's models, to sketches or fully worked out paintings and to theatrical representation. As the English theologian William Tyndale put it in 1530:

> And moreover, though sacrifices and ceremonies can be no ground or foundation to build upon; that is, though we can prove nought with them, yet when we have once found out Christ and his mysteries, then we may borrow figures, that is to say allegories, similitudes, or examples, to open Christ, and the secrets of God hid in Christ, even unto the quick, and to declare them more lively and sensibly with them than with all the words in the world. For similitudes have more virtue and power with them than bare words, and lead a man's wits farther into the pith and marrow and spiritual understanding of the thing, than all the words that can be imagined. And though also that all the ceremonies and sacrifices have, as it were, a star-light of Christ, yet some there be that have, as it were, the light of the broad day, a little before the sun-rising; and express him, and the circumstances and virtue of his death so plainly, as if we should his passion on a scaffold, or in a stage-play, openly before the eyes of the people; as the scape-goat, the brazen serpent, the ox burnt without the host, the passover lamb, &c. [. . .].[24]

What makes figural interpretation so important in the context of this book is that it is intensely visual in character. When the Church Father Tertullian introduced the word *figura* around 200 AD to discuss typological interpretation, it is the outward, living shape of persons and events that is both the focus of interpretation and that which gives them their mysterious significance.

Events and persons in the Old Testament (Moses, Noah) are called a 'figuram futuri', a figure of things to be. Christ's saying at the Last Supper while breaking bread – 'this is my body' – is interpreted to mean 'this is a figure of my body'. Tertullian adds that it could not have been a figure unless the bread had in truth been his body.[25] As the historian of European literature Erich Auerbach pointed out in his fundamental contribution to the study of figural interpretation:

> Its integral, firmly teleological, view of history and the providential order of the world gave it the power to capture the imagination [...] of the convert nations. Figural interpretation was a fresh beginning and a rebirth of man's creative powers.[26]

It provided one of the most widely used conceptual frameworks both for an understanding of the arts, an apology for their use and enjoyment, and a rationale for achieving and grasping their effect as persuasive statements. In John Donne's *Devotions upon Emergent Occasions* God is presented as both the creator of a system of types and antitypes, and compared to the light of early morning which, like a painter, gives life to all he paints with his brushes:

> Neither art thou thus a *figurative*, a *metaphoricall God* in thy *word* only, but in thy *workes* too. The *stile* of thy *works*, the *phrase* of thine *actions*, is *metaphoricall*. The institution of thy whole *worship* in the *old Law*, was a continuall *Allegory*; *types and figures* overspread all; and *figures* flowed into *figures*, and powred themselves out into *farther figures*; *Circumcision* carried a *figure* of *Baptisme*; and *Baptisme* carries a *figure* of that *purity*, which we shall have in *perfection* in the *new Jerusalem*.[27]

Even though typology as a strategy of invention in the visual arts became less common after 1500,[28] it was still used in a few conspicuous examples such as Michelangelo's frescoes for the Sistine Chapel and Rubens' *Triumph of the Eucharist* of 1625–7. But as a strategy of interpretation its use remained widespread.

Walter Montague's typological defence of courtly splendour

In Montague's defence of the court of King Charles, it now becomes clear that when he called it a type of heaven, he did not intend this in the sense of a prototype or model. Instead it receives a much more august status, as the prefiguration or foreshadowing of the heavenly court. By implication Charles' man-made environment becomes part of God's creation. While the uninitiated will remain content with enjoying its material riches and ceremonies, the true Christian will know that its outward forms and ceremonies are types of heavenly mysteries:

> In the Law of Moses, all the Rites and Ceremonies were not only declaratory formes of the present Religion, but significative figures of a future state; and howsoever, most of the vulgar looked no farther then the glosse and lustre of the exterior vaile, which was the beauty and decency of the forme, and order that affected them; yet the nobler sort passed their sight through their vaile, and fixed it upon the signification, and mysterie itselfe, and thereby, had not only their eye of sense delighted, but that of their understanding enlightened by these objects.[29]

Montague did not single out the handling of the orders, the use of classical models or proportion in his reflections on the Italianate forms introduced by Charles I and his wife Henrietta Maria. Instead, he used that typical rhetorical approach of staying with the appearance of works of art, whose beauty and splendour attract the attention of the viewer. The uninitiated can remain in that stage and be persuaded through that external splendour of the truth of Jewish religion; but those who look further than their 'gloss and lustre' would also grasp what these rites and ceremonies reveal about the new covenant. Montague explained this by taking Rome, the classical city par excellence, as an example:

> Such a figurative conception Saint Fulgentius framed out of these images, when he was asked, whether the beauty and Majesty of Rome did not worke upon his affections. He answered, if terrestiall Rome be so beautifull, how glorious must be celestiall Jerusalem? His minde was so little taken or retarded on her way, as she stayed not at all in the outward Court of the Gentiles, but passed on, as in her way through it, to the Holy of Holies [...].[30]

The beauties of the court and Rome are not a distraction, or something to be ignored in the process of ascetism that will lead to spiritual salvation, but types and shadows of heaven, and their close scrutiny will only help the believer on his way. The courtier or the visitor to Rome should not turn his or her eyes away from their splendour; they should not regard them as mirrors that only reflect their own status and importance, but as lenses that help them to see clearer. The imagination is here presented not as the faculty to create fancies, but literally as the power to create images. Helped by the vivid works of art and architecture at court, it creates true images of heaven. It is this vividness or visual attractiveness that affects the viewer and binds his or her attention:

> [...] by this method, who attend the offices of their mindes upon earth, and waite not upon the places of their bodies, concluding that they are but strangers and passengers through these courts, and Fellow-Citizens of the Saints and Domestikes of God; make excellent use of all the lustrous, and polished glories of the place; for instead of looking on them as flattering glasses, and mirrours which reflect only the materiall beauty of the earth, they make opticke glasses of them, through which they do the easier take the height of the celestiall glories: and surely, the sight of our minde is much helped by such materiall instruments, in the speculation of spiritualities, by reason that in this her prison, all the intelligence of our minde with immaterialities, passeth as I may say, through her keepers hands, which are her senses, that can carry nothing but corporeall images to her.[31]

The typological frame of mind transforms the mirrors of the court that reflect earthly pomp into telescopes with which heaven can be discerned. In other words, the court becomes a natural sign which through its resemblance with the heavenly court leads the soul to contemplation of spiritual reality; but the medium of this process is not allegory, or some other abstract intellectual process of reference. Since the soul can only be affected by images brought to her by the senses, it is only by the natural language of surrounding objects that this process can be effected. The medium of architectural persuasion is not some conventional, allegorical meaning attached to court architecture, but the visual and tactile impact of the buildings and objects themselves on the senses.

Sir Christopher Wren on the Temple of Peace

From the mid-1670s the architect and scientist Sir Christopher Wren worked on a treatise that was not finished or published during his lifetime. Tract IV offers some observations on a Roman building that at the time was taken to be the Temple of Peace in Rome, but is now generally considered to be the Basilica of Constantine and Maxentius (see Figs. 6.1–6.3 for the reconstruction by Palladio).[32] At present the Basilica is a large ruin, and very little remains of the original splendour of the building. But what intrigued Wren, and sparked off his extraordinary statement of what this building does to the beholder, was not its unprecedented scale or issues of reconstruction, but a relatively minor detail, the absence of the corona in the interior order. Today this can be discerned with some difficulty (Fig. 6.4); but Wren, who never set foot in Rome, probably used the reconstruction by Palladio

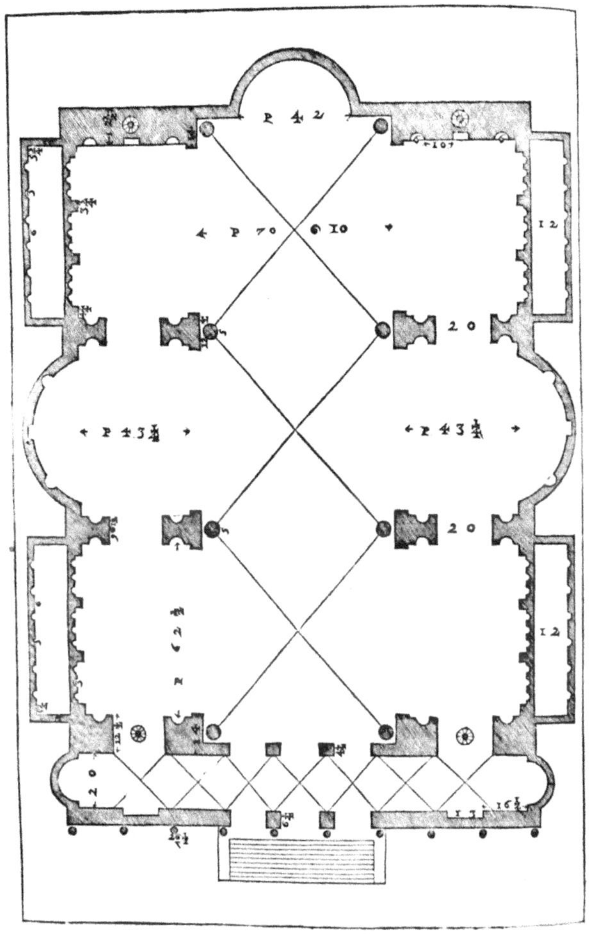

6.1 Andrea Palladio, plan of the Temple of Peace in Rome. From: Andrea Palladio, *I Quattro Libri dell'Architettura*, Book IV, p. 12 (photo: University Library, Leiden University, Leiden, Netherlands).

in the *Quattro Libri* as his source.[33] He began with some general observations on the design of the façade, noting the optical effect of the low and broad portico:

> I have admired the Greatness and Firmness of this Pile, but I cannot commend the Architect's Judgment for obscuring the majestick Stature of it with an humble Portico, and low Wings, which cause the visual Ray to cut off very much of the Height; so that in Perspective the Front will look exceeding broad and flat, and, to those that approach the Entrance, will seem as it were grafted upon the low Portico; though the Grace in the double Frontispice and Acroteria, doth something make amends, distinguishing the mighty Breadth into several Parts.[34]

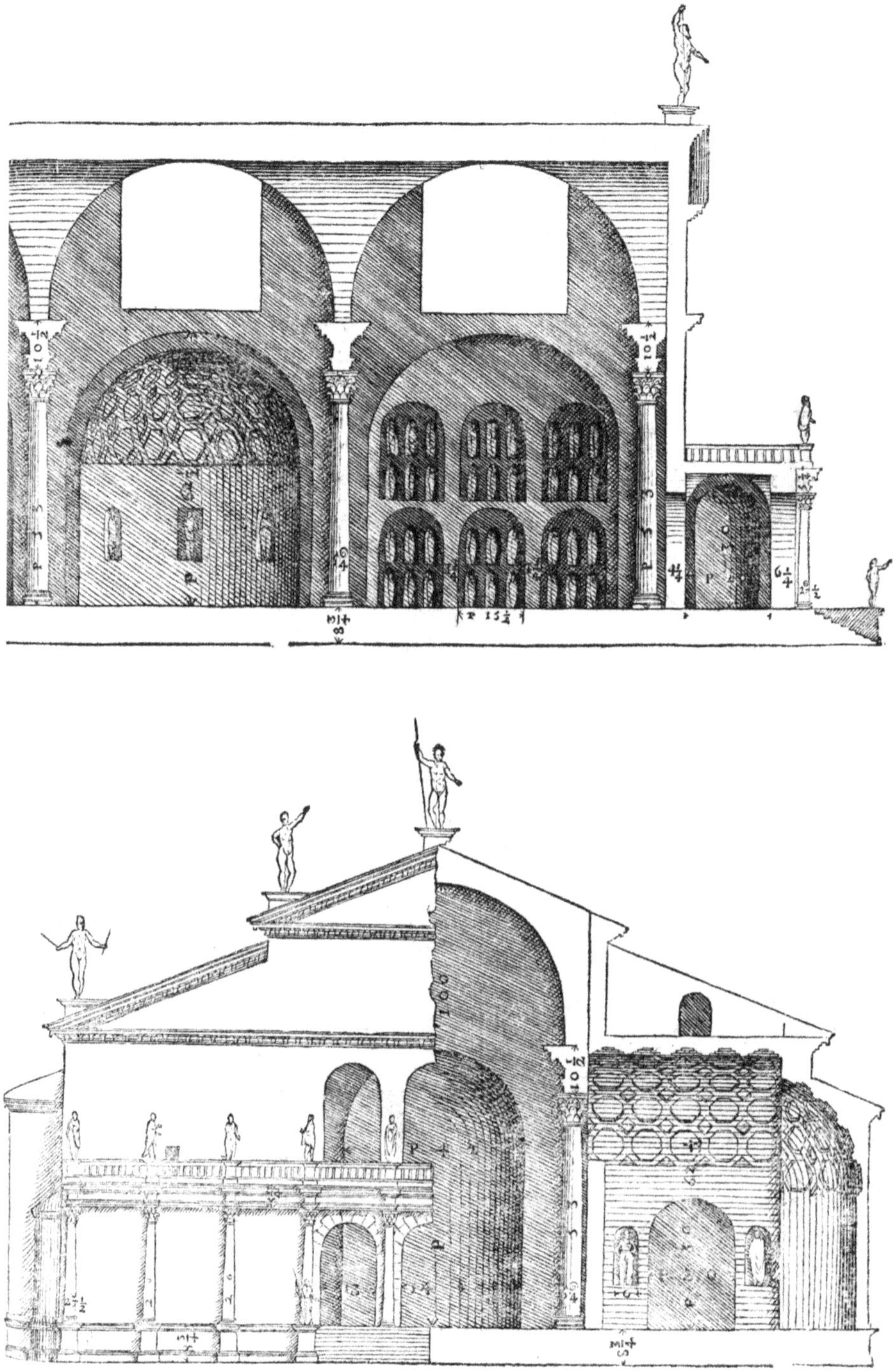

6.2 Andrea Palladio, interior and elevational section of the Temple of Peace in Rome. From: Andrea Palladio, *I Quattro Libri dell'Architettura*, Book IV, p. 13 (photo: University Library, Leiden University, Leiden, Netherlands).

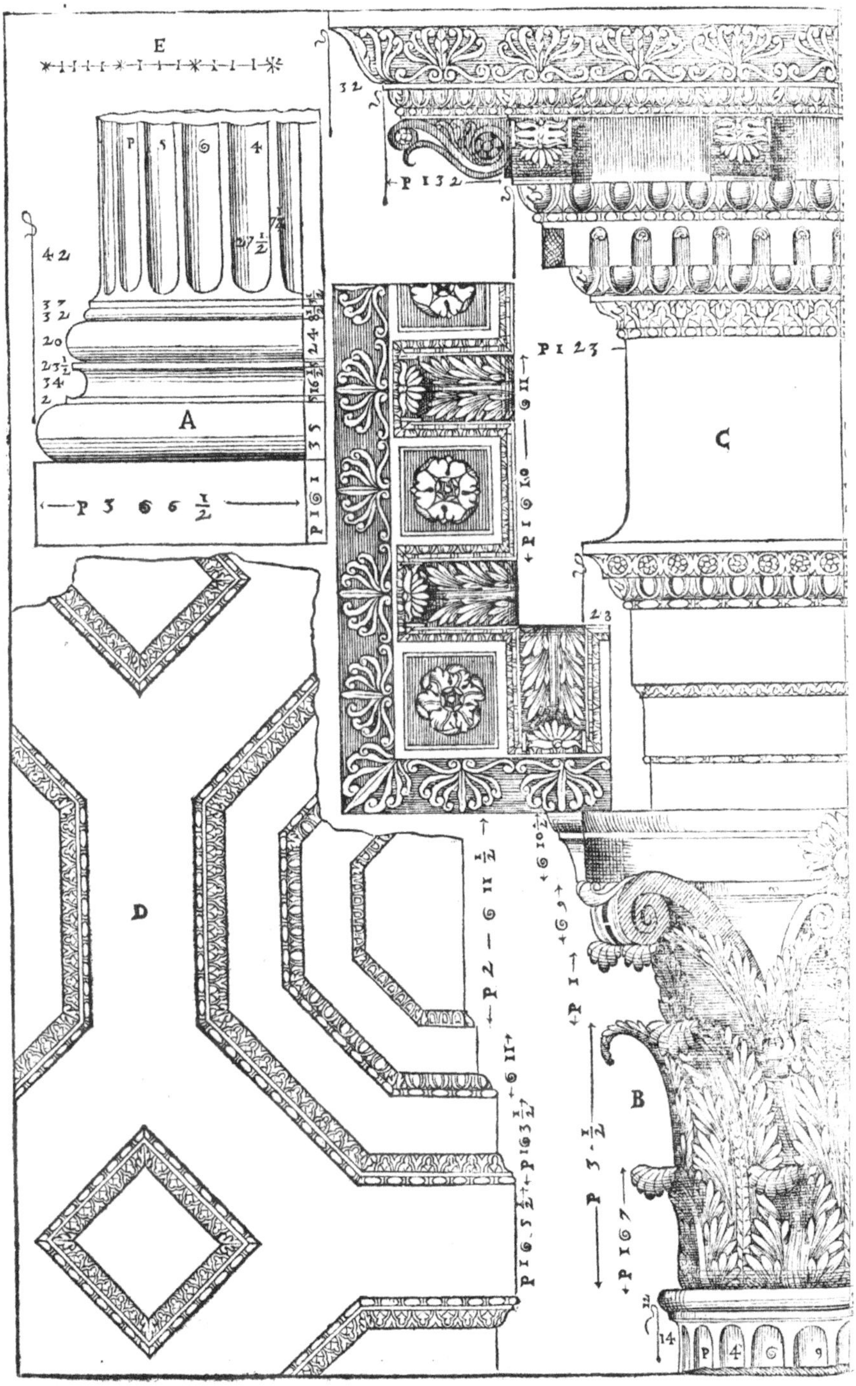

6.3 Andrea Palladio, detail of the order of the Temple of Peace in Rome. From: Andrea Palladio, *I Quattro Libri dell'Architettura*, Book IV, p. 14 (photo: University Library, Leiden University, Leiden, Netherlands).

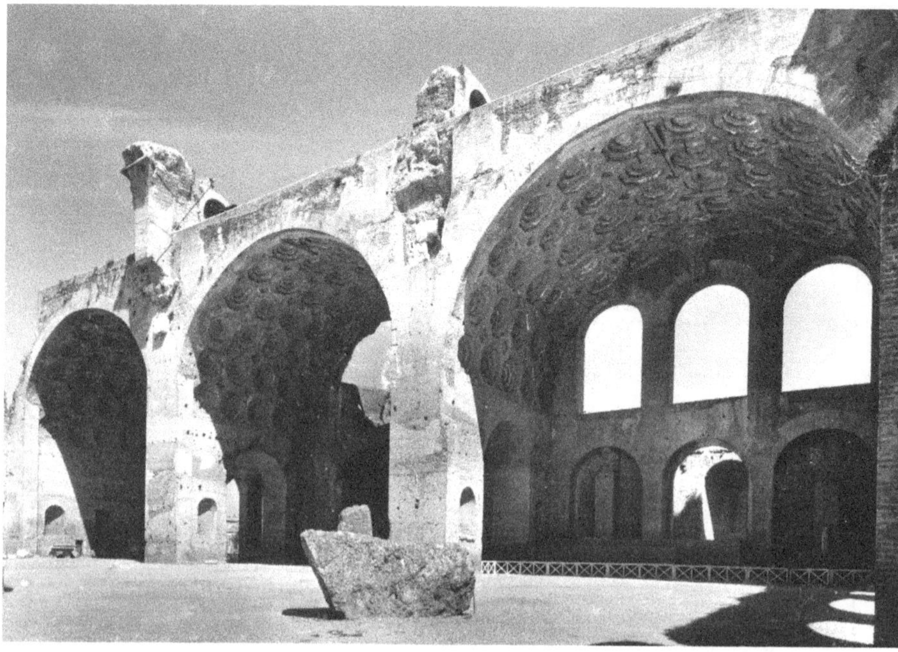

6.4 Basilica of Constantine and Maxentius. Rome: Forum Romanum AD 307 – after 312 (photo: Centre for Art-Historical Documentation, Radboud Universiteit Nijmegen).

He then zooms in on the absence of the corona:

> But shall I accuse Antiquity for want of Skill in Opticks, of which every where it shews such admirable Proofs? since particularly here the Architect hath given great Testimony of it in the Contrivance of his Cornice, wherein he hath left out the *Corona*, or Hanging-square, by an unusual Example. The *Corona* seems an essential Part in all Cornices, as that which gives Denomination to the whole, and is necessary to the Beauty of a Cornice; because, by its Projecture, it shadows all the lower Members, receiving upon its plane Surface a terse Light from above; this gives the Eminence and distinct Appearance which we see in the Parts of a Cornice at distance; but the Artist here ingenuously apprehending that his Lights in this Fabrick stood level with his Cornice, and therefore it would want the Effect for which it is used, and that the Hanging-face of it would be fore shortened to nothing, to the Eye which beholds it from beneath, wisely left out this Member [. . .].[35]

The corona is the projecting, beam-like part with a flat, undecorated surface below the cyma recta and reversa of a cornice.[36] The Arch of Titus in Rome, for instance, does have one, whereas it is absent in the Arco dei Leoni in Verona.

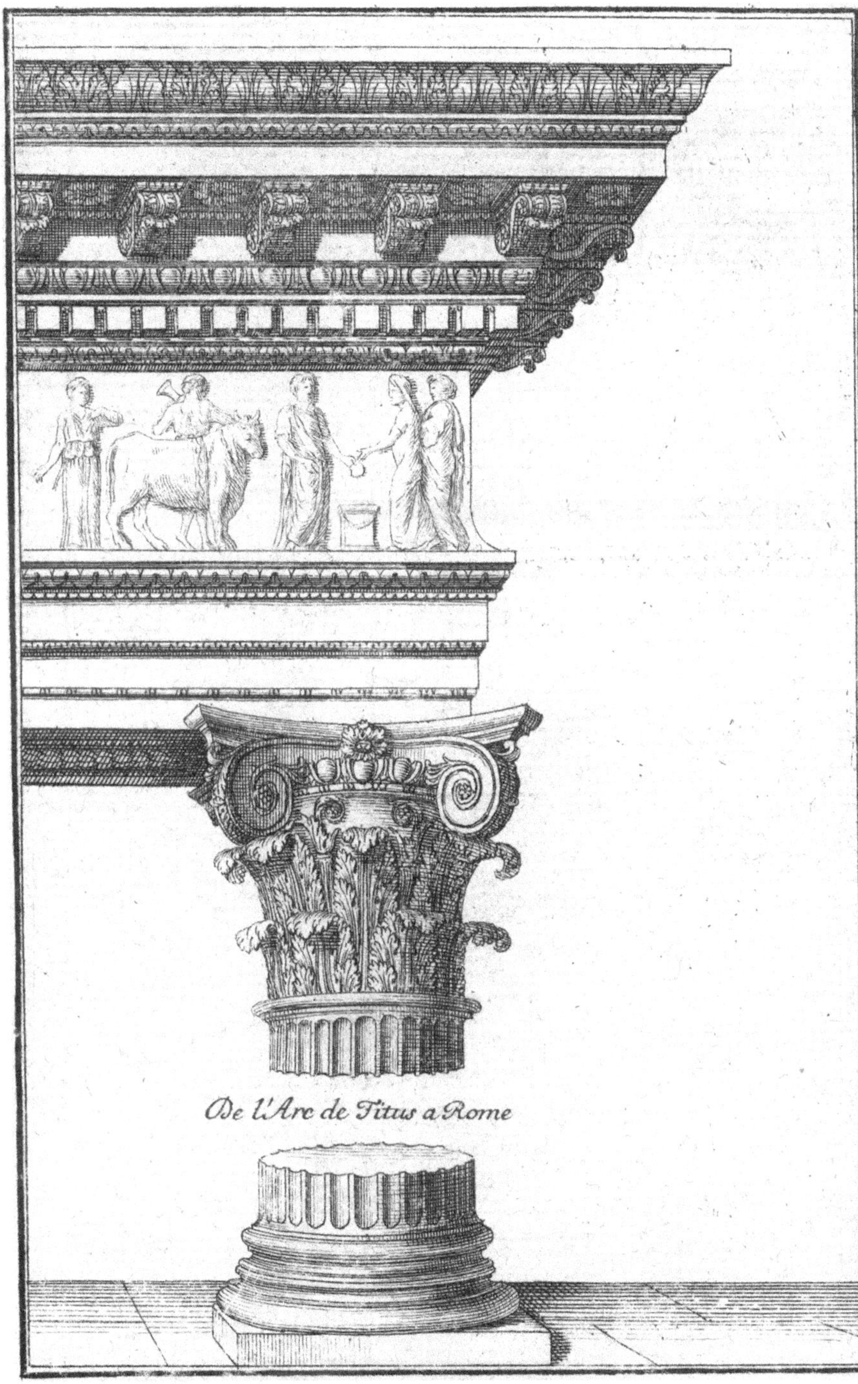

6.5 Arch of Titus. Rome, AD 81. From: R. Fréart de Chambray, *A Parallel of the Antient Architecture with the Modern* [...] *Made English for the Benefit of Builders* [...]. By John Evelyn Esq. London, 1664, p. 54 (photo: Koninklijke Bibliotheek, The Hague, Netherlands, 1296 B 29).

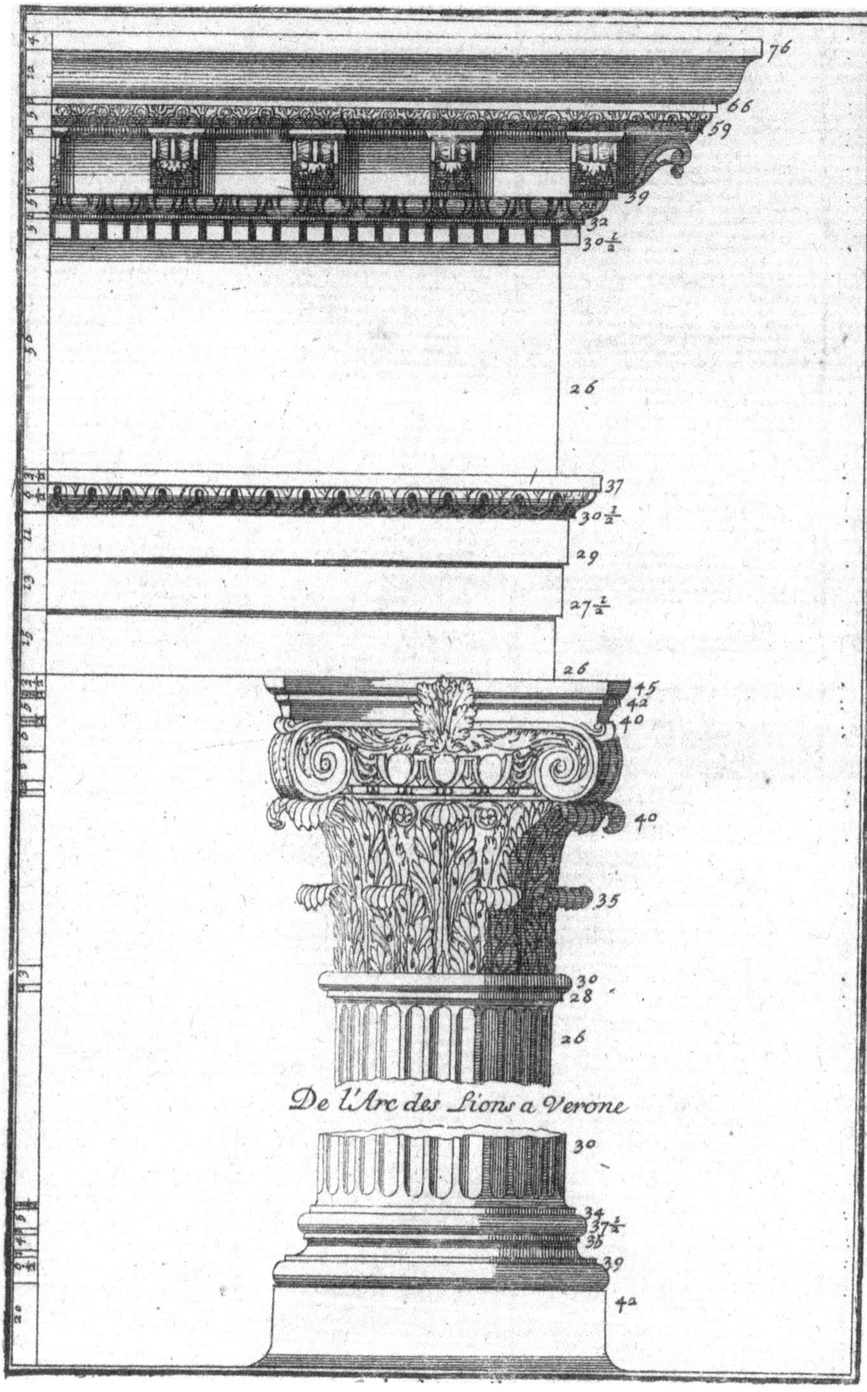

6.6 Arco dei Leoni, Verona, *c.* AD 50. From: R. Fréart de Chambray, *A Parallel of the Antient Architecture with the Modern* [. . .] *Made English for the Benefit of Builders* [. . .]. By John Evelyn Esq. London, 1664, p. 53 (photo: Koninklijke Bibliotheek, The Hague, Netherlands, 1296 B 29).

The illustrations in Fréart de Chambray's *Parallèle de l'Architecture antique et de la moderne*, originally published in 1650 and translated by John Evelyn in 1664 (Figs. 6.5 and 6.6) show the difference the corona makes in the visual appearance of a cornice. Omitting the corona might be the ground for severe criticism of the architect, but Wren refuses to go along with this. Instead he discusses the visual effect of the corona and tries to understand its absence in these terms.

Although Palladio and in his wake Inigo Jones had noted that the corona in the interior cornice had been replaced by modillions, Wren was the first to draw conclusions from its absence that go beyond the considerations of design and correct handling of the orders that had occupied previous authors.[37] His explanation of it is also very original. Wren tried to understand the reasons for its absence, and the explanation he provided starts from a thorough scrutiny of the entablature's surface. He did not consider it in terms of correct handling of the orders and their elements; nor did he attempt to give a structural or proportional rationale. Instead, his interest was in the visual aspect of this entablature. He observed that the corona is an essential part of all entablatures because it 'gives Denomination' to the whole cornice. Through its solid square mass it divides the upper and the lower parts of the cornice, and transforms the light that falls on the superior parts into shadow sheltering the lower parts from the glare of day light.

The optical considerations behind this visual effect are illustrated in the perspectival representation of the corona in the Arch of Titus in Rome as reproduced in Evelyn's *Parallel* (see Fig. 6.5).[38] The corona not only gives solidity and weight to the upper parts of the cornice and divides light and shadow, it also affects the degrees of plasticity of this part of the entablature: the parts above it are clearly detailed and sharply etched in the full blaze of sunlight falling on it, whereas the parts below it cannot be so clearly distinguished and form a dark mass of softer details. This play of light and shadow, sharp delineation and softer shadow, is an essential aspect of the aesthetic effect of classical design. It is hardly addressed in the Vitruvian treatises though, probably because scale models were used to calibrate the effect of mouldings, but possibly as well because until the development of projective geometry at the end of the eighteenth century, it was virtually impossible to give a mathematical analysis of the day light and shadow fall.[39] In this case, Wren observed, it would not do to include the corona, because the light of the sun did not strike the cornice from above, but was level with it (see Fig. 6.2 in the interior: the openings of the windows in the walls are on almost the same level as the top of the cornice).

Much has been made of Wren's empirical approach to the architecture of antiquity, and to design problems in general; of his preference for independent inquiry over the authority of history and religion, and his interest in experiment and trained observation which made him reject everything he could not observe and check himself.[40] This has been connected with his activities as an astronomer and mathematician, and his active role in setting up the agenda and contributing to the experiments of the Royal Society. Most commentators, however, have had far less to say about the sequel to this passage, in which Wren, in an unexpected lyrical outburst, praises the way in which the façade of this temple conveys the effect peace has on the human mind by purely visual and architectural means:

> It was not therefore Unskilfulness in the Architect that made him chuse this flat Kind of Aspect for his Temple, it was his Wit and Judgment. Each Deity had a peculiar Gesture, Face, and Dress hieroglyphically proper to it; as their Stories were but Morals involved: and not only their Altars and Sacrifices were mystical, but the very Forms of their Temples. No language, no Poetry can so describe Peace, and the Effects of it on Men's Minds, as the Design of this Temple naturally paints it, without any Affectation of the Allegory.[41]

At first sight he appears to reject the traditional ways of communicating meanings that lie outside of the visual object itself: gesture, face and dress, that is, the traditional iconographical attributes already listed in Vitruvius, such as the *boucrania* or skulls of sacrified animals sculpted in the metopes of the Doric order, or the Corinthian capital's reference to the maiden of Corinth. Wren's presentation of the ways in which this building conveys peace also focuses almost entirely on how it affects the beholder. It is not an attempt to show how the intrinsic properties of the building express or represent peace. Instead, it lists in what ways the temple makes the visitor experience peace by visual and architectural means, through the design of façade.

This interest in the effect of buildings on their beholders is a frequently recurrent theme in seventeenth-century English writing on architecture. These texts are distinguished by an interest in the particularities of the impressions buildings make, and by the attention paid to the gradual shifts in the experiences of spectators as they walk through a building. In 1638 for instance the unidentified author R.T. described the ways in which the architect can almost direct the experience of the spectator in a short treatise on church architecture called *De Templis*:

> [T]he man who enters the West door from farre beholding the Altar, where he seriously intends to offer his devotions to his God and Saviour, shall find his devout Soule, more rapt with divine awe and reverence, more inflamed with pure and holy zeale, in the delay and late approach unto it, than if at first he had entered upon it.[42]

Wren, who was an accomplished rhetorician, as his 1657 inaugural address as Gresham Professor of Astronomy shows, shared this interest in the visual impact of a building on its beholder.[43] Both his concentration on the emotional effect of the building on the mind and the aspects he singled out to illustrate the visual force of this building suggest rhetoric as the underlying model of communication. His praise for the openness of access of the temple, lack of arrogance, and disdain of invidious appearances recalls the characterizations by Cicero and Quintilian of the orator who has the best interests of his fellow-citizens and country at his heart: the *vir bonus dicendi peritus*, the skilled speaker who is first of all a gentleman:

> [This Temple] is easy of Access, and open, carries an humble Front, but embraces wide, is luminous and pleasant, and content with an internal Greatness, despises an invidious Appearance of all that Heighth it might otherwise justly boast of; but rather fortifying itself on every Side, rests secure on a square and ample Basis.[44]

But there is more to these notes on the Temple of Peace than an awareness of the visual impact of the absence of the corona and the suggestion that Wren connected its appearance with the impression a skilled orator should make on his public. What are we to make of Wren's references to hieroglyphs, involved morals, the mystical forms of pagan temples or the 'Affectation of the Allegory'? Much work has been done to situate Wren's work within the context of seventeenth-century science or natural philosophy; but here we must look at the contemporary background of his ideas on the meaning of architecture, which is rather less explored.

The observations on the Temple of Peace suggest that he believed architecture possessed, or was capable of expressing, a distinctly visual or architectural, as opposed to verbal, meaning: 'No language, no Poetry can so describe Peace, and the Effects of it in Men's Minds, as the Design of this Temple naturally paints it [. . .]'. That is, the temple becomes a representation of peace that the viewer understands immediately. He or she does not need any schooling in the conventions of allegory or embematics to grasp that this building is devoted to peace. Wren contrasts the conventional iconography of hieroglyphical gestures, attributes or dress traditionally used to represent deities in classical buildings with the natural way in which this temple represents peace.

Considered in these terms Wren's observations can be related to sixteenth- and seventeenth-century debates about natural versus conventional language, allegory, emblems and hieroglyphs. Defined in the broadest terms emblems are rhetorical inventions in which a novel or witty connection is suggested between a signifier and a signified, such as an image or motto and a concept or proverb; but at the same they were considered by early modern emblem theorists as an art resulting from inherent meanings already written in the Book of Nature by God. Originally the Greek word 'emblema' means something that is inserted, such as a badge. Quintilian discusses such insertions in his treatment of the use of common places in oratory, when he suggests that speakers improvise passages on commonplace themes in their speeches.[45] Emblems were not limited to the mixed media of word and image. As the sixteenth-century lexicographer Thomas Thomas put it in 1587: [emblems are] 'Picture works of wood, stone, or metall, finelie set or printed in divers colours'.[46]

Renaissance thought about verbal and visual meaning crystallized in discussions about the question whether emblems, imprese or heraldic signs were natural or conventional signs.[47] Andrea Alciato, the inventor of the emblem genre, had identified emblems with hieroglyphs as they were transmitted from Antiquity in the *Hieroglyphica* of Horapollo Nilus. Piero Valeriano, the latter's translator, considered hieroglyphs as part of the Book of Nature, and therefore as a language of natural signs, that is as a language created by God not man. In *De Re Aedificatoria* Alberti also alluded to this view when discussing the use of signs and images versus inscriptions:

> Inscriptions should be either written – these are called epigraphs – or composed of reliefs and emblems [*signis et imaginibus*]. [...] The Egyptians employed the following sign language: a god was represented by an eye, Nature by a vulture, a king by a bee [...]. They maintained that each nation knew only its own alphabet, and that eventually all knowledge of it would be lost [...] whereas the method of writing they used could be understood easily by expert men all over the world, to whom alone noble matters should be communicated.[48]

Bishop Joseph Hall, subsequently the very influential chaplain to King Charles I, neatly united emblematics and heraldry: 'God Himselfe was the first herald, and shall be the last'.[49] That is, every part of creation can be read as an emblem or impresa made by God. Seventeenth-century Italian and English authors tended to range emblems under natural language models, which seems to be Wren's intent as well. How widespread such views were is also shown by Lord Bacon, the intellectual precursor of Wren the empirical scientist. He grouped gesture and hieroglyphs together as natural signs in *The Advancement of Learning*. The passage paraphrases Aristotle's definition of language in *De Interpretatione*:

> These Notes of Cogitations are of two sorts; the one when the note hath some similitude or congruity with the notion; the other *ad placitum*, having force only by contract or acceptation. Of the former sort are Hieroglyphics and Gestures. For as to Hieroglyphics [...], they are but as continued impresses and emblems. And as for Gestures, they are as transitory Hieroglyphics, and are to Hieroglyphics as words spoken are to words written, in that they

> abide not; but they have evermore, as well as the other, an affinity with the things signified.[50]

Read against this background the 'Wit and Judgment' of the architect of the Temple of Peace made him design what we might call with Bacon an architectural emblem, using the natural language of gesture: it 'embraces wide'.

But classical architecture, because of its highly non-iconic character and culturally determined iconography, does not lend itself very well to become a natural emblem. So what can Wren have meant when he remarked that the Temple of Peace naturally paints peace? There is a clue in his remarks on its humble front and pleasant appearance. In Wren's description the building is transformed into a human being. By speaking of the Temple of Peace as if its façade were gesturing, and by stressing its accessible and noble character in a very interesting use of words that can be applied both to architecture and to human beings ('easy of access', 'carries an humble front', 'content with an internal Greatness'), this building is first naturalized, by aligning it with natural signs such as gesture, and then humanized. Human beings are part of God's creation and therefore are in themselves natural signs. This architectural gesture recalls the association of gesture with hieroglyphs and emblems in Francis Bacon's *Advancement of Learning*. He thought hieroglyphs to be natural signs, but their most notable variety was gesture. Wren transcends the abstract conventionality of traditional Vitruvian iconography. His description transforms the building from a conventional allegory into a natural sign that displays the outward characteristics of a living human being: gesture, expression and action. In doing so, he does not reduce the architecture of the Temple of Peace to a set of conventional textual signs. By describing its façade as a series of gestures and drawing attention to its spatial aspects he allows for a specifically architectural way of conveying meaning. The key to this is not only the naturalness of the Temple's design. The significance conveyed is not one fixed in the manner of verbal meaning. It is visual, and needs to be performed by the viewer in grasping the design of the façade as a series of gestures. Its ultimate foundation is a perception of the building as a human being, a person with an expressive face, who gestures and by all these expressive means exerts a benign agency on the viewer.[51]

Character and style in French architectural theory of the late eighteenth century

In Wren's analysis of the ways in which the Temple of Peace conveys meaning by architectural means the building is almost transformed into a person. Wren humanized the temple by describing its prominent features in terms of human behaviour: movement, gesture and expression. He also attributed a capacity to it which classical rhetorical theory saw as the defining characteristic of humanity: its capacity to speak. Both strategies featured very prominently in French architectural theory and criticism of the late eighteenth century. The first was the conceptual basis of the aesthetics of *caractère*; the second led to the introduction of the concept of style into architectural discourse.

Caractère

One of the topics the protagonists of Charles Perrault's *Parallèle des Anciens et des Modernes* (1688–92) discuss during their visit to Versailles is the universality of two core elements of classical culture: rhetoric and architecture, more in particular the five orders. Are they both a strictly European phenomenon, acquired by education and training, or is their knowledge and use innate and universal among humanity? The Abbé, who defends the Moderns, is put before us as a man of much learning, but more rich in his own ideas than in those taken from others. His opponent, the Président, is described as a man of genius, unlike the usual run of lovers of antiquity, who, because they cannot invent something new, always labour to fill through reading the void of their sterile imagination. According to the Président rhetoric is innate, but the use of the forms of classical architecture is not universal:

> Architectural ornaments are not the same as the ornaments of discourse. It is natural to man to make rhetorical figures, the Iriquois do it, and more abundantly than the best orators in Europe. But these same Iriquois do not use columns, architraves and cornices in their buildings.[52]

But his opponent, the Abbé, argues that using the classical orders, like the figures of speech, is open to everybody; true merit consists not in the simple fact that they are used, but in the manner in which they are employed:

> Just as the figures of rhetoric may be used by everybody, and present the same task to every speaker, the five Orders of architecture can be used by all architects. And just as the merit of orators lies not in using figures, but in using them well, an architect is praised not because he uses columns, pilasters and cornices, but because he employs them with judgment, and uses them to compose beautiful buildings.[53]

In this exchange the use of figures of speech is the defining feature of rhetoric, just as the use of the formal vocabulary offered by the orders defines ancient architecture. As we will see, a number of French architectural theorists of the eighteenth century followed the association of classical architecture and rhetoric developed in this conversation at Versailles. They also followed the Abbé in stressing that the use of the classical style has to be learned. Rhetoric offered a series of concepts to teach classical design as we have seen in Part One of this book. Associating architecture so closely with eloquence and the figures of speech also made it possible to understand it in the same rhetorical terms that were used to understand human speech.

Charles Perrault was one of the first French authors in the seventeenth century to connect architecture and rhetoric. Augustin-Charles d'Aviler compared mouldings to the letters of the alphabet in 1694.[54] In 1747 Charles Batteux had grouped rhetoric and architecture together in one category of his division of the fine arts, because they both combined the useful and the pleasant.[55] The comparison between elements of speech and elements of the orders, however, did not lead very far because the fundamental semantic indeterminacy of the parts of the orders prevents any interpretation of a building in the way one can construct the meaning of a sentence from the meaning of its constituent parts and the way these are combined. 'Man bites dog' and 'dog bites man', although composed of the same elements, unmistakably mean two different things; but a combination of various mouldings, such as a cyma recta, fascia and astragal in the Composite order does not have meaning in the same way, because classical architecture, like any other visual sign system, lacks the capacity to differentiate between verbs, adverbs and nouns. And besides, the meaning of these elements, placed in a different order, cannot be distinguished from its original arrangement in a Composite architrave.

A more interesting case of considering architecture and the impact it has on the spectator in terms of language and rhetoric is offered by Germain Boffrand in his *Livre d'Architecture* of 1745. One of the essays that precede the section showing his main buildings is based on the *Ars Poetica* by Horace. In the 'Principes tirés de l'Art Poétique d'Horace' passages from the Latin poem are quoted (and sometimes rewritten) to provide the basis for Boffrand's views on design. Although he compares profiles and mouldings to words because they are the constituents of buildings and discourse respectively, his position on the relation between buildings and language is in fact much more subtle and sophisticated, and had a great impact on subsequent French architectural theory.[56]

Boffrand was not unique in associating architecture and language or rhetoric, but he was probably the first theorist to apply the precepts of the *Art of Poetry* to architecture. The painter and theorist Roger de Piles had included a translation in his *Dialogue sur le Coloris* of 1673, together with an extensive commentary applying its precepts to painting.[57] The second chapter of the *Livre d'Architecture* opens with a consideration of the relations between the arts and sciences. They are so closely related that the principles of one art can serve as those of another.[58] In fact, the theoretical part of the *Livre d'Architecture* ends with an affirmation of Boffrand's belief in the unity of the arts: 'In general, every department of architecture, sculpture and painting must combine to make a single whole'.[59] Not only are all the arts and sciences so intimately linked that some of the principles of architecture are derived from mathematics but painting, sculpture and poetry are sisters. The first two speak to the eyes, the third to the ear, and music paints natural events. Up to this point, this is a rehearsal of what by then had become a commonplace in artistic theory, going back to Horace's *ut pictura poesis* and Cicero's statement in *Pro Archia* that the arts share each other's principles.

But Boffrand transformed this tradition. For him architecture is part of this sisterhood because it is a theatre; a building is a stage setting, announcing its function or destination just as the stage sets convey whether the piece to be acted is a comedy or tragedy; and a building itself is a character, which by its composition and ornament will disclose its personality to the spectator. Although architecture seems to be limited to the handling of building materials, it in fact becomes animated by its expression of the character of the various genres to which it belongs.

This expression of character is what makes architecture transcend its inanimate, material nature, and connects it to the other arts.[60] Design, structure and style depend on the character to be expressed, and are governed by considerations of decorum. In expressing character the architect should, like the dramatic poet, follow these considerations.

As the Latin version of Boffrand's book makes more explicit than the French, character here refers not only to the personality, so to speak, of the building, but is very closely associated to the genre the building belongs to: 'Architecture, although its object may seem to be no more than the use of material, falls into a number of genres'.[61] *Caractère* in French architectural theory of the eighteenth century is usually located within the context of discussions on the expression of the passions in painting, or linked to the physiognomy of Lavater. Robin Middleton, for instance, has recently argued that Boffrand's views on the expression of emotions in architecture had been influenced by the *Conférence sur l'Expression* of 1698 by the painter Charles Le Brun.[62] In it, Le Brun had argued, following Descartes' *Les passions de l'âme* (1649) that, since the face was closest to the soul, it was the most expressive part of the body. The eyes and eyebrows are the clearest indicators of the emotions because they are almost in direct contact with the soul. Four positions of the eyebrows show particular emotions, loving or irascible, simple or mixed. The mouth represented the movement of the heart. The basic modes could be combined, and in a later lecture Le Brun also demonstrated how the painter could use physiognomics, the study of the permanent characteristics of the body as they are moved by the passions, to give further refinement to the pictorial representation of the passions. According to Middleton, Boffrand followed Le Brun when he wrote that architecture can express all emotions by means of the straight, concave and convex line.[63] In this view, the façade and interiors of a building become a mask, expressing the passions associated with its destination by means of the lines of their mouldings, just as frowned eyebrows in the human face express anger or a threatening mood, and the upturned corners of the mouth cheerfulness.

There is, however, also another possible reading of *caractère*. As Boffrand put it, architecture can give life to its parts by expressing the characters belonging to the various genres.[64] The psychological and physiognomic origins and meanings of the term *caractère* are well known – although it should be noted that physiognomical readings of *caractère* based on the theories of Lavater postdate Boffrand's treatise.[65] But there is also a connection with rhetoric that has not yet been explored. Boffrand continued his discussion of genre and character by comparing architecture to poetry: they both have several genres, and within each art the style of one genre is not fitting for another. Genre and style are here closely associated. Classical handbooks on rhetoric used a number of terms when discussing style, varying from *stilus*, which means 'pen', but subsequently acquired the metaphorical meanings of the expression of thought and a writing manner that is characteristic of one particular author,[66] to *color scribendi* or the color of what one writes, a turn of phrase used by Boffrand as well. But when these handbooks discussed the topic of the styles appropriate to various genres, they spoke of the *genus dicendi*. The equivalent in Greek was *charaktèr*, from the verb *charassein*, to stamp, engrave or print, literally a mark or figure traced on paper, stone, or metal with some writing or drawing instrument to be the distinctive sign of something; in a figurative sense that what distinguishes something, and makes it stand out among others.[67] In this sense, it is clearly related to the Latin *species*, which can mean among other things an object's conspicuous aspect.[68] When considered with these rhetorical roots in mind, *caractère* can be seen to refer not only to Boffrand's theatrical view of architecture according to which a building, like an actor on the stage, expresses a character in the psychological sense. It also conveys the connotations of rhetorical theories of style, in which the various genres of speech are clearly distinguished and recognizable not only by the choice of vocabulary, but also by non-verbal means of communication such as gesture, facial expression and dress. Considered in this way *caractère* is not only part of a tendency to humanize architecture, of reading it in psychological terms, and of seeing a building as an individual. It also reflects the effort to consider the expressive qualities of a building in terms of persuasive and apt formulation, that is of style.

Style

The concept of style, the insight that a particular idea may be expressed in various ways, all with their specific connotations, was central to rhetoric.[69] It goes back to the rhetorical distinction between *res* and *verba*, the subject matter of a speech and its various formulations. Rhetorical handbooks generally distinguished three styles: grand or elevated (using many figures of speech and impressive words), intermediate (a more simple way of speaking, less florid), and plain (coming closest to everyday speech).[70] The selection of one of these styles depends on the effect the orator wants to achieve. The grand style is used to stir the emotions, the intermediate to exhort and deliberate, and the plain style to instruct. Academic doctrine took over the concept of style, both in the sense of the working manner characteristic of an individual artist, and in the sense of a hierarchy of styles that corresponded to a hierarchy of aims and genres: the grand style, for instance, was reserved for religious and historical scenes.

Boffrand not only gave new meaning to the traditional doctrine of the sister arts. He was also one of the first authors to use the term style in a systematic way when writing about architecture. Filarete had used the related terms 'stile' and 'maniera' around 1460 when he spoke of style as a means to recognize the work of an artist.[71] It was regularly applied to painting from the time of Poussin onwards.[72] The very first use of the term in an architectural context probably occurred in 1578, in documents related to the completion of San Petronio in Bologna.[73] A century later, Guarino Guarini used the term 'ordine' (e.g. 'ordine gotico') in his discussions of Gothic architecture, when he talks only about architecture, but 'style' when he placed architecture in the context of the other arts.[74] 'Style' began to be employed frequently in architecture from 1714 onwards in Great Britain, and from 1750 in France. Sir Christopher Wren used 'style' and 'manner' in his proposal for the completion of Westminster Abbey. Like Guarini, he used 'manner' to refer to the Gothic, and 'style' to refer to classical architecture or his own designs:

> This we now call the *Gothick* Manner of Architecture (so the *Italians* called what was not after the *Roman* Style) tho' the *Goths* were rather Destroyers than Builders; I think it should with more Reason be called the *Saracen* Style; [...]. I have made a Design, which will not be very expensive but light, and still in the *Gothick* Form, and of a Style with the rest of the Structure, which I would strictly adhere to, throughout the whole Intention: to deviate from the old Form, would be to run into a disagreeable Mixture, which no Person of a good Taste could relish.[75]

Well into the eighteenth century different types of architecture were described in terms of the architectural orders instead of stylistic terms. In France, Cordemoy's *Nouveau traité de toute l'architecture* (1714) did not contain an entry on style in the glossary attached to it. Instead, words like 'goût', 'manière', or 'genre' were used. And Montesquieu spoke in the same vein in his *De la manière gothique* of the 'goût' or 'ordre gothique'.[76]

Even if Boffrand did not directly apply the term 'style' to architecture, because of his close association of architecture and poetry he is the first to talk in a systematic way about architectural design in terms of style, instead of using it cursorily to draw the contrast between the Gothic and the classical as had been done by his predecessors:

> Through its composition a building expresses, as if in the theatre, that the scene is pastoral or tragic; that this is a temple or a palace, a public building destined for a particular purpose or a private house. By their planning, their structure and their decoration, all such buildings must proclaim their purpose to the beholder. If they fail to do so, they offend against expression and are not what they ought to be.
>
> The same is true of poetry: this, too, has its different genres; and the style of one does not suit another.[77]

He also spoke of the orders as if they were literary genres:

> As the genres of poetry are to its chosen subjects, so the orders of architecture used by the Greeks and Romans are to the various genres of building.[78]

Boffrand was not the first to make this connection. The Danish encyclopaedic writer Alsted, for instance, wrote in his *Encyclopaedia* of 1630 that 'columns are to the architect, what the modes are to the musician and the genres (*carminum genera*) to the poet'.[79] But by comparing architecture with poetry, and the orders of architecture with poetical genres, Boffrand could draw on the precepts of rhetoric to formulate his principles of architectural design. As we have seen, these principles concentrate on the appropriate use of ornament in accordance with the genre or character of the building; this reflects the rhetorical attention to the correspondence of the style of speaking (or *genus dicendi*) with the occasion, purpose, and audience of the speech, which should be guided by decorum.

This is not quite the same as the 'linguistic analogy' described by Peter Collins in *The Changing Ideals in Modern Architecture*.[80] He was concerned with the notion that the parts of a building can be compared to the parts of speech, or that architectural styles can be compared to languages since architecture, like language, is assumed to possess a syntax and a vocabulary. Even though Boffrand translated Horace's *verba* (words) and *syllaba* (syllables) with architectural terms such as 'parties' and 'profils', and compared the decorative parts of a building (profiles, mouldings – *profils, moûlures*) with the words of a building, he did not explicitly state that architecture is a language. Instead, his position is more subtle, and leaves room for specifically architectural means of expression such as the handling of space, ornament or the orders. The basis of the similarity between poetry and architecture is that both arts aim for expressive composition. In this Boffrand followed the precepts of rhetoric, which are based on the division of the process of writing or design into the *ratio rerum*, or subject matter, addressed in the stages of invention and disposition, and the *ratio verborum* or formulation of that subject matter in the stage of elocution and delivery.[81] The material, its composition and the means of expression – in architecture the use of ornament and even the choice of one of the orders – must be ordered by reference to decorum, and result in the use of a style (or *genus dicendi*) that is appropriate to the genre and character of the building. Boffrand here continued a line of thought that had begun with Vitruvius and Alberti, who both applied the conceptual apparatus of rhetoric to the theory of architecture. But Boffrand introduced a novel element because he gave a new interpretation to proportion, different from the meaning it was given in the Renaissance as a reflection of the divinely ordered proportion of the universe. Instead, for Boffrand:

> These orders of architecture, with their progression from the rustic to the sublime, have proportions relative to their character and to the impression that they are intended to make; each of the three possesses an elegance that is all its own by nature and inappropriate to any other.[82]

Such expressive composition employs the disposition of elements, structure and ornament, in particular the orders, to convey the character of the building.

Boffrand's buildings are like characters on a stage; but they speak and behave like Roman orators. This brings us back to a question that has puzzled earlier writers on Boffrand: why use Horace's *Art of Poetry* as a source for a treatise on the principles of architecture, particularly since it is such a fragmentary text, which does not at all offer the kind of systematic advice on poetical composition a writer of an architectural treatise might look for. But it was not a coherent system of individual precepts Boffrand seemed to be looking for in the first place. What he did look for was a text taking the theatrical character of poetry, and by extension all the arts, as its subject. The *Art of Poetry* itself is a dramatic monologue, spoken by a fictive character whose personality is revealed through the poem. Similarly for Boffrand, architecture by its composition and use of ornament reveals both its own character and that of the owner. Architecture for him is dramatic poetry, and as such should obey the rules of rhetoric.

Boffrand's aesthetic of character and style, in which the representation and evocation of emotional moods was so important, marks the transition from the object-oriented aesthetic concentrating on proportion developed in the late seventeenth century by the Académie Royale d'Architecture, to the subjectivist aesthetics of associationalism and the Picturesque that would become prominent in the last decades of the eighteenth century. Boffrand's writings on character were an important source for Sir William Chambers and Sir John Soane, who both echoed Boffrand's comparison of mouldings and words. Chambers wrote in his *Treatise of Civil Architecture* (1759) that

> materials in architecture are like words in phraseology; having separately but little power [...] they may be so arranged, as to excite ridicule, or even contempt; yet when combined with skill, expressed with energy, they actuate the mind with unbounded sway.[83]

Sir John Soane stated in his second Lecture for the Royal Academy that 'profiles and assemblages of mouldings are in architecture similar and of equal importance with those indescribable elegancies in poetry and painting which are not always sufficiently felt or duly appreciated'.[84] Elsewhere he noted, paraphrasing Quintilian that 'The art of architecture consists of the effect which the perfection of a work has upon the eye'.[85] In such passages, as in Boffrand's elucidation of the theatricality of architecture, building is compared to the use of language; not to argue that buildings are speeches in stone, but to demonstrate the rule-bound character of classical architecture, and its visual and spatial impact on the spectator. The spatial metaphors Chambers used suggest that the mind in looking at architecture becomes fully active; at the same time they suggest in terms that very much recall Longinus and the aesthetics of the sublime, that skilful design will dominate the mind, but at the same time will open endless and unlimited perspectives for it.

The most far-reaching of Boffrand's innovations was his association of architecture and style. In the *Cours d'Architecture* (published in 1771–6 but held from 1750 onwards), which was the result of his teaching at the Ecole des Arts, founded by him in 1743 against initial opposition by the Académie, Jacques-François Blondel devoted many pages to detailed analyses of the style and character of buildings that clearly take their starting-point in the *Livre d'Architecture*. In a passage that echoes many of the views of Boffrand, style becomes the regulative and unifying notion by which the design of a building is guided in such a manner that the beholder can recognize its function, genre and character. Choosing the style of a building then entails a system of possible choices of the *ordonnance* of the façade, the use of ornament and the disposition of the parts of the building:

> By *Style* in Architecture is meant the true genre which one must choose with respect to the motive which led to the construction of the building. The style in the *ordonnance* of the façade, and in the decoration of the apartments, is properly speaking the poetry of architecture, which alone contributes in making all the compositions of an Architect interesting; it is the style, proper to every kind of building

> that brings with it that infinite variety in buildings of the same kind, and of different kinds. The style can equally well paint the sacred genre, the heroic, and the pastoral genre; style can express in particular the character: regular or irregular, simple or composed, symmetrical or varied; and finally by the style one arrives at the sublime.[86]

In the context of Boffrand's theatrical view of architecture, another remark by Blondel on style is intriguing: 'by keeping of those orders simply their expression, which would bring *on the stage* now a grave and sublime style, now a masculine and terrible genre'.[87]

This rhetorical significance of the concept of style did not remain unchanged for long. Its further development can be observed in the writings of Antoine-Chrysostome Quatremère de Quincy, who wrote the entries on style and character for the *Encyclopédie Méthodique*, the successor to the *Encyclopédie* edited by Diderot and D'Alembert.[88]Although these articles were written before 1788, they were published in 1825, and by that time came to represent the canonical views of the author, who had become the Secrétaire Perpétuel of the Ecole des Beaux-Arts, the successor to the royal academies of painting and architecture. In these entries the meaning of style changed from the rhetorical one of Boffrand and Blondel to a view of style as the language of character. The notion of style, according to Quatremère, was taken from the *arts du discours*, where it has two meanings. In the first place, style is the form a writer gives to his or her thoughts according to the nature of the subject, the effect to be produced, and the harmony between the goal and the means to reach it. This is traditionally the domain of rhetoric, and Quatremère refers the reader to reference books on that subject for more details.

In the second place style is the expression of the individuality of a work of art, of its *caractère:*

> According to the second point of view, the word 'style' signifies, in a more generally accepted sense, that typical and characteristic form, which very general causes impress on products of the mind [. . .]. Style, as we say, becomes synonymous with *character*, or with the individual manner of the distinctive physionomy that belongs to each work of art, each genre, each school, each country, each period.[89]

Style became for Quatremère the language to express character. According to him the visual arts must anyway be considered as a language or way of writing because they are always trying to give a material, tangible form to ideas, to intellectual relations, moral affections or the products of the imagination. Therefore the idea of the mechanical activity of a writing instrument is transferred to an activity of the mind, namely the 'art of expressing one's ideas in the signs of writing'.[90] Thus, style refers to the most mechanical as well as the most spiritual of human activities: it signifies the instrument that gives readable form to our thoughts and feelings by means of graphic signs, but it also refers to the conception of ideas and the art of putting them into words and giving them visible and tangible form.

Although architecture at first sight seems to have very little in common with the art of writing, the rhetorical meaning of style, concerned with the formal choices the artist makes in order to give material form to his or her ideas, is nonetheless apt, because architecture is so much concerned with giving tangible and visible form to ideas and designs.[91] Quatremère thereby continues Barbaro and Scamozzi's advocacy to use rhetoric in the design process to aid the architect in presenting his designs.

Herein resides the novelty of Quatremère's view of style: he still adheres on the one hand to the traditional, rhetorical view of style as the apt and persuasive dress of thought, but he also identifies it with character, which for him is the expression of the circumstances that are attached to every work of art. Style here becomes the language or vocabulary of forms with which character can be expressed. It is therefore no longer the guiding and unifying notion, operative in the design process it was for Boffrand and Blondel. Instead, it acquires a new function: that of the chief instrument of historical classification. In the nascent academic discipline of art history works of art began to be studied with the aim of classifying them chronologically and geographically on the basis of formal characteristics that express circumstances such as climate, the availability of certain materials, or political circumstances that contributed to their creation. Quatremère identified these characteristics as the style of a work of art. In a move that is very close to that of Winckelmann, style becomes not only the expressive and persuasive dress of thought and feeling, but also the complex of formal properties that is both the basis and the instrument of art history.

NOTES

1 *De Re Aedificatoria* IX.x, ed. Rykwert p. 314. See Smith (1992), pp. 9–10, and Van Eck (2000).

2 For a widely read statement of that view see Collins (1965), pp. 173–82, and Lavin (1992). For a wide range of perspectives on the relation between architecture and language in the Middle Ages and Renaissance across Europe see Braegger (1982) and Clarke and Crossley (2000).

3 Quintilian, *Institutio Oratoria* II.iv.27.

4 Walter Montague, 'The ninth Treatise. Of the Condition of Courts, Princes and Courtiers. Divided into three Sections. Section I. The best Notion of Courts proposed'. In *Miscellanea Spiritualia or Devout Essays*, pp. 86–8. See Smuts (1987), pp. 217–45.

5 See Hart and Tucker (2001).

6 Samuel Daniel, *Defence of Rhyme* (1603), pp. 139–40 and 45.

7 Peacock (2007) offers a very thorough survey of the use of typology by seventeenth-century English viewers and artists.

8 Quoted in Galdon (1975), pp. 33–4.

9 There is a vast bibliography on figural or typological interpretation. The fundamental modern article is Auerbach (1967). The large majority of existing studies are devoted to the theological use of typology and its use in literature. A very useful collection of recent essays on the subject is Bohn (1988); Bercovitch (1972) and Korshin (1982) both contain

annotated bibliographies of relevant literature starting with Antiquity. For typology and the visual arts in general see Holländer (1988), even though this essay is in part a series of typological interpretations of paintings rather than a history documenting its use in the arts; and see the suggestive remarks in Prickett (1998). For the Renaissance see Bialostocki (1965) and Gordon (1975).

10 Quintilian, *Institutio Oratoria* IX.i.13–14.

11 *Institutio Oratoria* XII.ii.64; cf. IX.ii.92 and IX.ii.46; Virgil, *Aeneid* IV.550.

12 *Institutio Oratoria* IX.ii.65.

13 Pherecydes' interpretation was recorded in Diogenes Laertius, I.ii.119; cf. Woollcombe (1957), pp. 50–1.

14 Origenes, *Contra Celsum* 4.48, quoted in Woollcombe (1957) p. 51.

15 On the anthropological aspect of typology see Korshin (1982).

16 Cf. Holländer (1988), pp. 172 and 184.

17 On typology considered as a combination of a rhetorical figure and a particular view of history see Frye (1982), pp. 78–87.

18 Virgil, *Ecloga* IV.4–10; for Augustine see in particular *On the City of God* XII.14; cf. Frye (1982), pp. 96–7.

19 On the connection between the rhetorical use of *figura* as a figure of thought to hide the real meaning of what one is saying and the Jewish or early Christian use of types or *figurae* see Auerbach (1967), pp. 72–3.

20 On the hermeneutical and rhetorical aspects of Paul's use of typology see Prickett (1988), pp. 160–1.

21 See also 1 Cor. 10.6–11 and 15. 21; 2 Cor. 3.14; Gal. 4.21–31; Rom. 5.12ff. Apostles 8.32.

22 Melito of Sardis, *Homily on the Passion*, pp. 71–2.

23 Melito of Sardis, *Homily on the Passion*, p. 72.

24 William Tyndale, *A Prologue to the Book of Leviticus*, p. 60; cf. Davis (1988), p. 257.

25 Tertullian, *Adversus Marcionem* III.xvi.4, IV.xl in particular IV.xl.3: 'Professus itaque se concupiscentia concupisse edere pascha ut suum, – indignum enim, ut quid alienum concupisceret deus – acceptum panem et distributum discipulis corpus suum illum fecit hoc est corpus meum dicendo, id est "figura corporis mei". Figura autem non fuisset nisi veritatis esset corpus. Ceterum uacua res, quod est phantasma, figuram capere non posset'. See also the remarks on this passage in Auerbach (1967), pp. 66–7.

26 E. Auerbach (1967), p. 8.

27 J. Donne, *Devotions upon Emergent Occasions*, ed. John Sparrow (Cambridge: Cambridge University Press, 1923), p. 114.

28 For some background to its role in medieval painting see Acres (1998).

29 Walter Montague, *Devout Essays*, p. 85.

30 Ibid.

31 Walter Montague, *Devout Essays*, p. 86.

32 The remaining fragments were published by his grandson Christopher Wren in the *Parentalia: or, Memoirs of the Family of the Wrens* in 1750 under the title *Tracts on Architecture*. Cf. Soo (1998), p. 119. Tract IV was probably written in the mid-1670s. This is, however, only a tentative dating. See also Bennett (1973).

33 See Th. Buddensieg (1962) for a survey of reconstructions up to the nineteenth century. As far as I have been able to establish, the reconstruction by Palladio was the only one to include the portico until the nineteenth century. Important accounts of Roman monuments in Wren's library, such as A. Desgodetz's *Les Edifices Antiques de Rome dessinés et mesurés très exactement*, p. 105 describes it as the most majestic and magnificent of all Roman temples, and notes that one of the remaining columns of the interior had been transferred to the piazza in front of S. Maria Maggiore by Paul V in 1613. He does not mention the missing corona, and observes about the façade: 'Au devant il y avait une loge au porche de la longueur du Temple; on entroit dans ce porche par cinq portes, dont les trois au milieu estoient au droit de la partie du Temple que j'appelle la nef'. Cf. Minoprio (1932), p. 2, and Palladio, *Quattro Libri*, Part IV, p. 12. Another volume in Wren's library, G. Du Choul's *Veterum Romanum Religio* (Amsterdam: apud Janssonio-Waesbergio, 1685, pp. 4–5, lists the main Roman sources on the actual Templum Pacis: Plinius, *Natural History* XXXVI.5–7; 12–19; XXXV.8; XL.10; Josephus, *War of the Jews* VII.24. A. Nibby identified what had been generally known as the Temple of Peace as the Basilica of Constantine and Maxentius: see Nibby (1819) and Platner (1965).

34 Sir Christopher Wren, 'Observations on the Temple of Peace, built by the Emperor Vespasian', 'Tract IV on Architecture', p. 176.

35 Sir Christopher Wren, 'Tract IV', pp. 176–7.

36 See for instance Lever and Harris (1993), s.v. 'Corona'.

37 A. Palladio, *I Quattro Libri dell'Architettura*, Book IV, Chapter vi, p. 11: 'La Cornice ha i Modiglioni in vece di Gocciolatoio [i.e. a corona]'; cf. *Inigo Jones on Palladio*, p. 41: 'Thees Cartouses are insted of the Corrona'.

38 R. Fréart de Chambray, *A Parallel of the Antient Architecture with the Modern*, p. 68.

39 See Evans (1995), pp. xxxii–iii.

40 See for a recent summary of this view of Wren Soo (1998), pp. 119–53, and Bennett (1972).

41 Sir Christopher Wren, 'Tract IV', pp. 177–8. Wren's praise of the architect's 'Wit and Judgment' recalls the letter written to Wren in 1663 by Thomas Sprat, which sums up a conversation they had on the nature of wit, reproduced in *Parentalia* p. 102: 'Its chiefest Dominion is in forming new significations, and Images of Things and Persons. And this

may be so suddenly practised, that I have known in one Afternoon, new Stamps [imprese], and Proverbs, and Fashions of Speech raised, which were never thought of before, and yet gave Occasion to the most delightful Imaginations'. As Walter Montague's contemporary Owen Feltham put it: 'Beauty is the wit of Nature put into the frontispiece'. *Resolves, Divine, Morall, Politicall.* London 1623, p. 251, quoted in Sharpe (2000), p. 91.

42 R.T., *De Templis*, pp. 123–7.

43 Reprinted in *Parentalia*, pp. 200–6.

44 Wren, 'Observations on the Temple of Peace', pp. 176–7. Cicero, *De Oratore* I.viii.30–4; Quintilian, *Institutio Oratoria* XII.i.1–4.

45 *Institutio Oratoria* II.iv.27: '. . . ut quotiens esset occasio, extemporales eorum dictiones his velut emblemata exornaretur'.

46 Th. Thomas, *Dictionarium Linguarium Linguae Latinae et Anglicanae*, Cambridge 1587, s.v. 'emblema', quoted in Bath (1994), p. 8.

47 See Bath (1994), p. 155ff. for an overview of Renaissance discussions of the question whether emblems were natural or conventional signs. As Lisa Jardine has shown in her recent biography of Wren, he was very familiar with heraldry because his father was secretary to the Order of the Garter: Jardine (2002), pp. 25–44 and 478.

48 Alberti VIII.iv, ed. Rykwert p. 256. See also Wittkower (1972), in particular pp. 69–70.

49 Joseph Hall, Sermon at Court in 1610 and 1611 on Zachariah 14:20, reprinted in his *Collected Works*, pp. 430–1, and quoted in Bath (1994), p. 169. A similar combination of allegorical and typological interpretation of nature and the Bible occurs in Andrew Willett's *Emblematum Sacrarum Centuria* of 1592, where three categories of emblems are distinguished: typological or allegorical emblems (with an emphasis on images), historical and physical or natural emblems. The first group is called 'emblemata typica'.

50 Francis Bacon, *The Advancement of Learning*, Book II, 'De notis rerum', p. 231.

51 Bath (1994), p. 47, argues that, according to seventeenth-century English views, rhetoric needed nature to be persuasive, but nature needed rhetoric to raise the human mind to an understanding of divine truth through the means of persuasion it has: metaphor, imagery and similes. See, for instance, Obadiah Walker's *Of Education, Especially of Young Gentlemen*, p. 130, where he suggests to go about daily life composing emblems as the easiest way to exercise the writing skills and to read the book of nature. And see also Wren's description of the astronomer in his Gresham Inaugural Address as the 'conciliorum naturae particeps et interpres'. (*Parentalia*, p. 202), and the remarks on the Temple of Diana at Ephesus in Tract IV, where nature is presented as a source of architectural meaning (Soo [1998]), p. 172.

52 Ch. Perrault, *Parallèles des Anciens et des Modernes en ce qui regarde les Arts et les Sciences*. Tome Premier, p. 129: 'Il n'en est pas des ornemens de l'Architecture comme des ornemens du discours. Il est naturel à l'homme de faire des figures de Rhetorique, les Iroquois en font, & plus abondamment que les meilleurs Orateurs de l'Europe. Mais ces mesmes Iroquois n'employent pas des colonnes, des architraves & des corniches dans leurs bastimens'. For a modern, annotated edition see the 1964 edition by Jauss and Imdahl.

53 Ch. Perrault, *Parallèles des Anciens et des Modernes en ce qui regarde les Arts et les Sciences. Tome Premier*, p. 128.

54 A.-C. d'Aviler, *Cours d'Architecture qui comprend les Ordres de Vignole*, p. j: 'Les Moulures sont à l'Architecture ce que les Lettres sont à l'écriture. Or comme par la combinaison des caracteres il se fait une infinité de mots en diverses langues; aussi par le mélange des Moulures on peut inventer quantité de profils differens pour toutes sortes d'Ordres, & de compositions regulieres et irregulieres [. . .]'. Cf. also N. Goldmann, *Vollständige Anweisung zu der Civil-Bau-Kunst* [. . .], Preface: 'Die Glieder der Ordnungen sind gleichsam das Alphabet der Bau-Kunst: denn wie aus 24. Buchstaben unzehlich unterschiedene Wörter und Reden zusammen gesetzet werden, also kan man durch mancherley Zusammenfügungen der Glieder, derer nicht vielmehr als der Buchstaben sind, gantz unterschiedene Bau-Zierathe nach fünfferley Ordnungen zusammensetzen'. On this passage see Goudeau (2005), pp. 255–68; on this theme more in general see Oechslin (1982), pp. 216–55. On d'Aviler see also Kohler (1997).

55 Ch. Batteux, *Les Beaux Arts Réduits à un même Principe*, Chapitre VI: *En quoi l'Eloquence & l'Architecture different des autres Arts*, pp. 29–31.

56 Boffrand, *Book of Architecture*, p. 9.

57 Boffrand presented a paper on this topic to the Académie for the first time in 1734. Cf. Lemonnier (1911–29) vol. V, p. 151, session of 30 August 1734.

58 Boffrand here repeats the ancient conviction, held by Cicero and Vitruvius, among others, that what we now call the arts and sciences are very closely related. See the passage from Cicero's *Pro Archia Poeta* I.2, *De Oratore* III.vi.21 and Vitruvius' discussion of the education of the architect in I.i. Boffrand differs from the majority of French versions of *ut pictura poesis* because he applies Horace's poem to architecture not painting, but also because of his selection of similarities between the arts. Whereas De Piles and Batteux both stress the imitative character that poetry and painting have in common – not surprisingly, because the doctrine of *ut pictura poesis* focuses on the various means of representation in painting and poetry– the adaptation of the *Art of Poetry* in the *Livre d'Architecture* concentrates on decorum and character. It loosely follows the order

of topics in the original, moving from a discussion of decorum, unity and consistency to matters of style, how to move the public, the moral character of the audience, the relation between innate talent and training, and criticism.

59 Boffrand, *Book of Architecture*, p. 8.

60 For a survey of *caractère* in this period see Szambien (1986), pp. 174–200; and Picon (1988), pp. 87–8, who quotes J. F. Blondel's *Cours d'Architecture*, vol. II, pp. 230–1: 'Le peintre, par la variété qu'il fait répandre dans l'ordonnance de ses tableaux, n'étale-t-il pas aux yeux des spectateurs, l'image des passions fortes ou tempérées de l'action ou du repos? Dans la poésie, les genres héroïques, lyriques ou pastoraux, n'expriment-ils pas sous différentes formes, les diverses affections de l'âme? [...] Pourquoi donc l'architecture plus étendue dans ses préceptes, et non moins susceptible de goût que les autres arts, n'offrirait-elle pas aux architectes des ressources pour varier à l'infini leurs différentes espèces de productions?' Picon observes that Blondel never gave a clear definition of *caractère*. Its selection is based on *convenance*, but it remains unclear how the orders and their use should be coordinated. This issue is further obscured in theories of *caractère* such as those of Boffrand and Blondel because architectural forms and their effects on the sensibilities of the spectator are put together in one and the same category.

61 Boffrand, *Livre d'Architecture*, p. 16.

62 The English translation was published in 1701 under the title *The Conference upon Expression*; for a modern English edition and commentary see Montagu (1994).

63 N. Le Camus de Mézières, *The Genius of Architecture*, pp. 22–8; cf. Boffrand, *Livre d'Architecture*, p. 9. See also Szambien (1986), pp. 174–8.

64 Boffrand, *Livre d'Architecture*, p. 8.

65 For a late eighteenth-century overview of the various meanings of *caractère* see A.-C. Quatremère de Quincy, 'Caractère'; Johann Caspar Lavater's *Physiognomische Fragmente* were published in 1775–8. Cf. Gombrich (1963).

66 Cicero, *Brutus*, Section 100.

67 Cf. Liddell and Scott, *Oxford Greek Dictionary*, s.v. 'charaktèr'.

68 See Pollitt (1974), pp. 436–9.

69 Quintilian, *Institutio Oratoria* II.xv.13–14, III.v.1 and VII.Pr.32–3; Cicero, *De Oratore* III.xiv–xix.

70 See for instance Grube (1969).

71 See Filarete's *Treatise on Architecture*, vol. I, p. 12, corresponding to Book I, fol. 5v: 'E cosi d'ogni facultà si conosce lo stile di ciascheduno'. See also Germann (1972), pp. 11–12, and Onians (1988), p. 163.

72 Panofsky (1960), p. 115, n. 224.

73 Germann (1972), pp. 12–13.

74 Germann (1972), p. 16.

75 Sir Christopher Wren, 'Report on Westminster Abbey to Francis Atterbury, Dean' (1713).

76 J.-L. Cordemoy, *Nouveau traité de toute l'architecture ou l'art de bastir*, Paris, n.p. 1714 [1706]; Montesquieu, *De la manière gothique*, p. 966.

77 G. Boffrand, *Livre d'Architecture*, p. 8.

78 G. Boffrand, *Livre d'Architecture*, p. 10.

79 J. H. Alsted, *Encyclopaedia*, 1630 edition, col. 2198. See also Pochat (1986), p. 311.

80 Collins (1965), pp. 173–82, in particular 174.

81 See, for instance, Cicero *De Oratore* III. 55–73.

82 G. Boffrand, *Livre d'Architecture*, p. 10.

83 Sir William Chambers, *A Treatise of Civil Architecture*, p. iii.

84 Watkin (1996), p. 504. On Boffrand's influence on Soane see ibid., pp. 196–8.

85 Quoted in Watkin (1996), p. 187. The paraphrase is from Guthrie's edition of Quintilian, p. 130.

86 J.-F. Blondel, *Cours d'architecture*, vol. I, p. 401. See also vol. I, pp. 183 and 391–2. On Blondel see Middleton (1959).

87 Blondel, *Cours d'Architecture*, vol. II, p. 231: 'en ne retenant de ces ordres que leur simple expression, qui ameneroit sur scène, tantôt un style grave et sublime, tantôt un genre mâle ou terrible'. Note how Blondel uses the terminology of the rhetorical *genera dicendi* (*gravis, sublimis, tenuis*) to define architectural styles.

88 On Quatremère see Lavin (1992).

89 Quatremère de Quincy, 'Style' p. 411: 'Style [...] devient synonyme de caractère, ou de la manière propre de la physionomie distinctive qui appartient à chaque ouvrage, à chaque auteur, à chaque genre, à chaque pays, à chaque siècle'.

90 Quatremère de Quincy, 'Style', p. 410.

91 Ibid., pp. 412–13: 'Et pourquoi cette métaphore ne lui [i.e. architecture] seroit-il pas aussi justement applicable, s'il est vrai que, selon l'esprit qui constitue le genre de son imitation, cet art, par tel ou tel choix de formes et de proportions, sait rendre intelligible aux yeux, telles ou telles conceptions abstraites, telles ou telles combinaisons de l'intelligence; s'il est vrai que par un emploi diversement modifié de parties, de membres et d'ornemens, il sait, comme à l'aide des signes d'écriture, faire naître en nous des idées déterminées'.

CODA

Did the relevance of rhetoric for the arts end with the waning of the classical tradition in the nineteenth century? As befits a rhetorical subject, a case for both a positive and a negative answer can be made, presenting arguments *in utramque partem*.

Yes, we might argue, with the dismissal of rhetoric from secondary school curricula across Europe at the end of the nineteenth century people lost the training in rhetoric practically every educated person had possessed since the revival of classical education in the fifteenth century. More fundamental where the role of rhetoric in making and looking at art is concerned, was the rise of the new philosophical discipline of aesthetics from the 1750s. Baumgarten and Kant did not consider art primarily from the perspective of the maker, but claimed the viewer's experience of beauty as the territory of this new discipline. This viewer was not the public oratory was directed at, which aimed to instruct, delight and move, and ultimately sway the audience in whatever direction the orator intended, but the independent and free Enlightenment subject. The aesthetic experience was the domain where this new subject could enjoy the free play of its cognitive and emotional faculties, in a disinterested contemplation of art. After Plato, Kant was rhetoric's fiercest denouncer.[1]

In the new academic study of art history, rhetoric was dethroned as the main provider of terms, concepts and competences to use when analyzing art. Both the nineteenth-century German tradition of art history as *Geistesgeschichte*, which was much influenced by the aesthetic theories of Kant and Hegel, and practices of art history that were more directed towards archival research and documentation, developed originally by Rumohr, Schnaase and Kugler, took history, not rhetoric, as their model. After the 1850s, art historians increasingly looked as well to disciplines outside the humanities such as biology, ethnography or comparative linguistics to understand the development of art. Both varieties of academic art history tended to concentrate on the art work itself, often isolating it from the context in which it was commissioned, or the role it might have played in religious or secular settings. If they looked at its impact on the viewer, they did so in formal terms, not in terms of persuasion.

But the most damning argument against an ongoing relevance of classical rhetoric for any consideration of the arts today is that we have lost the foundation of classical culture: the conviction that there exists an unbroken thread connecting us to the past. Alberti could write of the *maiores nostri*, our forebears, when he delivered the first humanist analysis of Roman architecture, and by using these words suggested that he was part of an unbroken lineage reaching back to Republican Rome. As we have seen, a common cultural memory was considered essential to visual persuasion. After 1800, the defining characteristic of modernity is that the past is no longer accessible or even relevant. It is no longer self-evident that classical culture matters, or matters more than 1960s culture, or Chinese culture. Nor is the classical tradition the rich store of cultural memory it once was; neither can an artist or art historian these days assume the shared field of ideas, beliefs and convictions that provided the common ground on which persuasion could work. Studying the role of classical rhetoric in the arts of early modern Europe is therefore the pursuit of a cultural archivist.

Yet it is precisely when we step out of the archive and look at the films or politicians of our own time that arguments for the other side begin to emerge. We could point to the persistance of rhetorical ideas in historians and artists who contributed most to modern art history: John Ruskin's statement that a building should look well, speak well and act well; or Gottfried Semper's search for a discipline that would put architectural invention and disposition on a secure, scientific footing, thereby providing the architect with a repetoire of common places and save him from the dilemmas of style. But it is more interesting to leave the library entirely and look for a moment at present-day art, life and politics. George Bush and Tony Blair are masters – with depressing efficacy – of the rhetorical techniques Aristotle, Cicero and Quintilian developed: to create a sense of shared issues and beliefs; to draw on a supposed common history; to construct clear oppositions; to build an image of yourself as a reliable, only slightly superior version of the person next door. Publicity and election campaigns cannot operate without using these techniques to connect with customers. Hollywood films employ similar strategies to attract viewers. Now both Bush and Blair were educated at schools that still offered courses in rhetoric and public speaking, and it is no news that American popular culture is much influenced by the varieties of rhetorical training offered by most colleges. But ethnographical research by Geneviève Calame-Griaule, Alfred Gell and others has shown that rhetoric in the sense of the theory and practice of persuasive speech, art and actions is by no means limited to the Western world or classical and early modern Europe. In fact, it seems that rhetoric is just as universal as the making of images. Aniconic cultures are as rare as arhetorical cultures.[2]

The universality of rhetoric provides the main argument in favour of the ongoing relevance of classical rhetoric for the arts. In it, a way of thinking about art has crystallized that can no longer be taken at face value in the academic study of art, but nonetheless addresses one of its fundamental aspects: rhetoric looks at art as communication and then proceeds to ask how paintings, statues or buildings can be made to function, like any other human utterance, as persuasive communication. In the closed societies of ancient Greece and Rome or early modern Europe, where the variety of rhetoric was developed that is the subject of this book, persuasion was thought to function only on the basis of a common ground: artist, patron and public should be part of the same society or culture, and should have access to the same, common past. In this view a speech or a work of art sets out not simply to convince, but also to construct the public. In the words of Sir Henry Wotton: 'how to build a man'; as Sir Christopher Wren put it, 'architecture builds a nation'. The particular techniques developed in this tradition are no longer self-evident. But taking a close look at them to grasp how visual persuasion was thought to work, even within the confines and limitations of the classical tradition in Western art and culture, helps to understand more about art considered as communication and agency. There are striking resemblances between present-day anthropological views of art works functioning as agents in networks of social relationships and the way in which Aristotle, Cicero, Quintilian and the Renaissance artists and patrons, who were educated by them, conceived of art as a way to influence the emotions, beliefs and actions of the viewer. We might even say that rhetoric could help to liberate the study of art somewhat from the constraints imposed on it by the heritage of Kantian aesthetics. After all, looking with disinterested enjoyment at art deprived of its agency in museum vitrines, is a very recent Western invention, and by no means a universal phenomenon. Using art to get in touch with fellow human beings is.

Notes

1 See Vickers (1988), pp. 196–214 for Kant's attack on rhetoric and the disappearance of rhetoric from secondary school curricula.

2 Calame-Griaule (1955); Gell (1998); on the question whether aniconism actually occurs see Freedberg (1989), pp. 84–82.

BIBLIOGRAPHY

Primary sources

Alberti, L. B. *L'Architettura: De Re Aedificatoria.* Testo Latino e traduzione a cura di Giovanni Orlandi; introduzione e note di Paolo Portoghesi. Milan, 1966.

On Painting and Sculpture. Edited and translated by C. Grayson. London, 1972.

On the Art of Building in Ten Books. Translated, introduced and annoted by N. Leach, J. Rykwert and R. Tavernor. Cambridge, Mass. and London, 1991 [1988[1]].

Alberti, R. *Trattato della Nobiltà della Pittura.* Rome: Francesco Zanetti, 1585 [reprinted in Barocchi, P. *Scritti d'Arte del Cinquecento.* Turin, 1977, vol. I, pp. 900–50].

Alison, A. *Essay on the Nature and Principles of Taste.* Edinburgh, 1812 [1790[1]].

Alsted, J. H. *Cursus Philosophici Encyclopaedia Libris XXVII.* Heilbron, 1620.

[Anon.] *Rhetorica ad Herennium.* Edited with an introduction and English translation by H. Caplan. Cambridge, Mass. and London, 1977.

Aretino, P. *I Quattro Libri de la Humanità di Christo.* Venice, 1539.

Lettere. A cura di P. Procaccioli. Rome, 1997–2002.

Sur la poétique, l'art et les artistes (Michel-Ange et Titien). Introduction, traduction et notes de Paul Larivaille. Texte des lettres établi par Paolo Procaccioli. Paris, 2003.

La Vita di S. Maria Vergine, di Catarina Santa, & di Tomaso Aquinato Beato. Venice, 1539.

Aristotle, *Complete Works. The revised Oxford Translation.* Edited by J. Barnes. Princeton, 1995 [1984[1]].

The 'Art' of Rhetoric. Translated by J. H. Freese. Cambridge, Mass. and London, 1994 [1926[1]].

Armenini, G. B. *De' veri precetti della pittura di M. Gio vanni Battista Armenini da Faenza libri tre.* Ravenna, 1587.

Augustine. *The City of God Against the Pagans.* With an English translation by G. McCracken. Cambridge, Mass. and London, 1957–72.

Bacon, F. *The Advancement of Learning.* In *The Major Works.* Edited with an introduction and notes by B. Vickers. Oxford, 2002, pp. 120–300.

Barbaro, D. *Della Eloquenza. Dialogo Nuovamente mandato in Luce da Girolamo Ruscelli.* Venice, 1557.

I Dieci Libri dell'Architettura di M. Vitruvio Tradotti e Commentati da Monsignor Barbaro Eletto Patriarca d'Aquileia. Venice, 1556.

De architectura cum Commentariis. Venice, 1567a.

I Dieci Libri dell'Architettura di M. Vitruvio Tradotti e Commentati da Mons. Daniel Barbaro Eletto Patriarca d'Aquileia da Lui Riveduti et Ampliati. Venice, 1567b. Modern reprints: edited by M. Tafuri and M. Morresi, Milan, 1987; anastatic reprint Santa Cristina Gela, 1993.

La Prattica della prospettiva. Venice, 1569.

Barbaro, E. *Rhetoricorum Aristotelis Libri Tres. Hermolao Barbaro Patricio Veneto interprete Danielis Barbari Commentaria in eosdem libros.* Venice, 1544.

Barocchi, P. (ed.). *Scritti d'Arte del Cinquecento.* Milan and Naples, 1971.

Barocchi, P. (ed.). *Trattati dell'Arte del Cinquecento.* Bari, 1962.

Barozzi, P. 'In Leonis Baptistae libellum de pictura elegantissimum'. In Contarini, G. B., *Anecdota Veneta.* Venice, 1757. Reprinted in Baxandall (1971), p. 121.

Batteux, Ch. *Les Beaux Arts réduits à un même Principe.* Leiden, 1753 [1747[1]].

Bessarion, J. *De Natura et Arte adversus Georgium Trapezuntium Cretensem Liber Sextus* [=Appendix to *In Calumniatorem Platonis Libri IV*]. In idem, *Opera Omnia.* Venice, 1503.

Biondi, A. *Essequie della Sacra Cattolica Real Maestà del Re di Spagna Don Filippo II d'Austria. Celebrata in Firenze dalla Nobilissima Nazione Spagnuola.* Florence, 1598.

Biondo, M. *Della Nobilissima Pittura, et della sua arte, del modo, & della dottrina, di conseguirla.* Venice, 1549.

Blondel, J. F. *Cours d'Architecture, ou traité de la décoration, distribution et construction des bâtiments contenant les leçons données en 1750 et les années suivantes.* Paris, 1771–7.

Bocchi, Fr. *Opera sopra l'Imagine Miracolosa della Santissima Nunziata di Firenza.* In P. Barocchi, ed. *Scritti d'Arte del Cinquecento.* Milan and Naples, 1971, vol. I, pp. 1005–10.

Discorso sopra l'Eccellenza dell'Opere d'Andrea del Sarto, pittore fiorentino (1567), reprinted in Williams, R. (1989).

Eccellenza del San Giorgio di Donatello [published 1584 but written in 1571; reprinted in P. Barocchi, ed. *Trattati dell'Arte del Cinquecento* vol. III, pp. 125–9].

Le Bellezze della Città di Fiorenza. Florence, 1591.

Bocchi, F. *Oratio Francisci Bocchij de laudibus Michaelisangeli Florentini Pictoris, Sculptoris, atque Architecti Nobilissimi.* British Library Ms Egerton 1978 520 F, fols. 1–25.

Boffrand, G. *Livre d'Architecture.* Paris, 1754.

Book of Architecture. Translated by David Britt. Introduced and edited by C. A. van Eck. Aldershot, 2003.

Bolton, E. *Elements of Armouries.* London, 1610.

Bonifaccio, G. *L'Arte de' Cenni, con la quale formandosi Favella Visibile, si tratta della Muta Eloquenza, che non è altro che un Facondo Silentio.* Vicenza, 1616.

Borghini, R. *Il Riposo.* Florence: G. Marescotti, 1584, reprint Hildesheim, 1969.

Borghini, V. 'Selva di Notizie' published in Barocchi, *Scritti d'Arte del Cinquecento*, vol. I, pp. 611–73.

Bötticher, C. G. W. *Die Tektonik der Hellenen.* Berlin, 1874 [1844–52[1]].

Camillo, G. *L'Idee, ovvero forme della oratione da Hermogene considerate, & ridotte in questa lingua.* Udine, 1594.

Cassiodorus. *Variae* [reprint in *Monumentum Germaniae Historica* 12 (1961), p. 210].

Cennini, C. *The Craftsman's Handbook. The Italian 'Il Libro dell'Arte'.* Translated by D. V. Thompson Jr. New York, 1960 [1933[1]].

Cerva, E. L. *Opera latina.* In *Archivio Storico della Dalmazia* 16 (1935), pp. 525–7, reprinted in Settis 1999, p. 124.

Chambers, Sir W. *A Treatise of Civil Architecture, In Which the Principles of that Art are Laid Down.* London, 1759.

Chrysostomos, Johannes. *Homily 10.2 in Philippum.* In *Opera Omnia quae exstant*, vol. XI, 276. Edited by B. de Montfaucon. Paris, 1838.

Cicero. *De Natura Deorum.* With an English translation by H. Rackham. Cambridge, Mass. and London, 1956 [1933[1]].

De Amicitia. With a translation by W. A. Falconer. Cambridge, Mass. and London, 1979 [1923[1]].

De Legibus. With an English translation by C. W. Keyes. Cambridge, Mass. and London, 1977 [1928[1]].

De Oratore. With an English translation by E. W. Sutton. Completed, with an introduction, by H. Rackham. Cambridge, Mass. and London, 1976 [1942[1]].

De partitione oratoria. With an English translation by E. W. Sutton. Completed, with an introduction, by H. Rackham. Cambridge, Mass. and London, 1976 [1942[1]].

In Catilinam. With a New English translation by C. Macdonald. Cambridge and London, 1977.

Orator. Translated and edited by B. Krytzler. Munich and Zurich, 1988.

Philippicae. With a translation by W. C. A. Ker. Cambridge, Mass. and London, 1969 [1926[1]].

Pro Lege Manilia. With a translation by H. Grose Hodge. Cambridge, Mass. and London, 1979 [1927[1]].

Pro Sestio. With an English translation by E. Gardner. Cambridge, Mass. and London, 1984.

Clement of Alexandria. *Oratio contra Gentes.* With an English translation by G. W. Butterworth. Cambridge, Mass. and London, 1960.

Comanini, G. *Il Figino, ovvero del Fine della Pittura.* Mantua, 1591, reprint in P. Barocchi. *Trattati d'Arte del Cinquecento*, vol. III, pp. 237–383.

Contarini, G. *De magistratibus et Republica Venetarum.* Paris, 1543.

Cordemoy, J.-L. *Nouveau Traité de toute l'Architecture ou l'Art de Bastir.* Paris, 1714 [1706[1]].

Daniel, S. *Defence of Rhyme* (1603), reprint in Daniel, S. *Poems and a Defence of Rhyme.* Edited by A. C. Sprague. Chicago and London, 1965, pp. 139–40 and 45.

Daniello, B. *Della Poetica.* Venice, 1539, reprint in B. Weinberg, *Trattati di Poetica e Retorica del Cinquecento.* Bari, 1970, Vol. I, pp. 272.

D'Aviler, A.-C. *Cours d'Architecture qui comprend les Ordres de Vignole.* Paris, 1694.

Da Vinci, L. *The Notebooks of Leonardo da Vinci.* Edited by J. Richter. London and New York, 1970.

Treatise on Painting. Translated and edited by P. McMahon. New Jersey, 1956.

De' Capodiferro, E. M. *Laocoon in Titi imperatoris domo Julio II Pontifici Maximo repertus*, reprint in Settis (1999), p. 126.

Desgodetz, A. *Les Edifices Antiques de Rome dessinés et mesurés très exactement.* Paris, 1682.

Diogenes Laertius. *Lives of Eminent Philosophers.* With a translation by R. D. Hicks. Cambridge, Mass. and London, 1925.

Diodorus Siculus. *Historiae.* With a translation by C. H. Oldfather and others. Cambridge, Mass. and London, 1970–89.

Dionysius of Halicarnassus. *De Compositione Verborum.* Partially reprinted in Russell and Winterbottom, *Ancient Literary Criticism*, pp. 321–44.

Dolce, L. *Dialogo della Pittura di M. Lodovico Dolce, intitolato L'Aretino.* Venice, 1557, modern edition in M. W. Roskill, *Dolce's 'Aretino' and Venetian Art Theory of the Cinquecento.* Toronto, 2000 [1968[1]].

Doni, A. F. *Il Disegno.* Venice: Giolito de'Ferrari, 1549, reprint in Settis (1999), pp. 186–7.

Du Choul, G. *Veterum Romanum Religio.* Amsterdam, 1685 [1580[1]].

Fazio, B. *De Viris Illustribus.* Reproduced and translated in Baxandall (1964), pp. 90–107.

Fergusson, J. *A Historical Inquiry into the True Principles of Beauty in Art, More Especially with Reference to Architecture.* London, 1849.

Fioravanti, L. *Della Specchio di Scientia Universale.* Venice, 1612.

Filarete. *Filarete's Treatise on Architecture, Being the Treatise by Antonio di Piero Averlino, Known as Filarete.* Translated with an introduction by J. R. Spencer. New Haven and London, 1968.

Florus, *Epitome of Roman History.* With an English translation by E. S. Forster. Cambridge, Mass. and London, 1984.

Fréart de Chambray, R. *Parallèle de l'Architecture Antique et de la Moderne.* Paris, 1650.

A Parallel of the Antient Architecture with the Modern [...] *Made English for the Benefit of Builders.* By John Evelyn Esq. London, 1664.

Freigius, J. T. *Paedagogus.* Basel, 1582.

Gioioso, A. *Degli Errori de' Pittori circa l'Historie* [...] *et in che Modo vogliono esser Dipinte le Sacre Imagini.* Camerino, 1564, modern reprint in Barocchi, P. *Trattati d'Arte*, vol. II, pp. 1–115.

Goldmann, N. *Vollständige Anweisung zu der Civil-Bau-Kunst (...) vermehret von L. Chr. Sturm.* Leipzig, 1708 [1696[1]].

Guazzo, S. *La civil conversazione.* Venice, 1579 [1574[1]]. Modern edition edited by Amedeo Quondam. Ferrara and Modena, 1993.

Guillim, J. *A Display of Heraldrie.* London, 1610.

Hall, J. *Collected Works.* London, 1621.

Herodianus. *History of the Roman Empire after the Death of Marcus Aurelius.* Translated by C. R. Whittaker. Cambridge, Mass. and London, 1962.

Homer. *Iliad.* Translated by E. V. Rieu. Harmondsworth, 1950.

Horace, *Ars Poetica*, 'Epistula ad Pisones', *Epistulae* Book II, nr iii. Translated by H. Rushton Fairclough. Cambridge, Mass. and London, 1926.

Ars Poetica. Edited with Notes by A. S. Wilkins. London, 1971 [1939[1]].

Hoskyns, J. *Directions for Speech and Style.* Edited by H. Hudson. Princeton, 1935 [*c.* 1599[1]].

Hume, D. *An Enquiry Concerning Human Understanding.* Reprinted from the posthumous edition of 1777 and edited by L. A. Selby-Bigge. Oxford, 1975.

Hunt, J. D. and P. Wills, eds. *The Genius of the Place: the English Landscape Garden 1620–1820.* London, 1975.

Isocrates. Le Discours d'Isocrate sur Lui-Même, intitulé *Sur l'antidosis.* Traduit en français pour la première fois par Auguste Cartelier. Revu et publié avec le texte, une introduction et des notes par Ernest Havet. Paris, 1862.

Jeffrey, F. '*Essays on the Nature and Principles of Taste*, by Archibald Alison'. *The Edinburgh Review*, vol. 18 (1811), nr. xxxv, pp. 3–30.

Jones, I. *The Most Notable Antiquity of Great Britain, vulgarly called Stone-Heng: on Salisbury Plain. Restored by Inigo Jones*, edited by John Webb. London, 1655.

Jones, I. *Inigo Jones on Palladio. Being the notes by Inigo Jones in the copy of I quattro Libri della Architettura di Andrea Palladio 1601 in the Library of Worcester College Oxford.* Edited by B. Allsopp. Newcastle upon Tyne, 1970.

Jonson, B. *Works.* Oxford, 1925–52.

Junius, F. *The Paintings of the Ancients. De Pictura Veterum according to the English Translation (1638).* Edited by K. Aldrich, Ph. Fehl and R. Fehl. Berkeley and London, 1991.

Knight, R. P. *The Landscape, a Didactic Poem in Three Books. Addressed to Uvedale Price*, Esq. London, 1795.

Lancellotti, G. P. *Io. Pauli Lancellotti Perusiniiuris consulti de Lacoonte poema.* Reprinted in Settis (1999), p. 146.

Lebrun, C. *Conférence sur l'Expression Générale et Particulière* [1668]. Reprint in A. Merot, ed. *Les Conférences de l'Académie Royale de Peinture et Sculpture au XVIIe siècle.* Paris, 1996, pp. 98–113.

Lemonnier, H. ed. *Procès-Verbaux de l'Académie Royale d'Architecture.* Paris, 1911–29.

Le Camus de Mézières, N. *The Genius of Architecture; or, the Analogy of that Art with our Sensations.* Introduction by Robin Middleton. Translation by David Britt. Santa Monica, 1992.

Livy. *Ab Urbe Condita.* With an English translation by A. C. Schlesinger. Cambridge, Mass. and London, 1959.

Lomazzo, G. P. *Idea del Tempio della Pittura.* Edizione, commento e traduzione di Robert Klein. Florence, 1974.

Longinus. *On the Sublime.* Translated by W. H. Fyfe. Revised by D. Russell. Cambridge, Mass. and London, 1995.

On Sublimity. In D. A. Russell and H. Winterbottom (eds.). *Ancient Literary Criticism*, pp. 460–504.

Peri Hupsous, Or, Dionysius Longinus on the Height of Eloquence. Rendered out of the Originall by J. H. John Hall. London, 1652.

A Treatise of the Loftiness or Elegancy of Speech. Written originally in Greek ... and now translated out of French by Mr J. P. [James Pulteney]. London, 1698 [1680[1]].

An Essay on the Sublime. Translated from the Greek of Dionysius Longinus Cassius, the Rhetorician. Oxford, 1698.

Dionysius Longinus' Treatise on the Sublime. Translated by Leonard Wellsted. London, 1712.

Dionysius Longinus on the Sublime. Translated by William Smith. London, 1739.

Maranta, B. *Discorso all'ill.mo Sig. Ferrante Carrafa Marchese di Santo Lucido in Materia di Pittura nel quale si difende il Quadro della Cappella del Sig. Cosmo Pinelli, fatto per Tiziano, da alcune Opposizioni fattegli da alcune Persone.* Reprinted in P. Barocchi, ed. *Scritti d'Arte del Cinquecento*, vol. I, pp. 863–900.

Martial. *Epigrams.* Translated by D. R. Shackleton Bailey. Cambridge, Mass. and London, 1993.

Melito of Sardis. *Homily on the Passion.* Introduction, text, notes and translation from the Greek, by Campbell Bonner. London, 1940.

Merot, A. ed. *Les Conférences de l'Académie Royale de Peinture et Sculpture au XVIIe siècle.* Paris, 1996.

Minturno, A. *L'Arte Poetica.* Venice, 1563.

Molanus, J. *De Historia SS. Imagimum et Picturarum pro vero earum Usu contra abusus Libri IV.* Ingolstadt, 1594.

Montague, W. *Miscellanea Spiritualia or Devout Essays*, London, 1648.

Montesquieu, C. De Secondat de. 'De la manière gothique'. In *Oeuvres Complètes*. Texte présenté et annoté par Roger Caillois. Paris, 1976–99, vol. I, pp. 966–74.

Morosini, D. *De Bene Instituta Re Publica*. Venice, 1497.

Origenes, *Contra Celsum*. Edited by M. Marcovich. Leiden, 2001.

Origen: *Homilies on Leviticus*. Translated and edited by G. W. Barkley. Washington D.C., 1990.

Paleotti, G. *Discorso intorno alle Imagini Sacre e Profane, Diviso in cinque Libri. Raccolto & posto insieme ad utile delle Anime per Commissione di Monsignore Illustriss. & Reverendiss. Card. Gabriele Paleotti, Vescovo di Bologna*. Bologna, 1582, modern reprint in Barocchi, *Trattati*, vol. II, pp. 117–509.

Palladio, A. *I Quattro Libri dell'Architettura*. Venice, 1570.

Pascoli, L. *Vite de'Pittori Scultori ed Architetti Moderni*. Rome, 1736.

Peacham, H. *Garden of Eloquence*. Facsimile reprint with an introduction by W. G. Crane. Delham, 1977.

Perrault, Ch. *Parallèles des Anciens et des Modernes en ce qui regarde les Arts et les Sciences*. Tome Premier, seconde édition. Paris, 1692.

Parallèle des Anciens et des Modernes en ce qui regarde les arts et les sciences. Edited by Hans Robert Jauss and Max Imdahl. Munich, 1964.

Philo Judaeus. *De Migratione Abrahae*. Introduction, traduction et notes par J. Cazeaux. Paris, 1965.

Philostratus, *Imagines*. Translated and edited by E. Kalinka. Munich and Zurich, 1968.

Philostratus. *Imagines*. Translated by A. Fairbanks. Cambridge, Mass. and London, 1931.

Pico della Mirandola, G. *Commentary on a Canzona by Benviani*. New York and Frankfurt am Main, 1984.

Pino, P. *Dialogo di Pittura. Nuovamente Dato in Luce*. Venice, 1548. Modern editions in Barocchi, P., *Trattati*, vol. I, pp. 113–20; and Falabella, S. and B. Tavassi La Greca (eds.). *Paolo Pino. Dialogo di Pittura*. Rome, 2000.

Plethon, G. G. *Platonicae et Aristotelicae Philosophiae Differentiae* (1439). Reprinted in J. P. Migne. *Patrologia Cursus Completa. Series graeca*. Paris, 1857–68, vol. 160, cols. 889–932.

Pliny, *Naturkunde. Naturalis Historia Liber XXXV*. Herausgegeben und übersetzt von Roderich König in Zusammenarbeit mit Gerhard Winkler. Munich, 1997.

Plutarch. 'On the Fame of the Athenians'. In *Moralia*, vol. IV, pp. 501–3. Translated by F. C. Babbitt. London and New York, 1927.

De Audiendis Poetis. Translated by D. A. Russell and M. Winterbottom (eds.). In *Ancient Literary Criticism*, pp. 507–31.

Polybius. *The Histories*. Translated by W. R. Paton. Cambridge, Mass. and London, 1972–80 [1922–27[1]].

Pozzo, A. *Rules and Examples of Perspective for Painters and Architects. In English and Latin. Containing a most easie and expeditious Method to Delineate in Perspective All Designs relating to Architecture, after a New Manner, Wholly free from the Confusion of Occult Lines: by that Great Master thereof, Andrea Pozzo, Soc. Jes.* Engraven by John Sturt, done into English from the Original, printed in Rome 1693 in Latin and Italian by Mr John James of Greenwich. London, 1707.

Propertius. *Elegies Book I*. Edited by W. A. Camps. Cambridge and New York, 1977 [1961[1]].

Quatremère de Quincy, A.-Chr. *De l'Architecture Egyptienne considérée dans son origine, ses principes et son goût, et comparée sour les mêmes rapports à l'architecture grecque*. Paris, 1803.

'Caractère'. In *Encyclopédie Méthodique*, vol. V (Architecture), pp. 477–518. Paris, 1788–1825.

'Style'. In *Encyclopédie Méthodique*, Paris, vol. III, pp. 410–19. Paris, 1788–1825.

Quintilian. *Institutio Oratoria*. With an English translation by H. E. Butler, Cambridge, Mass. and London, 1996 [1921[1]].

Ridolfi, C. *Le Maraviglie dell'arte*. Venice, 1648. Modern edition edited by Detlev von Hagen, Berlin, 1919–24.

The Life of Titian. Edited by J. C. P. Bondanella, B. Cole and J. R. Shiffman. Translated by J. C. and P. Bondanella, University Park, 1996.

Russell, D. A. and M. Winterbottom (eds.). *Ancient Literary Criticism. The Principal Texts in New Translations*. Oxford, 1972.

Sadoleto, J. *De Laocoontis Statua Jacobi Sadoleti Carmen*. Reprinted in Settis (1999), pp. 118–21.

Sallust. *Bellum Iugurthinum*. Translated by J. C. Rolfe. Cambridge, Mass. and London, 1920.

Sansovino, F. *Dell'Arte Oratoria Libri Tre*. Venice, 1569.

Scamozzi, V. *Idea dell' Architettura Universale*. Venice, 1615. Reprint edited by Franco Barbieri and Werner Oechslin. Vicenza, 1997.

Serlio, S. *Il Settimo Libro dell'Architettura*. Frankfurt, 1575.

On Architecture. Volume One. Books I–V of 'Tutte l'Opere d'Architettura et Prospettiva by Sebastiano Serlio. Translated from the Italian with an introduction and commentary by Vaughan Hart and Peter Hicks. New Haven and London, 1996.

Shakespeare, W. 'The Tragedy of Coriolanus'. In S. Greenblatt, W. Cohen, J. E. Howard and K. E. Maus (eds.). *The Norton Shakespeare. Based on the Oxford Edition*. New York and London, 1997, pp. 2785–873.

Shenstone, W. *Unconnected Thoughts on Gardening* [1764]. Reprinted in J. Dixon Hunt, ed. *The Genius of the Place. The English Landscape Garden 1620–1820*. Cambridge, Mass. and London, 1997 [1975[1]].

Sidney, Sir P. *New Arcadia*. Edited with introduction and commentary by V. Skretkowicz. Oxford, 1987.

Soane, Sir J. *Royal Academy Lectures*. See Watkin (1996).

Unpublished manuscripts. Soane Museum Library, London: AL Case 161/4, convolute 'P'; Ms Lecture V 1819, AL Soane Case 156.

Soo, L. ed. *Wren's 'Tracts' on Architecture and other Writings*. Cambridge and New York, 1998.

Speroni, S. 'Della Rhetorica'. In *Dialoghi di M. Speron Speroni. Nuovamente ristampati, & con molte diligenza riveduti, & corretti*. Venice, 1544. Modern edition in P. Barocchi, (ed.). *Trattati*, vol. I, pp. 122–4, 261–3.

Spini, G. *I Tre Primi Libri sopra l'Instituzioni de' Greci et Latini Architettori intorno agl'Ornamenti che convengono a tutte le Fabbriche che l'Architettura compone*. In F. Borsi (ed.). *Il Disegno Interrotto. Trattati medicei d'architettura*. Florence, 1980.

Suetonius. *Galba. Otho. Vitellius*. Edited with introduction and notes by C. L. Murison. Bristol, 1992.

Tacitus, *Agricola*. translation from the Latin by P. Hutton. Revised edition by R. M. Ogilvie. Cambridge, Mass. and London, 2000 [1970[1]].

Annales. With an English translation by C. H. Moore and J. Jackson. Cambridge, Mass. and London, 1957.

Tasso, T. *Lezione del Signor Torquato Tasso sopra il sonnetto LIX di Monsignor G. della Casa*. In *Opera di M. G. della Casa. Milan*, 1806, vol. 3, p. 303.

Discorsi. Edited by F. Flora. Bari, 1960.

Tebaldi, A. *Rime*. Selection reprinted in Settis (1999), pp. 132–3.

Tertullian *Adversus Marcionem*. In *Q. Septimi Florentis Tertulliani Opera*, vol. I. Turnhout, 1954.

Theophrastus. *Enquiry into Plants*. With an English translation by A. Hort. Cambridge, Mass. and London, 1916.

T., R. *De Templis*. London, 1638. Reprinted in Ploeg (2006); fragments in C. A. van Eck (ed.). *British Architectural Theory*, pp. 123–7.

Tyndale, W. *A Prologue to the Book of Leviticus*. In *The Work of William Tyndale*. Edited and introduced by G. E. Duffield. Appleford, 1964.

Vanbrugh, Sir J. 'Mr Van-Brugg's Proposals about Building ye New Churches' 1712; reprinted in C. A. van Eck (ed.). *British Architectural Theory*. Aldershot, 2003, pp. 136–8.

Van Eck, C. A. (ed.). *British Architectural Theory 1540–1750. An Anthology of texts*. Aldershot, 2003.

Vasari, G. *Le Vite de' più eccellenti Pittori Scultori ed Architettori*. Edited by Paola della Pergola, Luigi Grassi and Giovanni Previtali. Novara, 1967.

Lives of the Painters, Sculptors and Architects. Translated by Gaston de Vere with an introduction and notes by David Ekserdjian. London, 1996 [1927[1]].

Veronese, G. *Oratio Guarini Veronensis quam recitavit in Principio Studii Ferrariae coram Marchione Leonello et aliis Famosiis Viris*. Reprinted in E. Garin (ed.). *Il Pensiero Pedagogico dello Umanesimo*. Florence, 1958.

Vickers, B. *English Renaissance Literary Criticism*. Oxford, 2002.

Walker, O. *Of Education, Especially of Young Gentlemen*. London, 1673.

Whately, Th. *Observations on Modern Gardening*. London and Dublin, 1770.

Willett, A. *Emblematum Sacrarum Centuria*. London, 1592.

Wotton, Sir H. 'A Panegyrick to King Charles [...] written in Latin by Sir Hen. Wotton [...] a little before his death. And now Englished by a Friend of the Authours, London 1651'. In I. Walton (ed.). *Reliquiae Wottonianae. Or, a Collection of Lives, Letters, Poems; With Characters of Sundry Personages* [...] *By the curious Pensil of the Ever Memorable Sr Henry Wotton Kt.* London, 1651. [3rd, enlarged edition London, 1672].

The Elements of Architecture. London, 1624. Reprint edited and introduced by F. Hard. London, 1968.

Wren, Sir C. 'Tract IV on Architecture'. In C. Wren Jr (ed.). *Parentalia: or, Memoirs of the Family of the Wrens*, pp. 362–4. Reprinted in Soo (1998), pp. 168–87.

'Report on Westminster Abbey to Francis Atterbury, Dean' (1713). In C. Wren, Jr (ed.). *Parentalia, or Memoirs of the Wrens*, Part 2, Section 7, pp. 295–302.

'Tract I'. In Soo (1998), pp. 153–7.

Wren Jr., C. *Parentalia: or, Memoirs of the Family of the Wrens*. London, 1750.

Secondary sources

Acres, A. 'The Columba Altarpiece and the Time of the World', *Art Bulletin* 80 (1998), pp. 423–51.

Aldrete, G. S. *Acclamations in Ancient Rome*. Baltimore, 1999.

Alpers, S. 'Ephrasis and Aesthetic Attitudes in Vasari's Lives'. *Journal of the Warburg and Courtauld Institutes* 23 (1960), pp. 190–215.

Ankersmit, F. *Sublime Historical Experience*. Stanford, 2005.

Arasse, D. 'Giovanni Bellini et les Limites de la Mimésis: la *Pietà* de la Brera', in Gaehtgens, W. (ed.). *Künstlerischer Austausch. Akten des XXVIII. Internationalen Kongresses für Kunstgeschichte Berlin 15–20 Juli 1002*. Berlin, 1993, pp. 503–9.

Attolini, G. *Teatro e spettacolo nel Rinascimento*. Bari, 1988.

Auerbach, E. 'Figura'. In *Gesammelte Aufsätze zur Romanischen Philologie*. Bern and Munich, 1967, pp. 55–93. English translation in *Scenes from the Drama of European Literature: Six Essays*. New York, 1959.

Badt, K. 'Raphael's *Incendio del Borgo*'. *Journal of the Warburg and Courtauld Institutes* 22 (1959), pp. 41–51.

Bann, S. *The True Vine. On Visual Representation and the Western Tradition*. Cambridge and New York, 1989.

Barasch, M. 'The Spectator and the Eloquence of Renaissance Painting'. In *The Language of Art. Studies in Interpretation*. New York and London, 1997, pp. 302–19.

'Character and Physiognomy: Bocchi on Donatello's *St George*, A Renaissance Text on Expression in Art'. In *Imago Hominis. Studies in the Language of Art*. Vienna, 1991, pp. 36–47.

Barbieri, B. (ed.). *Vincenzo Scamozzi 1548–1616*. Venice, 2003.

Barkan, L. 'Making Pictures Speak: Renaissance Art, Elizabethan Literature, Modern Scholarship'. *Renaissance Quarterly* 48/3 (1995), pp. 333–5.

Unearthing the Past. Archaeology and Aesthetics in the making of Renaissance Culture. New Haven and London, 1999.

'The Heritage of Zeuxis: Painting, Rhetoric, and History'. In A. A. Payne, A. Kuttner and R. Smick (eds.). *Antiquity and its Interpreters*. Cambridge and New York, 2000, pp. 99–110.

Baskins, C. L. 'Echoing Narcissus in Alberti's *Della Pittura*'. *Oxford Art Journal* 16 (1993), pp. 25–33.

Bath, M. *Speaking Pictures*. London, 1994.

Baxandall, M. 'Bartholomaeus Facius on Painting. A fifteenth-century Manuscript of *De Viris Illustribus*'. *Journal of the Warburg and Courtauld Institutes* 27, (1964), pp. 90–107.

Giotto and the Orators. Humanist Observers of Painting and the Discovery of Pictorial Composition. Oxford, 1971.

Painting and Experience. A Primer in the Social History of Pictorial Style. Oxford and New York, 1972.

'Jacopo Sadoleto's Laocoon'. In *Words for Pictures. Seven papers on Renaissance Art and Criticism*. New Haven and London, 2003, pp. 98–117.

Belkin, A. 'Ut Pictura Theatrum: the Adoration of the Magi by Leonardo da Vinci'. In N. Yaari (ed.). *On Interpretation in the Arts. Interdisciplinary Studies in Honor of Moshe Lazar*. Tel Aviv, 2000.

Belting, H. *Giovanni Bellini. Pietà, Ikone und Bilderzahlung in der venezianischen Malerei*. Frankfurt am Main, 1985.

Bild und Kult – Eine Geschichte des Bildes vor dem Zeitalter der Kunst. Munich, 1990.

Bennett, J. A. 'Christopher Wren: The Natural Causes of Beauty'. *Architectural History* 15 (1972), pp. 5–22.

'A Study of *Parentalia*, with two unpublished letters of Sir Christopher Wren'. *Annals of Science* 30 (1973), pp. 129–47.

Bercovitch, S. *Typology and Early American Literature*. Amherst, 1972.

Bialostocki, J. 'Das Modusproblem in den Bildenden Künsten'. *Zeitschrift für Kunstgeschichte* 24 (1961), pp. 128–52.

'Die Rahmenthemen und die archetypische Bilder'. In *Stil und Ikonographie*. Dresden, 1965.

Boehm, G. 'Bildsinn und Sinnesorgane'. *Neue Hefte für Philosophie* 18/19 (1980), pp. 118–32.

'Kunsterfahrung als Herausforderung der Ästhetik'. In W. Oelmüller (ed.). *Kolloquium Kunst und Philosophie I. Ästhetische Erfahrung*. Paderborn, 1981.

'Zu einer Hermeneutik des Bildes'. In H.-G. Gadamer and G. Boehm (eds.). *Seminar: die Hermeneutik und die Wissenschaften*. Frankfurt am Main, 1978.

Paul Cézanne: Montagne Sainte-Victoire Eine Künstlermonographie von Gottfried Boehm. Frankfurt am Main, 1988.

Bohn, V. (ed.). *Typologie. Internationale Beiträge zur Poetik*. Frankfurt am Main, 1988.

Bolzoni, L. *La Stanza della Memoria*. Turin, 1995. Translated as *The Gallery of Memory*, Toronto, 2000.

Borsi, F. *Leon Battista Alberti. The Complete Works*. New York and Milan, 1979 [1973[1]].

Braegger, C. (ed.). *Architektur und Sprache. Gedenkschrift für Richard Zürcher*. Munich, 1982.

Brilliant, R. 'Gesture and Rank in Roman Art. The Use of Gestures to denote Status in Roman Sculpture and Coinage'. *Memoirs of the Connecticut Academy of Arts and Sciences* 14 (1963).

The Arch of Septimius Severus in the Roman Forum. Rome, 1967 (=*Memoirs of the American Academy in Rome*, volume 29).

Buddensieg, Th. 'Die Konstantinsbasilica in einer Zeichnung Francesco di Giorgios und der Marmorkoloß Konstantins des Großen'. *Münchner Jahrbuch der bildenden Kunst* 13 (1962), pp. 37–48.

Calame, C. 'Quand dire c'est faire voir: l'évidence dans la rhétorique antique'. In *Etudes de lettres* 17 (1991), pp. 3–22.

Calame-Griaule, G. *La parole Griaule chez les Dogons*. Paris, 1955.

Carrier, D. 'Ekphrasis and Interpretation: Two Modes of Art History'. *British Journal of Aesthetics* 27 (1987), pp. 20–31.

Cave, T. 'Enargeia: Erasmus and the Rhetoric of Presence in the 16th Century'. *L'Esprit Créateur* 16 (1976), pp. 5–19.

The Cornucopian Text. Problems of Writing in the French Renaissance. Oxford, 1979.

Caye, P. *Le Savoir de Palladio. Architecture, Métaphysique et Politique dans la Venise du Cinquecento. Précédé du Commentaire au De architectura de Vitruve par Mgr Daniele Barbaro, Patriarche d'Aquilée (Livre I, 1, 2 et 3)*. Paris, 1995.

Chirelstein, E. 'Lady Elizabeth Pope: The Heraldic Body'. In L. Gent and N. Llewellyn (eds.). *Renaissance Bodies. The Human Figure in English Culture c. 1540–1660*. London, 1990, pp. 36–59.

Clarke, G. and P. Crossley (eds.). *Architecture and Language. Constructing Identity in European Architecture, c. 1000–c.1650*. Cambridge and New York, 2000.

Collins, P. *Changing Ideals in Modern Architecture*. London, 1965.

Corbeill, A. *Nature Embodied: Gesture in Ancient Rome*. New Jersey, 2004.

Curtius, E. R. *Europäische Literatur und Lateinisches Mittelalter*. Bern, 1948.

Damisch, H. *L'Origine de la Perspective*. Paris, 1987.

Davis, Th. M. 'Die Traditionen puritanischer Typologie'. In Bohn (1988), pp. 236–42.

De Jorio, A. *Gesture in Naples, Gesture in Classical Antiquity. La Mimica degli antichi investigata nel Gestire Napoletano*. Edited, translated and introduced by A. Kendon, Bloomington, 2000 [1832[1]].

Downes, K. *Hawksmoor*. London, 1979 [1959[1]].

Hawksmoor. London, 1996.

Drijepondt, H. L. F. *Die antike Theorie der 'varietas'. Dynamik und Wechsel im Auf und Ab als Charakteristikum von Stil und Struktur*. Hildesheim, 1979.

Du Prey, P. de la Ruffinière. 'Hawksmoor's "Basilica after the Primitive Christians": Architecture and Theology'. *Journal of the Society of Architectural Historians* 48 (1989), pp. 38–52.

Hawksmoor's London Churches. Architecture and Theology. Chicago, 2000.

Eden, K. *Hermeneutics and the Rhetorical Tradition. Chapters in the Ancient Legacy and Its Humanist Reception.* New Haven and London, 1997.

Eisenbichler, K. and P. Sohm (eds.). *The Language of Gesture in the Renaissance.* Toronto, 1983.

Elkins, J. *The Poetics of Perspective.* Ithaca and London, 1994.

Elsner, J. (ed.). *Art and Text in Roman Culture.* Cambridge and New York, 1994.

Art and the Roman Viewer. The Transformation of Art from the Pagan World to Christianity. Cambridge and New York, 1995.

'Between Mimesis and Divine Power: Visuality in the Greco-Roman World'. In Nelson (2000), pp. 45–70.

Evans, R. *The Projective Cast. Architecture and its Three Geometries.* Cambridge, Mass. and London, 1995.

Fontana, V. ' "Arte" e "Esperienza" nei Trattati d'Architettura Veneziani del Cinquecento'. *Architectura* 7 (1978), pp. 49–72.

'Il "Vitruvio" del 1556: Barbaro, Palladio, Marcolini'. In *Trattati Scientifici nel Veneto fra il XV e XVI secolo: Saggi e Studi.* Vicenza, 1985, pp. 39–72.

Freedberg, D. 'Johannes Molanus on provocative paintings. *De Historia Sanctarum Imaginum et Picturarum*, Book II, Chapter 42'. *Journal of the Warburg and Courtauld Institutes* 34 (1971), 229–45.

The Power of Images. Studies in the History and Theory of Response. Chicago and London, 1989.

Freedman, L. 'Bartolommeo Maranta on a Painting by Titian'. *HSLA. Hebrew University Studies in Literature and the Arts* 13 (1985), pp. 175–200.

Frye, N. *The Great Code. The Bible and Literature.* London, 1982.

Fuhrmann, M. *Das systematische Lehrbuch. Ein Beitrag zur Geschichte der Wissenschaften in der Antike.* Göttingen, 1960.

Fumaroli, M. *L'Ecole du silence. Le sens des images au XVIIe siècle.* Paris, 1994.

Gadamer, H. G. *Philosophical Hermeneutics.* Berkeley, 1976.

Galand-Hallyn, P. 'Le Songe et la Rhétorique de l'Enargeia'. In F. Charpentier (ed.). *Le songe à la Renaissance.* St Etienne, 1990, pp. 127–35.

'De la rhétorique des affects à une métapoétique: évolution du concept d'enargeia'. In H. Plett (ed.). *Renaissance-Rhetorik/Renaissance Rhetoric.* Berlin and New York, 1993, pp. 243–65.

Le Reflet des Fleurs: Description et Métalanguage poétique d'Homère à la Renaissance. Genève, 1994.

Les Yeux de l'Éloquence: Poétiques Humanistes de l'Évidence. Orléans, 1995.

Galdon, J. A. *Typology and 17th-century Literature.* The Hague and Paris, 1975.

Gell, A. *Art and Agency. An Anthropological Theory.* Oxford, 1998.

Gent, L. *Picture and Poetry: Relations between Literature and the Visual Arts in the English Renaissance.* Leamington Spa, 1981.

(ed.). *Albion's Classicism. The Visual Arts in Britain 1550–1660.* New Haven and London, 1995.

Germann, G. *Gothic Revival: Sources, Influences, Ideas.* London, 1972.

Gilbert, G. 'Antique Frameworks for Renaissance Art Theory: Pino and Alberti'. *Marsyas* 3 (1943–5), pp. 87–106.

Goffen, R. *Giovanni Bellini.* New Haven and London, 1989.

'Masaccio's *Trinity* and the Letter to the Hebrews'. In Masaccio's *Trinity.* Cambridge and New York, 1998, pp. 43–68.

Goldhill, S. and R. Osborne (eds.). *Art and Text in Ancient Greece.* Cambridge and New York, 1994.

'Ekphrasis and the Culture of Viewing'. In S. Goldhill and R. Osborne (eds.) (1994), pp. 197–224.

Goldstein, C. 'Rhetoric and Art History in the Italian Renaissance and Baroque'. *Art Bulletin* 73 (1991), pp. 641–52.

Visual Fact over Verbal Fiction. A Study of the Carracci and the Criticism, Theory, and Practice of Art in Renaissance and Baroque Italy. Cambridge and New York, 1988.

Gombrich, E.H. 'On Physiognomic Perception'. In *Meditations on a Hobby Horse and other Essays on the Theory of Art.* Oxford, 1963, pp. 45–56.

'Style'. In D. L. Sills (ed.). *International Encyclopedia of the Social Sciences.* New York, 1972.

'The Logic of Vanity Fair: Alternatives to Historicism in the Study of Fashions, Style and Taste'. In A. Schilpp (ed.). *The Philosophy of Karl Popper.* La Salle, 1974, pp. 925–57.

Goodman, N. 'How Buildings Mean'. In P. Alperson (ed.). *The Philosophy of the Visual Arts.* New York and Oxford, 1992, pp. 368–77.

Gordon, A. L. 'The Real and the Imaginary: Production and Religion in the Graeco-Roman World'. *Art History* 2 (1979), pp. 5–34.

Gordon, D.J. 'Ripa's Fate'. In *The Renaissance Imagination.* Essays and Lectures by D.J. Gordon collected by Stephen Orgel. Berkeley, 1975, pp. 51–77.

Goudeau, J. *Nicolaus Goldmann (1611–1665) en de wiskundige architectuurwetenschap.* Groningen, 2005.

Graf, F. 'Ekphrasis: Die Entstehung der Gattung in der Antike'. In G. Boehm and H. Pfotenhauer (ed.). *Beschreibungskunst - Kunstbeschreibung. Ekphrasis von der Antike bis zur Gegenwart.* Munich, 1995, pp. 143–55.

Grafton, A. *Leon Battista Alberti. Master Builder of the Italian Renaissance.* London, 2001.

'Alberti's Terminology in Context'. In J.J. Martin (ed.). *The Renaissance. Italy and Abroad.* London, 2003, pp. 199–214.

Grayson, C. 'Studi su Leon Battista Alberti II: Appunti sul Testo della *Pittura*'. *Rinascimento* 4 (1953), pp. 54–62.

Grayson, C. 'The Text of Alberti's *De Pictura*'. *Italian Studies* 23 (1968), pp. 71–92.

Grube, G.M. (ed.). *A Greek Critic: Demetrius on Style.* Toronto, 1969.

Gumbrecht, H.-U. and K.L. Pfeiffer, eds. *Stil: Geschichten und Funktionen eines kulturwissenschaftlichen Diskurselements*. Frankfurt am Main, 1986.

Hagstrum, J.H. *The Sister Arts. The Tradition of Literary Pictorialism and English Poetry from Dryden to Gray*. Chicago, 1974.

Hahn, R. *Die Allegorie in der antiken Rhetorik*. Tübingen: Tübingen University Ph.D. thesis, 1965.

Hall, M. *After Raphael. Painting in Central Italy in the Sixteenth Century*. Cambridge and New York, 1999.

Harris, E. and N. Savage. *British Architectural Books and Writers 1556–1785*. Cambridge and New York, 1992.

Hart, V. '"A Peece rather of Good Heraldry [...]" Heraldry and the Architectural Orders as Joint Emblems of British Chivalry'. *RES: Anthropology and Aesthetics* 23 (1993), pp. 51–66.

Nicholas Hawksmoor. Rebuilding Ancient Wonders. New Haven and London, 2002.

Hart, V. and R. Tucker. '"Immaginacy set free". Aristotelian ethics and Inigo Jones's Banqueting House at Whitehall'. *Res: Anthropology and Aesthetics* 39 (2001), pp. 151–67.

Haycock, D.B. *William Stukeley: Science, Religion and Archaeology*. Woodbridge, 2002.

Hazard, M. 'The Anatomy of "Liveliness" as a Concept in Renaissance Aesthetics'. *Journal of Aesthetics and Art Criticism* 33 (1975), pp. 407–18.

Elizabethan Silent Language. Lincoln and London, 2000.

Henderson, P. 'The Loggia in Tudor and Early Stuart England: the Adaptation and Function of Classical Form'. In L. Gent (1995), pp. 109–47.

Hendrickson, G.L. 'The Origins and Meaning of the Ancient Characters of Style'. *American Journal of Philology* 26 (1905), pp. 249–90.

Heninger, S.K. 'Sidney's Speaking Pictures and the Theatre'. *Style* 23 (1989), pp. 395–404.

Holanda, Fr. de. *Diálogos em Roma (1538). Conversations on Art with Michelangelo Buonarotti*. Edited by Grazia Dolores Folliero-Metz. With a Preface by Wolfgang Drost. Heidelberg, 1998.

Holländer, H. '"Inwendig voller Figur": Figurale und typologische Denkformen in der Malerei'. In Bohn (1988), pp. 166–206.

Hopkins, A. and A. Witte. 'From Deluxe Architectural Book to Builder's Manual: the Dutch editions of Scamozzi's L'Idea della Architettura Universale', *Quaerendo* 26/4 (1996), pp. 274–302.

Howard, W.G. 'Ut Pictura Poesis'. *Proceedings of the Modern Language Association*, n.s. 17 (1909), pp. 40–123.

Hyde, M.J. 'Rhetoric and Hermeneutics'. In Th.O. Sloane (ed.). *Oxford Encyclopaedia of Rhetoric*. Oxford: Oxford University Press, 2001.

James, L. and R. Webb. '"To Understand Ultimate Things and Enter Secret Places": Ekphrasis and Art in Byzantium'. *Art History* 14 (1991), pp. 1–17.

Jardine, J. *On a Grander Scale. The Outstanding Career of Sir Christopher Wren*. London, 2002.

Jost, W. and M. Hyde. *Rhetoric and Hermeneutics in our Time*. New Haven and London, 1997.

Kapp, V. 'Die Lehre von der *Actio* als Schlüssel zum Verhältnis der Kultur der früheren Neuzeit'. In *Die Sprache der Zeichen und Bilder. Rhetorik und non-verbale Kommunikation in der früheren Neuzeit*. Marburg, 1990, pp. 40–65.

Kemp, M. 'From "Mimesis" to "Phantasia": the Quatrocento Vocabulary of Creation, Inspiration and Genius in the Visual Arts'. *Viator* 8 (1977), pp. 347–98.

Kemp, W. *Der Betrachter ist im Bild*. Cologne, 1985.

Kennedy, G. 'Anthony's Speech at Caesar's Funeral'. *Quarterly Journal of Speech* 54 (1968), pp. 99–106.

Quintilian. New York, 1969.

The Art of Rhetoric in the Roman World, 300 BC–AD 300. Princeton, 1972.

'On Rhetoric'. *A Theory of Civic Discourse*. Oxford, 1991.

Kishlansky, M. *A Monarchy Transformed. Britain 1603–1714*. London, 1996.

Klein, R. *Form and Meaning*. Translated by M. Jay and L. Wieseltier. Princeton, New Jersey, 1979.

Kohler, B. '"Architektur ist die Kunst, gut zu bauen": Charles-Augustin d'Aviler's *Cours d'Architecture qui comprend les Ordres de Vignole*'. Zurich: Ph.D. thesis, Eidgenössische Technische Hochschule, 1997.

Kopperschmidt, J. (ed.). *Rhetorik*. Darmstadt, 1990.

Korshin, P.J. *Typologies in England 1650–1820*. Princeton, 1982.

Lagerlöf, M.R. *Ideal Landscape: Annibale Caracci, Nicholas Poussin and Claude Lorrain*. New Haven and London, 1990.

Land, N.E. 'Titian's Martyrdom of Saint Peter and the Limitations of Ekphrastic Art Criticism'. *Art History* 13 (1990), 293–317.

The Viewer as Poet. University Park: Penn State University Press, 1994.

Langdon, H. *Caravaggio: a Life*. London, 1998.

Lavin, S. *Quatremère de Quincy and the Invention of a Modern Language of Architecture*. Cambridge, Mass. and London, 1992.

LeCoat, G. *The Rhetoric of the Arts*. Berne and Frankfurt, 1975.

Lee, R.W. *Ut Pictura Poesis: The Humanistic Theory of Painting*. New York, 1967.

Lever, J. and J. Harris. *Illustrated Dictionary of Architecture 800–1914*. London, 1993.

Lewis, C.T. and C. Short. *A Latin Dictionary*. Oxford, 1975 [1879[1]].

Mandowsky, E. and C. Mitchell. *Pirro Ligorio's Roman Antiquities*. London, 1963.

Maier-Eichhorn, U. *Die Gestikulation in Quintilians Rhetorik*. Frankfurt am Main, 1989.

Manieri, A. *L'Immagine Poetica nella Teoria degli Antichi*. Phantasia *ed* enargeia. Pisa and Rome, 1998.

McKeon, R. *Introduction to Aristotle*. Second edition, revised and enlarged. Chicago and London, 1973 [1947[1]].

Middleton, R. 'Jacques-François Blondel and the *Cours d'architecture*'. *Journal of the Society of Architectural Historians* 18 (1959), pp. 140–8.

Minoprio, A. 'A Restoration of the Basilica of Constantine, Rome'. *Papers of the British School at Rome* 12 (1932), pp. 1–12.

Mitchell, W. J. T. *Picture Theory*. Chicago and London, 1994.

Montagu, J. *The Expression of the Passions: The Origin and Influence of Charles Le Brun's 'Conférence sur l'Expression Générale et Particulière'*. New Haven and London, 1994.

Moore, J. E. 'The Monument or Sir Christopher Wren's Roman Accent'. *Art Bulletin* 80 (1998), pp. 498–523.

Nelson, R. S. (ed.). *Visuality Before and Beyond the Renaissance*. Cambridge and New York, 2000.

Nibby, A. *Dello Tempio della Pace e della Basilica di Constantino*. Rome, 1819.

Niebuhr-Probsting, H. 'Das Schöne am Natürlichen: Architektur und Rhetorik bei Batteux'. In Y. Franke and H. Paetzold (eds.). *Ornament und Geschichte*. Bonn, 1996.

Oechslin, W. 'Architektur und Alphabet'. In Braegger (1982), pp. 216–55.

'Premesse a una nuova Lettura dell'Idea della Architettura Universale'. In V. Scamozzi, *L'Idea della Architettura Universale*. Vicenza, 1997, pp. xxxv–xxxvi.

Ong, W. *Ramus' Method and the Decay of Dialogue*. Cambridge, Mass., 1958.

Onians, J. 'Abstraction and Imagination in Late Antiquity'. *Art History* 3 (1980), pp. 1–24.

Bearers of Meaning. The Classical Orders in Antiquity, the Middle Ages, and the Renaissance. Cambridge and New York, 1988.

Classical Art and the Cultures of Greece and Rome. New Haven and London, 1999.

Orgel, S. 'Inigo Jones on Stonehenge'. *Prose* 3 (1971), pp. 109–25.

Orgel, S. and R. Strong *The Theatre of the Stuart Court*. London, 1973.

Panofsky, E. *Idea. Ein Beitrag zur Begriffsgeschichte der älteren Kunsttheorie*. Berlin, 1960 [1924[1]].

Pardo, M. *Paolo Pino's Dialogo di Pittura. A translation with commentary*. University of Pittsburgh, Unpublished Ph.D. thesis, 1984.

Pauly, A. F. von. *Paulys Realencyclopädie der classischen Altertumswissenschaft*. Neue Bearbeitung. Begonnen von Georg Wissowa. Stuttgart, 1894–1997.

Payne, A. A. *The Architectural Treatise in the Italian Renaissance: Architectural Invention, Ornament, and Literary Culture*. Cambridge and New York, 1999.

Peacock, J. *The Stage Designs of Inigo Jones. The European Context*. Cambridge and New York, 1995.

The Look of van Dyck. Anthony van Dyck's Self-Portrait with a Sunflower. Aldershot, 2007.

Pearsall Smith, L. *The Life and Letters of Sir Henry Wotton*. Oxford, 1906.

Pépin, J. 'Die frühe Hermeneutik. Worte und Vorstellungen'. In Bohn (1988), pp. 97–114.

Picon, A. *Architectes et Ingénieurs au Siècle des Lumières*. Marseilles, 1988.

Platner, S. B. *A Topographical Dictionary of Ancient Rome*. Completed and revised by Thomas Ashby. Rome, 1965 [1929[1]].

Plett, H.-F. 'Theatrum Rhetoricum: Schauspiel, Dichtung, Politik'. In *Renaissance-Rhetorik/Renaissance-Rhetoric*. Berlin and New York, 1993.

Ploeg, S. 'Staged Experiences: the church designs of Nicholas Hawksmoor'. In C. A. van Eck and E. Winters (2005), pp. 215–37.

Staged Experiences. Architecture and Rhetoric in the Architecture and Theory of Sir Henry Wotton, Nicholas Hawksmoor and Sir John Vanbrugh. University of Groningen, Unpublished Ph.D. thesis, 2006.

Pochat, G. *Geschichte der Ästhetik und Kunsttheorie. Von der Antike bis zum 19. Jahrhundert*. Cologne, 1986.

Pollitt, J. J. *The Ancient View of Greek Art: Criticism, History, and Terminology*. New Haven and London, 1974.

Prickett, S. 'The Bible in Literature and Art'. In J. Barton (ed.). *The Cambridge Companion to Biblical Interpretation*. Cambridge and New York (1988), pp. 160–4.

Puttfarken, T. 'The Dispute about *Colorito* and *Disegno* in Venice: Paolo Pino, Lodovico Dolce and Titian'. In P. Ganz (ed.). *Kunst und Kunsttheorie 1400–1900*. Wiesbaden, 1991 = Wolffenbüteler Forschungen 1991, pp. 75–101.

The Discovery of Pictorial Composition. Theories of Visual Order in Painting 1400–1800. New Haven and London, 2000.

'Aristotle, Titian, and Tragic Painting'. In D. Arnold and M. Iversen (eds.). *Art and Thought*. Oxford, 2003, pp. 9–27.

Titian and Tragic Painting. Aristotle's Poetics *and the Rise of the Modern Artist*. New Haven and London, 2005.

Ragusa, I. and R. B. Green (eds.). *Meditations on the Life of Christ. An illustrated manuscript of the 14th century*. Princeton, 1961.

Rehm, U. *Stumme Sprache der Bilder. Gestik als neuzeitlicher Bilderzählung*. Berlin, 2002.

Robertson, G. H. *Giovanni Bellini*. Oxford, 1968.

Roman D'Elia, U. *The Poetics of Titian's Religious Paintings*. Cambridge and New York, 2005.

Roodenburg, H. and J. Bremmer (eds.). *A Cultural History of Gesture*. London, 1993.

Rosand, D. *Painting in Cinquecento Venice: Titian, Veronese, Tintoretto*. New Haven and London, 1982.

'Ekphrasis and the Generation of Images'. *Arion* 3d series, vol. 1 (1990), pp. 61–105.

Painting in Sixteenth-Century Venice. Titian. Veronese. Tintoretto. Revised edition. Cambridge and New York, 1997.

Rubin, P. L. 'Raphael and the Rhetoric of Art'. In P. Mack (ed.). *Renaissance Rhetoric*. New York, 1994.

Giorgio Vasari. Art and History. New Haven and London, 1995.

Russell, D. A. *Criticism in Antiquity*. London and Berkeley, 1981.

Rüther-Weiss, V. *Studien zu Albertis Architektursystem. Venustas – Dignitas – Pulchritudo – Ornamentum.* University of Bonn, Unpublished Ph.D. thesis, 1991.

Salerno, L. 'Seventeenth-Century Literature on Painting'. *Journal of the Warburg and Courtauld Institutes* 14 (1951), pp. 234–58.

Scaglione, A. *The Classical Theory of Composition from its Origins to the Present. A Historical Survey.* Chapel Hill, 1972.

Scholz, B. F. *'Ekphrasis and Enargeia in Quintilian's Institutionis Oratoriae Libri xii'.* In P. L. Oesterreich and T. O. Sloane (eds.). *Rhetorica Movet: Studies in Historical and Modern Rhetoric in Honour of Heinrich F. Plett.* Leiden, 1999, pp. 3–24.

Schütte, U. ' "Als wenn eine ganze Ordnung da stünde [. . .]" Anmerkungen zum System der Säulenordnungen und seiner Auflösung im späten 18. Jahrhundert'. *Zeitschrift für Kunstgeschichte* 44 (1981), pp. 15–37.

Sekler, E. F. *Wren and his Place in European Architecture.* London, 1956.

Settis, S. *Laocoonte. Fama e stile.* Con un apparato documentario a cura di Sonia Maffei su "La fama di Laocoonte nei testi del Cinquecento". Rome, 1999.

Sharpe, K. *Remapping Early Modern England. The Culture of Seventeenth-Century Politics.* Cambridge and New York, 2000.

Shearman, J. *Only Connect [. . .]. Art and the Spectator in the Italian Renaissance.* Washington and Princeton: Princeton University Press, 1992.

Sittl, C. *Die Gebärden der Griechen und Römer.* Leipzig, 1890.

Smith, C. *Architecture in the Culture of Early Humanism: Ethics, Aesthetics, and Eloquence 1400–70.* Oxford, 1992.

Smuts, M. R. *Court Culture and the Origins of a Royalist Tradition in Early Stuart England.* Philadelphia, 1987.

Sohm, Ph. *Style in the Artistic Theory of Early Modern Italy.* Cambridge and New York, 2001.

Soo, L. (ed.). *Wren's 'Tracts' on Architecture and other Writings.* Cambridge and New York, 1998.

Spencer, J. R. 'Ut Pictura Rhetorica: a Study in Quattrocento Theory of Painting'. *Journal of the Warburg and Courtauld Institutes* 20 (1957), pp. 26–44.

Stewart, P. 'The Image of the Roman Emperor'. In R. Maniura and R. Shepherd (eds.). *Presence. The Inherence of the Prototype within Images and Other Objects.* Aldershot, 2006, pp. 243–59.

Summers, D. 'Contrapposto: Style and Meaning in Renaissance Art'. *Art Bulletin* 59 (1977), pp. 336–72.

Michelangelo and the Language of Art. Princeton, 1981.

'Conditions and Conventions: On the Disanalogy of Art and Language'. In I. Gaskell and S. Kemal (eds.). *The Language of Art History.* Cambridge and New York, 1991, pp. 181–213.

Summerson, J. *Georgian London.* Harmondsworth, 1978 [1945¹].

Szambien, W. *Symmétrie, Goût, Caractère. Théorie et terminologie de l'architecture à l'âge classique 1550–1800.* Paris, 1986.

Tafuri, M. *Venice and the Renaissance.* Cambridge, Mass. and London, 1995.

Trexler, R. *Public Life in Renaissance Florence.* New York, 1980.

Trimpi, W. 'The Meaning of Horace's Ut Pictura Poesis'. *Journal of the Warburg and Courtauld Institutes* 36 (1973), pp. 1–35.

Üding, G., G. Kalivoda and H.-F. Robling (eds.). *Historisches Wörterbuch der Rhetorik.* Tübingen, 1992.

Ullmann, S. *Style in the French Novel.* Cambridge, 1957.

Van Eck, C. A. *Organicism in 19th-century Architecture. An Inquiry Into its Theoretical and Philosophical Background.* Amsterdam, 1994.

' "Par le style on atteint au sublime": the Meaning of the Term "Style" in French Architectural Theory of the late eighteenth Century'. In C. A. van Eck, J. W. McAllister and R. van de Vall (eds.). (1995), pp. 89–108.

Van Eck, C. A., J. W. McAllister and R. van de Vall (eds.). *The Concept of Style in Philosophy and the Arts.* Cambridge and New York, 1995.

Van Eck, C. A. 'Giannozzo Manetti on Architecture: the *Oratio de saecularibus et pontificalibus pompis in consecratione basilicae Florentinae* of 1436'. *Renaissance Studies* 12/4 (1998), pp. 449–75.

'The Structure of Alberti's *De re aedificatoria* Reconsidered'. *Journal of the Society of Architectural Historians* 56 (1998a), 280–97.

'Language, Rhetoric and Architecture in *De Re Aedificatoria*'. In G. Clarke, G. and P. Crossley (2000), pp. 72–82.

'The Retrieval of Classical Architecture in the Quattrocento: the Role of Byzantine and Humanist Observers'. In W. Reinink and J. Stumpel (eds.). *Memory and Oblivion. Acts of the XXIXth International Congress for the History of Art.* Dordrecht, 2000a, pp. 231–9.

'Verbal versus Visual Abstraction: The Role of Images in Renaissance Architectural theory'. In C. Anderson and K. Koehler (eds.). *The Built Surface. Volume 1. Architecture and the Pictorial Arts from Antiquity to the Enightenment.* Aldershot, 2002, pp. 162–80.

Vickers, B. *In Defence of Rhetoric.* Oxford, 1988.

Vinge, L. *The Narcissus Theme in Western European Literature up to the Early Nineteenth Century.* Lund, 1967.

Von Rosen, V. 'Die Enargeia des Gemäldes: Zu einem vergessenen Inhalt des *Ut-pictura-poesis* und seiner Relevanz für das cinquecenteske Bildkonzept'. *Marburger Jahrbuch für Kunstwissenschaft* 27 (2000), pp. 171–208.

Walker, A. D. 'Enargeia and the Spectator in Greek Historiography'. *Transactions of the American Philological Association* 123 (1993), pp. 353–77.

Walliser-Wurster, M. *Fingerzeige. Studien zu Bedeutung und Funktion einer Geste in der bildenden Kunst der Italienischen Renaissance.* Frankfurt am Main, 2001.

Watkin, D. *Sir John Soane. Enlightenment Thought and the Royal Academy Lectures.* Cambridge and New York, 1996.

Watson, G. *Phantasia in Classical Thought*. Galway, 1988.

Williams, R. 'A Treatise by Francesco Bocchi in Praise of Andrea del Sarto'. *Journal of the Warburg and Courtauld Institutes* 52 (1989), pp. 122–39.

Wittkower, R. 'Hieroglyphics in the Early Renaissance'. In B. S. Levy (ed.). *Developments in the Early Renaissance*. Albany, 1972, pp. 58–98.

Art and Architecture in Italy 1600–1750. Harmondsworth, 1980.

Woollcombe, K.J. 'The Biblical Origins and Patristic Development of Typology'. In G. Lampe and K.J. Woollcombe. *Essays on Typology Studies in Biblical Theology* 22. London, 1957.

Wright, D. R. E. 'Alberti's *De Pictura*: its Literary Structure and Purpose'. *Journal of the Warburg and Courtauld Institutes*, vol. 47 (1984), pp. 52–71.

Wright, G. 'Caravaggio's *Entombment* Considered *In Situ*'. *Art Bulletin* 60 (1978), pp. 35–42.

Yale French Studies. 'Towards a Theory of Description'. Special Issue. vol. 61 (1981).

Zanker, P. 'Enargeia in the Ancient Criticism of Poetry'. *Rheinisches Museum* 124 (1981), pp. 207–311.

INDEX: NAMES AND CONCEPTS

Figures in italics indicate illustrations

INDEX: RHETORICAL TERMS

Lightning Source UK Ltd.
Milton Keynes UK
UKHW051929191221
395951UK00010B/73

9 781107 687851